P9-AGP-647

KF
9227
.C2
P47
2013

Perlin, Michael L.,
1946-
    Mental disability
and the death penalty

DISCARD

JAN 2 2 2015

Mental Disability and the Death Penalty

Mental Disability and the Death Penalty

The Shame of the States

Michael L. Perlin

ROWMAN & LITTLEFIELD PUBLISHERS, INC.
Lanham • Boulder • New York • Toronto • Plymouth, UK

Published by Rowman & Littlefield Publishers, Inc.
A wholly owned subsidiary of The Rowman & Littlefield Publishing Group, Inc.
4501 Forbes Boulevard, Suite 200, Lanham, Maryland 20706
www.rowman.com

10 Thornbury Road, Plymouth PL6 7PP, United Kingdom

Copyright © 2013 by Rowman & Littlefield Publishers, Inc.

All rights reserved. No part of this book may be reproduced in any form or by any electronic or mechanical means, including information storage and retrieval systems, without written permission from the publisher, except by a reviewer who may quote passages in a review.

British Library Cataloguing in Publication Information Available

Library of Congress Cataloging-in-Publication Data
Perlin, Michael L., 1946–
  Mental disability and the death penalty / Michael L. Perlin.
    p. cm.
  Includes bibliographical references and index.
  ISBN 978-1-4422-0056-2 (cloth : alk. paper) — ISBN 978-1-4422-0058-6
(electronic) 1. Capital punishment—United States. 2. Mental health laws—United
States. 3. Mentally ill offenders—United States. 4. Insanity (Law)—United States. 5.
Legal assistance to people with mental disabilities—United States. I. Title.
  KF9227.C2P47 2013
  345.73'0773—dc23   2012032790

∞™ The paper used in this publication meets the minimum requirements of
American National Standard for Information Sciences—Permanence of Paper
for Printed Library Materials, ANSI/NISO Z39.48-1992.

Printed in the United States of America

Contents

Preface

$\mathcal{I}$ started work as a public defender in August 1971. Some four months later, the New Jersey Supreme Court declared the state death penalty statute unconstitutional.[1] In the summer of 1972, in *Furman v. Georgia*, the United States Supreme Court declared *all* state death penalty statutes unconstitutional as applied.[2] In the summer of 1974, I became director of the New Jersey Division of Mental Health Advocacy in the newly created state Department of the Public Advocate, and I no longer represented criminal defendants at trial (although I continued to represent patients at the Vroom Building, the state psychiatric hospital for the criminally insane, a cohort that included individuals who had faced the death penalty over the prior half century). In 1982—some six years after the Supreme Court's decision in *Gregg v. Georgia*,[3] declining to find the death penalty unconstitutional in all circumstances—the death penalty was reinstated in New Jersey,[4] at the time when I was special counsel to the commissioner of the public advocate. In this position, I drafted legislative testimony for the state public advocate in opposition to the death penalty,[5] coauthored a law review article on the need for a proportionality review as an element of any death penalty legislation,[6] and "second sat" *Strickland v. Washington*[7] at the US Supreme Court.

I became a law professor at New York Law School in 1984 and soon thereafter created the Federal Litigation Clinic. Although the bulk of our work was civil—mostly appeals from administrative decisions involving SSI and SSDI benefits—we also did some appellate *amicus curiae* work in criminal cases. One of the cases in which we were involved was *Ake v. Oklahoma*,[8] in which the US Supreme Court ultimately held, in a death penalty case, that an indigent defendant is constitutionally entitled to psychiatric assistance when he makes a preliminary showing that his sanity "is [likely] to be a significant factor at trial."⁹ Among the classes that I have taught are Criminal Law, Criminal Procedure: Adjudication, and Criminal Law and Procedure: The Mentally Disabled Defendant. I began to write law review articles, treatises, and monographs, and in this literature, death penalty issues were always a major part of my focus, almost always from the perspective of the representation of a defendant with serious mental disabilities.¹⁰ I consulted with legal aid and public defender offices providing legal services to this clientele, and I sometimes served as an expert witness—on *Strickland* issues—in cases involving defendants with mental disabilities.

In short, although I never represented a defendant at a death penalty trial, death penalty issues have always been part of my professional life. Thus, when I was approached to write this book, I eagerly accepted the invitation since it would give me an opportunity to put together all the thoughts that I had about this issue and to focus on some of the main reasons why the death penalty can never be administered in an equitable and rational way.

The death penalty is used disproportionately in cases of persons with serious mental disabilities, and there are multiple cases in which defendants who are factually innocent have been sentenced to death. Jurors misconstrue evidence introduced ostensibly in mitigation of punishment and instead perversely turn it into aggravating evidence. Invalid and unreliable testimony by alleged "experts" paints pictures of universal "future dangerousness." In spite of decisions ostensibly banning the practice, defendants with mental retardation and serious mental disabilities continue to be executed. The prosecutorial apparat is universally silent and turns its head in the face of gross evidence of prosecutorial misconduct. And there is no contradiction of Stephen Bright's aphorism that "[t]he death penalty will too often be punishment not for committing the worst crime, but for being assigned the worst lawyer."¹¹ In too many cases, the lawyers assigned to represent death penalty defendants are, in the immortal words of Judge David Bazelon, "walking violations of the Sixth Amendment."¹²

Why is this? I believe that we cannot hope to find the answers until we come to grips with the pernicious power of sanism¹³ and pretextuality.¹⁴ I have written frequently about how these factors have contaminated all aspects of the judicial process,¹⁵ and I believe this contamination is nowhere more virulent— and, self-evidently, more deadly—than in the death penalty decision-making process. As I said in an article about counsel and the death penalty,

> [S]anism in the death penalty decision-making process . . . is often irrational, rejecting empiricism, science, psychology, and philosophy, and substituting in its place myth, stereotype, bias, and distortion. It resists educational correction, demands punishment regardless of responsibility, and reifies medievalist concepts based on fixed and absolute notions of good and evil and of right and wrong.¹⁶

But I do not believe that all is hopeless. As I discuss throughout this work, I believe that therapeutic jurisprudence[17] offers the best hope of redemption of all mental disability law,[18] including death penalty law.[19] And I explore that hope throughout this work.

I also call the reader's attention to the importance of international human rights law in this enterprise.[20] The United States stands shoulder to shoulder with many authoritarian and repressive nations in its support of the death penalty, a position rejected flatly by international human rights treaties and covenants. Although we have, for the most part, regularly ignored this body of law, the recent ratification of the UN Convention on the Rights of Persons with Disabilities[21] should force us to rethink our position from this fresh and new perspective—one that promises to infuse a measure of sadly lacking dignity[22] into the entire process.

Much of this book is entirely new, but parts of it draw upon articles and book chapters I have previously published.[23] I have also presented many of the ideas here at conferences over the years sponsored by the American Academy of Psychiatry and Law, the American Psychology-Law Society, the International Academy of Law and Mental Health, the Association of American Law Schools, the American College of Forensic Psychology, the Canadian Psychological Association, the Western Psychological Association, the American College of Forensic Psychiatry, Mt. Sinai Medical School, and the University of Pennsylvania Forensic Psychiatry Workshop Series; at symposia put on by New Mexico Law School, Akron Law School, Stanford University Law School, and the University of Miami Law School; in guest lectures hosted by National Taipei University and the University of Auckland Law School; and at multiple faculty workshops at New York Law School. Most recently, I presented a paper—"Mental Illness, Factual Innocence and the Death Penalty"—at National Chingchi Law School in Taipei, Taiwan, and at the Asian Criminological Society annual conference in Seoul, Korea, that became the centerpiece of the second half of chapter 1, and I am especially grateful to have had those opportunities.

My team of research assistants—Alison Lynch, Megan Crespo, Jessica Cohn, and Cambridge Peters—has been superb. I want to add my thanks to past research assistants who helped me so much in the preparation of earlier articles on which I've drawn in this book: Naomi Weinstein, Jeanie Bliss, Jayne South, Lori Kranczer, Ilene Sacco, Jennifer Burgess, Jenna Anderson, and Marisa Costales. I am so appreciative of all you have done for me. I also want to thank former New York Law School dean Richard A. Matasar, interim dean Carol Buckler, and associate deans Jethro Lieberman and Stephen Ellmann for their support and for the financial support of the NYLS Summer Grant program, and Sonja Davis for her excellent administrative assistance.

But most, of course, I wish to thank my family—my wife, Linda, my daughter, Julie, and my son, Alex—for their love and laughter and strength over all these years, and for keeping me "forever young." Alex, who was just one year old when I first wrote about the *Barefoot* and *Ake* cases,[24] is now an assistant deputy public defender in Trenton, New Jersey—the office in which I started my legal practice over four decades ago.[25] Luckily, he does not need to deal with death penalty issues.

It is to Linda, Julie, and Alex that this book is dedicated.

Michael L. Perlin
Trenton, New Jersey
September 4, 2012

An Introduction and the Dilemma of Factual Innocence

AN OVERVIEW

The story of the death penalty has been told many times.[1] But there is no single-volume work exploring the relationship between mental disability and the death penalty.[2] There is no question that the death penalty is disproportionately imposed in cases involving defendants with mental disabilities (referring both to those with mental illness and those with intellectual disabilities, more commonly referred to as mental retardation).[3] Estimates of those with mental retardation range from 10 to 30 percent,[4] and of those with mental illness from 10 to 70 percent.[5] Conservatively, over sixty persons with serious mental disabilities have been executed in the past three decades.[6] It is "a rare case in which the capital defendant has no mental problems."[7] All clinical studies report the frequent observation of neurological abnormalities and neurological deficits among death row prisoners.[8] Notwithstanding the bars against the execution of persons with mental disabilities,[9] there are multiple cases in which this has happened,[10] and many of the cases involving exonerations[11] involve defendants with mental disabilities (especially intellectual disabilities).[12] As Harold Koh points out, "The intellectually disabled rank among the world's most vulnerable and at-risk populations, both because they are different and because their disability renders them less able either to assert their rights or to protect themselves against blatant discrimination."[13] The American Bar Association has promulgated a resolution that "defendants should not be executed or sentenced to death if, at the time of the offense, they had significant limitations in both their intellectual functioning and adaptive behavior, as expressed in conceptual, social, and practical adaptive skills, resulting from mental retardation, dementia, or a traumatic brain injury";[14] yet such executions continue. There is clear bias, and it is systemic.[15]

Finally, none of this is a surprise; the state of Tennessee legislatively created a commission to study "[w]hether the law provides adequate protection for specific vulnerable populations such as the mentally retarded . . . and the mentally ill; whether persons suffering from mental illness constitute a disproportionate number of those on death row and what criteria should be used in judging the level of mental illness involved; and whether or not people with mental illness should be executed."[16] And all of this is made worse by the "arbitrary or capricious patterns" reflected in many states in which the death penalty is frequently sought in some counties and almost never sought in others.[17]

This is all problematic for many reasons:

- Execution of such persons flies in the face of a US Supreme Court decision *barring* the execution of persons with mental retardation.[18]
- Execution of such persons flies in the face of a US Supreme Court decision *barring* the execution of persons whose mental illness obstructs them from having a "rational understanding" of the reasons for their execution.[19]
- Execution of such persons reflects the reality that defendants with mental disabilities are more likely to be represented by ineffective counsel who fail miserably in providing the sort of vigorous legal advocacy envisioned by case law and legal standards.[20]
- Execution of such persons reflects the reality that, at the penalty stage of a death penalty prosecution, at the time when defense counsel is constitutionally obligated to introduce *mitigating* evidence,[21] jurors regularly misconstrue evidence of mental disability and view it as *aggravating* evidence,[22] making imposition of the death penalty more likely. In this context, jurors make gross—and often fatal errors—in evaluating whether the defendant appears to be sufficiently "remorseful,"[23] errors that flow from jurors' reliance on their self-referential (and flawed) "ordinary common sense."[24]
- Execution of such persons reflects the propensity of jurors to improperly see evidence of mental illness as evidence of "future dangerousness," again making a decision to impose the death penalty more, rather than less, likely.[25]
- Execution of such persons often reflects juror (and judicial) bias (that I elsewhere call *sanism*),[26] prosecutorial conduct that often borders (or crosses the border) of unethical behavior,[27] and cynical expert testimony that reflects a "high propensity [on the part of some experts] to purposely distort their testimony in order to achieve desired ends"[28] (that I elsewhere call *pretextuality*),[29] resulting in a system of constitutional, moral, and ethical flaws that fosters an atmosphere in which a significant percentage of the public believes that virtually *all* persons with mental disabilities involved in the criminal-court process

(at *any* level) are disproportionately dangerous, are immune to efforts at rehabilitation, and are deserving of more retaliatory punishment.[30]

- Execution of such persons flies in the face of international human rights standards[31] and is inimical to both the principles of therapeutic jurisprudence[32] and the concept of dignity.[33]
- Persons with serious mental disabilities generally have difficulties in obtaining a fair hearing in "regular cases."[34] The likelihood of unfairness is self-evidently increased in cases involving capital murders.[35]

The questions I raise in this book are underdiscussed—shockingly underdiscussed—in the literature.[36] I have chosen to write this book to explore the relationship between mental illness and the death penalty so as to explain why and how this state of affairs has come to be, to identify the factors that have contributed to this shameful policy morass, to highlight the series of policy choices that need immediate remediation, and to offer some suggestions that might meaningfully ameliorate the situation.[37]

This is a question of great legal, moral, political, and social significance. Assuming, as we must, that the death penalty remains constitutional in the United States,[38] the choices of whom we execute, how we exclude (or do not exclude) certain classes from the category of "potentially executable," the ways that mentally disabling conditions are constructed in the trial and penalty phases of death penalty cases, and the assumptions we make about individuals at every stage of the death penalty process are of significance to scholars, policy makers, students, and informed citizens alike.

The book will follow this road map. First, I will consider the reality that it is more likely that a person with a serious mental disability will be convicted and sentenced to death in a case in which he is factually innocent.[39] Then I will look at the ways that sanism and pretextuality dominate this entire area of law and social policy, and I will consider both the role that dignity should play in this consideration and the meaning of therapeutic jurisprudence in this context.[40] Then I will consider the role of mental disability in all aspects of the death penalty process. In this context, I will first consider substantive questions about which there is a corpus of US Supreme Court case law: the significance of the "future dangerousness" inquiry in death penalty decision making,[41] and the textures of the mitigation doctrine, paying special attention to the ways that mitigation evidence is often misunderstood and misapplied by jurors as *aggravation* evidence.[42]

I will next focus on questions of execution competency: first, I will look at the ways that Supreme Court case law that ostensibly bars the execution of some defendants with mental retardation is regularly ignored and trivialized by trial courts;[43] next, I will consider the ways that Supreme Court case law that ostensibly bars the execution of some defendants with serious mental illness is regularly ignored and trivialized by trial courts.[44] As part of this inquiry, I will pay special attention to the question of whether a defendant with severe mental illness can be medicated so as to make him competent to be executed,[45] as well as to the potential role of neuroimaging evidence in such cases.[46]

I will then consider the roles of the participants in the death penalty litigation system: the ways that jurors, in general, tend to distort mental disability evidence at every stage of the death penalty case;[47] the impact of prosecutorial misconduct;[48] the ways that, in some states, judges—seeking to pander to voters in reelection campaigns—use a legislatively sanctioned "override" power to impose death sentences in cases in which jurors had voted to sentence the defendant to life imprisonment;[49] and the abject and global failure of counsel to provide effective assistance to this most vulnerable cohort of defendants.[50]

I will then consider how international human rights conventions and case law—although acknowledged by a bare majority of the Supreme Court—are ignored by trial courts in cases involving this same cohort of defendants, and in this context consider how this body of law might aid us in reconstructing this area of jurisprudence.[51] In all of these chapters, I will reconsider the issues that I raise in chapter 2 about sanism, pretextuality, the role of dignity, and the potential of therapeutic jurisprudence as offering us a way of (at least modestly) ameliorating the situation.

I will then conclude with some recommendations and some policy suggestions. These recommendations and suggestions will include the following:

- An acknowledgment of the ubiquity and the pernicious powers of sanism and pretextuality, especially in cases involving violent crime;
- A reexamination of the Supreme Court's pallid effectiveness-of-counsel decision of *Strickland v. Washington*,[52] in an effort to—finally—ameliorate the situation described some thirty-five years ago by Judge David Bazelon, who characterized lawyers appearing before him (in cases involving mentally disabled criminal defendants) as "walking violations of the Sixth Amendment";[53]
- A serious reevaluation of the roles of expert witnesses in testifying to "future dangerousness";
- The need for promulgation of a set of guidelines and standards to be employed in cases involving a defendant's competency to be executed; and
- Some strategies that would lead to a greater role for international human rights in this entire inquiry (especially the recently ratified United Nations Convention on the Rights of Persons with Mental Disabilities),[54] with a "readers' guide" as to how this body of law can and should be used in domestic death penalty cases.

My hope is that this book will call attention to this cluster of issues that, sadly, still remain "under the radar" (or perhaps more pessimistically but accurately, "*off* the radar") for almost all participants in the criminal justice system, and that it will eventually lead to invigorated thinking and ameliorative action.

In 1948, the journalist Albert Deutsch wrote *The Shame of the States*,[55] an exposé of the state of American mental institutions at that time. In it he expressed sadness and outrage that this "rich, busy, idealistic, sympathetic, growing country"[56] could allow such a state of affairs to continue. Today, the same words that he used could be used about the way we have countenanced the imposition of the death penalty upon persons with severe mental disabilities. If anything, the word "shame" is an understatement.

ACTUAL INNOCENCE AND "DEATH WORTHINESS"

Introduction

The issue of innocence has had—and continues to have—"a profound impact" on the death penalty debate.[57] Any consideration of the topic that is central to this volume—the relationship between mental disability and the death penalty—reveals one undeniable truth that colors this entire investigation: that there are factors that make it significantly more likely that a person with a serious mental disability will falsely confess to a crime that he did not commit, and other factors that make it far more likely that such a person will seem "death worthy" because of his inability to "present" in ways that fact finders are likely to interpret as being remorseful or taking responsibility for the act in question. It is necessary to consider these factors at the outset of this inquiry.[58]

False Confessions

> When a defendant has confessed to committing a crime, the vast majority of police, prosecutors, and jurors see it as rock-solid evidence of guilt. Most people are baffled by the notion that someone would confess to a crime he or she did not commit. In 25 percent of all DNA exonerations, however, defendants have done just that—confessed to crimes that they did not commit.[59]

Mental disability is a significant confounding factor at every stage of the criminal justice system—from precontact to initial contact to intake and interrogation, to prosecution and disposition, and to incarceration.[60] In the context of capital punishment, these coalesce most vividly in the context of the false confession.[61]

William Follette and his colleagues point out,

> the *ability* to resist interrogative influence is derived from three broad sources: relevant knowledge, intact cognitive resources, and self-regulatory

capacity—or the ability to control emotions, thinking, and behavior. In turn, *motivation* to resist interrogative influence can be enhanced or undermined by a variety of chronic or acute individual characteristics.[62]

A person must be able to exert self-control to resist the pressures of interrogation and "withstand the relentless pressures to confess."[63] Self-evidently, this is more difficult for a person with mental disabilities, especially if she is (1) uncertain what happened or what is true; (2) lacks confidence in her own memories or ability to understand—for example, due to long-standing subjectively known cognitive impairments; or (3) suffers impaired "reality monitoring."[64] Self-evidently, mental disorders render individuals more susceptible to suggestion through one or more of these mechanisms.[65]

There are many reasons why persons with mental disabilities are sentenced to death for murders they did not commit,[66] and other reasons why they are sentenced to death in cases in which individuals without mental disabilities might have been spared the death penalty. There are multiple case studies to consider. By way of example, Anthony Porter was convicted of murdering Marilyn Green and Jerry Hillard in Chicago in 1982. Largely from the investigative efforts of the Innocence Project, it was discovered that Porter was mentally disabled and innocent. Their investigative efforts resulted in an interview of the prosecution's chief eyewitness, who recanted his testimony and explained that he falsely accused Porter under police pressure.[67] The cases of Douglas Warney, a person with a history of mental disabilities who confessed falsely to his involvement in a murder after twelve hours of interrogation, and Earl Washington, a mildly mentally retarded man who gave a false confession that led to his wrongful conviction,[68] are not dissimilar.[69]

As the above cases suggest, the most prevalent issue is that of false confessions. Of the first 130 exonerations that the New York–based Innocence Project obtained via DNA evidence,[70] 85 involved people convicted after false confessions.[71] Mental impairment is a commonly recognized risk factor for false confessions.[72] There is no disputing that false confessors have been found to score higher on measures of anxiety, depression, anger, extraversion, and psychoticism, as well as being more likely to have seen a mental health professional or taken psychiatric medications in the year prior.[73] Defendants with mental retardation "have diminished capacities to understand and process information, to communicate, to abstract from mistakes and learn from experience, to engage in logical reasoning, to control impulses, and to understand the reactions of others."[74] Go to the Internet and scan the websites of the various Innocence Projects. In every instance, mental impairment is listed as a major reason why innocent persons confess to crimes they did not commit.[75] On this point, the US Supreme Court is clear: "Mentally retarded defendants in the aggregate face a special risk of wrongful execution."[76]

Studies have repeatedly shown that a substantial proportion of adults with mental disabilities, and "average" adolescents below age sixteen, have impaired understanding of *Miranda* warnings when they are exposed to them,[77] often lack the capacity to weigh the consequences of a rights waiver, and are more susceptible to waiving their rights as a matter of "mere compliance with authority."[78]

Although false confessions cover the full gamut of crimes, over 80 percent occur in murder cases.[79] Of the false pleaders studied by the Innocence Project and independent scholars, more than one-quarter are either mentally ill or intellectually disabled.[80] Here are the sobering statistics:

> Sixteen of the 340 [Innocence Project] exonerees were mentally retarded; 69% of them—over two thirds—falsely confessed. Another ten exonerees appear to have been suffering from mental illnesses; seven of them falsely confessed. Among all other exonerees (some of who may also have suffered from mental disabilities of which we are unaware) the false confession rate was 11% (33/313). Overall, 55% of all the false confessions we found were from defendants who were under eighteen, or mentally disabled, or both. Among adult exonerees without known mental disabilities, the false confession rate was 8% (23/272).[81]

On average, these defendants served eleven to twelve years prior to their exonerations.[82]

But there are other reasons as well. In *Atkins v. Virginia*,[83] the US Supreme Court's 2002 decision that executing a person with mental retardation violated the Cruel and Unusual Punishment Clause of the Constitution, Justice John Stevens explained the concerns that were among the motivating factors leading to the Court's conclusion:

> First, there is a serious question as to whether either justification that we have recognized as a basis for the death penalty [retribution and deterrence] applies to mentally retarded offenders. . . .
>
> The reduced capacity of mentally retarded offenders provides a second justification for a categorical rule making such offenders ineligible for the death penalty. The risk "that the death penalty will be imposed in spite of factors which may call for a less severe penalty" is enhanced, not only by the possibility of false confessions, but also by the lesser ability of mentally retarded defendants to make a persuasive showing of mitigation in the face of prosecutorial evidence of one or more aggravating factors. Mentally retarded defendants may be less able to give meaningful assistance to their counsel and are typically poor witnesses, and their demeanor may create an unwarranted impression of lack of remorse for their crimes.[84]

In spite of the *Atkins* decision, there are still countless cases of defendants with mental retardation who are sentenced to death. Consider these cases:

- The Court in *Howell v. State*[85] speculated that the defendant did not exert enough "effort" on those of his IQ tests on which he scored under 70,[86] and that the jury could have thus concluded he "functioned at a higher level" [87] (a case which might be read hand in glove with *State v. Strode*,[88] which approvingly cited legislative testimony that retardation was a "birth defect" that you are "born with for the most part"). [89]
- In the same vein, the Court in *State v. Grell*[90] stressed the "risk of malingering" as justification for imposing the burden of proving mental retardation on the defendant by clear and convincing evidence, reasoning that defendants had "significant motivation to attempt to score poorly on an IQ test."[91]

In short, the *Atkins* decision has *not* been a palliative for the resolution of this issue.

The Trial Presentation of Persons with Mental Disabilities

Inappropriate Demeanor   Recall what the Supreme Court said in the *Atkins* case: the demeanor of a defendant with mental disabilities "may create an unwarranted impression of lack of remorse for their crimes."[92] Professor Blume and his colleagues have noted, "[D]evelopmentally disabled people typically lack social skills and have not had the same opportunities or peer group contact so critical in the development of appropriate social behavior that normal individuals have had."[93] The cognitive limitations of individuals with mental retardation often result in poor impulse control and inattentiveness, which may lead the defendant to be perceived as cold, aloof, and avoidant. Finally, if a defendant with mental retardation is trying to hide his disability behind a "cloak of competence," he may adopt a "tough guy" persona by bragging about his physical strength and intellectual prowess—or by assuming posture and expressions that are read as braggadocio."[94] All of these make it more likely that such a defendant will be subjected to the death penalty in spite of actual innocence.

Vulnerability to Exploitation   Finally, Professor Blume considers how vulnerability to exploitation makes it more likely that such a person will "invent" participation in a crime, "particularly if a trusted 'friend' is urging such an account of the crime." Likewise, when it comes time to make a deal, the person of normal intellectual ability is likely to be the one to turn state's evidence in exchange for reduced charges. Finally, all of these vulnerabilities together make the defendant with mental retardation a probable target of a "snitch" once he is incarcerated; he is likely to be willing to talk to a snitch, more likely than other defendants to say something incriminating (whether true or not) to the snitch, and less likely to be able to muster convincing evidence that the snitch made it all up.[95]

CONCLUSION

In short, the decks are severely stacked against a defendant with serious mental disabilities in death penalty cases,[96] and it is far more likely that a false conviction will be entered in such a case than in the instance of a mentally able defendant.

In subsequent chapters, I will discuss how defendants with mental disabilities fare poorly—fatally poorly—in the death penalty process at every stage of the proceeding. But these later chapters must be read in the context of the realities I raise here.

Sanism, Pretextuality, the Role of Dignity, and Therapeutic Jurisprudence

INTRODUCTION

$\mathscr{I}$ have been writing about mental disability law my entire career, and much of that work relates to criminal law and procedure in general,[1] and to the death penalty in particular.[2] I am convinced—beyond any doubt whatsoever—that it is impossible to remotely understand any aspect of mental disability law—civil or criminal—without understanding the insidious and corrosive power of sanism and of pretextuality.[3] I am also convinced in the same manner that any investigation of mental disability law must seriously consider the absence of dignity in the way persons with such disabilities are treated at every stage of the criminal justice system.[4] Finally, I am convinced—again beyond any doubt—that only the application of therapeutic jurisprudence principles[5] can explain the contamination of sanism and pretextuality, can serve as a mechanism "to expose pretextuality and strip bare the law's sanist facade,"[6] and optimally can redeem mental disability law.[7] In this chapter, I will discuss each of these concepts. As the book progresses, I will apply these ideas to all aspects of my inquiry into the relationship between mental disability and the death penalty.

SANISM[8]

"Sanism" is an irrational prejudice of the same quality and character as other irrational prejudices that cause (and are reflected in) prevailing social attitudes of racism, sexism, homophobia, and ethnic bigotry.[9] It infects both our jurisprudence and our lawyering practices.[10] Sanism is largely invisible and largely

11

socially acceptable. It is based predominantly upon stereotype, myth, super-stition, and deindividualization, and it is sustained and perpetuated by our use of alleged "ordinary common sense" (OCS) and heuristic reasoning in an unconscious response to events both in everyday life and in the legal process.

In a series of papers, I have explored the roots of the assumptions that are made by the legal system about persons with mental disabilities[11]—who they are, how they got that way, what makes them different, what there is about them that lets society treat them differently, and whether their condi-tion is immutable.[12] These assumptions—that reflect societal fears and ap-prehensions about mental disability, persons with mental disabilities, and the possibility that any individual may become mentally disabled[13]—ignore the most important question of all: Why do we feel the way we do about people with mental disabilities?[14]

These conflicts lead us to inquire about the extent to which social science data does (or should) inform the development of mental disability law juris-prudence.[15] If there is societal consensus that individuals with mental disabili-ties can be treated differently (because of their mental disability, or because of behavioral characteristics that flow from that disability), it would appear logi-cal that this difference in legal treatment is—or should be—founded on some sort of empirical database that confirms both the *existence* and the *causal role* of such difference. Yet we tend to ignore, subordinate, or trivialize behavioral research in this area, especially when acknowledging that such research would be cognitively dissonant with our intuitive (albeit empirically flawed) views.[16]

One might optimistically expect, though, that this gloomy picture would be subject to change because of a renewed interest in the integration of social science and law, and greater public awareness of defendants with mental dis-abilities. One might also expect that litigation and legislation in these areas would draw on social science data in attempting to answer such questions as the actual impact that deinstitutionalization has had on homelessness, or whether experts can knowledgeably testify about criminal responsibility in so-called "volitional prong" insanity cases.[17]

What are some reasons for this expectation? First, scholars such as John Monahan and Laurens Walker have constructed a jurisprudence of "social science in law,"[18] articulating coherent theories about the role of social science data and research in the trial process and outlining specific proposals for ob-taining, evaluating, and establishing the findings of such research.[19] Second, a series of social and political developments (primarily the public awareness of psychiatric hospital deinstitutionalization and its purported link to home-lessness,[20] and a series of sensational criminal trials in which mental status defenses have been raised)[21] has resulted in significantly increased visibility of some persons with mentally disabilities in predominantly negative ways.[22]

And yet any attempt to place mental disability law jurisprudence in con-text results in confrontation with a discordant reality: social science is rarely a coherent influence on mental disability law doctrine.[23] Rather, the legal system selectively—teleologically[24]—either accepts or rejects social science data depending on whether or not the use of that data meets the a priori needs of the legal system.[25] In other words, social science data is privileged when it supports the conclusion the fact finder wishes to reach, but it is subordinated when it questions such a conclusion.[26]

These ends are sanist.[27] In other words, decision making in mental disability law cases is inspired by (and reflects) the same kinds of irrational, unconscious, bias-driven stereotypes and prejudices that are exhibited in racist, sexist, homophobic, and religiously and ethnically bigoted decision making.[28] Sanist decision making infects all branches of mental disability law and distorts mental disability jurisprudence.[29] Paradoxically, while sanist decisions are frequently justified as being therapeutically based, sanism customarily results in anti-therapeutic outcomes.[30]

Judges are not immune from sanism. "[E]mbedded in the cultural presuppositions that engulf us all,"[31] judges also take refuge in heuristic thinking and flawed, nonreflective "ordinary common sense." They reflect and project the conventional morality of the community, and judicial decisions in all areas of civil and criminal mental disability law continue to reflect and perpetuate sanist stereotypes.[32]

Judges are not the only sanist actors. Lawyers, legislators, jurors, and witnesses (both lay and expert) all exhibit sanist traits and characteristics.[33] Until system "players" confront the ways that sanist biases (selectively incorporating or misincorporating social science data) inspire such pretextual decision making, mental disability jurisprudence will remain incoherent. Behaviorists, social scientists, and legal scholars must begin to develop research agendas so as to (1) determine and assess the ultimate impact of sanism, (2) better understand how social science data is manipulated to serve sanist ends, and (3) formulate normative and instrumental strategies that can be used to rebut sanist pretextuality in the legal system. Practicing lawyers need to articulate the existence and dominance of sanism and of pretextual legal behavior in their briefs and oral arguments so as to sensitize judges to the underlying issues.

There is no question that sanism is inextricably linked to our death penalty jurisprudence.[34] In later chapters, I will explore the significance of this link.

PRETEXTUALITY

Sanist attitudes also lead to pretextual decisions. "Pretextuality" means that courts regularly accept (either implicitly or explicitly) testimonial dishonesty, countenance liberty deprivations in disingenuous ways that bear little or no relationship to case law or to statutes,[31] and engage in dishonest (and frequently meretricious) decision making, specifically where witnesses, especially expert witnesses, show a "high propensity to purposely distort their testimony in order to achieve desired ends."[35] This pretextuality is poisonous; it infects all participants in the judicial system, breeds cynicism and disrespect for the law, demeans participants, and reinforces shoddy lawyering, blasé judging, and, at times, perjurious and/or corrupt testifying.

Pretextual devices such as condoning perjured testimony, distorting appellate readings of trial testimony, subordinating statistically significant social science data, and enacting purportedly prophylactic civil rights laws that have little or no "real-world" impact dominate the mental disability law landscape.[36] Judges in mental disability law cases often take relevant literature out of context,[37] misconstrue the data or evidence being offered,[38] and/or read such data selectively[39] and/or inconsistently.[40] Other times, courts choose to flatly reject this data or ignore its existence.[41] In other circumstances, courts simply "rewrite" factual records so as to avoid having to deal with social science data that is cognitively dissonant with their view of how the world "ought to be."[42] Even when courts do acknowledge the existence and possible validity of studies that take a contrary position from their decisions, this acknowledgment is frequently little more than mere "lip service."[43]

As with sanism, the notion of pretextuality is part and parcel of death penalty law.[44] Again, this will be explored in subsequent chapters.

THE ROLE OF DIGNITY

In the Supreme Court's plurality opinion in *Ford v. Wainwright*,[45] barring execution of the "currently insane,"[46] Justice Marshall focused on the significance of dignity values, searching for "objective evidence of contemporary values before determining whether a particular punishment comports with the fundamental human dignity that the [Eighth] Amendment protects."[47] Professor Carol Sanger suggests that dignity means that people "possess an intrinsic worth that should be recognized and respected," and that they should not be subjected to treatment by the state that is inconsistent with their intrinsic worth.[48] Treating people with dignity and respect makes them more likely to view procedures as fair and the motives behind law enforcement's actions as well meaning.[49] The legal process upholds human dignity by allowing the litigant—including the criminal defendant—to tell his own story.[50] A notion of individual dignity, "generally articulated through concepts of autonomy, respect, equality, and freedom from undue government interference, was at the heart of a jurisprudential and moral outlook that resulted in the reform, not only of criminal procedure, but of the various institutions more or less directly linked with the criminal justice system, including juvenile courts, prisons, and mental institutions."[51]

One way of best assuring such dignity is the provision of dedicated and effective counsel.[52] As the Montana Supreme Court noted in a civil commitment case, "'Quality counsel provides the most likely way—perhaps the only likely way' to ensure the due process protection of dignity and privacy interests in cases such as the one at bar [an involuntary civil commitment]."[53] Professor Tom Tyler's research in procedural justice has demonstrated, beyond doubt, that individuals subject to involuntary civil commitment hearings, like all other citizens, are affected by such process values as participation, dignity, and trust, and that experiencing arbitrariness in procedure leads to "social malaise and decreases people's willingness to be integrated into the polity, accepting its authorities and following its rules"[54]

In his exhaustive evaluation of dignity in the specific context of international human rights law, Professor Christopher McCrudden reviews cases from the International Court of Justice, the European Court of Human Rights, the European Court of Justice, and the constitutional courts of many nations and finds multiple categories of cases in which "dignity" is relied on as a basis for a court's judgment:

- cases involving prohibition of inhuman treatment, humiliation, or degradation by one person over another;[55]
- cases involving individual choice and the conditions for self-fulfillment, autonomy, and self-realization;
- cases involving protection of group identity and culture; and
- cases involving the creation of necessary conditions for individuals to have essential needs satisfied.[56]

The connection between these principles and the administration of the death penalty should be clear. The South African Constitutional Court has struck down the death penalty because it "annihilates human dignity."[57] Twenty years ago, in a death penalty context, Hugo Adam Bedau wrote that human dignity is "perhaps the premier value underlying the last two centuries of moral and political thought."[58] Concurring in *Furman v. Georgia*, Justice Brennan articulated this precise value: the death penalty was unconstitutional because "it does not comport with human dignity" in that it fails to respect people "for their intrinsic worth as human beings."[59] The question before us here is this: To what extent has this value been effectuated in cases involving death penalty defendants with mental disabilities?[60]

THERAPEUTIC JURISPRUDENCE[61]

One of the most important legal theoretical developments of the past two decades has been the creation and dynamic growth of therapeutic jurisprudence

(TJ).[62] Initially employed in cases involving individuals with mental disabilities, but subsequently expanded far beyond that narrow area, therapeutic jurisprudence presents a new model for assessing the impact of case law and legislation, recognizing that, as a therapeutic agent, the law can have therapeutic or anti-therapeutic consequences.[63] The ultimate aim of therapeutic jurisprudence is to determine whether legal rules, procedures, and lawyer roles can or should be reshaped to enhance their therapeutic potential while not subordinating due process principles.[64] There is an inherent tension in this inquiry, but David Wexler clearly identifies how it must be resolved: "the law's use of mental health information to improve therapeutic functioning [cannot] impinge upon justice concerns."[65] As I have written elsewhere, "An inquiry into therapeutic outcomes does not mean that therapeutic concerns 'trump' civil rights and civil liberties."[66]

Therapeutic jurisprudence "asks us to look at law as it actually impacts people's lives"[67] and focuses on the law's influence on emotional life and psychological well-being.[68] It suggests that "law should value psychological health, should strive to avoid imposing anti-therapeutic consequences whenever possible, and when consistent with other values served by law should attempt to bring about healing and wellness."[69] By way of example, therapeutic jurisprudence "aims to offer social science evidence that limits the use of the incompetency label by narrowly defining its use and minimizing its psychological and social disadvantage."[70]

In recent years, scholars have considered a vast range of topics through a therapeutic jurisprudence lens, including, but not limited to, all aspects of mental disability law, domestic relations law, criminal law and procedure, employment law, gay rights law, and tort law.[71] As Ian Freckelton has noted, "it is a tool for gaining a new and distinctive perspective utilizing socio-psychological insights into the law and its applications."[72] It is also part of a growing comprehensive movement in the law towards establishing more humane and psychologically optimal ways of handling legal issues collaboratively, creatively, and respectfully.[73] These alternative approaches optimize the psychological well-being of individuals, relationships, and communities dealing with a legal matter and acknowledge concerns beyond strict legal rights, duties, and obligations. In its aim to use the law to empower individuals, enhance rights, and promote well-being, therapeutic jurisprudence has been described as "a sea-change in ethical thinking about the role of law . . . a movement towards a more distinctly relational approach to the practice of law . . . which emphasises psychological wellness over adversarial triumphalism."[74] That is, therapeutic jurisprudence supports an ethic of care.[75]

One of the central principles of therapeutic jurisprudence is a commitment to dignity. Amy Ronner describes the "three Vs": voice, validation, and voluntariness,[76] arguing,

> What "the three Vs" commend is pretty basic: litigants must have a sense of voice or a chance to tell their story to a decision maker. If that litigant feels that the tribunal has genuinely listened to, heard, and taken seriously the litigant's story, the litigant feels a sense of validation. When litigants emerge from a legal proceeding with a sense of voice and validation, they are more at peace with the outcome. Voice and validation create a sense of voluntary participation, one in which the litigant experiences the proceeding as less coercive. Specifically, the feeling on the part of litigants that they voluntarily partook in the very process that engendered the end result or the very judicial pronunciation that affects their own lives can initiate healing and bring about improved behavior in the future. In general, human beings prosper when they feel that they are making, or at least participating in, their own decisions.[77]

Although there has been some substantial literature on the relationship between therapeutic jurisprudence and all aspects of the criminal justice system and the correctional system,[78] it is only in recent years that scholars have begun to seriously assess its relationship to the imposition of the death penalty.[79] Through this volume, I expect to add to that corpus of literature.

CONCLUSION

I will seek to unify subsequent chapters by demonstrating the impact of sanism and pretextuality on every substantive topic that I discuss in this volume by arguing on behalf of strategies to enhance dignity and by exploring how therapeutic jurisprudence might provide some solutions to the seemingly insoluble problems that contaminate death penalty jurisprudence. It is, I believe, the only way that we can make any meaningful social progress in this area of the law.

· 3 ·

Future Dangerousness and the Death Penalty

INTRODUCTION

In an effort to ensure that the "worst of the worst" receive death sentences, many jurisdictions encourage jurors to consider the danger a defendant will pose to society in the future by including "future dangerousness" as an aggravating factor.[1] The inclusion of this factor, however, assumes the existence of three important facts not in evidence: that mental health professionals can accurately predict dangerousness, that defense counsel can effectively cross-examine state experts on this issue, and that jurors can competently assess this sort of testimony. A review of the case law and the professional literature makes it clear that none of these questions can be answered affirmatively. In short, the Supreme Court's future-dangerousness methodology and jurisprudence is built on a flimsy house of cards and has little or no support in valid and reliable social science or behavioral studies. The Court, however, blithely ignores this and perpetuates a fraudulent system based on magical thinking.

This, stunningly, is not news. Commentators have understood the enormity of the Court's blunder on this question since days after the decision in *Barefoot v. Estelle*[2] nearly thirty years ago. Tragically, a majority of the Court does not appear interested in revisiting that decision and the harm that it has wreaked. And it goes without saying that the damage created by *Barefoot* is most severe in cases involving defendants with mental disabilities, a cohort feared, despised, and grievously misunderstood by jurors.[3]

In this chapter, I will first briefly discuss *Barefoot*'s predecessor in this saga, *Jurek v. Texas*,[4] one of the so-called "July 2 cases" that reinstated the death penalty.[5] Next I will examine *Barefoot* and consider the early responses to it. Then I will consider the subsequent valid and reliable research that

19

exposes the vacuity and meretriciousness of that decision, especially in the context of cases involving defendants with mental disabilities, and will then consider some options that might ameliorate the problem we face. I will conclude by considering the ways that sanism and pretextuality infect this entire process, and then offer some suggestions for amelioration based upon the teachings of therapeutic jurisprudence.

TESTIMONY AS TO DANGEROUSNESS AT THE PENALTY PHASE[6]

In *Jurek v. Texas*, the Supreme Court specifically upheld the constitutionality of a state statutory scheme which required, inter alia, that the jury determine, beyond a reasonable doubt, whether there was a "probability that the defendant would commit criminal acts of violence that would constitute a continuing threat to society."[7] On this issue, the controlling plurality opinion[8] established its guidelines as to such a "dangerousness"[9] finding:

> It is, of course, not easy to predict future behavior. The fact that such a determination is difficult, however, does not mean that it cannot be made. Indeed, prediction of future criminal conduct is an essential element in many of the decisions rendered throughout our criminal justice system.[10] The task that a jury must perform in answering the statutory question in issue is thus basically no different from the task performed countless times throughout the American system of criminal justice. What is essential is that the jury have before it all possible relevant information about the individual defendant whose fate it must determine. Texas law clearly assures that all such evidence will be adduced.[11]

The decision in *Jurek* was immediately criticized as "appalling,"[12] and as "difficult to reconcile" with the Court's recognition in *Gregg v. Georgia*[13] that "the concept of human dignity underlying the Eighth Amendment demands a principled application of the death penalty."[14] This aspect of the opinion was specifically seen as flawed by vagueness[15] and prejudicially misleading to the defendant.[16]

Although *Jurek* was subsequently partially overruled by *Abdul-Kabir v. Quarterman*[17]—in light of intervening cases that had emphasized that "the Constitution guarantees a defendant facing a possible death sentence not only the right to introduce evidence mitigating against the death penalty but also the right to *consideration* of that evidence by the sentencing authority"[18]—nothing in the latter decision appears to have had any impact on the questions under consideration in this chapter. And the Texas scheme continues to be "universally considered to be the worst" of all death penalty statutes.[19] Writing recently about *Jurek*, Professors Carissa Byrne Hessick and F. Andrew Hessick noted the circularity of the Court's logic: "[D]ue process objections to future dangerousness as a sentencing factor have essentially been rejected based on nothing more than a statement of fact that courts frequently use future dangerousness as a sentencing factor."[20]

Barefoot's *Significance*[21]

While psychiatric testimony was not at the core of the *Jurek* opinion, that issue emerged clearly and explicitly several terms later in *Barefoot v. Estelle*.[22]

After Thomas Barefoot was convicted of murdering a Texas police officer, two psychiatrists[23] testified in response to hypothetical questions[24] at the penalty phase[25] that the defendant "would probably commit further acts of violence and represent a continuing threat to society."[26] The jury subsequently accepted this testimony,[27] and the death penalty was imposed.[28]

The defendant's conviction was affirmed in the state courts, and his application in federal district court for a writ of habeas corpus was denied,[29] a denial that was affirmed by the Fifth Circuit.[30] The Supreme Court then agreed to hear the case.[31]

In affirming the denial of habeas corpus, the Court summarized the defendant's claim on the psychiatric issue:

> First, it is urged that psychiatrists, individually and as a group, are incompetent to predict with an acceptable degree of reliability that a particular criminal will commit other crimes in the future, and so represent a danger to the community. Second, it is said that in any event, psychiatrists should not be permitted to testify about future dangerousness in response to hypothetical questions and without having examined the defendant personally. Third, it is argued that in the particular circumstances in this case the testimony of the psychiatrists was so unreliable that the sentence should be set aside.[32]

The Court first rejected the argument that psychiatrists could not reliably predict future dangerousness in this context,[33] noting that it made "little sense" to exclude *only* psychiatrists from the "entire universe of persons who might have an opinion on this issue,"[34] and that the defendant's argument would also "call into question those other contexts in which predictions of future behavior are constantly made."[35] In the course of this argument, the Court rejected the views presented by the American Psychiatric Association as *amicus* that (1) such testimony was invalid due to "fundamentally low reliability,"[36] and (2) long-term predictions of future dangerousness were essentially lay determinations that should be based on "predictive statistical or actuarial information that is fundamentally nonmedical in nature."[37]

The Court construed its decision in *Estelle v. Smith*[38] to in "no sense disapprov[e] [of] the use of psychiatric testimony on future dangerousness."[39] On the hypotheticals issue, the Court simply held that expert testimony "is commonly admitted as evidence where it might help the fact finder do its assigned job,"[40] and that the fact that the witnesses had not examined the defendant "went to the weight of their testimony, not to its admissibility."[41]

Justice Blackmun dissented (for himself, and Justices Brennan and Marshall),[42] rejecting the Court's views on the psychiatric issue:

> The Court holds that psychiatric testimony about a defendant's future dangerousness is admissible, despite the fact that such testimony is wrong two times out of three. The Court reaches this result—even in a capital case—because, it is said, the testimony is subject to cross-examination and impeachment. In the present state of psychiatric knowledge, this is too much for me. One may accept this in a routine lawsuit for money damages,[43] but when a person's life is at stake—no matter how heinous his offense—a requirement of greater reliability should prevail. In a capital case, the specious testimony of a psychiatrist, colored in the eyes of an impressionable untouchability of a medical specialist's words, equates with death itself.[44]

Relying on the American Psychiatric Association's *amicus* brief, Justice Blackmun made four main points: (1) no "single, reputable source" was cited by the majority for the proposition that psychiatric predictions of long-term violence "are wrong more often than they are right";[45] (2) laymen can do "at least as well and possibly better" than psychiatrists in predicting violence;[46] (3) it is "crystal-clear" from the literature that the state's witnesses "had no expertise whatever";[47] and (4) such "baseless" testimony cannot be reconciled with the Constitution's "paramount concern for reliability in capital sentencing."[48]

Because such purportedly scientific testimony—"unreliable [and] prejudicial"[49]—was imbued with an "aura of scientific infallibility,"[50] it was capable of "shroud[ing] the evidence[, leading] the jury to accept it without critical scrutiny."[51] Justice Blackmun charged, "When the court knows full well that psychiatrists' predictions of dangerousness are specious, there can be no excuse for imposing on the defendant, on pain of his life, the heavy burden of convincing a jury of laymen of the fraud."[52]

Responses to Barefoot[53]

The "amazingly naive"[54] psychiatric testimony prong of *Barefoot* has been criticized uniformly by commentators[55] and flies in the face of carefully crafted guidelines suggesting limitations on expert testimony in such areas,[56] a problem made especially pernicious by the reality that appraisals of future violence "may obscure or *even supplant* judgments of the defendant's moral culpability."[57] By way of example, on the question of prediction accuracy, Professor James Marquart and his colleagues characterize predictions of future dangerousness in this context as akin to "gazing into a crystal ball."[58] As Professor Richard Bonnie artfully noted, "Even the best clinical testimony merely casts some light into a room that remains very dark."[59] Professor O. Carter Snead is certainly accurate when he says, "[T]he aggravating factor of future dangerousness [is] no friend to the capital defendant."[60] Mark Cunningham and his colleagues are clear: "The issue of future dangerousness is the *crux* of a juror's preference for death."[61]

To some extent, the Court's decision in *Barefoot* reflected a post hoc, defensive posture. It appears to be saying: we have already decided (in *Jurek v. Texas*)[62] that predictions of dangerousness are acceptable at the penalty phase, so—even in the light of the overwhelming evidence before us—how can we exclude "psychiatrists, out of the entire universe of persons who might have an opinion on the issue"?[63] This attitude partially mirrored the chief justice's position in *Addington v. Texas*: given "the lack of certainty and the fallibility of psychiatric diagnosis, there is a serious question as to whether the state could *ever* prove beyond a reasonable doubt that an individual is both mentally ill and likely to be dangerous."[64] A student note written in 1967 augured both of these positions: "If ever it be proven that psychiatry is not reliable, there will be created a doctrinal abyss into which will sink the whole structure of commitment law, not just those portions which deal with the harmless mentally ill."[65] The court in *Barefoot* appeared unwilling to confront the implications of this potential "doctrinal abyss." In an earlier article, this author suggested that

> *Barefoot* appears to be indefensible on evidentiary grounds, on constitutional grounds, and on common sense grounds. It flies in the face of virtually all of the relevant scientific literature. It is inconsistent with the development of evidence law doctrine, and it makes a mockery of earlier Supreme Court decisions cautioning that *extra* reliability is needed in capital cases.[66]

No subsequent developments[67] have suggested that this assessment is in need of any major substantive revision. *Barefoot* has seen surprisingly little legally significant subsequent litigation,[68] with courts generally—especially in Texas[69]—applying the doctrine relatively mechanically.[70]

The evidence revolution engineered by the Supreme Court's decisions in *Daubert v. Merrill Dow Pharmaceuticals Inc.*[71] and *Kumho Tire Co. v. Carmichael*[72] has had negligible impact on this state of affairs.[73] Writing some twelve years after *Daubert* in this context, Professor John Edens and his colleagues concluded, "Although . . . *Daubert* [and] *Kumho* . . . may have a constraining effect on the use of clinical predictions of violence risk in capital cases, *at present these predictions continue relatively unabated.*"[74] Although in a Fifth Circuit concurring opinion,[75] Judge Emilio Garza has pointed out that in light of *Daubert*, the continuing vitality of *Barefoot* is questionable,[76] there is little if any evidence that there has been any "real-life" impact of *Daubert* on *Barefoot* in this context.

By way of example, in *Coble v. State*,[77] where the court noted that the "'gatekeeping' standards of the trial court must keep up with the most current understanding of any scientific endeavor, including the field of forensic psychiatry and its professional methodology of assessing long-term future dangerousness," that a testifying expert must employ "the same professional standards of intellectual rigor in the courtroom as is expected in the practice of the relevant field," that the "validity of the expert's conclusions depends upon the soundness of the methodology,"[78] and that *Daubert* and its progeny "have significantly altered the evidentiary threshold requirements of reliability and relevance of any expert's testimony, including psychiatric or psychological expertise,"[79] it nonetheless affirmed the defendant's conviction under the harmless error rule.[80] Indeed, all of the most recent empirical research—studying Texas cases—concludes that there is "little support" for any claim that these predictions have improved over the past two decades.[81]

We also know that courts generally "lower the bar" on the resolution of *Daubert* issues in criminal cases,[82] and that in *Daubert* cases, the prosecutor's position is sustained (either in support of questioned expertise or in opposition to it) "vastly more often" than is that of the defense counsel.[83] As Professor Paul Gianelli has ruefully noted, "*Daubert* required a far higher standard of admissibility for money-damages than *Barefoot* required for the death penalty."[84] Although *Daubert*'s gatekeeping role for judges and demand for reliability as well as relevance would seem to have raised the standards high enough that such testimony should be excluded,[85] again, there is little or no evidence that this has ever happened.[86] In short, *Barefoot*'s legacy continues in spite of *Daubert* and its progeny. Professor Michael Gottesman is absolutely correct: "*Daubert* cannot be squared with *Barefoot*."[87]

This is all more problematic in light of what we know about the ineffectiveness of counsel in death penalty cases.[88] One of the slender reeds that appears, on the surface, to support the holding in *Barefoot* is the assumption that defense counsel can effectively cross-examine state witnesses who testify as to future dangerousness.[89] *Barefoot* offered no empirical support for this proposition (the majority merely expressing its confidence that the fact finder "would have the benefit of cross examination and contrary evidence by the opposing party").[90] The frequently lackluster quality of counsel in death penalty cases in no way supports this brave assertion.[91]

It is also assumed that *jurors* will be able to adequately assess this testimony.[92] The majority noted pointedly,

> Petitioner's entire argument, as well as that of Justice Blackmun's dissent, is founded on the premise that a jury will not be able to separate the wheat from the chaff. We do not share in this low evaluation of the adversary process.[93]

The uncontroverted facts paint a dismal picture and show how misguided the majority was. Violence risk assessment errors continue at capital sentencing.[94] At the best, future dangerousness determinations are "wildly speculative."[95] One study concluded that jurors making a prediction of future violence—the factor that is the jurors' "overriding concern"[96] or "predominant consideration"[97]—were wrong 97 percent of the time, showing only "chance-level" performance of capital juries in predicting future dangerousness.[98] Compare these findings to the recommendation of Professor Chris Slobogin: "The death penalty should never be based on a finding of dangerousness, unless the prediction can be made with virtual certainty."[99]

In an exhaustive study, Professors Mark Cunningham and Thomas Reidy identify multiple factors suggesting the potential for "fundamental error" in jury decision making in this context:

1. Individuals undertaking violence risk assessment are likely to commit a number of fundamental errors unless guided by reliable scientific methodology and group data, often resulting in an overestimation of violence risk.
2. A capital jury's familiarity with the heinousness of the capital offense and knowledge of other aggravating factors or acts encourages an expectation of high future violence risk in prison that is not justified by research.
3. The combination of these factors is likely to result in a capital sentencing jury that is strongly biased toward overestimation of violence risk when scientifically grounded expert testimony is excluded.
4. A federal capital jury is at best almost certain to be ignorant of reliable violence risk assessment methodology, rates of prison violence, prison population demographics and characteristics, and federal prison confinement options and security procedures. At worst, federal capital jurors come to a capital sentencing risk assessment holding intuitive assumptions regarding future dangerousness that are false. It must be emphasized that much of the research data on the violence risk assessment of prison inmates is counterintuitive.
5. In the absence of expert testimony, a capital jury has no mechanism to discount memorable but infrequent events (anecdotal evidence), understand or incorporate base rate data, appreciate the importance of context, avoid illusory correlations, maintain skepticism of clinical methods, understand the minimal implications of antisocial personality disorder or related characterizations, incorporate the effects of aging, reliably evaluate patterns of behavior, factor in preventive measures, acquire the broad information relevant to violence risk considerations, appreciate the probabilistic nature of their task, or critically evaluate the arguments of the government or the defense.[100]

Barefoot is especially troubling because research shows that future dangerousness plays a part in almost all jury determinations to impose a death sentence. By way of example, between 1995 and 2006, "future violence was alleged as a non-statutory aggravating factor in [77]% of the federal capital prosecutions," and a "death [sentence] occurred in over 80% of the federal cases where the jury found that future prison violence was likely."[101] The incapacitation rationale of the death penalty is "severely undermined by alarmingly unreliable predictions of future threat."[102] Yet, as Professor Berry underscores, this prediction is "the strongest determinant of whether an individual receives the death penalty."[103]

On Sanism

In the context of the insanity defense, I made this point nearly twenty years ago:

> Careful research studies have thus found that judges, attorneys, legislators and mental health professionals all inappropriately employ irrelevant, stereotypical negative information in coming to conclusions on the related question of the potential future dangerousness of a mentally disabled criminal defendant. What we call "common sense" is frequently nothing more than sanism: the irrational thought processes, founded on stereotype, that are at the roots of our incoherent insanity defense jurisprudence.[104]

The sort of testimony that had regularly been offered in death penalty cases by Dr. Grigson[105] appealed to the basest sanist instincts of jurors.[106] Certainly, jurors' fears of false negatives[107]—driven by sanism—help account for juries' willingness to accept expert predictions of future dangerousness in capital cases.[108] And expert witnesses are no less culpable. Consider *Francois v. Henderson*,[109] in which the testifying doctor conceded that he "hedged" testimony "because he did not want to be criticized should (the patient) be released and then commit a criminal act."[110] Writing about the relationship between sanism and the death penalty in this context, John Parry is clear:

> The whole notion upon which almost every execution depends—a finding of dangerousness—is a disgraceful sham, particularly when applied to persons who already are stigmatized, feared by society, and often viewed by judges and jurors as being dangerous before sentencing even begins.[111]

On Pretextuality

This entire area of law and policy is based on pretextuality.[112] We profess our faith in expert witnesses' ability to predict dangerousness,[113] in jurors' ability to "separate the wheat from the chaff,"[114] and in lawyers' ability to effectively cross-examine such experts.[115] All the valid and reliable evidence tells us that this is not so.[116] To continue to express our beliefs in these propositions in spite of this database is pretextual at best, and delusional at worst.[117]

On Therapeutic Jurisprudence

There has been little written about the relationship between therapeutic jurisprudence (TJ) and the error rate/predictions of dangerousness dilemma. Self-evidently, it is not therapeutic to sentence someone to death when that sentence is predicated, in significant part, on juror misunderstanding about the likelihood of future violence.[118] Beyond this, TJ scholars have, in other contexts, critically examined the entire "dangerousness prediction" enterprise, recommending that it be abandoned and replaced by a "risk assessment" or "risk management" model,[119] an approach that "should lead to greater accuracy" and be more consonant with "considerations valued by therapeutic jurisprudence."[120] And, in the civil commitment context, colleagues and I have written about the TJ implications of a "more formal" system of dangerousness assessments:

> For the first time, psychiatrists were subjected to rigorous cross-examination and were required to substantiate their medical opinions rather than merely make medical conclusions. At the same time, psychiatric diagnostic and predictive skills were more closely scrutinized. Lawyers were often successful in convincing courts that psychiatric diagnoses and predictions of dangerousness were inaccurate. The meaning of dangerousness also became an important area of litigation. Critics charged that the concept was "vague" and "amorphous," and its "elasticity" has made it "one of the most problematic and elusive concepts in mental health law."[121]

Although the issues in death penalty litigation (and the stakes of the litigant) are self-evidently very different from the ones discussed in these articles, I believe that these perspectives are important as well for the topic discussed in this chapter.

CONCLUSION

Few Supreme Court decisions in the past forty years have been criticized as uniformly or as scathingly as the opinion in *Barefoot*. The Court's sanctioning of (in its most charitable light) highly questionable expert testimony on future dangerousness is deeply troubling, especially in a death penalty context. There is no doubting the accuracy of the conclusions drawn by Professors Mark Cunningham and Thomas Reidy that *Barefoot* reflects "grossly inadequate" methodology and is "profoundly flawed in overestimating both the magnitude of risk and the accuracy of the prediction."[122]

Writing with other colleagues, Professor Cunningham concludes that "there is a chasm between the predictions of capital jurors that serious violence is likely in the future and the science demonstrating that capital jurors cannot reliably make this prediction."[123] Our system of purportedly assessing future dangerousness—fueled by sanism and pretextuality—thus disproportionately taints death sentences involving defendants with serious mental disabilities and robs the capital sentencing process of any modicum of dignity.

· 4 ·

Mental Disability
Evidence and Mitigation[1]

INTRODUCTION

$\mathscr{N}$early thirty-five years ago, when surveying the availability of counsel to mentally disabled litigants, President Carter's Commission on Mental Health noted the frequently substandard level of representation made available to mentally disabled criminal defendants.[2] Nothing that has happened in the intervening years has been a palliative for this problem; if anything, it is confounded by the myth that adequate counsel is available to represent both criminal defendants in general, and mentally disabled litigants in particular.[3] And as the importance of the construction of "mitigating" and "aggravating" evidence grows, so does the need for counsel to be able to understand and utilize this mental disability evidence.

In this chapter, I will first explain how "aggravating" and "mitigating" circumstances are statutorily characterized, then trace the Supreme Court's case law in this area, discuss the significance of the ABA guidelines, speculate as to the potential "backlash effect" that may arise in mitigation cases, and finally sketch out some of the significant operative issues in the presentation of mitigation evidence in cases involving defendants with mental disabilities who face the death penalty. Then, as I have done in other chapters, I will again contextualize these variables through the jurisprudential filters of sanism, pretextuality, and therapeutic jurisprudence.

"AGGRAVATORS" AND "MITIGATORS"[4]

Contemporaneous death penalty statutes require findings of what are called "mitigating" and "aggravating" factors.[5] This is done to ensure (ostensibly)

29

that the death penalty is reserved for only the vilest of crimes and the worst offenders[6]—ones for which there is no reasonable excuse or justification.[7] By way of example, in Pennsylvania, a typical death penalty jurisdiction for these purposes, "aggravators" include, but are not limited to, such circumstances as the commission of a murder of a prosecution witness, of a murder in the perpetration of a felony, the knowing creation of a "grave risk of death to another person in addition to the victim of the offense," the use of torture, a prior murder conviction, or a murder for hire.[8] In the same statutory scheme, mitigators include age, lack of significant criminal history, acting under "extreme duress,"[9] and two others especially significant to this chapter:

> (2) The defendant was under the influence of extreme mental or emotional disturbance[10] [and]
> (3) The capacity of the defendant to appreciate the criminality of his conduct or to conform his conduct to the requirements of law was substantially impaired.[11]

Aggravating factors in Pennsylvania must be proven beyond a reasonable doubt, and the mitigating circumstances must be proved by the defendant by a preponderance of the evidence.[12] In the same sentencing scheme, the verdict must be a sentence of death if the jury unanimously finds at least one aggravating circumstance and no mitigating circumstance or if the jury unanimously finds one or more aggravating circumstances which "outweigh" any mitigating circumstances.[13] The verdict must be a sentence of life imprisonment in all other cases. On this point, the New Jersey Supreme Court has spoken clearly about the then-operative New Jersey law which was substantially similar to the one in Pennsylvania: "We can think of no judgment of any jury in this state in any case that has as strong a claim to the requirement of certainty as does this one."[14]

The importance of mitigating evidence at the penalty stage "cannot be overestimated,"[15] although what actually is construed by jurors to be mitigation, in the words of a veteran death penalty defense counsel, "remains a mystery."[16] The sentencing authority must[17] consider any relevant mitigating evidence that a defendant offers as a basis for a sentence less than death,[18] a holding that flows from *Gregg v. Georgia*[19] and the Court's other initial "modern" decisions upholding the death penalty, in which it mandated that the sentencing authority be provided with adequate individualized information about defendants and be guided by clear and objective standards.[20] These cases led Professor James Liebman and a colleague to craft a four-part test to be employed in determining the degree to which mitigation based on mental disorder would be proper in a capital case:

1. Whether the offender's suffering evidences expiation or inspires compassion;
2. Whether the offender's cognitive and/or volitional impairment at the time he committed the crime affected his responsibility for his actions, and thereby diminished society's need for revenge;
3. Whether the offender, subjectively analyzed, was less affected than the mentally normal offender by the deterrent threat of capital punishment at the time he committed the crime; and
4. Whether the exemplary value of capitally punishing the offender, as objectively perceived by reasonable persons, would be attenuated by the difficulty those persons would have identifying with the executed offender.[21]

Notwithstanding this careful formulation, there is little disputing Kevin Doyle's conclusion that "every step [of the penalty phase] carries a significant risk of error."[22]

THE IMPORTANCE OF *LOCKETT* AND *EDDINGS*[23]

In *Lockett v. Ohio*,[24] the Supreme Court substantially widened the scope of mitigating evidence allowed at the penalty phase of a capital case, concluding that "the Eighth and Fourteenth Amendments require that the sentencer, in all but the rarest kind of capital case, not be precluded from considering, as a mitigating factor, any aspect of a defendant's character or record . . . that defendant proffers as a basis for a sentence less than death."[25]

Four years later, the Court expanded on its *Lockett* rule in *Eddings v. Oklahoma*,[26] holding that the sentencing authority must consider any relevant mitigating evidence.[27] In *Eddings*, during the sentencing hearing, the defendant presented testimony that he was the product of a broken family and the victim of child abuse.[28] Psychological testimony also showed that Eddings was emotionally disturbed and that his mental and emotional development was at a level below his chronological age.[29] Further, a psychiatrist and a sociologist testified that Eddings could be treated and rehabilitated.[30] Despite this testimony, the trial judge considered only Eddings' youth as a mitigating factor, which, while important, did not outweigh the aggravating factors presented by the prosecution.[31]

Reversing and remanding the sentence, the Supreme Court concluded that the sentencer must consider all mitigating evidence and then weigh this evidence against the aggravating circumstances.[32] Thus, *Eddings'* restatement of the *Lockett* rule requires the sentencing tribunal to "listen" to any relevant evidence proffered to mitigate in a death penalty case.[33] Testimony found relevant as to Eddings' mental disorder, then, could not be ignored. Read together, *Lockett* and *Eddings* thus "require the courts to admit into evidence, and to consider, *any* claim raised by the defendant in mitigation."[34]

Subsequent Supreme Court decisions have reconfirmed the Court's commitment to this approach. By way of example, in *Porter v. McCollum*,[35] the Supreme Court reversed an Eleventh Circuit decision that had reversed a grant of habeas corpus in a case in which the state court had not considered expert testimony for purposes of nonstatutory mitigation and "unreasonably discounted the evidence of [the defendant's] childhood abuse and military service."[36]

PENRY, TENNARD, AND MITIGATION[37]

Then, in *Penry v. Lynaugh*,[38] the Supreme Court held that evidence as to the defendant's mental retardation was relevant to his culpability and that, without such information, jurors could not express their "reasoned moral response" in determining the appropriateness of the death penalty.[39] There, the court found that assessment of the defendant's retardation would aid the jurors in determining whether the commission of the crime was "deliberate."[40] Without a special instruction as to such evidence, a juror might be unaware that his evaluation of the defendant's moral culpability could be informed by his handicapping condition.[41] Also, in attempting to grapple with questions of future dangerousness or of the presence of provocation (both questions that must be considered under the Texas state sentencing scheme), jurors were required to have a "vehicle" to consider whether the defendant's background and childhood should have mitigated the penalty imposed.[42] Without such testimony, the jury could not appropriately express its "reasoned moral response" on the evidence in question.[43]

On remand, Penry was again sentenced to death, and appealed on the question of whether the jury instructions at his second sentencing comported with the mandate in the first *Penry* case.[44] The court agreed with Penry that the jury directions failed to "provide the jury with a vehicle for expressing its reasoned moral response to the mitigating evidence of Penry's mental retardation and childhood abuse,"[45] and found:

> As we made clear in *Penry I*, none of the special issues is broad enough to provide a vehicle for the jury to give mitigating effect to the evidence of Penry's mental retardation and childhood abuse. . . . In the words of Judge Dennis below, the jury's ability to consider and give effect to Penry's mitigating evidence was still "shackled and confined within the scope of the three special issues." 215 F.3d, at 514 (dissenting opinion). Thus, because the supplemental instruction had no practical effect, the jury instructions

at Penry's second sentencing were not meaningfully different from the ones we found constitutionally inadequate in *Penry I.*[46]

The trial court's supplemental instructions, the Supreme Court concluded, provided an "inadequate vehicle for the jury to make a reasoned moral response to Penry's mitigating evidence."[47]

The Supreme Court had another opportunity to consider application of its *Penry* jurisprudence three years later in *Tennard v. Dretke.* [48] That case again involved the question of whether Texas' capital sentencing scheme provided an adequate vehicle for consideration of the defendant's low intelligence. Directly at issue in this case, however, was the propriety of a "screening test" employed by the Fifth Circuit for determining whether mitigating evidence was "constitutionally relevant" for habeas corpus purposes. Justice O'Connor, writing for the majority, ruled that the Fifth Circuit erred in refusing to grant a Certificate of Appealability (COA) on the basis that the petitioner had failed to show that his low intelligence was a "uniquely severe permanent handicap" that bore a "nexus" to the crime.[49]

The Court stated that in so ruling, the Fifth Circuit had "invoked its own restrictive gloss on *Penry I.*"[50] The appeals court had determined that Tennard's evidence that he had an IQ of 67 failed both prongs of its test for "constitutional relevance"—it was not evidence of mental retardation or another "uniquely severe permanent handicap," and Tennard had not shown that it bore any nexus to the crime.[51] After noting that the Fifth Circuit appeared to apply its "screening test" uniformly to *Penry* claims, the Court held that such a test "has no foundation in the decisions of this Court." [52] The Court began its analysis by noting that the standard of relevance applicable to mitigating evidence in capital cases was no different than the standard applied in other contexts. [53] In the capital sentencing context, mitigating evidence is any evidence that the jury could reasonably find warrants a sentence less than death. [54] Once this low threshold of relevance was met, the Eighth Amendment required that the jury be able to consider and give effect to the mitigating evidence. [55]

"To say that only those features and circumstances that a panel of federal appellate judges deems to be 'severe' (let alone 'uniquely severe') could have such a tendency is incorrect. Rather, the question is simply whether the evidence is of such a character that it might serve as a basis for a sentence less than death." [56] Moreover, requiring a nexus between Tennard's low IQ and the crime was also an incorrect application of the law in that "impaired intellectual functioning is inherently mitigating." [57] Applying the proper analysis to the facts of the case, the Court held that reasonable jurists could conclude that evidence of low IQ was relevant mitigating evidence and that the Texas Court of Criminal Appeals' application of *Penry* to the facts of Tennard's case was unreasonable. The Court noted that in the case at hand, the prosecutor's comments pressed exactly the most problematic interpretation of the special issues, suggesting that Tennard's low IQ was irrelevant in mitigation, but relevant to the question whether he posed a future danger.[58] The Court thus reversed the denial of the COA and remanded the case for further proceedings.

AFTER *LOCKETT, EDDINGS, PENRY,* AND *TENNARD*[59]

Building on these decisions, lower court cases have considered the guidance that must be given to juries in determining whether mitigating circumstances have been presented, including both statutory and nonstatutory factors.[60] In most cases, it was required that the judge tell the jury what a mitigating circumstance is, and what its function is in the jury's sentencing deliberation.[61] This responsibility would not have been fulfilled simply by telling the jurors that they may "consider" such circumstances.[62]

As testimony of mental disorder at the penalty phase is warranted by the serious responsibility that devolves on the fact finder (usually the jury) in a capital case, it is not strictly relegated in some jurisdictions to mitigating factors but may also be presented by the prosecution so as to evidence aggravating factors as well.[63] Also, courts will weigh what is perceived as the clarity and lucidity of conflicting expert testimony in determining whether a mitigating factor is present.[64] Other courts have explored the implications of defendants' wishes to waive the production of mitigating evidence,[65] requirements that defendants file pretrial notice of their intent to present expert testimony at the mitigation stage,[66] what is a reasonable decision-making process to not produce mitigating evidence,[67] and the circumstances that arise when defense counsel fails to present/investigate mitigating mental health history and personal history and the prosecution uses this lack of mitigating evidence against the defendant.[68]

Testimony as to mental disorder need not support a finding of insanity.[69] On the other hand, courts are split on the question of the relevance of testimony as to the defendant's capacity for rehabilitation.[70] Further, testimony at the sentencing phase must be admitted even where a defense of not guilty by reason of insanity has been specifically rejected at the guilt phase of the trial,[71] or where the issue was never previously raised.[72]

THE BACKLASH ISSUE[73]

Professor George Dix has noted that, in certain cases where the same evidence that demonstrates diminished responsibility also suggests that the offender poses a serious and continuing risk to society, the integration of such testimony into the sentencing process might "almost inevitably result in practical pressure to *increase* the severity of the penalty."[74] On this point, Professor Christopher Seeds has noted, "Given the frequency with which a defendant's future dangerousness is alleged as an aggravating factor in capital cases, concern about presenting mitigation, such as evidence of mental illness, that could turn against the client (or open the door to counterargument that would portray the client as a psychopath or otherwise support a propensity for violence) is perhaps warranted."[75] There are also differences at play here in cases involving defendants with mental retardation and those with mental illness,[76] although the American Psychiatric Association has found that jurors err in both subsets of cases, "tend[ing] to give too little weight to mitigating evidence of severe mental disorder, leading to inappropriate execution of offenders whose responsibility was significantly diminished by mental retardation *or* mental illness."[77] A study—of both mock and actual jurors—by Professor Marla Sandys and her colleagues reveals that "mere perceptions" of future dangerousness are enough to tilt the balance in the direction of a death sentence.[78] The reverse side of this coin is important as well: Might arguing mitigation evidence during the penalty phase undermine a defendant's *factual innocence* argument?[79] On this point, Professor Gary Kowaluk concludes,

> This study provides support for the defense experts' recommendations that the best argued denial and admission defense cases involves a thorough pre-trial investigation which uncovers as much lingering doubt and mitigation evidence on behalf of the defendant as possible and introduces mitigation evidence early in the form of a coherent theme regardless of what kind of strategy is being argued.[80]

Veteran defense lawyer Danalynn Recer stresses, "The idea is to use the mitigation process to tell the life story of the defendant in a way that explained the conduct that brought him into court."[81]

ON THE CONSTRUCTION OF MITIGATION EVIDENCE

What is the lawyer's role in confronting the mitigation dilemmas? Lawyer-anthropologist Jessie Chang articulates the lawyer's task this way: "Death penalty mitigation involves the extensive, humanizing practices of investigation and representation that go into producing a thickly contextual social biography of capital defendants, to be used in advocating against a sentence of death."[82]

Writing about this issue, Professor Laura Jochnowitz recently underscored the dilemma:

> Death row inmates are often afflicted with severe psychological problems and/or below average intelligence, as well as with some related disabling factors like head injuries, drug and childhood abuse histories. Yet claims by capital defendants of extenuating mental impairments may sometimes be investigated poorly or strategically omitted,[83] and even when the claims are presented, they are not well understood by jurors. Defendants' history of mental impairments may be perceived by jurors as stigmatizing, threatening, or not believable. Jurors respond differently and more punitively to some types of mental illness and addiction, than to cognitive impairments. Their personal attributes and criminal justice attitudes may affect their receptivity. Jurors' exposure to mental health and other issues early in the case, at voir dire or the guilt phase of a bifurcated capital trial, may affect whether they pre-judge its significance at the penalty phase. Yet, jurors' exposure to long guilt phase prosecution evidence and bloody crime scene photos, without evidence foreshadowing diminished capacity or reduced culpability may desensitize jurors, before they hear penalty phase evidence.[84]

Professor Jochnowitz's thoughtful observations underscore the absolute connection between the presentation of mitigation evidence and the quality and effectiveness of counsel in the presentation of this evidence.[85] As I discuss extensively elsewhere, the role of counsel is critical in any mitigation inquiry. Professor Christopher Seeds characterizes the issue in this manner:

> My hypothesis—rooted in the principles of the prevailing professional guidelines and supported by the existing studies and analysis regarding how jurors make decisions and what matters to them—is that jurors who hear complete and coherent mitigation presentations are more likely to find double-edged explanatory life history evidence mitigating, not aggravating. Jurors respond to consistency and coherence, and those inclined by personal experience to vote for a life sentence, in particular, will respond to detail. In short, how jurors perceive explanatory mitigation may depend less on the "double-edged" nature of the evidence, and more on how the evidence is presented.[86]

Beyond this, it is important to understand that "mitigation" cannot be left solely for the mitigation phase.[87] As Professor Sean O'Brien notes,

> the mitigation case is intricately woven into every step of the case, including the prosecutor's decisions as to the degree of the charge or whether to seek the death penalty, and the defense team's approach to settlement negotiations, jury selection, and first-stage trial issues. It is universally understood by experienced capital trial lawyers and mitigation specialists

that waiting to unveil the mitigation case at the penalty phase of a capital trial is simply too late.[88]

Defense counsel often misses mental health claims entirely. Professor Jochnowitz's research reveals that "missed mental health claims made up almost one third, 31.1% or 119/383, of all occurrences of missed claims" in a sample studied, and that "[t]hese included mental culpability mitigation claims, 29/36 cases (80.6%), and missed mental assessment claims, 28/36 cases (77.8%)."[89]

In recent years, there has, finally, been some guidance. In 2003, the ABA significantly elevated the standard of representation in death penalty cases. Its revised "Guidelines for the Appointment and Performance of Defense Counsel in Death Penalty Cases" (*Guidelines*) provided the partial basis for the 2003 Supreme Court decision in *Wiggins v. Smith*,[90] which established the requirement for a thorough and comprehensive mitigation review. *Wiggins* found that the defendant's attorney failed to conduct a comprehensive social history of his client, thus violating his Sixth Amendment rights.[91] Specifically, the Court set forth the requirement that mitigation investigations include efforts to discover "all reasonably available" mitigating evidence, as well as evidence to rebut any aggravating evidence that may be introduced by the prosecutor.[92] *Wiggins* incorporated the *Guidelines*, whose objective was to "set forth a national standard of practice for the defense of capital cases in order to insure high quality legal representation for all persons facing the possible imposition or execution of a death sentence by any jurisdiction."[93]

Included among the *Guidelines'* recommendations is the need for at least one member of the defense team to be "qualified by training and experience to screen individuals for the presence of mental or psychological disorders or impairments." The *Guidelines* address this issue:

> Creating a competent and reliable mental health evaluation consistent with prevailing standards of practices is a time consuming and expensive process. Counsel must compile extensive historical data, as well as obtaining a thorough physical and neurological examination. Diagnostic studies, neuropsychological testing, appropriate brain scans, blood tests or genetic studies, and consultation with additional mental health specialists may also be necessary.[94]

The *Guidelines* also recommend the inclusion of a mental health professional/mitigation specialist who possesses

> clinical and information-gathering skills and training that most lawyers simply do not have. They have the time and ability to elicit sensitive, embarrassing and often humiliating evidence that the defendant may have never disclosed. They have the clinical skills to recognize such things as

congenital, mental or neurological conditions, to understand how these conditions may have affected the defendant's development and behavior, and to identify the most appropriate experts to examine the defendant or testify on his behalf.[95]

The mitigation specialist is an indispensable member of any capital defense team.[96] Notes Professor Seeds, "The 'science of mitigation' that [has] developed . . . combined advances in social work, psychology, anthropology, and related fields with legal understanding of how best to communicate information to a sentencing judge or jury."[97]

Elliot Atkins and his colleagues have also provided detailed guidelines for conducting mitigation in capital cases with the goal of humanizing the client:[98]

1. Clinical evaluation including interviewing and psychological testing exploring psychological syndromes, neurological impairment, psychosocial/familial issues, and substance abuse history. Academic, occupational, and mental health records are essential to this stage.
2. Social and cultural factors affecting the defendant's development and in particular his involvement in the offense, including poverty, institutionalization, race, age, foreign culture, military experience, gang involvement, and sexual identity.
3. Prison experience must be gathered if present, including adaptation to prison life, respect for corrections officers, assistance to other inmates, and any other accomplishments during incarceration.
4. Factors related to the offense, including the defendant's intention at the time of the crime, moral justification, and role in the offense. This is a particularly important area in which cultural sensitivity is critical, especially with regard to motivation and anticipation of outcome or consequences.
5. The defendant's character, including a lack of criminal history, cooperation with authorities, remorse, and rehabilitation.[99]
6. Victim-related variables, including whether the offense was provoked by the victim and/or the extent to which the victim was a participant in the offense.[100]

It is critical that the jury be made aware of the extent to which the defendant's mental health issues had an impact upon the defendant's thoughts, emotions, and behaviors, not only at the time of the crime but throughout the course of his/her life. Will this information be sufficient to disavow jurors of their belief (perhaps their conviction?) that the defendant is so evil that a sentence of life without the possibility of parole is perceived to be inadequate punishment for the crime committed?[101] In order to overcome such perceptions, the forensic practitioner must present the jury with evidence-based mitigating factors—factors that are the product of a thorough and objective evaluation of both the defendant and the mitigation being presented. Opinions presented that are not the product of a methodologically reliable evaluation will be assailable, particularly during cross-examination. It is in this effort to humanize the defendant that the forensic mental health practitioner is charged with the responsibility of conveying the mitigation evidence that will make the difference between life and death.[102]

SOME JURISPRUDENTIAL FILTERS

Sanism[103]

In this environment, it is easy to see how evidence of mental illness ostensibly introduced for mitigating purposes can be construed by judges or by jurors as aggravating instead.[104] In one notorious Florida case, for example, a trial judge concluded that because of the defendant's mental disability (paranoid schizophrenia manifested by hallucinations in which he "saw" others in a "yellow haze"), "the only assurance society can receive that this man never again commits to another human being what he did to [the brutally murdered decedent] is that the ultimate sentence of death be imposed."[105]

To a great extent, sanism in the death penalty decision-making process mirrors sanism in the context of insanity defense decision making.[106] Such decision making is often irrational, rejecting empiricism, science, psychology, and philosophy, and substituting in its place myth, stereotype, bias, and distortion. It resists educational correction, demands punishment regardless of responsibility, and reifies medievalist concepts based on fixed and absolute notions of good and evil and of right and wrong. In such cases, "[T]he public has always demanded that mentally ill defendants comport with its visual images of 'craziness,'"[107] that they demonstrate "outward signs of craziness or bizarre behavior."[108]

Myths similar to those that infect the insanity defense process apply when a mentally disabled defendant is being prosecuted in a capital case. And to confound matters, "enormous pressures" will often be placed on defense counsel to play into the hands of these myths and paint an exaggerated picture of a "totally crazy" defendant to assuage jurors whose "ordinary common sense"[109] demands an all-or-nothing representation of mental illness.[110] The importance of competent, trained, and specialized counsel to identify and rebut these sanist myths should be clear on its face.

A sampling of cases decided under the Federal Sentencing Guidelines similarly demonstrates the ways in which judges are frequently sanist.[111] Although these are not death penalty cases, the judicial attitudes reflected are instructive. In rejecting a defendant's "suicidal tendencies" as a possible basis for a downward departure in an embezzlement case, the Sixth Circuit held that departure would never be permissible on this basis because any consideration of this argument would lead to "boilerplate" claims and force courts to "separate the wheat of valid claims from the chaff of disingenuous ones," a "path before which we give serious pause."[112] This argument tracks, nearly verbatim, the reasoning of the Fourth Circuit, which refused to depart downward in the case of a defendant who had suffered severe childhood sexual abuse, referring to the "innumerable defendants" who could plead "unstable upbringing" as a potential departure ground.[113]

Underlying many of these Guidelines cases is a powerful current of blame:[114] the defendant succumbed to temptation by not resisting drugs or alcohol and by not overcoming childhood abuse.[115] This sense of blame mirrors courts' sanist impatience with mentally disabled criminal defendants in general, attributing their problems in the legal process to weak character or poor resolve.[116] Thus, we should not be surprised to learn that a trial judge, responding to a National Center for State Courts survey, indicated that incompetent-to-stand-trial defendants could have understood and communicated with their counsel and the court "if they [had] only wanted."[117]

The threat to dismantle the mitigation doctrine becomes even more troubling when considered in light of both the empirical findings (as to juror rejection of mental disability as a proper mitigator and as to the reality of what happens to mentally disabled criminal defendants facing the death penalty); the unheralded case law (mental disability issues are often ignored or poorly presented; counsel's failures here will rarely be seen as reversible error); and the theoretical perspectives that I have pointed out in this work (the ways that sanist jurors use heuristic cognitive devices to shape their schemas about these defendants, acts sanctioned explicitly or implicitly by pretextual or teleological courts).[118]

Pretextuality[119]

All of this data must be read in the context of other information about mental disability, criminal law, and jury behavior. We know that jurors adhere firmly to the belief that mental status pleas are overused in the face of a unanimous empirical database as to their rarity, the greater rarity of success, and the high risk to defendants raising such pleas.[120] We know that defendants are more likely to feign sanity rather than insanity (even where the evidence of their mental disability might qualify as mitigating evidence under Supreme Court doctrine).[121] We know how, as a result of the vividness heuristic, one salient case can lead to the restructuring of an entire body of jurisprudence.[122] We know how jurors overpredict future dangerousness in death penalty cases.[123] We know how the

Supreme Court's "death qualification" jurisprudence for jury selection makes it more likely that seated jurors will see mental nonresponsibility defenses "as a ruse and as an impediment to the conviction of criminals."[124] We know that there is "a clear 'fit' between the retribution-driven punitive response favored by authoritarians and the authoritarian's resentment of the insanity defense and his general hostility toward psychiatry."[125]

This data must be read side by side with what we know about juror use of schemas: that they are especially confused and confusing in death penalty cases;[126] that they "play to" menacing and dangerous stereotypes of mentally disabled persons;[127] and that when there are dissonances in these schemas, they are interpreted in ways "consistent with criminality."[128] It must be read further against the backdrop of ongoing judicial hostility toward mental disability–based excuses for crime and toward mental disability evidence in general.

As a result of these factors, application of the mitigation doctrine is revealed, in certain individual cases, to be a pretextual hoax. Consider the Florida case of *Mason v. State*.[129] Mason was convicted of murder after the trial court failed to inform the jury about his "long history of mental illness, the fact that he suffered from organic brain damage, that he suffered from mental retardation, had a history of drug abuse, that he attempted suicide on four occasions during [the prior year], and that he [had] a history of suffering from depression and hallucinations."[130] The dissonance between the trial court's behavior in this case and the Supreme Court's line of cases from *Eddings*[131] and *Lockett*[132] to *Penry*[133] to *Tennard*[134] suggests that mere doctrinal analysis and recalibration can never be a solution to the underlying problems.

Further, there is now an impressive body of social science research that suggests that jurors frequently do not understand jury instructions as to the construction of mitigating evidence.[135] What could be more pretextual than a system that relies on the transmission of information to fact finders who cannot understand the information being transmitted? Again, the presence of frequently inadequate counsel exacerbates this problem even more and heightens the pretextuality of the entire capital punishment process. Refusal by courts to acknowledge the regularly substandard job done by counsel in this most demanding area of the law is simply pretextual.[136]

In short, as discussed earlier in this chapter, mental illness, rather than serving as a mitigating factor, is often seen in reality as an aggravating factor.[137] If competent counsel is present, the dilemma may paradoxically be even further confounded: if she should rely on certain kinds of "empathy" evidence—evidence of abuse, stress, retardation, institutional failure, and substance abuse—she runs the risk of putting before the jury the evidence that "has the greatest potential for turning into evidence in aggravation."[138] In the hands of sanist fact finders, the presentation of such evidence can be deadly to the defendant.[139]

Therapeutic Jurisprudence[140]

If therapeutic jurisprudence principles are applied to the questions raised in this chapter, several inquires immediately surface. First, if mental disability evidence can be seen as aggravating rather than mitigating, what a powerful incentive this may be for criminal defendants with mental disabilities to deny their mental illness and simultaneously refuse to seek ameliorative treatment.[141] If jurors especially turn "empathy" evidence into evidence of aggravating circumstances, how will that affect the already compromised relationship between counsel and the client with a mental disability?[142]

In short, any death penalty system that provides inadequate counsel and that, at least as a partial result of that inadequacy, fails to ensure that mental disability evidence is adequately considered and contextualized by death penalty decision makers, fails miserably from a therapeutic jurisprudence perspective.[143] Interestingly, it is important to note that sentencing and mitigation trainings offered nationwide by the National Association of Sentencing Advocates ("NASA") are grounded in core principles of therapeutic jurisprudence.[144]

The founders of therapeutic jurisprudence—David Wexler and Bruce Winick—have carefully sketched out how TJ principles are compatible with the criminal defense counsel's role.[145] The *humanizing* aspect of the mitigation presentation[146] is totally consonant with TJ's mission to "humanize the law,"[147] in part by adding human emotions and psychological aspects to the legal process.[148] As one example, the use of a mitigation specialist or interpreter who is familiar with the language, values, ethics, and laws of the defendant's cultural background can greatly facilitate information gathering, leading to a much more effective mitigation presentation.[149] This sort of culturally competent mitigation practice[150] demonstrates the utility (and necessity) of TJ practices at the death penalty stage. Not unimportantly, it is also the best means of seeking to expunge pervasive sanism from this system as well.[151]

To be consonant with TJ values, defense attorneys must draw connections between mental health and behavior by presenting a full personal history of the defendant, and demonstrate the value of the defendant's life to the jurors.[152] Not only will this make it more likely that jurors will reject the death penalty—if they can see and understand why the defendant behaved the way he did[153]—but also it is likely that the defendant will be more cooperative with counsel if he believes counsel understands him and what caused him to commit what might otherwise be seen as an inexplicable crime.

Counsel must, again in consonance with TJ, be able to explain to jurors that mitigation evidence is not an excuse but rather an explanation.[154] Counsel must be able to explain to the jurors that someone can be a beloved father, son, and husband and can still commit a seemingly horrible act, that these are not mutually exclusive categories.[155]

It is essential that defense counsel be able to explain, in lay terms, the essence of the defendant's mental illness and its relationship to the acts in question. This is an essential strategy in stripping away the sanist facade from the death penalty proceeding.[156]

CONCLUSION

In a series of cases decided over the past thirty-four years, the Supreme Court has clarified the necessity of a constitutionally coherent system of ensuring that all potentially mitigating evidence be introduced at the sentencing phase of a death penalty trial. The stark reality, however, is that, operationally, this system has, in many instances, failed spectacularly, and that such evidence is often misconstrued as aggravating evidence, leading to an improper death sentence. Sanism and pretextuality are to blame here, and until we begin to take seriously the need to incorporate therapeutic jurisprudence principles into all phases of the death penalty trial, efforts to implement a constitutionally based process for the introduction and consideration of mitigation evidence will continue to fail miserably.

• 5 •

Competency to Be Executed:
The Case of Mental Retardation

INTRODUCTION[1]

$\mathcal{A}$nyone who has spent any time in the criminal justice system—as a defense lawyer, as a district attorney, or as a judge—knows that our treatment of criminal defendants with mental disabilities has been a scandal forever. Such defendants receive substandard counsel,[2] are treated poorly in prison,[3] receive disparately longer sentences,[4] and are regularly coerced into confessing to crimes (many of which they did not commit).[5] And those of us who know about this system know that it is a scandal of little interest to most lawyers, most citizens, and most judges.

This is not news and has not been so for decades. We are content to bury our heads in the sand and ignore the ramifications of the morally corrupt system we have created.[6] But every once in a while, a case is decided that makes us reconsider this question and forces us to see what we do on a regular basis in that system. The United States Supreme Court decision in *Atkins v. Virginia*[7]—holding that the execution of individuals with mental retardation[8] violates the Eighth and Fourteenth Amendments[9]—was such a case. Although *Atkins*, on paper, appears to be an impressive victory for advocates for persons with mental disabilities, that victory may be illusory unless we look carefully at a constellation of legal, social, and behavioral issues that have combined to poison this area of the law for decades. *Atkins* provides a blueprint, but it is by no means "the end of the road."

The chapter will proceed in this manner. First, it will briefly look at some earlier signposts—*Ford v. Wainwright*,[10] the Supreme Court's predecessor case barring execution of the "currently insane,"[11] and also the Court's earlier decision in *Penry v. Lynaugh*[12] (with a brief nod at *Penry v. Johnson*[13]) in an attempt to uncover which meta-issues were really animating the majority and dissenting justices in those opinions. Next, it will briefly summarize the key points of *Atkins* and then consider what I characterize as the seventeen "pressure points" in *Atkins*, pressure points that must be taken extraordinarily seriously if the *Atkins* decision is, in fact, to have authentic meaning. It will then consider the post-*Atkins* case law and commentary. Finally, it will offer some brief conclusions—both prescriptions and proscriptions—focusing primarily on what the likely meaning of *Atkins* will be for persons with mental retardation facing the death penalty and for lawyers who represent these individuals.

THE ROAD FROM *FORD* TO *PENRY* TO *ATKINS*

The Ford *Decision*

In *Ford v. Wainwright*,[14] a fractured Supreme Court concluded that the Eighth Amendment did prohibit the imposition of the death penalty on an insane prisoner.[15] Justice Marshall—writing in the only portion of any of the four opinions that captured a majority of the court—pointed out that since the Court decided *Solesbee v. Balkcom* in 1950,[16] its Eighth Amendment jurisprudence had "evolved substantially."[17] Its ban on "cruel and unusual punishment embraced, at a minimum, those modes or acts of punishment that had been considered cruel and unusual at the time that the Bill of Rights was adopted"[18] and also recognized the "evolving standards of decency that mark the progress of a maturing society."[19] In coming to its determination, the Court took into account "objective evidence of contemporary values before determining whether a particular punishment comports with the fundamental human dignity that the Amendment protects."[20]

As I will discuss extensively in a subsequent chapter,[21] *Ford* was modified some two decades later in *Panetti v. Quarterman*,[22] clarifying *Ford*'s substantive test to demand that the prisoner possess a "rational understanding"[23] of the reasons he is to be executed.[24]

The Penry I *Decision*

While *Ford* initially clarified the question of the constitutionality of executing persons with mental illness, it did not answer the collateral and equally important issue of the constitutionality of executing individuals who have mental retardation. In *Penry v. Lynaugh*,[25] the Supreme Court approached the question from a significantly different perspective and reached a strikingly different conclusion.[26]

Penry was a person with moderate mental retardation (with an IQ of 50 to 63, the mental age of a six-and-a-half-year-old, and the social maturity of a nine- to ten-year-old).[27] In addressing the question of whether the Constitution banned the execution of persons with mental retardation, the Supreme Court turned to the Eighth Amendment issue. While the Court conceded that it might be cruel and unusual punishment to execute those who are "profoundly or severely retarded and wholly lacking the capacity to appreciate the wrongfulness of their actions,"[28] it suggested that, because of "the protections afforded by the insanity defense today," such persons were not likely either to be convicted or to face punishment.[29] Further, it distinguished the case before it on factual grounds: Penry had been found competent to stand trial, and the jury had rejected his insanity defense, reflecting their conclusion that he did know right from wrong at the time of the offense.[30] It further dismissed Penry's argument that there was an "emerging national consensus" against execution of persons with retardation, noting that only one state had legislatively banned such executions and rejecting Penry's evidence on this point from public opinion surveys as an "insufficient basis" upon which to ground an Eighth Amendment prohibition.[31]

On the question of whether such punishment was disproportionate, Justice O'Connor[32] rejected Penry's argument that individuals with mental retardation do not have the same degree of culpability because they do not have the same "judgment, perspective and control as persons of normal intelligence."[33] On the record before the Court, she could not conclude that all mentally retarded persons—"by virtue of their mental retardation alone, and apart from any individualized consideration of their personal responsibility—invariably lack the cognitive, volitional, and moral capacity to act with the degree of culpability associated with the death penalty."[34] Further, she rejected the concept that there was a baseline "mental age" beneath which one could not be executed, arguing that this sort of a bright line test might have a "disempowering effect" on the mentally retarded if applied in other areas of the law (such as contracts or domestic relations).[35] Thus, she concluded that, while mental retardation might "lessen" a defendant's culpability, the Eighth Amendment did not preclude the execution of any mentally retarded person.[36]

In partial dissent, Justice Brennan (for himself and for Justice Marshall) stated that he would ban capital punishment in the case of any mentally retarded offender who "thus lack[ed] the full degree of responsibility for [his] crimes that is a predicate for the constitutional imposition of the death penalty."[37] First, on the question of proportionality, while Justice Brennan agreed that the treatment of persons with mental retardation as a homogeneous group is inappropriate for many reasons, he argued that the dangers associated with that sort of overgeneralization disappear in the context of the controlling clinical definition for the purposes of punishment. Quoting from documents prepared by the American Association of Mental Retardation, he reasoned that all mentally retarded individuals share the common attributes of "low intelligence and inadequacies of adaptive behavior" as well as "reduced ability" in such areas of functioning as "ability to control impulsivity [and] moral development."[38] Such impairment so limits the individual's culpability so as to make capital punishment "always and necessarily disproportionate to . . . blameworthiness and hence . . . unconstitutional."[39]

Second, Justice Brennan found that the execution of an individual with mental retardation does not further the punishment aims of deterrence or of retribution. Because such individuals lack the requisite culpability, execution can never be a "just desert" for a retarded offender.[40] Similarly, the factors that make capital punishment disproportionate when applied to persons with mental retardation give the penalty "the most minimal deterrent effect" as far as retarded potential offenders are concerned; the potential death penalty will not, for such individuals, "figure in some careful assessment of different courses of action."[41]

In a separate opinion, Justice Scalia (writing for himself, Justice White, Justice Kennedy, and the chief justice) parted company with those aspects of Justice O'Connor's opinions that dealt with proportionality, arguing that the concerns she expressed "ha[ve] no place in our Eighth Amendment jurisprudence."[42]

In an early analysis of this aspect of *Penry*, a student commentator characterized it as a "troubling decline in the Court's death penalty jurisprudence,"[43] concluding that its Eighth Amendment analyses relied upon "overly narrow considerations [while] ignor[ing] the broader social and political context in which public sentiment and defendant culpability must be evaluated."[44] The author focused on those aspects of the opinion that relied on legislative silence as indicia that public opinion did not oppose such executions:

> Even if one assumes that legislation reflects the collective will, the absence of legislation may only reflect a failure to secure a place on the legislative agenda. A strong consensus may never be articulated through legislation if the issue never comes to a vote. Therefore, in construing legislative silence, the Court should pay special heed to the political enactment and hesitate to draw substantive conclusions from the products of process failure. Because mentally retarded citizens have difficulty participating in the political process, the Court's assumption that legislative silence signified more than public misunderstanding and political inattention was unreasonable.[45]

In sharp contrast to Justice O'Connor's opinion, Justice Brennan's focus on issues of moral development engrafted an important subject of philosophical and psychological speculation into one of the most contentious areas of the law. Although consideration of this issue came slowly,[46] the question as to its implications for subsequent developments still remained open.[47]

Writing seven years after *Penry*, I had this to say about that case and *Ford*:

> To some extent, *Ford* and *Penry* serve as paradigms for the Court's confusion about cases involving mentally disabled criminal defendants. Justice Rehnquist's and Justice O'Connor's opinions in *Ford* and Justice O'Connor's opinion in *Penry* remain infused with the obsessive fear that defendants will raise "false" or "spurious claims" in desperate attempts to stave off execution. This fear—a doppelganger of the public's "swift and vociferous outrage" over what it perceives as "abusive" insanity acquittals, thus allowing "guilty" defendants to "beat the rap"—remains the source of much of the friction in this area.[48]

THE *ATKINS* DECISION[49]

The opening paragraph of *Atkins* provides important signposts as to the development of the case. This is how Justice Stevens begins the majority opinion:

> Those mentally retarded persons who meet the law's requirements for criminal responsibility should be tried and punished when they commit crimes. Because of their disabilities in areas of reasoning, judgment, and control of their impulses, however, they do not act with the level of moral culpability that characterizes the most serious adult criminal conduct. Moreover, their impairments can jeopardize the reliability and fairness of capital proceedings against mentally retarded defendants. Presumably for these reasons, in the 13 years since we decided *Penry*, the American public, legislators, scholars, and judges have deliberated over the question whether the death penalty should ever be imposed on a mentally retarded criminal. The consensus reflected in those deliberations informs our answer to the question presented by this case: whether such executions are "cruel and unusual punishments" prohibited by the Eighth Amendment to the Federal Constitution.[50]

Atkins had been convicted of capital murder stemming from an ATM robbery.[51] In the penalty phase, the defense called a forensic psychologist, who testified that Atkins was "mildly mentally retarded" (with an IQ of 59).[52] The jury convicted Atkins and sentenced him to death; after that sentence was set aside (for unrelated reasons), the same witness testified at the rehearing.[53] At this time, the state called its own witness (Dr. Stanton Samenow) in rebuttal.[54] Dr. Samenow testified that the defendant was not retarded, that he was "of average intelligence, at least," and that the appropriate diagnosis was antisocial personality disorder.[55] The jury again sentenced Atkins to death, and this sentence was affirmed by the Virginia Supreme Court (over a dissent that characterized the state's expert's testimony as "incredulous as a matter of law" and argued that the imposition of the death sentence on one "with the mental age of a child between the ages of 9 and 12 [was] excessive").[56]

In weighing the case, the Supreme Court first looked at the meaning of "excessive" in Eighth Amendment jurisprudence, stressing,

> A claim that punishment is excessive is judged not by the standards that prevailed in 1685 when Lord Jeffreys presided over the "Bloody Assizes" or when the Bill of Rights was adopted, but rather by those that currently prevail. As Chief Justice Warren explained in Trop v. Dulles, "The basic concept underlying the Eighth Amendment is nothing less than the dignity of man. The Amendment must draw its meaning from the evolving standards of decency that mark the progress of a maturing society."[57]

In engaging in a proportionality review,[58] the Court pointed out that its inquiry should be guided by "objective factors," and that, in assessing these factors, the "clearest and most reliable objective evidence of contemporary values is the legislation enacted by the country's legislatures."[59] As part of this inquiry, it noted the significant changes since it decided *Penry* in 1989 when only two states banned the execution of persons with mental retardation; in the intervening thirteen years, at least another sixteen (and the federal government) enacted similar laws,[60] leading the Court to this conclusion:

> It is not so much the number of these States that is significant, but the consistency of the direction of change. Given the well-known fact that anticrime legislation is far more popular than legislation providing protections for persons guilty of violent crime, the large number of States prohibiting the execution of mentally retarded persons (and the complete absence of States passing legislation reinstating the power to conduct such executions) provides powerful evidence that today our society views mentally retarded offenders as categorically less culpable than the average criminal. The evidence carries even greater force when it is noted that the legislatures that have addressed the issue have voted overwhelmingly in favor of the prohibition. The practice, therefore, has become truly unusual, and it is fair to say that a national consensus has developed against it.[61]

Further, the Court perceived that this consensus "unquestionably reflects widespread judgment about the relative culpability of mentally retarded offenders and the relationship between mental retardation and the penological purposes served by the death penalty."[62] The Court added that "it suggests that some characteristics of mental retardation undermine the strength of the procedural protections that our capital jurisprudence steadfastly guards."

Mental retardation, the Court found, involves "not only subaverage intellectual functioning, but also significant limitations in adaptive skills such as communication, self-care, and self-direction that became manifest before age 18."[63] It continued in the same vein:

> Mentally retarded persons frequently know the difference between right and wrong and are competent to stand trial. Because of their impairments, however, by definition they have diminished capacities to understand and process information, to communicate, to abstract from mistakes and learn from experience, to engage in logical reasoning, to control impulses, and to understand the reactions of others. There is no evidence that they are more likely to engage in criminal conduct than others, but there is abundant evidence that they often act on impulse rather than pursuant to a premeditated plan, and that in group settings they are followers rather than leaders. Their deficiencies do not warrant an exemption from criminal sanctions, but they do diminish their personal culpability.[64]

In light of these deficiencies, the Court found that its death penalty jurisprudence provided two reasons "consistent with the legislative consensus that the mentally retarded should be categorically excluded from execution."[65]

> First, there is a serious question as to whether either justification that we have recognized as a basis for the death penalty applies to mentally retarded offenders. *Gregg v. Georgia* identified "retribution and deterrence of capital crimes by prospective offenders" as the social purposes served by the death penalty.[66] Unless the imposition of the death penalty on a mentally retarded person "measurably contributes to one or both of these goals, it 'is nothing more than the purposeless and needless imposition of pain and suffering,' and hence an unconstitutional punishment."[67]

On the question of retribution, the Court reasoned that, in light of its precedents in this area,[68]

> [i]f the culpability of the average murderer is insufficient to justify the most extreme sanction available to the State, the lesser culpability of the mentally retarded offender surely does not merit that form of retribution. Thus, pursuant to our narrowing jurisprudence, which seeks to ensure that only the most deserving of execution are put to death, an exclusion for the mentally retarded is appropriate.[69]

On the question of deterrence, the Court again looked at earlier cases for a restatement of the proposition that "capital punishment can serve as a deterrent only when murder is the result of premeditation and deliberation,"[70] and added,

> Exempting the mentally retarded from that punishment will not affect the "cold calculus that precedes the decision" of other potential murderers. Indeed, that sort of calculus is at the opposite end of the spectrum from behavior of mentally retarded offenders. The theory of deterrence in capital sentencing is predicated upon the notion that the increased severity of the punishment will inhibit criminal actors from carrying out murderous conduct. Yet it is the same cognitive and behavioral impairments that make these defendants less morally culpable—for example, the diminished ability to understand and process information, to learn from experience, to engage in logical reasoning, or to control impulses—that also make it less likely that they can process the information of the possibility of execution as a penalty and, as a result, control their conduct based upon that information. Nor will exempting the mentally retarded from execution lessen the deterrent effect of the death penalty with respect to offenders who are not mentally retarded. Such individuals are unprotected by the exemption and will continue to face the threat of execution. Thus, executing the mentally retarded will not measurably further the goal of deterrence.[71]

The reduced capacity of mentally retarded offenders provided an additional justification for a categorical rule making such offenders ineligible for the death penalty.[72] The Court went on to note that there was an "enhanced" risk of improperly imposed death penalties in cases involving defendants with mental retardation because of the possibility of false confessions, as well as "the lesser ability of mentally retarded defendants to make a persuasive showing of mitigation in the face of prosecutorial evidence of one or more aggravating factors."[73] The Court also stressed several additional interrelated issues: the difficulties that persons with mental retardation may have in being able to give meaningful assistance to their counsel, their status as "typically poor witnesses," and the ways in which their demeanor "may create an unwarranted impression of lack of remorse for their crimes."[74]

Here the Court acknowledged an important difficulty: "[R]eliance on mental retardation as a mitigating factor can be a two-edged sword that may enhance the likelihood that the aggravating factor of future dangerousness will be found by the jury,"[75] raising the specter that "mentally retarded defendants in the aggregate face a special risk of wrongful execution."[76] Thus, the Court concluded, "Construing and applying the Eighth Amendment in the light of our 'evolving standards of decency,' we therefore conclude that such punishment is excessive and that the Constitution 'places a substantive restriction on the State's power to take the life' of a mentally retarded offender."[77]

There were two dissents. Chief Justice Rehnquist, dissenting for himself and Justices Thomas and Scalia, criticized that part of the majority's methodology that had relied upon public opinion polls, the views of professional and religious organizations, and the status of the death penalty in other nations as part of the basis for its decision.[78] According to the chief justice, only "two sources—the work product of legislatures and sentencing jury determinations—ought to be the sole indicators by which courts ascertain the contemporary American conceptions of decency for purposes of the Eighth Amendment."[79]

Justice Scalia also dissented (for himself, the chief justice, and Justice Thomas), noting immediately, "Seldom has an opinion of this Court rested so obviously upon nothing but the personal views of its members."[80] Justice Scalia's dissent flatly rejected the notion that there was a "consensus" against the execution of persons with mild mental retardation (relying both on historical sources that had exempted only persons with severe or profound mental retardation from that punishment[81] and on his alternative reading of the data cited by the majority that led him to conclude that, at best, a "fudged" 47 percent of death penalty jurisdictions had barred such executions).[82]

Rather than being based on a consensus, Justice Scalia continued, "what really underlies today's decision [is] pretension to a power confined neither by the moral sentiments originally enshrined in the Eighth Amendment (its original meaning) nor even by the current moral sentiments of the American people."[83] In his view, it was nothing more than "the feelings and intuition of a majority of the Justices that count—'the perceptions of decency, or of penology, or of mercy, entertained by a majority of the small and unrepresentative segment of our society that sits on this Court.'"[84] Here he specifically rejected the majority's assumption that judges and jurors were unable to "take proper account of mental retardation."[85]

Justice Scalia assessed the majority's retribution and deterrence analyses and found them both wanting. On the question of retribution, he noted rhetorically, "The fact that juries continue to sentence mentally retarded offenders to death for extreme crimes shows that society's moral outrage sometimes demands execution of retarded offenders. By what principle of law, science, or logic can the Court pronounce that this is wrong? There is none."[86] He continued in the same vein: "As long as a mentally retarded offender knows 'the difference between right and wrong,' only the sentencer can assess whether his retardation reduces his culpability enough to exempt him from the death penalty for the particular murder in question."[87]

On the deterrence issue, Justice Scalia concluded that "the deterrent effect of a penalty is adequately vindicated if it successfully deters many, but not all, of the target class,"[88] and again he flatly rejected the majority's "flabby" argument that persons with mental retardation faced a "special risk" for wrongful execution (suggesting that "just plain stupid, inarticulate or even ugly people" might face a similar risk, but that, if this were in fact so, it was not an issue that came within the ambit of the Eighth Amendment).[89]

Finally, he expressed his "fear of faking":

> One need only read the definitions of mental retardation adopted by the American Association of Mental Retardation and the American Psychiatric Association to realize that the symptoms of this condition can readily be feigned. And the capital defendant who feigns mental retardation risks nothing at all.[90]

"Nothing has changed," he concluded, in the nearly three hundred years since Hale wrote his *Pleas of the Crown*:

> [Determination of a person's incapacity] is a matter of great difficulty, partly from the easiness of counterfeiting this disability and partly from the variety of the degrees of this infirmity, whereof some are sufficient, and some are insufficient to excuse persons in capital offenses.[91]

ATKINS' PRESSURE POINTS

Atkins leaves open many unanswered questions:[92]

- the extent to which states will adopt new prophylactic implementation procedures,[93]
- the dangers in using a numerical IQ score as the primary retardation determination "cutoff factor,"[94]
- the scope of the hearing to determine whether a defendant is a person with mental retardation,[95]
- the difficulties in assessing mental retardation in persons who are not English speaking,[96]
- the allocation of the burden of proof in making that assessment,[97]
- the application of *Atkins* in cases of "borderline" mental retardation,[98]
- the interplay between judge and jury in the determination of who is "mentally retarded" (no matter how that term is ultimately defined),[99]
- the question of retroactivity of application,[100] and
- the costs of implementation.[101]

I believe that it is impossible for *Atkins* to have any authenticity unless we restructure the ways in which counsel represent persons with mental retardation and we ensure that such individuals have competent experts assisting them.[102] In this context, I identify seventeen "pressure point" issues in *Atkins* on questions of *substantive* implementation—issues that must be taken seriously if we are to understand the greater significance of the *Atkins* case.

1. The capacity of lawyers to "get" mental retardation;
2. The extent to which defense lawyers can "explain away" what may appear to jurors as a lack of remorse on the part of defendants;
3. The ways that failures to develop retardation evidence are treated in *Strickland v. Washington*[103] cases;
4. The underlying sanism of jurors in assessing mental retardation;[104]
5. The ability of fact finders to "unpack" the difference between cases involving the types of violent crimes more likely to be committed by persons with mental retardation (nondeliberate) and the types more likely to be committed by some persons with severe mental illness (very deliberate and planful, but equally immune from deterrence);[105]
6. The extent to which jurors will use retardation evidence as an aggravator rather than as a mitigator;[106]
7. The capacity of jurors to empathize with persons with mental retardation;[107]
8. The role of experts in explaining the meanings of IQs, functional abilities, capacity for moral development, and so forth, of persons with mental retardation;[109]
9. The willingness of states to read *Ake v. Oklahoma*[108] expansively to ensure access to appropriate experts;
10. The reluctance of criminal defendants, even those facing the death penalty, to identify themselves as "mentally retarded";[110]
11. The ability of post-*Atkins* defendants to provide meaningful assistance to counsel (assuming a finding of competence to stand trial);[111]
12. The impact of *Godinez v. Moran*,[112] *Indiana v. Edwards*,[113] and the dilemma of self-representation;
13. The willingness of judges to enforce *Atkins*;[114]
14. The extent to which Justice Scalia's fear-of-faking concerns will dominate post-*Atkins* jurisprudence;[115]
15. The ability of all participants to understand the relationship between such cases and the insanity defense;[116]
16. The attitude of prosecutors toward such cases;[117] and
17. The ability of society to accept the reality of the number of death-eligible defendants with mental retardation.[118]

These seventeen issues can be "sorted" as to the interest group whose attitudes and/or behaviors are most at issue (although there are certainly many overlaps): defense counsel, jurors, experts, defendants, trial court judges, appellate court judges, prosecutors, and, for lack of a better phrase, society as a whole. I will address them in order.

Defense Counsel[119]

Issue 1.   The capacity of lawyers to "get" mental retardation.

Lawyers have traditionally done a terrible job of being able to identify mental disability, being able to differentiate mental illness from mental retardation, and "seeing" mental disability if the defendant does not "look crazy."[120]

The dangers here should be self-evident. If a lawyer does not "get" the fact that his client is mentally retarded, then the issues raised in *Atkins* may never be brought to the court's attention.[121] As is discussed extensively in another chapter in this book, there are countless cases of lawyers' failures to identify a client's mental disability, often resulting in an "effectiveness of counsel" challenge.[122] This issue is the first one that must be confronted; if counsel fails here, it is impossible for *Atkins* to be given any kind of meaningful life.[123]

Issue 2.   The extent to which defense lawyers can "explain away" what may appear to jurors as a lack of remorse on the part of defendants.

Jurors frequently look for visual cues and clues in determining whether a defendant should be sentenced to death. In this process, they determine—based on their own flawed, pre-reflective "ordinary common sense"[124]—whether a defendant looks sufficiently "remorseful." This behavior was noted accurately by Justice Kennedy in his concurrence in *Riggins v. Nevada*,[125] relying on research by William Geimer and Jonathan Amsterdam,[126] demonstrating that an assessment of the defendant's level of remorse may be the most determinative factor in the decision as to who will live and who will die.[127]

Nonetheless, this remains a significant obstacle for lawyers representing persons with mental retardation, some of whom may gesture inappropriately, grimace, giggle, or manifest other behaviors that jurors may translate into meaning "I don't care."[128] A person with mental retardation may not understand the consequences of the proceedings; consequently, he may alienate the jury by "sleeping, smiling, or staring at nothing while in court."[129] This "unavoidable and inappropriate conduct" may also convey a "false impression of a lack of remorse or compassion for the victim."[130] A juror, by way of example, may perceive a defendant's sitting slumped down in his chair as acting "cool" and not showing "proper respect for the proceedings."[131] The lawyer must be able to neutralize these interpretations.

Beyond this, a defendant with mental retardation may not truly understand what is transpiring in court. Even if he meets the minimalist competency-to-stand-trial test set out in *Dusky v. United States*,[132] the defendant may not be able to adequately participate meaningfully in his or her own defense. Also, persons with mental retardation quite often suffer from very poor memory, an impediment that, when coupled with the tendency to fall prey to others' suggestions, may render communication of the facts to the defense lawyer, especially the most mitigating facts, "next to impossible."[133]

There is an ominous "flip side" to this coin, and it is one that cannot be understood without a nuanced appreciation of the extent to which "sanism" dominates attitudes in such cases. Jurors often expect people with mental retardation to be extremely low functioning and may not be expecting a quiet, mild-mannered individual. When the defendant fails to exhibit any stereotypical behaviors (such as drooling, giggling, smiling with a vacant appearance, or rocking), jury members may think that the mental retardation defense is untrue or unwarranted.[134] Courts see facial expressions—purportedly "decodable" by any layperson—as evidence of mental retardation.[135] In a recent case granting habeas corpus to a defendant with mental retardation, the court rejected the state's arguments that the defendant's ability to talk about "typical" conversational topics proved his lack of retardation:

> A recording of [defendant] Brumfield's outgoing phone calls from prison (Ex. S-35) shows nothing extraordinary that a normal ten-year-old child could not do. Talking about making purchases online, conversing about sports scores and stats, and the like are simply not sufficient to show adaptive strength in communication abilities.[136]

The burdens here on defense counsel are self-evidently immense. A leading article summarizes: "Counsel must explain mental retardation and its diagnostic process thoroughly and carefully so jurors will have a clear understanding of this often misunderstood disability. The defense lawyer must educate the jury about mental retardation, its various presentations, and the distinct difference between mental retardation and mental illness."[137]

The majority in *Atkins* clearly understood this (as evidenced by its focus on the ways that the demeanor of persons with mental retardation "may create an unwarranted impression of lack of remorse for their crimes").[138] It is an open question whether defense lawyers will pay heed to this warning.

Issue 3.   The ways that failures to develop retardation evidence are treated in *Strickland v. Washington*[139] cases.

As I discuss extensively in a subsequent chapter,[140] the quality of counsel in providing legal representation to mentally disabled criminal defendants is a disgrace. This is not news to commentators;[141] however, the rich body of descriptive, analytical, anecdotal, and prescriptive literature has had little impact on the realities of practice in this area of the law.[142] If lawyers continue this pattern of ineffectiveness, it raises the critical question as to the extent to which the universe of defense lawyers who are *generally* ineffective in their representation can *ever* develop evidence of mental retardation in a way contemplated by *Atkins*.

Jurors

    Issue 4. The sanism of jurors.

    In a subsequent chapter, I challenge the Supreme Court's assumption that jurors can be relied upon to apply the law in this area conscientiously and fairly, concluding that the reality is the opposite of this assumption: that jurors generally distrust mental disability evidence, that the most mentally disabled persons are treated the most harshly by jurors, and that jurors tend to overimpose the death penalty on severely mentally disabled defendants.[143]

    These issues must be addressed seriously if *Atkins* is to be implemented in a meaningful and coherent manner.[144]

    Issue 5. The ability of fact finders to "unpack" the difference between cases involving the types of violent crimes more likely to be committed by persons with mental retardation (nondeliberate) and the types more likely to be committed by some persons with severe mental illness (often very deliberate and planful, but equally immune from deterrence).

    Fact finders confuse and conflate mental retardation and mental illness.[145] This confusion may be fatal to the chances of a reasoned judgment in a death penalty case involving a defendant with mental retardation. First, the defendant may not appear to be "mad to the man on the street."[146] Second, the criminal conduct of a person with mental retardation often "stem[s] from an impulsive reaction against the painful awareness, hammered home by frustration, failure, and humiliation, of the cruel trick that biology has played on him."[147] Because persons with mental retardation often lack the ability to control impulsive behavior, they are far less likely to have planned out the commission of capital crimes[148] in the bizarre ways that some persons with profound mental illness do.[149] Thus, in many instances, given limitations in intellectual reasoning, control of impulsive behavior, and moral development, "it is not possible for a mentally retarded defendant to freely choose to commit a crime."[150] Again, I am not particularly optimistic about jurors' ability to make these discriminating judgments.

    Issue 6. The extent to which jurors will use retardation evidence as an aggravator rather than as a mitigator.

    In a prior chapter,[151] I demonstrated how mental illness—although ostensibly a mitigating factor in death penalty cases—is often improperly used as an aggravator.[152] Paradoxically, if a defendant is represented by competent counsel, the dilemma may be even further confounded: if she should rely on certain kinds of "empathy"[153]—evidence of abuse, stress, retardation, institutional failure, or substance abuse—she runs the risk of putting before the jury the evidence that "has the greatest potential for turning into evidence in aggravation."[154] Such a distortion has appropriately been called "the disempathetic effect."[155]

The *Atkins* Court took this issue seriously, cautioning that "reliance on mental retardation as a mitigating factor can be a two-edged sword that may enhance the likelihood that the aggravating factor of future dangerousness will be found by the jury,"[156] and warning of "the lesser ability of mentally retarded defendants to make a persuasive showing of mitigation in the face of prosecutorial evidence of one or more aggravating factors."[157] Given some jurors' propensity to use evidence of mental disability as an *aggravator* rather than as a *mitigator*,[158] this adds to the ambiguity and complexity of post-*Atkins* cases.

Issue 7. The capacity of jurors to empathize with persons with mental retardation.[159]

The persistence of the mental retardation stereotype also frequently precludes the development of juror empathy.[160] In cases in which the crime is especially violent and inexplicable, we may "simply shut our eyes to the reality of his madness in order to reap the rewards of our revenge."[161] In the context of a capital trial, "empathy evidence," such as mental problems, substance abuse, or family background difficulties, "can facilitate the jury's image of the defendant as an 'irreparable monster' who was so retarded, scarred, or disturbed by child abuse that he just could not contain his rage."[162] Will *Atkins* have any impact on this issue?

Experts

Issue 8. The role of experts in explaining the meanings of IQs,[163] functional abilities, capacity for moral development, and so forth, of persons with mental retardation.[164]

There are multiple roles for experts in death penalty cases involving defendants with mental retardation.[165] A mental retardation expert may be utilized to explain the relevance of mental retardation in either the guilt or penalty phases of trial, or both (including relevant aspects of confessions, waivers of *Miranda* rights, culpability, and potential future dangerousness).[166] Often, a multidisciplinary team of experts is critical to the defense of capital defendants with mental retardation. One of the leading practice articles instructs that defense counsel should "always contact a mitigation or mental health expert to determine the existence of mental retardation and complete a social-medical history before requesting the assistance of a psychologist or psychiatrist."[167] The article also cautions that "ordinary psychiatrists and most psychologists are not trained in areas involving mental retardation and courts frequently fail to make the distinction between these experts."[168]

What are some of the factors that the expert must consider? "Speech, language and memory impairments, physical and motor disabilities, IQ examinations and other tests require a professional evaluation and assessment by various mental health experts."[169] Such experts should also be able to convey to the jury "the effects that mental retardation has on behavior and decision making, explain the vulnerable and suggestible nature of a mentally retarded individual, and educate juries about the full spectrum of mental retardation, irrespective of the defendant's appearance or demeanor," and must be able to "state their findings in plain, comprehensible language and common sense terms used by the average person."[170]

Finally, the expert must be able to rebut sanist myths (recall my earlier discussion about the defendant who failed to exhibit any stereotypical behaviors, such as drooling, giggling, smiling with a vacant appearance, or rocking).[171] In short, *Atkins* will be an empty shell without the aggressive participation of such experts.

Issue 9.   The willingness of states to read *Ake* expansively to ensure access to appropriate experts.

In *Ake v. Oklahoma*,[172] the Supreme Court held that an indigent defendant is constitutionally entitled to psychiatric assistance when he makes a preliminary showing that his sanity "is [likely] to be a significant factor at trial."[173] Courts have split on the requisite professional background to satisfy *Ake*'s command, for instance on the question of whether a defendant is entitled to the appointment of an expert psychologist[174] (certainly the appropriate professional in many cases involving defendants with mental retardation).[175] A leading criminal procedure treatise concludes that, "[g]enerally speaking, the courts have read *Ake* narrowly, and have refused to require appointment of an expert unless it is absolutely essential to the defense."[176] The problems here are heightened by some experts' lack of expertise. Commentators have noted that even mental disability professionals often inappropriately confuse mental retardation with mental illness,[177] an error that could be literally fatal in a post-*Atkins* case.

Will narrow readings of *Ake* (coupled in some cases with inexpert experts) rob fact finders of the full and rich explanation of mental retardation and its relationship to the commission of the charged criminal act?[178] This is an issue that cannot be ignored.

Defendants

Issue 10.   The reluctance of criminal defendants, even those facing the death penalty, to identify themselves as "mentally retarded."

One of the basic sanist myths is that defendants regularly feign mental disability, and that they similarly succeed regularly in befuddling experts when they do so.[179] Here we are faced with the inverse: criminal defendants *mask* their retardation from their counsel (and often from themselves).[180] Dr. Dorothy Lewis documented that juveniles imprisoned on death row were quick to tell her and her associates, "I'm not crazy," or "I'm not a retard."[181] Moreover, a person with mental retardation will often attempt to conceal his condition from lawyers, not realizing that his condition could constitute a major part of his defense.[182] Especially in a case in which counsel is substandard, this could—again—be fatal to a defendant who ought otherwise come under the *Atkins* umbrella.[183]

Issue 11. The ability of post-*Atkins* defendants to provide meaningful assistance to counsel (assuming a finding of competence to stand trial).[184]

Many defendants of ordinary intelligence do not contribute much help to their attorneys in extracting pertinent mitigating information.[185] This is certainly "exacerbated in the situation of a [defendant with mental retardation], who may not even understand what type of information her attorney needs, let alone begin to know how to provide it."[186] The *Atkins* Court stressed the difficulties that persons with mental retardation may have in being able to give meaningful assistance to their counsel, their status as "typically poor witnesses," and the ways that their demeanor "may create an unwarranted impression of lack of remorse for their crimes."[187] This is an extremely important issue to which scant attention has been paid, and it is one that is intensified by the reality that state criminal justice systems are ill equipped to deal with mentally ill or retarded defendants unable to aid their defense attorneys.[188]

Surveys of case law underscore the inability of criminal defendants with mental disabilities to aid their counsel, even in cases in which no *Dusky* violation has been found.[189] This issue must be reexamined carefully in the post-*Atkins* generation of death penalty cases.

Issue 12. The impact of the *Godinez v. Moran/Indiana v. Edwards* morass.

The Supreme Court has held in *Godinez v. Moran*[190] that the standard for pleading guilty and for waiving counsel is no higher than for standing trial, rejecting the notion that competence to plead guilty must be measured by a higher (or even different) standard from that used in incompetence-to-stand-trial cases.[191] It reasoned that a defendant who was found competent to stand trial would have to make a variety of decisions requiring choices: whether to testify, whether to seek a jury trial, whether to cross-examine his accusers, and, in some cases, whether to raise an affirmative defense.[192] While the decision to plead guilty is a "profound one," "it is no more complicated than the sum total of decisions that a defendant may be called upon to make during the course of a trial."[193] Finally, the Court reaffirmed that any waiver of constitutional rights must be "knowing and voluntary."[194] It concluded on this point,

> Requiring that a criminal defendant be competent has a modest aim: It seeks to ensure that he has the capacity to understand the proceedings and to assist counsel. While psychiatrists and scholars may find it useful to classify the various kinds and degrees of competence, and while States are free to adopt competency standards that are more elaborate than the Dusky formulation, the Due Process Clause does not impose these additional requirements.[195]

Fifteen years later, *Edwards* modified *Godinez* by ruling that the Constitution permits states to insist upon representation by counsel for those who are competent enough to stand trial but who still suffer from severe mental illness to the point where they are not competent to conduct trial proceedings by themselves.[196] *Edwards* is significant for several reasons: although it goes out of its way to suggest that it is deciding matters "that [it] did not consider in *Godinez*," it is fairly clear that *Edwards* does modify and limit *Godinez* (which suggested that the *only* question to consider was the minimalistic one posed in *Dusky*) by implicitly rejecting the unitary standard that *Godinez* had established for all aspects of the criminal trial, and by explicitly recognizing that mental illness is not an all-or-nothing dyadic concept (mentally ill/ not mentally ill), a concept that is frequently endorsed by trial courts and by jurors. [197]

Notwithstanding the decision in *Edwards*, *Godinez* may still lead to a potentially absurd scenario in which a defendant with a history of mental illness or mental retardation may be found competent to stand trial if he is found to have some ability to assist counsel in some way, but later may be allowed to remove counsel and represent himself.[198] The trial of Colin Ferguson, by way of one vivid example, "graphically symbolizes the dangerous implications of courts using *Godinez*'s low standard of competency."[199]

Atkins, of course, is silent on this issue, as counsel represented the defendant. But it is an issue—how the *Atkins* standards can possibly be met in the case of a *pro se* defendant with mental retardation—that must be taken seriously.

Trial Judges

Issue 13. The willingness of judges to enforce *Atkins*.

In an earlier chapter, I discussed the corrosive impact of pretextuality in mental disability law jurisprudence.[200] A careful examination of mental disability law reveals that judges are often pretextual because of their own "instrumental, functional, normative and philosophical" dissatisfaction with non-sanist constitutional decisions that grant a measure of dignity to persons with mental disabilities.[201] Trial judges who are similarly dissatisfied with *Atkins*—and it does not require research or citations to assert that there will be many—can easily sabotage it in hidden ways. This is an area that demands extraordinary vigilance.

A recent habeas corpus grant underscores this point. In granting the writ because of the defendant's mental retardation, Federal District Judge James Brady admonished his colleagues to "disregard whatever preconceptions they might have about this intellectual disability,"[202] and continued:

> Mildly mentally retarded persons usually do not have obvious physical manifestations of their shortcomings, as may be the case with persons diagnosed with Down's Syndrome. Nor are their intellectual capabilities so severely impaired as to be immediately noticeable to most people in casual conversation, as is the case with profoundly mentally retarded individuals. Indeed, the line between the upper range of mildly mentally retarded persons and the borderline cases where mild mental retardation is not shown can be exceedingly blurry and subjective. Yet if we as a society are to effectuate the evolving standard of decency contemplated by the Eighth Amendment's prohibition on cruel and unusual punishment, we must accept as a given that certain cases will present unfortunate facts which, when viewed under the law, result in an outcome at odds with majoritarian sentiment. This may be one of those cases in the eyes of some.[203]

Appellate Courts

Issue 14. The extent to which Justice Scalia's fear-of-faking concerns will dominate post-*Atkins* jurisprudence.[204]

Again, the sanist "fear-of-faking" myth dominates mental disability law.[205] Justice Scalia's dissent in *Atkins* is a pathetic recapitulation of this dreary myth and may prove to be the most significant roadblock to the implementation of *Atkins*. His fears—similar to ones that Chief Justice Rehnquist and Justice O'Connor expressed in *Ford* and in *Penry*[206]—reflect "society's suspicion that the defendant is faking the illness and, together with her defense lawyers, will hoodwink an unsuspecting jury into accepting fallacious medical testimony."[207] Despite the lack of empirical support, judges deciding legal questions related to sanity frequently appeal to what they perceive as the "significant dangers presented by feigned or spurious claims of insanity."[208] Historically, society believed that insanity was too easily feigned, that such simulation easily deceived psychiatrists, and that the use of the defense was "an easy way to escape punishment."[209] The fear is one that has held some of this century's most respected jurists in its thrall, regardless of the fact that it is an axiom of criminal procedure that rights are not ordinarily denied to all because of the fear that a few might abuse them.[210]

This helps to explain why there is increasing support for relaxing the legal protections available to persons with mental illness, by making those persons equally subject to the same draconian penalties now generally in favor. Thus, in analyzing the decision of the legislature in Idaho to reduce the insanity defense to solely a consideration of mens rea, Geis and Meier found that Idaho residents concluded that mentally disabled criminal defendants should not be able to avoid punitive consequences of criminal acts by reliance on either a "real *or* faked plea of insanity."[211] A member of the Louisiana Supreme Court subsequently endorsed this sentiment.[212] Again, reconsider Justice Scalia's curious reference to the feigning insanity defense pleader who then "risks commitment to a mental institution until he can be cured (and then tried and executed)."[213]

The empirical realities are very different:

> Malingering by mentally disabled criminal defendants is statistically rare. Research reveals that defendants attempt feigning in less than eight percent of all competency to stand trial inquiries. Yet, in deciding incompetency to stand trial cases, courts continue to focus, in some cases almost obsessively, on testimony that raises the specter of malingering. The fear of such deception has "permeated the American legal system for over a century," despite the complete lack of evidence that such feigning "has ever been a remotely significant problem of criminal procedure." This fear is a further manifestation of judicial sanism.[214]

Again, this most compelling of all mental disability law myths must be taken seriously in the aftermath of *Atkins*.[215]

Issue 15. The ability of all participants to understand the relationship between such cases and the insanity defense.

Sanism similarly infects competency-to-stand-trial jurisprudence in critical ways. Courts stubbornly refuse to understand the distinction between competency to stand trial and insanity, even though the two statuses involve different concepts, different standards, and different points on the "time line," and courts frequently misunderstand the relationship between incompetency and subsequent commitment.[216] Justice Scalia's curious reference to feigned insanity defenses suggests that this confusion persists. It is an issue that must be taken seriously in the world after *Atkins*, especially when we consider the extent to which the act of pleading the insanity defense may significantly increase the likelihood of a jury returning a death penalty verdict.[217]

Prosecutors

Issue 16. The attitude of prosecutors toward such cases.[218]

There has been little written about the ways that prosecutors construct cases involving defendants with mental retardation.[219] Jamie Fellner, an attorney with Human Rights Watch, has had this to say:

Even when a defense lawyer presents evidence of the client's retardation, prosecutors are all too often more concerned with the professional or political ramifications of obtaining a "victory"—a death sentence—than with giving serious consideration to the ways mental retardation has affected the defendant's comprehension and conduct. Faced with pressure from the community and the victim's family, they do not want to "excuse" the crime or let an offender "off too easy." During trials they vigorously challenge the existence of mental retardation, minimize its significance, and suggest that although a capital defendant may "technically" be considered retarded, he nonetheless has "street smarts"—and hence should receive the highest penalty.[220]

Nothing in the body of *Atkins* touches on this issue, but, operationally, its importance cannot be overstated.[221] Again, those of us who watch post-*Atkins* developments must scrutinize this carefully.

Society

Issue 17.   The ability of society to accept the reality of the number of death-eligible defendants who are mentally retarded.[222]

It has been estimated that up to 30 percent of all persons on death row are mentally retarded.[223] Other surveys range from 4 to 20 percent.[224] Jonathan Bing's research reveals that

> [o]f the first 157 convicted murderers executed since capital punishment was reinstituted in 1976, at least eleven of them (seven percent) were known to be mentally retarded, although the incidence of mental retardation among the population at large is estimated at only three percent. Of the 2,500 people on death row [in 1995], it is estimated that twelve to twenty percent of them are mentally retarded.[225]

These are numbers that many find jarring and that all should find troubling. They show, dramatically, that there is little that is exceptional or idiosyncratic about the facts of the *Atkins* case.

Post-Atkins *Litigation*

Although post-*Atkins* decisions explore many of the issues left unresolved by the case, there is certainly no consensus in the lower courts on many of the unresolved issues. By ways of example,

- In *Bowling v. Commonwealth*,[226] the Court rejected an argument that fused *Atkins* and *Roper v. Simmons*[227] and that asserted that the Constitution prohibited executing an offender with the *mental* age of a juvenile.
- In *Rodriguez v. Quarterman*,[228] the Court considered carefully the conundrum of a case involving an individual who did not manifest

mental retardation until after he was eighteen, but who suffered brain injury or neurological illness after that date, characterizing this as the central "conundrum facing . . . courts in the post-*Atkins* era."[229]

- In *Dickerson v. Bagley*,[230] the Court linked its *Atkins* analysis to a consideration of what constitutes ineffective assistance of counsel under the *Strickland* test in a case where counsel failed to investigate that the defendant functioned at "an intellectual level little above the retarded level."[231]

- As discussed in chapter 1, in a very different sort of opinion, the Court in *Howell v. State*[232] speculated that the defendant did not exert enough "effort" on those of his IQ tests on which he scored under 70,[233] and that jury could have thus concluded he "functioned at a higher level"[234] (a case which might be read hand in glove with *State v. Strode*,[235] which approvingly cited legislative testimony that retardation was a "birth defect" that you are "born with for the most part,"[236] and

- In the same vein, the Court in *State v. Grell*[237] stressed the "risk of malingering" as justification for imposing the burden of proving mental retardation on the defendant by clear and convincing evidence, reasoning that defendants had "significant motivation to attempt to score poorly on an IQ test."[238]

- And, most recently in *Black v. Bell*,[239] the Sixth Circuit concluded that a state appellate court's assessment of a Tennessee capital defendant's level of intellectual and adaptive functioning for the purposes of *Atkins*' prohibition against execution of mentally retarded defendants was contrary to federal law.[240]

There are, in sum, many issues still unexplored and unresolved in this area of the law.

CONCLUSION

What must be done so as to ensure that *Atkins* has meaning for the universe of death-penalty-eligible defendants with mental retardation?

The judiciary must—for the first time—take these issues seriously. Judges, like jurors and other lay people, continue to take ordinary-common-sense-like refuge in stereotyping persons with mental retardation, especially in the cases of such persons charged with serious crimes. Legal resources are now available to all judges that help dispel these myths,[241] but it is not at all clear whether judges have availed themselves of these resources. It is time they do.

It is time for prosecutors to stop posturing.[242] It is black letter law that the role of the prosecutor is not simply to win convictions but to seek justice.[243] It is time that this happens in these cases.

Again, we must confront the corrosive and malignant impact of sanism and pretextuality, an impact that is at its most insidious in this sort of case. Concludes Bryan Dupler,

> Both judges and jurors initially regard mental retardation claims with such extreme skepticism and "fear of faking" that only the most abject demonstration of retardation seems to have a reasonable chance of a favorable verdict or judicial finding. It is far more likely that the judicial system will refuse to acknowledge a capital defendant's mental retardation than a feigning defendant will whip justice. Professor Michael Perlin's theory of "sanism"—and its characteristically irrational fear of feigned mental illness—finds its corollary in a pernicious "average-ism" that subtly conspires against a finding of mental retardation even when sufficient evidence supports it.[244]

If we fail to consider this, then *Atkins* can be no more than a paper victory.

We must also consider the application of therapeutic jurisprudence to this area of the law.[245] The late Professor Bruce Winick has written about how TJ values are intertwined into the determination of who is mentally retarded for *Atkins* purposes, and he has urged that, when states adopt procedures to effectuate this aspect of *Atkins*, such procedures "should take into account considerations of therapeutic jurisprudence."[246] Beyond this, however, I believe that the full range of questions that I raise in this chapter—questions involving the roles of judges, juries, lawyers, and experts—could all be profitably considered with the use of a TJ lens. As discussed earlier in this work, Professor Amy Ronner has argued persuasively that, consonant with TJ principles, "litigants must have a sense of voice or a chance to tell their story to a decision maker."[247] Here this question must be posed, to what extent do court procedures ensure that the defendant has a "voice"? Will there be expert witnesses to disentangle meanings of reports, to contextualize IQ scores, to explain acts that might seem to be otherwise inexplicable and contrary to jurors' "ordinary common sense"? Will the defense counsel be able to adequately represent the defendant with mental retardation and illuminate all these issues to the jury? If experts and counsel cannot perform these tasks, then it is unlikely that therapeutic jurisprudence mandates will be fulfilled.

· 6 ·

Competency to Be Executed:
The Case of Mental Illness

INTRODUCTION[1]

$\mathcal{D}$r. Paul Appelbaum, in regarding the question of the constitutional appropriateness of standards and procedures required to determine whether a death row
prisoner with mental illness is competent to be executed, aptly characterized it as
"one of the more perplexing issues in criminal justice today."[2] While in *Ford v.*
Wainwright[3] the Supreme Court finally gave a partial answer, and while it partially clarified its *Ford* holding some two decades later in *Panetti v. Quarterman*,[4]
to a significant extent the "conundrum" perceived by Dr. Appelbaum still exists.[5]

In this chapter, I will first provide a historical overview of the issue,
one which dates back centuries. I will next carefully consider the Supreme
Court's *Ford* decision, the first modern decision constitutionally proscribing
execution of the "currently insane." Then I will look at the ways that the Supreme Court's 2007 *Panetti* decision modified the *Ford* holding. After that,
I will speculate on *Panetti's* likely future influence on this complex issue of
law and social policy, I will highlight some areas touched on by *Panetti* that
require further consideration, and I will examine the scholarly response to
Panetti, focusing on projected links between *Panetti* and *Atkins v. Virginia*,[6]
the Supreme Court's 2002 decision that applied the Eighth Amendment to
the execution of persons with mental retardation.

HISTORICAL OVERVIEW

The issue of executing "the insane"[7] is one that has plagued the legal system for
centuries.[8] In their seminal study,[9] Professors Hazard and Louisell examined

arguments made by Blackstone,[10] Hale,[11] and Coke[12] specifically opposing such execution, and looked also at the writings of St. Thomas Aquinas[13] and Shakespeare[14] for the religious and cultural roots of the doctrine.[15] In his classic treatise on *Insanity and the Criminal Law*, Dr. William White focused almost ninety years ago on the "general feeling of abhorrence against executing a person who is insane."[16]

Although the Supreme Court had rejected as recently as 1950 the argument that there was a due process right to a pre-execution judicial sanity determination,[17] that decision predated by twelve years the court's incorporation of the Eighth Amendment to be applied to the states,[18] and the court had not considered the argument again since that time. In short, while the slate was not a clean one when *certiorari* was granted in *Ford*, neither was there much in the way of binding precedent for the court to uphold, distinguish, or overrule.

Given the significance of capital punishment in contemporary American political debates,[19] it should be no surprise that the "conundrum"[20] raised by Dr. Appelbaum has begun, again, to assume greater significance as an issue to be confronted both by forensic psychiatrists and the law.[21] What can be expected, simply, is that more offenders with mental illness[22] will be represented in prison,[23] and that a significant number of death row inmates[24] will suffer serious mental disorder.

THE *FORD* CASE

The issues involved in psychiatric participation in capital punishment decision making[25] raise a series of "intractable"[26] operational problems for mental health professionals: the responsibility of psychiatrists to construe appropriately the key terms in operative statutes' assessment of the appropriate standard of proof,[27] the reliability of diagnoses, and the possibility of regression between evaluation and execution.[28] They also raise core ethical problems that have not yet been resolved.

The Supreme Court's decision to hear *Ford v. Wainwright* suggested some recognition of the depth of the problem and appeared to promise a relatively broad-based solution, since Florida's "competency-to-be-executed" law[29] was similar in critical aspects to the statutes enacted in over a half dozen other states.[30] Alvin Ford was convicted in 1974 of murdering a police officer during an attempted robbery[31] and was sentenced to death.[32] While there was no suggestion that he was incompetent at the time of the offense, his trial, or his sentencing,[33] he began to manifest behavioral changes in 1982, nearly eight years after his conviction.[34] He developed delusions[35] and hallucinations,[36] and his letters—focusing on the local activities of the Ku Klux Klan[37]—revealed "an increasingly pervasive delusion that he had become the target of a complex conspiracy, involving the Klan and assorted others, designed to force him to commit suicide."[38]

Counsel requested that a psychiatrist continue to see Ford and recommend appropriate treatment.[39] After fourteen months of evaluation and interviews, the treating psychiatrist concluded that the defendant suffered from "a severe, uncontrollable mental disease which closely resembles 'Paranoid Schizophrenia With Suicide Potential'"—a "major mental disorder . . . severe enough to substantially affect [defendant's] present ability to assist in the defense of his life."[40]

Ford's lawyer then invoked Florida procedures governing the determination of competency of an inmate sentenced to death.[41] In accordance with the statute, the governor appointed three psychiatrists to evaluate whether the defendant had "the mental capacity to understand the nature of the death penalty and the reasons why it was imposed upon him."[42] After a single thirty-minute meeting, each psychiatrist reported separately to the governor. While each produced a different diagnosis,[43] all found him to have sufficient capacity to be executed under state law.[44]

The governor subsequently, and "without explanation," signed Ford's death warrant.[45] After the state courts rejected Ford's application for a *de novo* hearing to determine competency,[46] he applied for a writ of habeas corpus in federal court, seeking an evidentiary hearing on his sanity, "proffering the conflicting findings of the Governor-appointed commission and subsequent challenges to their methods by other psychiatrists."[47]

In the only portion of any of the four separate opinions in the *Ford* case to command a majority of the Court,[48] Justice Marshall concluded that the Eighth Amendment did prohibit the imposition of the death penalty on an insane prisoner.[49]

First, he pointed out that, since the Court decided *Solesbee v. Balkcom*[50] in 1950, its Eighth Amendment jurisprudence had "evolved substantially,"[51] and that its ban on "cruel and unusual punishment embraces, at a minimum, those modes or acts of punishment that had been considered cruel and unusual at the time that the Bill of Rights was adopted,"[52] and recognizes the "evolving standards of decency that mark the progress of a maturing society."[53] In coming to its determination, the Court must take into account "objective evidence of contemporary values before determining whether a particular punishment comports with the fundamental human dignity that the Amendment protects."[54]

The opinion traced the common-law development of the doctrine barring execution of the insane,[55] noting that, while the reasons for the rule were not precisely clear, "it is plain the law is so."[56] It concluded that there was "virtually no authority condoning the execution of the insane at English common law,"[57] and that "this solid proscription was carried to America."[58]

This "ancestral legacy" has not "outlived its time," the court added.[59] No state currently permits execution of the insane,[60] and it is "clear that the ancient and humane limitation upon the State's ability to execute its sentences has as firm a hold upon the jurisprudence of today as it had centuries ago in England":[61]

> [T]he natural abhorrence civilized societies feel at killing one who has no capacity to come to grips with his own conscience or deity is still vivid today. And the intuition that such an execution simply offends humanity is evidently shared across the Nation. Faced with such wide-spread evidence of a restriction upon sovereign power, this Court is compelled to conclude that the Eighth Amendment prohibits a State from carrying out a sentence of death upon a prisoner who is insane. Whether its aim be to protect the condemned from fear and pain without comfort or understanding, or to protect the dignity of society itself from the barbarity of exacting mindless vengeance, the restriction finds enforcement in the Eighth Amendment.[62]

On the question of what procedures were appropriate in such a case, the Court was sufficiently fragmented that no opinion commanded a majority of justices. In a four-justice opinion, Justice Marshall concluded that a *de novo* evidentiary hearing on Ford's sanity was required, unless "the state-court trier of fact has after a full hearing reliably found the relevant facts."[63] Further, if some sort of state judgment were rendered, the habeas statute compels federal courts to hold an evidentiary hearing if state procedures were inadequate,[64] or insufficient,[65] or if the applicant did not receive a "full, fair and adequate hearing" in state court.[66]

In cases such as the one before the Court—where fact-finding procedures must "aspire to a heightened standard of reliability"[67]—the ascertainment of a prisoner's sanity "as a lawful predicate to execution calls for no less stringent standards than those demanded in any other aspect of a capital proceeding,"[68] a standard particularly demanding in light of the reality that "the present state of the mental sciences is at best a hazardous guess however conscientious."[69] Under this analysis, Florida's procedures failed to pass muster. The state procedure was "wholly within the executive branch, ex parte, and provides the exclusive means of determining sanity."[70] That this "most cursory form of procedural review[71] fails to achieve even the minimal level of reliability required for the protection of any constitutional interest, and thus falls short of adequacy under *Townsend* [*v. Sain*], is self-evident."[72]

There were three significant deficiencies in the Florida procedures. First, state practice failed to allow any material relevant to the ultimate decision to be submitted on behalf of the prisoner,[73] in contravention of Court doctrine that the fact finder must have before it "all possible relevant information about the individual defendant whose fate it must determine."[74] Any procedure that precludes the prisoner or his counsel from presenting material relevant to his sanity or bars consideration of such material by the fact finder is "necessarily inadequate."[75]

Second, under Florida law, the defendant had no opportunity to challenge or impeach the opinion of the state-appointed experts through cross-examination,[76] thus creating a "significant possibility that the ultimate decision made in reliance on those experts will be distorted."[77]

Third, and "[p]erhaps the most striking defect," was the placement of the decision entirely in the executive branch: "The commander of the State's corps of prosecutors[78] cannot be said to have the neutrality that is necessary for reliability in the factfinding proceeding."[79] "In no other circumstance of which we are aware," Justice Marshall concluded on this point, "is the vindication of a constitutional right entrusted to the unreviewable discretion of an administrative tribunal."[80]

The opinion thus left it to the state to develop appropriate procedures "to enforce the constitutional restriction upon its execution of sentences,"[81] noting that it was not suggesting that "only a full trial on the issue of sanity will suffice to protect the federal interests."[82] The "lodestar" of any such procedures, however, "must be the overriding dual imperative of providing redress for those with substantial claims and of encouraging accuracy in the factfinding determination."[83] Because the state's procedures failed to provide adequate assurance of accuracy to satisfy the *Townsend* doctrine, the defendant was thus entitled under the habeas corpus statute to a *de novo* evidentiary hearing on the question of his competence to be executed.[84]

Justice Powell concurred, joining fully in the majority's opinion on the substantive Eighth Amendment issue,[85] but differing substantially from Justice Marshall's opinion on the issue of the appropriate procedures which states must follow pursuant to the habeas statute.[86] Writing for herself and Justice White, Justice O'Connor concurred in part and dissented in part. While she agreed fully with Justice Rehnquist's two-justice dissent that the Eighth Amendment did not create a substantive right not to be executed while insane (and she thus did not join in the Court's opinion or reasoning),[87] she found further that it was "inescapable" that Florida state law provided a protected liberty interest in not being executed while incompetent.[88]

As Florida did not provide "even those minimal procedural protections required by due process,"[89] she would have vacated the judgment and remanded for a state court hearing in a manner "consistent with the requirements of the Due Process Clause."[90] She emphasized, however, that, in her view, the federal court should have no role "whatever in the substantive determination of a defendant's competency to be executed."[91]

Finally, Justice Rehnquist dissented on behalf of himself and the chief justice.[92] In his view, the Florida procedures were "fully consistent with the 'common-law heritage' and current practice on which the Court purports to rely,"[93] and, in their reliance on executive branch procedures, they were "faithful to both traditional and modern practice."[94] Further, he saw no reason to abandon *Solesbee*, which had sanctioned procedures vesting decision making in "the solemn responsibility of a state's highest executive with authority to invoke the aid of the most skillful class of experts on the crucial questions involved."[95] He concluded that Florida law did not grant the defendant the sort of entitlement "that gives rise to the procedural protections for which he contends."[96] To create a constitutional right to a judicial determination of sanity prior to execution "needlessly complicates and postpones still further any finality in this area of the law,"[97] in an area where yet another adjudication "offers an invitation to those who have nothing to lose by accepting it to advance entirely spurious claims of insanity."[98]

Of special note here is that aspect of both Justice Rehnquist's and Justice O'Connor's opinions that remained obsessed with the fear that defendants will raise "false"[99] or "spurious claims"[100] in desperate attempts to stave off execution. This fear—a *doppelganger* of the public's "swift and vociferous . . . outrage"[101] over what it perceives as "abusive"[102] insanity acquittals, thus allowing "guilty" defendants to "beat the rap"[103]—was dispatched more than adequately almost 150 years ago by Dr. Isaac Ray, the father of American forensic psychiatry:

> The supposed insurmountable difficulty of distinguishing between feigned and real insanity has conduced, probably more than all other causes together, to bind the legal profession to the most rigid construction and application of the common law relative to this disease, and is always put forward in objection to the more humane doctrines.[104]

On the other hand, at least one inevitable outcome of *Ford* has been that more clinicians became aware of the problems involved and began to stake out the competing positions outlined by Radelet and Barnard, Ward, and Appelbaum, as a step toward, perhaps, "achieving consensus within the professions."[105] A study of the aftermath of the *Ford* case glumly concluded that, despite the decision in that litigation, "it remains all but impossible" for defense counsel to prove that a death row client is incompetent to be executed.[106]

IN THE AFTERMATH OF *FORD*: THE MEANING OF *PANETTI*

Subsequent to *Ford*,[107] courts split in their assessment of whether individual defendants were competent to be executed under the standards set out in that case.[108] As with other important areas of criminal procedure, the question of whether a defendant was "malingering" remains an important question in this context.[109] Other cases decided on related questions reveal a continued failure on the part of many courts to authentically implement the *Ford* decision.[110]

Generally, however, *Ford* was interpreted narrowly, the lower courts regularly finding that competency was determined solely by an inquiry into whether a prisoner was aware "that he was going to be executed and why he was going to be executed."[111] *Certiorari* was granted in the *Panetti* case—at least in part—to clarify the *Ford* ruling.[112]

Panetti, who had been convicted of capital murder in the slayings of his estranged wife's parents, had been hospitalized numerous times for serious psychiatric disorders.[113] Notwithstanding his "bizarre," "scary," and "trance-like" behavior, he was found competent to stand trial and competent to waive counsel.[114] He was convicted (the jury rejecting his insanity defense) and was sentenced to death.[115] After his direct appeals and initial petition of habeas corpus were rejected,[116] Panetti filed a subsequent habeas writ petition, alleging that he did not understand the reasons for his pending execution.[117] This petition was rejected, the court concluding that the test for competency to be executed "requires the petitioner know no more than the fact of his impending execution and the factual predicate for the execution."[118] The Fifth Circuit affirmed,[119] and the Supreme Court granted *certiorari*.[120]

The Court reversed in a 5–4 decision, and in the course of its opinion[121] significantly elaborated on its *Ford* opinion on two dimensions:[122] as to the procedures that are to be afforded to a defendant seeking to assert a *Ford* claim, and as to the substance of the *Ford* standard.

On the first matter, it found error below in the trial court's failure to provide the defendant an adequate opportunity to submit expert evidence in response to the report filed by the court-appointed experts,[123] thus depriving him of his "constitutionally adequate opportunity to be heard."[124] The fact-finding procedures on which the trial court relied, it concluded, were "'not adequate for reaching reasonably correct results' or, at a minimum, resulted in a process that appeared to be 'seriously inadequate for the ascertainment of the truth.'"[125]

On the second, it carefully elaborated on—and clarified—*Ford*. It reviewed the testimony that demonstrated the defendant's "fixed delusion" system,[126] and quoted with approval expert testimony that had pointed out that "an unmedicated individual suffering from schizophrenia can 'at times' hold an ordinary conversation and that 'it depends [whether the discussion concerns the individual's] fixed delusional system.'"[127] Here, it rejected the court of appeals' interpretation of the *Ford* standard—that competency-to-be-executed depends only on three findings: that the prisoner is aware he committed the murders, he is aware he is going to be executed, and he is aware of the reasons the state has given for his execution.[128]

This narrow test, the Supreme Court concluded, unconstitutionally foreclosed the defendant from establishing incompetency by the means that Panetti sought to employ in the case at bar: by making a showing that his mental illness "obstruct[ed] a rational understanding of the State's reason for his execution."[129] The Fifth Circuit had squarely confronted this issue and had found that "awareness" was "not necessarily synonymous with 'rational understanding'";[130] the Supreme Court rejected this position, finding that it was "too restrictive to afford a prisoner the protections granted by the Eighth Amendment."[131]

In this case, the Court found, the Fifth Circuit improperly treated a prisoner's delusional belief system "as irrelevant if the prisoner knows that the State has identified his crimes as the reason for his execution."[132] Nowhere, the Court continued, did *Ford* indicate that "delusions are irrelevant to 'comprehen[sion]' or 'aware [ness]' if they so impair the prisoner's concept of reality that he cannot reach a rational understanding of the reason for the execution."[133] If anything, the court continued, "the *Ford* majority suggests the opposite."[134]

After quoting the "simply offends humanity" language from *Ford*,[135] the Court focused on the reasons why executing an insane person "serves no retributive purpose":[136]

> [I]t might be said that capital punishment is imposed because it has the potential to make the offender recognize at last the gravity of his crime and to allow the community as a whole, including the surviving family and friends of the victim, to affirm its own judgment that the culpability of the prisoner is so serious that the ultimate penalty must be sought and imposed. The potential for a prisoner's recognition of the severity of the offense and the objective of community vindication are called in question, however, if the prisoner's mental state is so distorted by a mental illness that his awareness of the crime and punishment has little or no relation to the understanding of those concepts shared by the community as a whole. This problem is not necessarily overcome once the test set forth by the Court of Appeals is met. And under a similar logic the other rationales set forth by *Ford* fail to align with the distinctions drawn by the Court of Appeals.[137]

There was no support in *Ford* ("or anywhere else"), the Court added, for the proposition that "a prisoner is automatically foreclosed from demonstrating incompetency once a court has found he can identify the stated reason for his execution."[138] Although it conceded that concepts such as "rational understanding" could be difficult to define, and that some might fail to be punished on account of "reasons other those stemming from a severe mental illness," it concluded, on this point: "The beginning of doubt about competence in a case like petitioner's is not a misanthropic personality or an amoral character. It is a psychotic disorder."[139] In this case, it again underlined, it was the prisoner's "severe, documented mental illness that is the source of gross delusions preventing him from comprehending the meaning and purpose of the punishment to which he has been sentenced."[140]

After coming to this conclusion, the Court added that it was not attempting to set out a rule to govern all competency determinations, and then remanded so that the "underpinnings of petitioner's claims [could] be explained and evaluated in further detail on remand."[141] Among the questions it sought to be explored in greater depth was "the extent to which severe delusions may render a subject's perception of reality so distorted that he should be deemed incompetent," citing here to an aspect of the *amicus* brief by the American Psychological Association that had discussed ways in which mental health experts can inform competency determinations.[142]

PANETTI'S LIKELY INFLUENCE

Panetti will be an enormously significant opinion with regard to the underlying issues for at least two reasons: it fleshes out the constitutionally adequate procedural standards for making a determination on execution competency (by demanding that defendants have the opportunity to submit adequate expert evidence to respond to evidence on competency "solicited by the state court" as part of the defendant's "constitutionally adequate opportunity to be heard"),[143] and it clarifies *Ford*'s substantive test to demand that the prisoner possess a "rational understanding"[144] of the reasons he is to be executed.[145]

The Court's opinion also expands the role of the expert witness in competency determinations.[146] First, its procedural prong tells us that the trial court's failure to allow the defendant to introduce evidence on this question was a failure of constitutional dimensions. Second, its conclusion's citation to the American Psychological Association's *amicus* brief (that had discussed the ways that experts can inform competency determinations) tells us that a majority of this Court (albeit a bare majority) is comfortable with (and responsive to) a greater role for mental health experts in judicial proceedings. We cannot underestimate the significance of this attitude.

Panetti leaves untouched a question recently articulated in this context by Professor Christopher Seeds: Should the question of whether a death row prisoner has the capacity to assist counsel "be a part of the Eighth Amendment prohibition on executing people who have severe mental illness?"[147] Professor Seeds argues that this capacity was basically discarded by *Ford v. Wainwright*,[148] which dismissed it "as obsolete given procedural protections and collateral opportunities for appeal that now exist in capital cases,"[149] but that it should be reinstated under *Panetti* so as to "protect the reliability of judgments and add more certainty (less arbitrariness) to a determination that, as courts and commentators have long recognized, is problematically moral."[150] Although Professor J. Amy Dillard subsequently relied on Professor Seeds' reasoning—characterizing the ability to assist counsel in preparing an adequate defense as operating "as a lifeline in capital litigation"[151]—this theory has not yet been relied upon in reported post-*Panetti* litigation.[152]

Post-*Panetti* cases have not been enormously helpful in clarification of many of the issues discussed here, although several have underscored the fundamental difference between the *Panetti* holding and the *Ford* holding[153] and have considered the application of *Panetti* to claims brought under *Atkins v. Virginia*,[154] the application of the *Panetti* reasoning in non-death-penalty cases to determinations of competency to be sentenced,[155] and the number of opportunities a defendant might have to raise a *Panetti* claim.[156]

IN NEED OF FURTHER CONSIDERATION

Although *Panetti* chose not to consider the issue below on which much attention had been focused—the question of medicating defendants so as to make them competent to be executed[157]—it will remain significant with regard to the underlying issues for at least two reasons: the fact that it fleshes out the constitutionally adequate procedural standards for making a determination on execution competency (by demanding that defendants have the opportunity to submit adequate expert evidence to respond to evidence on competency "solicited by the state court" as part of the defendant's "constitutionally adequate opportunity to be heard"),[158] and the fact that it clarifies the *Ford* substantive test to demand that the prisoner possess a "rational understanding"[159] of the reasons he is to be executed. Moreover, there are several other aspects of *Panetti* that need further consideration:

- Although the Court does not state this directly, it was clear that, in the Fifth Circuit at least (the federal circuit that includes Texas, the state in which Panetti was convicted), the *Ford* test was no test at all. Panetti's lawyers told this to the court in their petition for *certiorari*:

  > Two decades have passed since this Court decided *Ford*, and the Fifth Circuit has yet to find a *single* death row inmate incompetent to be executed. During this same period, the State of Texas has executed 360 people.[160]

  In other areas of the law, the Supreme Court has considered the (lack of) value of a "paper" remedy that had never been invoked.[161] Although this aspect of Panetti's *certiorari* petition is never directly addressed in the majority's opinion, it is certainly reasonable to speculate that this sorry "track record" might have had some impact on the Court's thinking.

- Many states have still never defined criteria for competency to be executed.[162]
- The Court clarifies that it is limiting its decision to individuals with "severe mental illness," as opposed to those with a "misanthropic personality disorder."[163] The question of whether a personality disorder might be the basis for an insanity defense has plagued the courts for years,[164] and it can be expected that this aspect of the Court's opinion will provoke significant new future case law and scholarship.
- The Court's focus on the "rational understanding"[165] of an individual condemned prisoner invites reconsideration of whether one can ever sufficiently generalize his mental state. Notes a perceptive student commentator:

> That is, examining the context of an individual's state of mind means considering its causes and consequences. Looking within and beyond the individual in this way contextualizes the concept of rational individual choice that is often imagined abstractly. This appeal to causation, combined with the epistemic impossibility of knowing if we judge rationality accurately—even for prisoners not diagnosed as mentally ill—casts doubt on the legitimacy of the ultimate punishment of death, if indeed that legitimacy depends on finding that the condemned's mental state is objectively rational, and is his alone.[166]

It is by no means clear that lower courts will understand the wisdom of this message.

- The Court's expansion of the role of the expert witness in competency determinations, again, constitutionalizes this important aspect of the hearing process and tells us that a majority of this Court (albeit a bare majority) is comfortable with (and responsive to) a greater role for mental health experts in judicial proceedings.

SCHOLARLY CONSIDERATIONS

Even before the Supreme Court's decision in *Atkins v. Virginia*,[167] scholars had begun to sketch out reasons why the ban on imposing the death penalty on persons with mental illness should be extended so that "most" such individuals should not be executed.[168] Professor Christopher Slobogin gave three reasons:

> First, such executions would violate equal protection of the laws in any jurisdiction in which execution of children and people with mental retardation is

barred. Second, many death sentences imposed on people with mental illness violate due process because their mental illness is treated by the factfinder as an aggravating factor, either directly or to bolster a separate aggravating circumstance. Third, many mentally ill offenders who are sentenced to death will be so impaired at the time of execution that they can not emotionally appreciate the significance of their punishment and thus cannot be executed under the eighth amendment; the latter conclusion is required even if they are restorable through treatment, given the unethical and medically inappropriate role in which such treatment casts mental health professionals.[169]

Following the *Atkins* decision, Professor Slobogin expanded upon his earlier thoughts, focusing primarily on the equal protection argument, noting, "Because murderers with proven significant mental illness at the time of the offense are no more culpable or deterrable, nor any more dangerous, than juvenile murderers or murderers who suffer from mental retardation, the only possible basis for the states' continued willingness to execute members of the first group is the type of 'irrational prejudice' against which *Cleburne*[170] inveighed."[171] Here, Slobogin stressed the "irrationality" of the "disproportionate fear of people with mental illness" as a reason why executions of such persons have continued over the years.[172] This echoes other arguments made by this author as to how sanism dominates this area of the law,[173] and can be read hand in glove with Professor Richard Bonnie's post-*Panetti* criticism that, in death penalty cases, "courts trivialize mental illness."[174]

Subsequently, the Individual Rights and Responsibilities Section of the American Bar Association (ABA-IRR) established a Task Force on Mental Disability and the Death Penalty, and that task force endorsed an almost identical position, recommending,

> Defendants should not be executed or sentenced to death if, at the time of the offense, they had a severe mental disorder or disability that significantly impaired their capacity (a) to appreciate the nature, consequences, or wrongfulness of their conduct; (b) to exercise rational judgment in relation to conduct; or (c) to conform their conduct to the requirements of the law.[175]

Here, the Task Force drew on *Atkins*, arguing that one of *Atkins'* key rationales—that neither deterrence nor retribution were justifications for the execution of persons with mental retardation[176]—similarly applied to persons with mental illness. Again, speaking of this task force, Professor Slobogin noted that its recommendations focused "on their role as a corrective for the insidious impact of 'sanist' attitudes on the part of legal decision-makers in capital cases."[177] His position was supported by other scholars,[178] advocates,[179] and student authors.[180] Professor Pamela Wilkins, by way of example, buttresses her support of a categorical Eighth Amendment ban in large part on jurors' inherent sanism: that in the case of defendants with serious mental illness, "there is a substantial risk that the fact-finder will give more weight to future dangerousness than to culpability."[181]

In the years since the *Panetti* decision, more and more other scholars have expressed similar positions.[182] Again, Richard Bonnie flatly states that, to execute Panetti "in this condition is an affront to his dignity as a person and to the 'dignity of man,' the core value of the Eighth Amendment."[183] The late Professor Bruce Winick relies on an "emerging conception of proportionality under the Eighth Amendment,"[184] arguing that "it can and should be extended to offenders with severe mental illness at the time of the offense,"[185] and that the imposition of capital punishment on those whose mental illness significantly diminished their blameworthiness "would be a disproportionate penalty. It would constitute an affront to human dignity. It should be banned as cruel and unusual punishment."[186] Professor Pamela Wilkins focuses squarely on Scott Panetti's condition:

> In the end, competency for execution is a narrow issue affecting very few inmates. However, strict adherence to a realistic substantive test and to generous procedural standards not only is required by the Eighth Amendment, but is a measure of our commitment to a just society. Adherence to these standards may be inconvenient, but the alternative is that we kill pitiful, ill men like Scott Panetti with no penological justification whatsoever. For the Scott Panetti's of the world, attention must be paid.[187]

Although Professor Lyn Entzeroth is not optimistic about a categorical ban being imposed in all cases involving persons with mental illness,[188] I expect that Professor Wilkins' prediction—that "sooner or later the Court will accept a petitioner's invitation to consider whether the Eighth Amendment permits death sentences for those with such severe mental illnesses at the time of their crimes"[189]—will eventually be borne out.[190]

Dignity values are at play here too.[191] Professor John Castiglione argues that the most promising construction of the "dignity interest" focuses on "concepts like degradation, cruelty, and humiliation."[192] These concepts are the *basso continuo* of cases involving defendants with serious mental disabilities and the death penalty. In discussing, globally, the role of dignity in American jurisprudence, Professor Rex Glensy focuses on this issue:

> Thus, the Court has noted that any punishment must comport "with the basic concept of human dignity" that animates the "core" of the Eighth Amendment. This relationship between the Amendment and human dignity would be examined in every case regarding cruel and unusual punishment, and the court would therefore square the accused state practice with the individual's dignitary interest. Some cases have implicitly employed

this approach, such as when the Court was tasked to decide whether executing the insane constituted a violation of the Eighth Amendment. The Court ruled that the "execution of an insane person simply offends humanity," and that a "person under the shadow of death should have the opportunity to make the few choices that remain available" under those circumstances. The Court hinged its opinion on the notion that awareness of one's own surroundings was a necessary component to humane punishment and that the absence of this component negated an individual's dignitary interest. According to the Court, "a cruel punishment is one that treats the offender as though he or she were not a human person with a claim to our concern as fellow persons, but as a mere animal or thing lacking in basic human dignity."[193]

Finally, there are other therapeutic jurisprudence values that can be implemented.[194] Perhaps most importantly, there are important TJ threads in the *Panetti* opinion itself. In explaining its decision, the Court stressed that, in a case in which a prisoner's mental state "is so distorted by a mental illness" that he does not share with "the community as a whole" an understanding of the concepts of crime and punishment, the objective "of community vindication [is] called in question."[195] For years, scholars have been tentatively exploring the relationship between therapeutic jurisprudence[196] and its implications for the execution of persons with severe mental disabilities.[197] Here, the Court frontally considers the implications of this dilemma, and it can be safely forecast that more attention will be paid to this specific issue in the coming years.

There are other TJ questions to be considered as well. Bruce Winick persuasively argues that it is consonant with TJ principles if the determination of competency to be executed is conducted, whenever possible, pretrial, rather than after conviction and sentencing.[198] In a thoughtful article considering the death penalty from an international human rights perspective,[199] Liliana Lyra Jubilut recommends the adoption of a series of procedural remedies that would result in fewer death sentences being meted out to individuals with serious mental disabilities:

> Adequate procedural protections would, at a minimum, involve a panel of doctors to evaluate the disease (to avoid personal bias and prejudice and guarantee an opinion less fallible than the one obtained by relying on just one expert). The evaluation should: (1) involve meeting not only the defendant but also people connected to him or her (to gather more information and also because the mere existence of the disease sometimes prevents the defendant from being able or willing to assist in his or her own evaluation); (2) be a product of more than one interview with the defendant (so to be true to the process-like features of diagnosis and of the disease); (3) not be the result of just a standard test but rather a combination of personal interviews, interviews with relatives or members of the personal circle,

and tests (because experts seem to diverge on which of these strategies is the best one); and (4) should not be focused only on pretrial, in-trial, and preexecution procedures (to avoid the above-mentioned underinclusiveness of time-framed diagnosis), and a follow-up evaluation. The panel should be composed of: (1) both men and women with diverse ethnic backgrounds (because diagnoses are culturally influenced, it is important to have a more comprehensive panel in order to minimize the possibility of prejudices interfering with the result), and (2) either disinterested doctors or doctors chosen by both the defendant and the state (to avoid biased opinions depending on who hired the doctor and also due to the burden-sharing notion mentioned above). Adequate procedural protections should also include a mandatory psychiatric evaluation in all capital cases (due to the fact that the disease may be of such a type that the defendant or his or her defense counsel do not recognize the fact that he or she is sick, or because lack of money is often an obstacle in assessing the mental health of a defendant).[200]

CONCLUSION

The question of competency in the death penalty context continues to be an important one, both with regard to the number of cases in which this status is raised, the scope of type of cases in which it is raised, and the practical implications of adopting one standard or another. It is a question to which the United States Supreme Court has returned on many occasions, and will return again.[201]

The case law in this area is far from coherent, but some of the more recent decisions—such as *Panetti*—do reflect more nuanced decision making. Also, scholars have begun to consider the deeper textures of the underlying issues much more carefully and thoughtfully.[202] Even though the Supreme Court failed to address the medication question in *Panetti*, its decision to clarify *Ford* must be seen as a positive step.

Several years ago, I wrote this about the court process in these cases:

> The abdication on the part of lawyers (leaving it to mental health professionals to develop their own competence assessment standards with little assistance) and on the part of judges (refusing to independently assess clinical testimony), the failure of most clinicians to use standardized and validated tests, the lack of meaningful dialogue between the lawyer and the evaluator, are all symptoms of the same malignancy: the corrosive impact of sanism on the legal process.[203]

If *Panetti* is, in fact, implemented and if it is given life in lower courts, then perhaps the first step toward the eradication of sanism in the death penalty decision-making process will have taken place.

· 7 ·

Competency to Be Executed:
The Question of Medication

INTRODUCTION[1]

The question of whether a defendant facing execution can be involuntarily medicated so as to make him competent to be executed has been the topic of strenuous and pointed debate among academic and forensic psychiatrists for decades.[2] In 1996, Drs. Alfred Freedman and Abraham Halpern laid down the gauntlet:

> The rationale that physicians should assist in the administration of justice, insofar as capital punishment is concerned, is frighteningly reminiscent of how German physicians justified their involvement in the torture and killing of thousands of innocent human beings and carried out the Nazi programs of sterilization and "euthanasia" by murdering countless children and adults.[3]

In contrast, Dr. Robert Phillips argued,

> While many hold strong opinions about the propriety of involvement of a psychiatrist that may lead to execution, there is no ethical barrier to testifying at the pre-trial, trial, or sentencing phase in a capital case. Despite the heavy reliance on psychiatric testimony, the psychiatrist is neither the judge nor the executioner.[4]

Other psychiatrists remain ambivalent and freely share their ambivalence. In the words of Dr. Julie Cantor:

> Though the *Singleton* case[5] has ended, its legacy is a paradox. I believe in the arguments set forth here. I believe that psychiatrists have an ethical

duty to medicate prisoners in clinical situations like that of Charles Single-ton. I believe that psychotic inmates deserve treatment, the kind of care that they would get in the outside world, and that psychiatrists should not deny that treatment because the inmate may become competent for execution. But that does not mean that I would have cheered at Singleton's execution, nor would I dance on his grave. The reasons that death penalty opponents cite are convincing—killing Singleton will not bring back his victim; execution may not deter future killers; a life sentence is cheaper than the requisite appeals by orders of magnitude; given a different lawyer/skin color/jurisdiction, the outcome would have been different; and so on. To even the most callous observer, the inconsistencies in the punishment and the innocents exonerated from death rows around the country makes capital punishment seem "irrational, arbitrary, and unfair." Still, I would have treated Charles Singleton. And yet I remain troubled by the point-lessness of his crime and uneasy with the manner of his death.[6]

CASE LAW DEVELOPMENT

In the aftermath of *Ford v. Wainwright*[7] (and eventually *Panetti v. Quarter-man*)[8] this separate-but-related policy issue demands resolution. As new de-velopments in psychiatry and psychotropic medication have enabled the state to render death row inmates competent for execution,[9] an issue self-evidently never contemplated at the time of the drafting of the Eighth Amendment, the question of the legality, morality, and ethics of the use of such medica-tions to "make competent" a defendant so as to allow an execution to proceed now confronts the courts.[10]

The Supreme Court had, over two decades ago, granted *certiorari* in *Perry v. Louisiana*[11] (presenting this precise question), thus making it appear that this gap would be resolved. However, the Court declined to rule on the merits, remanding the case, instead, to the Louisiana Supreme Court for re-consideration[12] in light of its then-contemporaneous decision in *Washington v. Harper*.[13]

Perry had been charged with the murder of five family members, includ-ing his parents.[14] After he was found competent to stand trial, Perry withdrew his previously entered not-guilty-by-reason-of-insanity plea (over counsel's advice) and entered a not-guilty plea.[15] He was convicted and sentenced to death.[16] On appeal, the Louisiana Supreme Court affirmed both his convic-tion and death sentence, but ordered an adversarial hearing on his present competence to be executed.[17]

At that competency hearing, the four expert witnesses agreed that Perry was psychotic and that his condition improved when he was properly medicated.[18] Two of the witnesses found that he would be competent to be executed if he were to receive medication; a third, who did not believe Perry understood the purpose of his sentence, was not sure if the medication would make him competent; the fourth remained unconvinced that the defendant understood that he had really committed the murders in question.[19]

Following this hearing, the trial court, after it had received new reports from the prison hospital, ordered two of the experts to reexamine the defendant.[20] At this hearing (held five months after the initial hearing), testimony was adduced that Perry was now aware of the reason he was to be executed.[21]

The trial court then found that Perry was competent to be executed, adopting Justice Powell's definition of competence from the *Ford* opinion.[22] It further found that any due process right to refuse medication that Perry might have had was outweighed by two compelling state interests: the provision of proper psychiatric care, and carrying out a valid death penalty.[23] It thus ordered that Perry be medicated—by force if necessary—so that he would remain competent to be executed.[24] The Louisiana Supreme Court declined to review this order.[25]

The United States Supreme Court subsequently granted *certiorari* to resolve, inter alia, the question of whether the Eighth Amendment prohibits states from forcibly medicating death row inmates for the purpose of making them competent to be executed.[26] However, as noted above, instead of deciding the case on the merits, the Court ultimately vacated and remanded[27] to the Louisiana Supreme Court for further reconsideration in light of its decision in *Washington v. Harper*.[28]

It is unclear why the Supreme Court chose to deal with *Perry* in this manner. It may be that the justices, after considering the case, felt that the only issue presented was that of forcible medication, finding the execution consequences irrelevant, and that they thus felt it was essential for the state court to consider, after *Harper*, whether the difference in long-term harm in a case such as *Perry* (his execution) outweighed the state's interests in involuntarily medicating him.[29] It may also be that, since one of the justices—Justice Souter—did not participate in *Perry*,[30] the court felt the issue was too important to decide without the benefit of a full court.

On remand, the Louisiana Supreme Court found, under *state* constitutional law,[31] that the state was prohibited from medicating Perry to make him competent to be executed.[32] Concluded the court:

> For centuries no jurisdiction has approved the execution of the insane. The state's attempt to circumvent this well-settled prohibition by forcibly medicating an insane prisoner with antipsychotic drugs violates his rights under our state constitution. . . . First, it violates his right to privacy or personhood. Such involuntary medication requires the unjustified invasion of his brain and body with discomforting, potentially dangerous and painful drugs, the seizure of control of his mind and thoughts, and the

usurpation of his right to make decisions regarding his health or medical treatment. Furthermore, implementation of the state's plan to medicate forcibly and execute the insane prisoner would constitute cruel, excessive and unusual punishment. This particular application of the death penalty fails to measurably contribute to the social goals of capital punishment. Carrying out this punitive scheme would add severity and indignity to the prisoner's punishment beyond that required for the mere extinguishment of life. This type of punitive treatment system is not accepted anywhere in contemporary society and is apt to be administered erroneously, arbitrarily or capriciously.[33]

This decision was not re-appealed to the Supreme Court (no doubt because of its state constitutional law basis).

While the Supreme Court's disposition of *Perry* did not clarify the underlying issues,[34] it appeared inevitable that this question would arise again in the future, thus giving the Court, if it so chose, a second chance to weigh the competing values. Yet this never happened, and the only relevant developments were in the lower federal courts and the state courts.[35] By way of examples, the South Carolina Supreme Court relied upon the Louisiana Supreme Court's decision in *Perry* to support its conclusion that medicating a defendant to make him competent to be executed would violate the South Carolina *state* constitution.[36] On the other hand, in *Singleton v. Norris*,[37] the Arkansas Supreme Court ruled that the state had the burden to administer antipsychotic medication as long as a prisoner was alive and was a potential danger either to himself or to others, and that the collateral effect of the involuntary medication—rendering him competent to understand the nature and reason for his execution—did not violate due process. The Supreme Court subsequently denied *certiorari*.[38]

Later, in the *Singleton* litigation, Singleton filed a petition for a writ of habeas corpus seeking a stay of execution. Denial of the writ was affirmed by the Eighth Circuit, which held that neither due process nor the Eighth Amendment prevented the state from executing an inmate who has regained competency as the result of forced medication that is part of "appropriate medical care."[39]

Turning to the substantive question, the Court noted that it was guided by both *Harper* and *Ford* and that its task was to weigh the state's interest in carrying out a lawfully imposed sentence against Singleton's interest in refusing medication. The Court found that Singleton "prefers to take the medication rather than be in an unmedicated and psychotic state" and that he suffered no substantial side effects.[40] It held that as a result, the state's interest in carrying out its lawfully imposed sentence was the "superior one."[41] The Court went on to note that Singleton had proposed no less intrusive means of ensuring his competence and never argued that he was not competent with the medication—other than to put forth what the Court termed his "artificial competence theory."[42]

The Court then turned to what it deemed the "core of the dispute" namely "whether the antipsychotic medication is medically appropriate for Singleton's treatment."[43] The Court found Singleton to have "implicitly conceded" that the treatment was in his short-term medical interest.[44] In addressing his central claims, the Court reasoned,

> Singleton's argument regarding his long-term medical interest boils down to an assertion that execution is not in his medical interest. Eligibility for execution is the only unwanted consequence of the medication. The due process interests in life and liberty that Singleton asserts have been foreclosed by the lawfully imposed sentence of execution and the *Harper* procedure. In the circumstances presented in this case, the best medical interests of the prisoner must be determined without regard to whether there is a pending date of execution. . . . Thus, we hold that the mandatory medication regime, valid under the pendency of a stay of execution, does not become unconstitutional under *Harper* when an execution date is set.[45]

The Court also rejected Singleton's claim, based on *State v. Perry*, that the Eighth Amendment prohibited execution of one who is made "artificially competent":

> Closely related to his due process argument, Singleton also claims that the Eighth Amendment forbids the execution of a prisoner who is "artificially competent." Singleton relies principally on a case construing an analogous provision in the Louisiana Constitution. State v. Perry, 610 So. 2d 746 (La. 1992). . . . We note, however, that the *Perry* court accepted the view of "best medical interests" that we have rejected. 610 So. 2d at 766. The court also found Perry's medication was ordered solely for purposes of punishment and not for legitimate reasons of prison security or medical need. 610 So. 2d at 757. We decline to undertake a difficult and unnecessary inquiry into the State's motives in circumstance [*sic*] where it has a duty to provide medical care.[46]

Citing *Estelle v. Gamble*,[47] for the proposition that the government has an obligation to provide medical care to those whom it incarcerates, the Court reasoned that "any additional motive or effect is irrelevant." It concluded,

> *Ford* prohibits only the execution of a prisoner who is unaware of the punishment he is about to receive and why he is to receive it. A State does not violate the Eighth Amendment as interpreted by *Ford* when it executes a prisoner who became incompetent during his long stay on death row but who subsequently regained competency through appropriate medical care.[48]

In a dissenting opinion, Judge Heaney stated,

> I believe that to execute a man who is severely deranged without treat-
> ment, and arguably incompetent when treated, is the pinnacle of what
> Justice Marshall called "the barbarity of exacting mindless vengeance."[49]

Judge Heaney went on to cite facts from the record that indicated
that even in a *medicated* state, Singleton appeared not to fully or rationally
comprehend death or the nature of his sentence. After noting examples of
Singleton's beliefs regarding death, including the belief that his victim was
not truly dead and that a person can be executed by correctional officers and
then have his breathing "started up again" by judges, he turned to a discussion
of "synthetic" sanity:

> Singleton's case is exemplary of the unpredictable result antipsychotic
> treatment has on mentally ill prisoners. . . . Based on the medical history
> in this case, I am left with no alternative but to conclude that drug-induced
> sanity is not the same as true sanity. Singleton is not "cured"; his insan-
> ity is merely muted, at times, by the powerful drugs he is forced to take.
> Underneath this mask of stability, he remains insane. *Ford's* prohibition
> on executing the insane should apply with no less force to Singleton than
> to untreated prisoners.[50]

Finally, noting the impact of the majority's ruling not only on mentally
ill prisoners but on the integrity of the medical profession, the dissent concluded,

> I would hold that the State may continue to medicate Singleton, volun-
> tarily or involuntarily, if it is necessary to protect him or others and is in
> his best medical interest, but it may not execute him. I continue to believe
> that the appropriate remedy is for the district court to enter a permanent
> stay of execution.[51]

Cases that followed Singleton were inconclusive, and absolutely no
coherent jurisprudential threads could be drawn from them.[52] The next important development in this area of the law came several years later when, in
Panetti v. Dretke,[53] the Fifth Circuit found that a medicated defendant was
competent to be executed. There, it affirmed a decision of the district court
that had found that the defendant suffered from schizoaffective disorder,
and had a "delusional belief system in which he viewed himself as being
persecuted for his religious activities and beliefs," believing that the state is
"in league with the forces of evil to prevent him from preaching the Gospel."
Nonetheless, as the defendant was aware that he was to be executed, that he
had committed the murders for which he was convicted and sentenced to
death, and that the "State's stated reason for executing him is that he commit-

ted two murders," the district court held that Panetti was competent to be executed.[54] The Supreme Court subsequently granted *certiorari*[55] and ultimately reversed, holding that the defendant was denied the constitutional procedures to which he was entitled under *Ford*.[56] The decision, however, did not discuss the issue of involuntary medication, so this question remains unresolved.[57]

Few of the cases in this cohort pay particular attention to the trilogy of US Supreme Court cases that deal with involuntary medication in cases involving convicted prisoners, competent defendants pleading the insanity defense, or incompetent defendants whom the state seeks to medicate so as to make them competent to stand trial.[58] Professor Lyn Entzeroth, in writing about this trilogy in this context, suggests that "forcible administration of antipsychotic medication [to make one competent to be executed] seems at the very least inconsistent with the principles of *Harper*, *Riggins*, and even *Sell*."[59]

I have written extensively elsewhere about the relationship between sanism, pretextuality, and the right to refuse treatment.[60] In a cohort of civil cases, I found that "the data suggests that, in many jurisdictions, such counsel is woefully inadequate—disinterested, uninformed, roleless, and often hostile."[61] Certainly, in death penalty cases—where counsel's inadequacy is often the norm[62]—the likelihood that applications for involuntary medication will be met with vigorous advocacy is negligible.

CONCLUSION

It is virtually impossible to reconcile the conflicting positions. A student commentator thus concludes,

> A prisoner allowed to refuse anti-psychotic drugs is a prisoner forever trapped in madness. He must be isolated and shunned by prison officials and staff for their own safety. He will be a constant danger to himself. This result ignores the state's affirmative duty of care and may harm the prisoner in ways that cannot be contemplated by sane persons. One wonders how the Constitution could tolerate this extreme example of individualism despite an obligation of care.[63]

On the other hand, in a recent article on the ethical issues that face physicians who medicate death row inmates, Dr. Howard Zonana concludes this way:

> As a species we are too good at rationalizing what we are doing or decided to do in the past. A little known example from World War II is the story of Japan's Unit 731 and Hisato Yoshimura ("the scientific devil"). Here are examples of physicians poisoning prisoners with cyanide and potassium chloride, performing vivisection, and deliberately inoculating prisoners

with deadly pathogens. Hundreds of Japanese physicians took part in such murders. Their rationale, according to surviving physicians, was that the prisoners were condemned to die regardless, but this way their deaths would contribute useful knowledge. We have good ethical guidelines, and we need to follow them.[64]

Professor Bruce Arrigo and a colleague have approached this question from the perspective of therapeutic jurisprudence[65] and have concluded that involuntarily medicating death row prisoners to make them competent to be executed violates therapeutic jurisprudence principles from both the perspectives of the effects such drugging has on medical personnel engaged in administering the drugs, and the effects it has on the inmate being medicated.[66] Further, Professor Bruce Winick underscores how the use of therapists as an adjunct to capital punishment may "undermine their roles as healers,"[67] speculating that medicating prisoners to make them competent to be executed could "drive many ethical and sensitive practitioners from the field or deter them from entering it."[68] I believe that these positions and Dr. Zonana's position are, by far, the more persuasive in this inquiry.

Neuroimaging and the Death Penalty

INTRODUCTION

$\mathcal{T}$he robust debate over neuroimaging has highlighted a series of law-and-policy questions dealing primarily with reliability, admissibility, and availability. I address this as a separate issue in this book, since I believe that the resolution of this debate sheds light on multiple issues that we face in all inquiries related to the imposition of the death penalty on defendants with mental disabilities. Also, I believe that this debate is of great relevance to two specific substantive issues of death penalty procedure, one of which is discussed extensively elsewhere in this volume (the competency of persons with mental illness to be executed),[1] and one which is not (the availability of expert witnesses to indigent defendants in cases in which the state seeks to prove the defendant's future dangerousness).[2]

Thus, in this chapter, after first discussing the neuroimaging literature as it relates to the criminal process in general, I will consider a series of questions that are essential to resolving the underlying policy dilemma: (1) What impact will such evidence—apparently less inherently easy to falsify—have on jurors whose inherent suspicion of mental state opinion testimony is well documented? (2) Will this "falsifiability" issue even *matter* to jurors whose personal values/moral codes reject the notion of mitigation because it is dissonant with their heuristics-driven and false "ordinary common sense"?[3] (3) To what extent will sanism and pretextuality drive juror behavior in such cases?[4] and (4) What are the therapeutic jurisprudence implications of the answers to all of these questions?[5] I will then consider the implications of this evidence, in cases involving applications under *Ake v. Oklahoma*,[6] on an indigent defendant's access to expert testimony. Finally, I will consider its implications in the context of the Supreme Court's 2007 decision in *Panetti v. Quarterman*,[7] recrafting the standard originally set out in *Ford v. Wainwright*[8] on the executability of a mentally ill defendant.

THE NEUROIMAGING LITERATURE AND DEBATE[9]

A review of the literature on neuroimaging predictably reveals a broad array of positions, promises, and prophecies. O. Carter Snead argues that the ambition of cognitive neuroscientists is "to use the claims of their discipline and the new powers conferred by neuroimaging to overthrow retributive justice as a legitimate justification for criminal sanctions."[10] Jonathan Marks quotes William Uttal's warning that neuroimaging may be simply a "neo-phrenological fad."[11] David Eagleman claims that "[t]here is a new potential to use detailed combinations of behavioral tests and neuroimaging to better predict recidivism."[12] Perhaps most emphatically, Bruce Arrigo levels this critique:

> In short, the mass marketing and wholesale circulation of fMRI technology for medicolegal purposes endorses capitalist status quo dynamics and, as such, breeds, nurtures, and sustains the very structural inequalities (both social and psychological) that result in destructiveness, violence and crime. Indeed, through reliance on such cognitive neuroscience advances, it is assumed that the path to "correcting" the ills of the individual are discoverable through reliance on the novel (though simulated or computer-generated) breakthroughs of science.[13]

For the purposes of this book, I do not believe it is necessary to "take sides" on this debate. I set it out here because it is relevant to the related, but distinctly separate, issue: Which of these positions will *jurors* think is "right," especially in the context of their deciding death penalty cases? The primary and robust debate that has taken place so far over neuroimaging in law and medical journals has highlighted a series of law-and-policy questions dealing primarily with reliability,[14] admissibility,[15] and availability.[16] Scholars have already expressed an extensive range of opinions on the value, and perhaps even the *ethics*, of this testimony. Thus, when we consider the topic that I will be addressing in this chapter—the impact of neuroimaging evidence on juror decision making—we need to recalibrate our focus so as to incorporate *other* questions that I listed above (as to the evidence's apparent nonfalsifiability, as to the impact of heuristic-thinking/false "ordinary common sense" and sanism/pretextuality on the resolution of the underlying issues, and of the potential therapeutic jurisprudence implications of that resolution).

Overview

Definitions of neuroimaging and brain imaging in the law and in the behavioral literature immediately warn us of some land mines. "A brain image is the *vivid* representation of anatomy or physiology through a pictorial or graphic display of data."[17] Neuroimaging modalities offer "an *objective*, non-invasive *quantifiable* image, which can provide useful information, especially when the clinical examination may otherwise be normal."[18] Through advances in neuroscience, "the ability of mental health professionals to assess [frontal lobe dysfunction] and its impact on impulse control *is now sufficiently established* to merit the introduction of such evidence in support of an insanity defense under a control test."[19] Neuroscience seems "advanced enough to enter forensic psychiatry."[20] "Advances in neurobiological research methods allow one to address the nature and biological basis of human behavior."[21] And we assume that jurors can be counted on to critically evaluate such evidence.[22]

Some of this language jumps off the page: *vivid, objective, quantifiable, advanced.* I note this because these are all factors that might have a significant impact on jury decision making in cases in which neuroimaging evidence is critically important to the case's ultimate disposition, as they are all factors that might lead unwitting fact finders to believe that the story told by the neuroimaging picture is susceptible to only one interpretation. And that, at the outset, is troubling.

The reality is that neuroimaging is "fraught with uncertainties,"[23] and the steps used in the production and presentation of neuroimaging evidence are "not only . . . not standardized, they are easily manipulated by a person with the knowledge of the technology."[24] Some researchers characterize it as "indistinct."[25] Similarly, Amanda Pustilnik concludes, "neuroscience cannot provide complete, or even sufficient, explanations of criminal violence by reference primarily to purported neurobiological dysfunctions within isolated parts of offenders' brains."[26] Other scholars charge that "researchers, clinicians, and lawyers are seduced into becoming true believers in the merits of [brain imaging] for understanding the relationship between brain and behavior."[27] On this point, Professors Tancredi and Brodie stress,

> [A]n ideological approach to understanding the brain of those claiming insanity for their criminal actions would be one that holds on to an image as though it were the truth of what is being asserted about the brain.[28]

Scholars vacillate between positions that neuroimaging is like or is unlike other scientific evidence.[29] Dov Fox finds "no reason to think that jurors will be any less capable of critically evaluating EEG or fMRI tests than they are of evaluating other types of scientific evidence."[30] Alexandra Roberts considers analogies to both DNA and polygraph testimony and finds them both wanting.[31] But there is little doubt that "hard science"—and neuroimaging certainly appears to be "hard science"—at the very least, in the words of a veteran death penalty defense lawyer, makes "Legislators stand up and listen."[32] Already, there has been a flurry of activity focusing on the question on whether neuroimaging can finally and conclusively shed light on (1) the roots and etiology of psychopathic behavior, and (2) accurately identifying *who* is a "psychopath."[33] Neuroimaging has even been discussed as a potential tool of counterterrorism.[34]

My point is simple: the *existence* of neuroimaging techniques has changed the contours of the playing field, and that reality must be acknowledged.

FACTORS/FACT FINDERS' CONSTRUCTIONS

I have identified a cluster of factors that we must think about seriously in an effort to understand how neuroimaging evidence will be construed by fact finders: visualization, reductionism, the attribution heuristic, and the impact of a belief in "the CSI effect." I will discuss each of these briefly.

Visualization

We start with the obvious. Neuroimaging testimony is colorful[35] and grabs the viewer's attention with representations that may "appear like holograms."[36] The visual "allure"[37] can "dazzle" and "seduce" jurors[38] in ways that are "inappropriately persuasive."[39] The fact that neuroimaging appears "interesting" may make it more impressive and probative to jurors than clinical or actuarial testimony.[40] It is thus *vivid* and forces us to reconsider the dominance and the power of the *vividness heuristic*, a cognitive simplifying device through which a "single vivid, memorable case overwhelms mountains of abstract, colorless data upon which rational choices should be made";[41] in this context, *visual* images are particularly vivid.[42]

Reductionism

Professor Neil Feigenson concludes that these colorful depictions are inappropriately reductionist; neuroimaging testimony has the meretricious capacity to "reduce . . . psychosocial complexity,"[43] an error that encourages jurors to improperly misuse the cognitively simplifying attribution heuristic—through which we "interpret a wide variety of additional information to reinforce pre-existing stereotypes"[44]—in this sort of decision making. This is the charge that Bruce Arrigo has thus asserted:

In short, cognitive neuroscience's ability to detect neuronal activity that allows the fMRI investigator to visualize and, presumably, understand how the brain reacts/thinks when presented with a series of questions such that these scanned activities can be measured accurately, is an overly reductionistic and deterministic perspective.[45]

Attributionism

The attribution heuristic teaches us that we "overattribute others' behavior to the kinds of people they are rather than to the circumstances in which they find themselves."[46] We have always sought to attribute human behavior, in the words of Laura Khoshbin and Shahram Khoshbin, "to a physical source in the head."[47] This desire is intensified when we seek to explain violence, especially either otherwise inexplicable violence or political violence.[48] The potential for concern is exacerbated further here by what Professor David Faigman and his colleagues have characterized as "the general lack of science literacy among Americans, including lawyers and judges."[49]

"The CSI Effect"

All participants in the criminal justice system agree on one thing: the existence of what is called "the CSI effect."[50] What this means is fairly clear: that jurors (and presumably also judges) are so inured to the ubiquity of forensic evidence—as depicted by the "leave-no-doubt" crime solver in TV police procedural shows—that there is an expectation that such evidence will be presented in *all* criminal trials.[51] In truth, this idea that jurors believe in the CSI effect is based on anecdotal evidence (some of it stupefying),[52] and the valid and reliable evidence that such a CSI effect exists in jurors' minds—to the extent that they demand the "money shot" of hard forensic evidence in all trials—is scant.[53] Rather, the evidence shows that jurors' expectations of such evidence vary with the type of case.[54] But the fact remains that participants in the criminal justice system believe that *jurors* believe in this effect.[55] And that is what needs to be confronted: this perception, and whether or not it is seriously flawed.

Conclusion

I believe that the key to an answer here is a consideration of sanism: to what extent will our prejudices, our stereotypes, our slotting, and our typification overwhelm all other evidence and all other issues in this conversation? In every aspect of mental disability law that I have ever studied—especially as it relates to questions of criminal procedure—the answer has been "to a great extent." Is there any reason to think it will be less so here? Perhaps the seductive dazzle of colorful pictures will trump millennia of fear and superstition.[56] But there is no body of evidence that yet suggests that this may happen.

RIGHT TO AN EXPERT

Introduction

Consider next the implications of (1) *Ake v. Oklahoma*[57] (an indigent defendant's access to expert testimony) in cases where neuroimaging tests might be critical, (2) the defendant's competency to consent to the imposition of a neuroimaging test or examination, and (3) the impact of medications—specifically, antipsychotic medications—on a defendant's brain at the time that such a test is performed.

The Ake Case[58]

The vast majority of criminal defendants are indigent.[59] Neuroimaging testing is expensive, and it is more expensive in cases in which the examined defendant is in jail awaiting trial.[60] The question before us here is relatively simple: Does the defendant have a right to an independent neuroimaging expert in a death penalty case?

Over twenty-five years ago, the US Supreme Court addressed the question of a defendant's right to an expert in a criminal trial. In *Ake v. Oklahoma*, which was a death penalty case, the Supreme Court ruled that an indigent criminal defendant who makes a threshold showing that insanity is likely to be a significant factor at trial is constitutionally entitled to a psychiatrist's assistance.[61] The Court observed that it had "long recognized that when a State brings its judicial power to bear on an indigent defendant in a criminal proceeding, it must take steps to ensure that the defendant has a fair opportunity to present his defense."[62] This principle, grounded in the due process clause's guarantee of "fundamental fairness," derives from the belief "that justice cannot be equal when, simply as a result of his poverty, a defendant is denied the opportunity to participate meaningfully in a judicial proceeding in which his liberty is at stake."[63]

"Meaningful access to justice" is the theme of the relevant cases, the Court found,[64] noting that "mere access to the courthouse door does not by itself assure a proper functioning of the adversary process."[65] A criminal trial is "fundamentally unfair if the State proceeds against an indigent defendant without making certain that he has access to the raw materials integral to the building of an effective defense."[66]

In determining whether access to a psychiatrist is one of the "basic tools of an adequate defense,"[67] the Court set out three relevant factors:

> The first is the private interest that will be affected by the action of the State. The second is the governmental interest that will be affected if the safeguard is provided. The third is the probable value of the additional or substitute procedural safeguards that are sought, and the risk of an erroneous deprivation of the affected interest if those safeguards are not provided.[68]

The Court quickly disposed of the first prong, characterizing the private interest in accuracy of a criminal proceeding as "almost uniquely compelling."[69] In the same way, it summarily rejected the argument that a reversal would "result in a staggering burden to the state,"[70] noting that at least forty states and the federal government already made such services available.[71] The Court also found it "difficult to identify *any* interest of the state, other than in its economy, that weighs against recognition of this right."[72] Finally, it considered the "pivotal role" psychiatry has come to play in criminal proceedings,[73] reflecting the "reality that when the State has made the defendant's mental condition relevant to his criminal culpability and to the punishment he might suffer, the assistance of a psychiatrist may well be crucial to the defendant's ability to marshal his defense."[74]

The Court set out what it perceived as the role of the psychiatrist in such cases:

> [P]sychiatrists gather facts, both through professional examination, interviews, and elsewhere, that they will share with the judge or jury; they analyze the information gathered and from it draw plausible conclusions about the defendant's mental condition, and about the effects of any disorder on behavior at the time in question. They know the probative questions to ask of the opposing party's psychiatrists and how to interpret their answers. Unlike lay witnesses, who can merely describe symptoms they believe might be relevant to the defendant's mental state, psychiatrists can identify the "elusive and often deceptive" symptoms of insanity, Solesbee v. Balkcom, 399 U.S. 9, 12 (1950), and tell the jury why their observations are relevant. Further, where permitted by evidentiary rules, psychiatrists can translate a medical diagnosis into language that will assist the trier of the fact, and therefore offer evidence in a form that has meaning for the task at hand. Through this process of investigation, interpretation and testimony, psychiatrists ideally assist lay jurors, who generally have no training in psychiatric matters, to make a sensible and educated determination about the medical condition of the defendant at the time of the offense.[75]

Because psychiatry is not an exact science, however, and because of frequent psychiatric disagreement on the classification and diagnosis of mental illness and the likelihood of future dangerousness, it is often necessary for juries to resolve differences in opinion.[76] On such a determination, "the testimony of psychiatrists can be crucial and 'a virtual necessity if an insanity plea is to have any chance of success.'"[77] This finding led the Court "inexorably" to conclude:

> [W]ithout the assistance of a psychiatrist to conduct a professional examination on issues relevant to the defense, to help determine whether the insanity defense is viable, to present testimony, and to assist in preparing the cross-examination of a State's psychiatric witnesses, the risk of an inaccurate resolution of sanity issues is extremely high. With such assistance, the defendant is fairly able to present at least enough information to the jury, in a meaningful manner, as to permit it to make a sensible determination.[78]

As the risk of error from denial of such assistance is highest "when the defendant's mental condition is seriously in question,"[79] the defendant would thus qualify for such assistance when he is able to make an "*ex parte* threshold showing that his sanity is likely to be a significant factor in his defense."[80] The Court thus held that, when a defendant is able to demonstrate that his sanity was such a "significant factor," the state must "assure the defendant access to a competent psychiatrist who will conduct an appropriate examination and assist in evaluation, preparation and presentation of the defense."[81]

Finally, the Court held that a defendant was similarly entitled to psychiatric expert assistance to rebut the state's evidence of future dangerousness at the penalty phase of a death penalty trial.[82] Where the consequence of error is so great, the relevance so evident, and the burden to the state so slim, due process requires "access to a psychiatric examination" for assistance in the preparation of the sentencing phase.[83]

The courts have generally read *Ake* narrowly and have refused to require appointment of an expert unless it is "absolutely essential to the defense."[84] By way of examples, courts have split on whether there is a right to an expert *psychologist* to perform psychological testing under *Ake*,[85] and have also, without citing *Ake*, rejected an application for the right to the appointment of a social psychologist to aid in jury selection.[86] *Ake*, on the other hand, was relied on so as to require the appointment of a pathologist in a criminal case.[87] On the perhaps closer question of the requirement of the appointment of a DNA expert, after an intermediate appellate court in Virginia relied on *Ake* to require the appointment of such an expert, that decision was subsequently vacated, with no discussion of *Ake* in the subsequent opinion.[88]

In his exhaustive survey article about the implementation of *Ake*, Professor Paul Giannelli points out, in a slightly different context, that "in 1985, the *Ake* Court could not have anticipated how the advent of DNA evidence

would revolutionize forensic science."[89] Nor, of course, could it have anticipated the new significance of neuroimaging evidence. To this point in time,
however, lower courts have been generally reluctant to extend *Ake* to requests
for funding for neuroimaging tests.[90] In *Bates v. State*,[91] no *Ake* violation was
found where a defendant sought additional expert assistance in establishing
functional organic brain damage, and in *Smith v. Kearney*,[92] there was no *Ake*
error where the defendant sought funds for a PET scan.[93] Although the court
in *Walker v. Oklahoma*[94] found that it was an *Ake* error to fail to provide funds
for additional neurological testing "to flesh out the etiology [of the defendant's] mental illness,"[95] it deemed that error harmless.[96] On the other hand,
People v. Jones[97] did reverse a conviction because of the lower court's refusal
to fund brain scans.

The constitutional analysis here cannot be undertaken without serious
consideration of likely juror response to the glitter of neuroimaging evidence,
what Dean Mobbs has called the "Christmas tree phenomenon"[98] in writing
about the *seductiveness* of this evidence.[99] Certainly, this analysis argues persuasively for an expansive reading of *Ake* and its progeny.[100]

ON QUESTIONS OF COMPETENCY TO BE EXECUTED[101]

As discussed earlier in this book,[102] in *Panetti v. Quarterman*,[103] the Supreme
Court clarified and expanded upon its holding in *Ford v. Wainwright*,[104] finding that a person cannot be executed unless the prisoner possess a "rational
understanding"[105] of the reasons he is to be executed.[106]

Few of the post-*Panetti* cases have illuminated the underlying issues.
Few discussed neuropsychological testing at all, and none have examined the
questions I am raising here in the context of the *Panetti* holding.[107]

This all leads to an examination of the questions I raised earlier: How
will neuroimaging testimony be dealt with in post-*Panetti* cases? Again, to
the best of my knowledge, this issue has not yet been raised in any reported
case, but I believe that it is inevitable that the issue will be confronted by the
courts in the near future. I think these are some of the questions that will be
considered in the future:

1. Will defense counsel seek to introduce such testimony, and what,
exactly, can we expect such testimony will say?

My answer here is a qualified "maybe," dependent on multiple inter-
locked variables: Will courts be receptive to neuroimaging testimony that
seeks to answer the specific substantive question posed by *Panetti*: did the
defendant possess "a *rational understanding* of the State's reason for his execution"?[108] Such testimony has been introduced—with mixed results—in cases
where defendants have sought to assert their incompetency to stand trial or

their lack of responsibility for the underlying criminal offense.[109] The two most notorious cases in this cohort are the (non–death penalty) cases of Vincent "The Chin" Gigante and John Hinckley,[110] but such evidence has also been introduced in a range of less familiar cases dealing with such questions as potential reduction in degrees of homicide,[111] the capacity of a defendant to plead guilty,[112] and the penalty phase of a death penalty trial.[113] How will courts react when the question is whether the defendant is even eligible for the death penalty?

There are certainly cautions and concerns involving the use of this testimony, and I believe the admonitions by Professor John Blume and Emily Paavola are absolutely on point:

> Neuroimaging is *never* the first option in a capital case, and it should only be considered after (1) a comprehensive social history investigation has been conducted; (2) a comprehensive neuropsychological battery of tests has been administered to the client; and (3) the client has been evaluated by a neuropsychiatrist or neurologist who is familiar with neuropsychological testing and its social history and who is sensitive to the dangers of neuroimaging. In sum, neuroimaging is not an investigative tool; it is a confirmatory and explanatory tool (and even then, only in the right case).[114]

Will defense counsel even think about this question? This returns us to the question of the inevitability of a substandard quality of counsel often made available to defendants in death penalty cases.[115] All too often, such lawyers are, once again in Judge Bazelon's unforgettable phrase, "walking violations of the Sixth Amendment."[116] Is it too much to hope for to expect counsel to "get" the potential value of such testimony in *Panetti*-type cases?

Assuming counsel doesn't "get it," how will the courts construe the "pallid"[117] standard of *Strickland v. Washington*[118] in this context? Is it likely that counsel will be held ineffective for not seeking this sort of testing?[119] Or, if it is used, for not understanding its limitations?[120] An interesting parallel can be found in an investigation by Professor Deborah Denno of the use of behavioral genetics evidence in criminal cases.[121] Although Professor Denno discusses a handful of cases in which failure to consider such evidence resulted in *Strickland*-based remands, these cases, she concludes, are a "minority," and courts generally "place . . . less importance on [this] evidence."[122] I would expect courts assessing the issue I am discussing here to fall in line.

Assuming that counsel does get it, who pays? Neuroimaging testing is expensive, and it is more expensive in cases in which the examined defendant is incarcerated—as will inevitably be the case in a death penalty prosecution—when the test is performed.[123] The services of experts skilled to testify about this testing are also expensive. I will return to this question shortly, but I raise it here as well since I believe its resolution may also help to resolve this issue.

2. In cases involving indigent defendants, will *Ake v. Oklahoma*[124] be interpreted expansively or restrictively?[125] I addressed this issue in an earlier section of this chapter, but it is confounded by language in *Panetti* that appears to envision an expanded role for expert witnesses in this sort of inquiry, language finding that trial court's failure to allow the defendant to introduce evidence on this question was a failure of constitutional dimensions.[126] Will this aspect of *Panetti* be given life in subsequent decisions? In the subsequent non-death-penalty case of *Lewis v. Zon*,[127] *Panetti* was relied on to support the grant of a writ of habeas corpus, the court noting that "not allowing a defendant the opportunity to respond to evidence solicited by the state court to determine trial competency is inconsistent with a defendant's procedural due process right."[128] To what extent will other courts follow this language from *Lewis*? We simply do not know yet.[129]

In a related context, there has been sparse litigation on the application of *Ake* to the need for *neurological* evaluations. In denying such an application, a federal district court in Mississippi cursorily dismissed this request as "a fishing expedition in an attempt to show a mental disorder resulting from brain damage due to injuries suffered as a child."[130]

3. Will prosecutors seek to introduce such testimony to rebut defendant's *Panetti* applications?

In a law review article, I have considered the impact that antipsychotic medication might have on a defendant's neuroimaging results.[131] Even the boldest commercial technology (the so-called "No Lie MRI") warns of limitations on its valid use in the case of subjects who are "brain damaged."[132] Jane Moriarty underscores that such testimony is able to produce "false positives."[133] To what extent will prosecutors introducing such evidence "come clean" and share this information with jurors?

4. To what extent are judges more or less impervious to the "dazzle" or "Christmas tree effect" of such testimony than are jurors?

Steven Erickson writes about the "gloss of intrigue and seduction" inherent in neuroimaging testimony.[134] Others have noted that the visual "allure"[135] of such testimony can "dazzle" and "seduce" jurors[136] in ways that are "inappropriately persuasive."[137] Joelle Moreno says, flatly, "[B]rain research is *sexy*."[138] I have noted that the vividness of this testimony may have a distortive impact on jurors;[139] the open question is whether judges are less susceptible than jurors to the vividness heuristic in this setting?

Judges have the same predisposition to uncritically use the vividness heuristic in a variety of other legal settings, whether it be competency to stand trial, the applicability of the Americans with Disabilities Act to persons with mental disability, or dealing with lawyers with mental disability.[140] Should we have any confidence that they will be immune to its ravages here?[141]

5. How will such testimony be dealt with if there is a *Daubert* challenge?[142]

Scholars have expressed concern that many of the claims made in support of some uses of neuroscience testimony in courts are "wholly unsupportable."[143] Courts have been mixed in their assessment of neuroscience evidence under both *Frye* and *Daubert*. In at least three instances, *Frye* jurisdictions have rejected PET scan and SPECT scan evidence, in all cases finding that the evidence in question was not "generally accepted,"[144] whereas in two cases—both personal injury–based—PET and SPECT scans were admissible under the *Frye* rule.[145] In other *Daubert* cases, though, such evidence has been accepted, albeit in matters involving civil causes of actions.[146] For the purposes of this chapter, one of the most intriguing (albeit cryptic) cases is that of *Hoskins v. State*.[147] There, in a death penalty case, the state Supreme Court vacated the sentence, noting, "Following the PET-scan and the evidentiary hearing, the trial judge concluded that the PET-scan did show an abnormality and that, as conceded by the State, Dr. Krop's testimony changed as a result of the PET-scan. Because the trial judge has found in the affirmative, we vacate the sentence of death imposed on Hoskins and remand this cause for a new penalty phase proceeding."[148]

In a footnote, the court noted that no *Frye* hearing was held, but that "[t]he fact that the trial judge did not consider these issues at the evidentiary hearing does not affect our decision to remand this case."[149]

What is most critical here is the fundamental unfairness of the *Daubert* process:

> It is obligatory to note the disparity in decisionmaking; that is, that, in *Daubert* cases, the prosecutor's position is sustained (either in support of questioned expertise or in opposition to it) vastly more often than is that of defense counsel's.[150] The implications of these findings must be considered as well.[151]

By way of comparison, in a critique of how courts treat bite-mark testimony (offered "dressed in the illusion of science"),[152] Professor Erica Beecher-Monas notes that judges in criminal cases "overwhelmingly circumvent their [*Daubert*-mandated] gatekeeping responsibilities."[153] Writing about the use of *Daubert* in vaccine court cases, Professor Joelle Moreno has perceptively noted,

> Law does not happen in a vacuum. The idea that gatekeeping judges reflect on only the case-specific in-court impact of proffered scientific claims and theories ignores the real world outside the courthouse, the fact that information about science-based legal issues also travels from the bottom-up, and the genuine interdependence of law, science, and society. It is inarguable that judges must focus on the specific facts and issues in each case and the application of proffered scientific evidence to these facts.

But, as Justice Breyer observed, this type of perpetual *Daubertista* focus is an incomplete description of the judicial task because "[t]he importance of scientific accuracy in the decision of such [science-based] cases reaches well beyond the case itself."[154]

Consider also the dangers of teleology in the context of mental disability law jurisprudence: how judges "teleologically . . . privilege [certain evidence] (where that privileging serves what they perceive as a socially-beneficial value) and subordinate [such evidence] (where that subordination serves what they perceive as a similar value)."[155] The post-*Daubert* case law is a textbook example of teleology. I raise this issue here as a red flag to those who are concerned about the ways that judges "teleologically 'cherry pick . . .' social science evidence so as to justify [their] decisions"[156] in this area of the law.

6. How will fact finders deal with such testimony in cases where the evidence revealed by neuroimaging testimony does not comport with their (false) "ordinary common sense" (OCS) view of "crazy" criminal defendants?[157]

I have identified—as one of the prime "sanist myths"[158]—the use by jurors of "a fixed vision of popular, concrete, visual images of craziness" in their decision making in cases involving mentally disabled criminal defendants.[159] Michael Pardo thus states flatly that neuroimaging evidence is significant in part because it "provides jurors with information . . . beyond their common-sense background understanding."[160] Joshua Greene and Jonathan Cohen predict that neuroscience evidence will "undermine people's common sense," referring specifically to the public's "libertarian conception of free will and the retributivist thinking that depends on it."[161]

Just as false OCS "contaminate[s]" insanity defense practice,[162] we need to consider how fact finders may respond to contrary-to-OCS evidence in *Panetti* cases. Confounding this issue is the research cited by Professor Daniel Martell showing that jurors are more likely to be convinced by "'bad,' logically irrelevant explanations" for behavior if such explanations are couched in terms of neuroscience."[163]

In writing about neuroimaging evidence and the insanity defense, I recently had this to say:

> Neuroimaging is (or isn't) hard science. It is (or isn't) relatively easy for jurors to interpret. It is (or isn't) immune to falsification efforts. It is (or isn't) objective. It will (or won't) lead jurors to "better" verdicts in insanity cases. It will (or won't) be used disproportionately in news-friendly cases. It will (or won't) "trump" jurors' inherent suspicion of the insanity defense. It does (and here there is no contradictory or antipodal position) raise a variety of important and provocative legal, behavioral, and social issues, none of which has received nearly enough attention by the courts or by commentators.

So what are we to make of this? I believe that the key to an answer here is a consideration of sanism: to what extent will our prejudices, our stereotypes, our slotting, and our typification overwhelm all other evidence and all other issues in this conversation? In every aspect of mental disability law that I have ever studied, the answer has been, "To a great extent." Is there any reason to think it will be less so here? Perhaps the seductive dazzle of colorful pictures will trump millennia of fear and superstition. But, as of today, I wouldn't bet on it (and this analysis again completely and consciously sidesteps the question of whether this evidence is as valuable in litigation as its proponents argue).[164]

Is it likely that similar attitudes will be affected by conflicting or contradictory evidence in *Panetti* cases? I am certainly not confident that the answer is a resounding yes.

7. How will the less well-known aspect of *Panetti* (that which deals with the need for additional expert testimony)[165] be treated in such cases?

As I have already discussed, there appears likely to be a significant law-practice conflict between the expansive language in *Panetti* (seeing a broader role for experts) and the reality as to how *Ake* has been construed in the quarter century since that case was decided. The issue is especially pressing here, given the potential miscomprehension of neuroimaging evidence by both judges and jurors, the distortions inherent in the evidence's "Christmas tree effect," and the "stacked deck" *Daubert* issue. If this aspect of *Panetti* is ignored, then it appears that the problems to which I allude throughout this chapter will only be exacerbated.

8. What, actually, will neuroimagers *do* in such cases?

The technology in question seeks to identify brain abnormalities in individuals with serious mental disabilities.[166] The examining neuropsychologist or neuropsychiatrist must review available historical information from the defendant's life history that might potentially point to possible brain impairment (e.g., documented head injuries or other neurological disease processes), or psychiatric disorders that indicate potential chemical and neurotransmitter abnormalities.[167] Best practices dictate that neuropsychological testing should be employed to further clarify any neurobehavioral deficits and to pinpoint functional deficits that correlate with behavioral issues related to both the crime and the proposed neuroimaging study.[168]

Whether structural (CT, MRI) or functional (PET, SPECT) approaches are employed will depend on the defendant's mental and neurological history.[169] Standard protocols typically used would include ensuring an awareness and appreciation of the procedure, as well as of the potential risks and benefits from the procedure, and the ability to make a decision regarding these issues.

In the case of a defendant alleging incompetency to be executed, this will all be far more challenging. To the best of my knowledge, it is an issue that has not been addressed either in the case law or in the academic literature.[170] But it is an issue that inevitably will need to be resolved in the aftermath of *Panetti*.

9. Will prosecutors seek to use neuroimaging evidence to support findings of future dangerousness in such cases?

In a recent article, a sitting Arkansas state judge raised his concerns about this possibility. Judge J. W. Looney warned that, while "it does not seem out of the ordinary to use such technology to evaluate brain structure and, to some degree, brain function, it is less likely that such technology will be used in the immediate future to explain behavior or to predict future behavior." "Nevertheless," he added, "such technology could be used in the types of proceedings outlined above—to predict future dangerousness."[171] Such use, he direly concluded, would "vindicate the nineteenth century Italian criminologist, Lombroso."[172]

CONCLUSION

There has been an explosion of commentary and academic literature in recent years about the impact of neuroimaging testimony on the criminal trial process, but, to the best of my knowledge, no one has yet considered the relationship between that issue and the standards for determining competency to be executed as set out in the *Panetti* case. The issues that I have raised in this section of this chapter cover a fairly wide range of questions—questions of counsel behavior, juror attitudes, and evidentiary considerations—that, when looked at together, reflect so many of the tensions and ambivalences that are inherent in criminal trials, especially those of death-eligible defendants.[173]

Panetti builds on, clarifies, and expands the *Ford* standard by adding the requirement that the defendant possess a "rational understanding" of the purposes of the forthcoming execution.[174] But it also enhances the role of expert witnesses at competency-to-be-executed hearings.[175] As more attention is paid to the role of neuroimaging in the courts, it is inevitable that the use of this testimony will be used (or at least sought to be used) at such hearings, both by defendants and by prosecutors. We are still faced with unanswered questions as to how judges and jurors will assess such testimony.

The *Ford* test has all too often been no test at all.[176] Professor Richard Bonnie refers to the "appalling failures" of the criminal justice system that are "amply documented" by *Panetti*.[177] In its *Panetti* decision, the Court stressed that, in a case in which a prisoner's mental state "is so distorted by a mental illness" that he does not share with "the community as a whole" an understanding of the concepts of crime and punishment, the objective "of community vindication [is] called in question."[178] Scholars have made tentative explorations concerning the implications of therapeutic jurisprudence[179] for the execution of persons with severe mental disabilities.[180] Here, the Court frontally considers the implications of this dilemma. But it does not consider how neuroscience evidence—as this was not before the Court in the *Panetti* case—might be used (or misused) in seeking to resolve these difficult questions.

We are just scratching the surface of the world of neuroscience. I conclude by repeating my conclusions from an article that I published about this topic several years ago, simply because I think these words are the best I can do:

> I sense the power of the evidence in question, and because of my fears that its seductive dazzle may hold jurors in thrall, leading to outcomes that are both factually and legally inaccurate and constitutionally flawed. My hope is that a consideration of the issues that I am raising here will lead all of us to think a little harder about the road ahead.[181]

· 9 ·

The Role of Jurors, Prosecutors, and Judges[1]

INTRODUCTION

$\mathcal{T}$he Supreme Court's death penalty jurisprudence is based in large part on the assumption that jurors can be counted on to apply the law in this area conscientiously and fairly. And all our criminal procedure jurisprudence is based in large part on the assumption that prosecutors and judges will act fairly. I believe that these assumptions are based on nothing more than wishful thinking,[2] and that the record of death penalty litigation in the thirty-five years since the "modern" penalty was approved in *Gregg v. Georgia*[3] gives the lie to them.

First, as to jurors: A review of case law, controlled behavioral research, and "real-life" research not only casts grave doubt on its validity but tends to reveal the opposite: that jurors generally distrust mental disability evidence; that they see it as a mitigating factor only in a handful of circumscribed situations (most of which are far removed from the typical scenario in a death penalty case); that lawyers representing capital defendants are intensely skeptical of jurors' ability to correctly construe such evidence; that jurors actually impose certain preconceived schemas in such cases that, paradoxically, result in outcomes where the most mentally disabled persons (those regularly receiving doses of powerful antipsychotic medications) are treated the most harshly; and that jurors tend to *over*impose the death penalty on defendants with severe mental disabilities. I draw these conclusions on a backdrop that has never been seriously challenged: that jurors, in *all* criminal cases, fail to adequately comprehend judicial instructions,[4] a failure that has inevitably important (often fatal) consequences in death penalty cases,[5] especially when the instructions make reference to mental disability concepts.[6]

Why is this? I believe it results from a combination of important factors: jurors' use of cognitive simplifying devices (heuristics)—in which vivid, negative experiences overwhelm rational data (and a death penalty case is a fertile environment for such cognitive distortions)—that reify their sanist attitudes, courts' pretextuality in deciding cases involving mentally disabled criminal defendants, and courts' teleological decision making in reviewing such cases.

In earlier chapters, I discussed how jurors respond to mitigation testimony[7] and how they construe future dangerousness in the penalty phase of death penalty cases.[8] In each instance, I linked my findings to what we know about the pernicious impact of sanism and pretextuality on the questions at hand. In the first section of this chapter, I will first consider juror attitudes, seeking to explain how and why jurors act as they do. I will then discuss the significance of the use of heuristic devices in these actions and the power of teleological thinking in this context. Finally, in my conclusion, I will attempt to demonstrate the depths of the problem under consideration and will focus on the actual animators on juror and judicial behavior in these cases.

In the subsequent sections, I move on to the roles of prosecutors and judges. I will discuss how, in some jurisdictions, the political incentives to seek and enforce more death sentences lead to prosecutorial misconduct and judicial irresponsibility, and how this disproportionately affects persons with mental disabilities.

JUROR ATTITUDES

As I have discussed earlier,[9] scholars have expressed their skepticism about the use of a mental illness defense in a capital punishment penalty phase, suggesting that such testimony raises issues of unpredictability and dangerousness to potentially suggest to the jury that the defendant "poses a continuing risk to society."[10] While expert witnesses have predicted (with near unanimity) that such a defense would be successful,[11] research with mock jurors (and archival research in cases involving actual jurors) has revealed that (1) a defendant's unsuccessful attempt to raise an insanity defense positively correlates with a death penalty verdict,[12] (2) a mental illness defense is rated as a less effective strategy than other alternatives at the penalty phase (even including the alternative of raising no defense at all),[13] and (3) jurors who are "death qualified"[14] are more likely to convict capital defendants who suffer from nonorganic mental disorders.[15] And this analysis needs to be considered in the context of the reality that voir dire in most capital cases is "woefully inadequate at the most elementary task—weeding out unqualified jurors."[16]

Fact finders demand that defendants conform to popular, commonsensical visual images of "looking crazy."[17] This is accentuated in the case of death-qualified jurors who "have a tendency to believe that, if you cannot see something, it does not exist."[18] This further "ups the ante" for defendants raising such a defense. On the other hand, some empirical evidence suggests that a mental illness defense may be successful where the defendant presents expert testimony, where he has a history of psychiatric impairment (especially where he has sought treatment), and where he is able to present "objective" evidence of psychopathology,[19] perhaps through evidence of organic brain damage.[20] Also, empirical evidence reveals that fact finders will be more receptive to a mental status defense that does not involve "planful" behavior,[21] and that, in coming to their conclusions, jurors are likely to rely upon "implicit theories about the causes of violence,"[22] an especially odious state of affairs given the reality that as much as 75 percent of the public view people with mental illness as "violent."[23]

Reconciliation of jurors' attitudes with court doctrine is made even more difficult by juror confusion over the proper role of mitigating evidence, their lack of recognition of mitigating evidence when presented with it, and their misunderstanding of its expected impact on their death penalty deliberations.[24] The dilemma here is compounded further by the fact that many mental disorders of death row inmates are never identified.

> Either no one looks for them, or the defendants do not consider themselves impaired, so they never request specialized evaluations. Even when defendants are examined, they often are unaware of what symptoms might mitigate their sentences. Their inadequacies may make them less capable than other defendants of obtaining competent representation or assisting their attorneys in documenting types of neurological impairments that might be important for purpose of mitigation.[25]

The riskiness of a mental illness defense must be considered in the context of yet other evidence that a significant percentage of actual jurors saw certain aspects of a defendant's demeanor—whether he looked passive, unremorseful, or emotionless—as a critical operative factor in determining whether or not to return a death sentence.[26] Other studies reveal that a defendant's *attractiveness* is a significant trial variable (with jurors treating attractive defendants more leniently than unattractive defendants)[27] and that a defendant's "emotionless appearance" will have negative trial consequences.[28]

These findings are particularly problematic in light of the fact that a significant percentage of mentally disabled criminal defendants receive powerful psychotropic medication while awaiting trial.[29] Among the side effects of such medications are akinesia and akathesia, conditions that may mislead jurors by making the defendant appear either apathetic and unemotional or agitated and restless.[30] Another important side effect, tardive dyskinesia—marked by "tic-like movements of the lips," "worm-like contractions of the tongue," "pouting, sucking, smacking and puckering lip movements," and "expiratory grunts and noises,"[31]—will inevitably make a defendant appear less "attractive" to jurors. It is precisely behaviors of this sort that "fit" into jurors' preexisting "schemas"[32] about defendants with mental disabilities who face the death penalty. What is worse, the more complex the subject, the more juror performance is reduced,[33] and the more likely it is that jurors will rely on "load-reducing information 'structures,'"[34] the sorts of heuristics that contaminate all fact finding in these sorts of cases.[35]

We know that death-qualified jurors are disproportionately hostile to mental health testimony, defenses, and mitigation[36] and are more likely to assume that the defendant is guilty before hearing any evidence presented.[37] Further, death-qualified jurors more willingly accept aggravating circumstances than mitigating factors—many of which involve mental health issues.[38] They may be left more susceptible to what Professor Craig Haney has termed the "media model" of willfully violent criminality.[39] Juries also may misunderstand clinical evidence concerning the offender's mental illness and its impact on his functioning at the time of the offense, may incorrectly equate mental illness with dangerousness, and may incorrectly think that the death penalty is the only way to protect the community from the defendant's future violence.[40] Death-qualified jurors are also much less likely to accept the insanity defense,[41] believing it to be a "loophole allowing too many guilty people to go free."[42] The Capital Jury Project's study revealed, on this point, that "future dangerousness[43] is on the minds of most capital jurors . . . , *even if the prosecution says nothing about it.*"[44]

Professor Brooke Butler summarizes the prevailing valid and reliable research:

> Previous research has demonstrated that death-qualified jurors tend to be demographically, attitudinally, dispositionally, and behaviorally distinguishable from their excludable counterparts. For example, they are more likely to be male, Caucasian, financially secure, politically conservative, and Christian. . . . Death-qualified jurors are more likely to trust prosecutors; view prosecution witnesses as more believable, credible, and helpful; consider inadmissible evidence even if a judge has instructed them to ignore it; and infer guilt from a defendant's failure to take the witness stand. . . . Death-qualified jurors tend to be hostile to psychological defenses . . . , more likely to believe in the infallibility of the criminal justice process, and less likely to agree that even the worst criminals should be considered for mercy. . . . Death-qualified jurors, when compared to excludables, are also more likely to have a high belief in a just world, an internal locus of control, and espouse legal authoritarian (i.e., pro-government) beliefs. . . . Perhaps more importantly, the aforementioned factors translate into behavior: Death-qualified jurors are significantly more likely than excludables to both find capital defendants guilty and sentence them to death.[45]

We also know that the presumption that jurors are capable of distinguishing true from false confessions[46] is flawed.[47] As Saul Kassin and his colleagues tell us,

> Research on the impact of confessions throughout the criminal justice system is unequivocal. Mock jury studies have shown that confessions have more impact than other potent forms of evidence . . . and that people do not fully discount confessions—even when they are judged to be coerced . . . and even when the confessions are presented secondhand by an informant who is motivated to lie.[48]

There are multiple reasons for this: (1) generalized common sense[49] leads people to trust confessions the way they trust other behaviors that counter self-interest, (2) jurors are typically not adept at detecting deception, and (3) police-induced false confessions often contain *content* cues presumed to be associated with truthfulness.[50] Until we acknowledge the reality of these factors, we will continue to willfully blind[51] ourselves to the possibility (in some cases, probability) of serious error in this cohort of cases.

WHY JURORS DO WHAT THEY DO

Introduction

I believe that it is impossible to understand the underlying dilemmas here without considering a bundle of motivating factors that affect the behaviors of jurors and judges. Specifically, it is necessary to "unpack" juror "schemas" in an effort to determine *why* jurors so frequently misuse rational data in decision making, especially in cases involving mentally disabled criminal defendants. I contend that the schemas that jurors employ are driven by the use of heuristics. These heuristic devices reflect jurors' sanist attitudes. These attitudes are shared by judges who decide cases pretextually and justify those decisions teleologically. In this part, I will first explore the meaning of each of these concepts and will then consider how they "play out" in this context in two different dimensions: in the ways that lay persons rely inordinately on visual imagery as the most persuasive evidence of mental illness, and in the ways that the question of mental disability as a mitigating factor in death penalty cases is a Rorschach test for these attitudes.

Heuristics[52]

Heuristics are cognitive psychology constructs that involve the implicit thinking devices that individuals use to simplify complex information-processing tasks.[53] The use of heuristics causes decision makers to "ignore or misuse items of rationally useful information"[54] and frequently leads to distorted and systematically erroneous decisions. One single, vivid, memorable case overwhelms mountains of abstract, colorless data upon which rational choices should be made.[55] Empirical studies reveal jurors' susceptibility to the use of these devices.[56]

Thus, through the "availability heuristic," we judge the probability or frequency of an event based upon the ease with which we recall it. Through the "typification heuristic," we characterize a current experience via reference to past stereotypic behavior, and through the "attribution heuristic," we interpret a wide variety of additional information to reinforce preexisting stereotypes. Through the "hindsight bias," we exaggerate how easily we could have predicted an event beforehand. Through the "outcome bias," we base our evaluation of a decision on our evaluation of an outcome.[57] In short, heuristic thinking dominates all aspects of mental disability law processes, both civil and criminal.[58]

Teleology[59]

The legal system selectively—teleologically—either accepts or rejects social science evidence depending on whether or not the use of that data meets the a priori needs of the legal system.[60] In cases where fact finders are hostile to social science teachings, such data thus often meets with tremendous judicial resistance, and courts express their skepticism about, suspicions of, and hostilities toward such evidence.[61] Specifically, the skepticism toward statistical data and evidence about the behavioral sciences appears to stem directly from the belief that such data are not "empirical" in the same way that "true" sciences are and therefore are not trustworthy.[62] Social science data is seen as overly subjective, falsifiable, and subject to researcher bias.[63]

Courts are often threatened by the use of such data. Social science's "complexities [may] shake the judge's confidence in imposed solutions."[64] Additionally, judges may be especially threatened by social science when it is presented to a jury, as such presentation may appear to undermine "judicial control" of trial proceedings.[65]

Courts' general dislike of social science is reflected in the self-articulated claim that judges are unable to understand the data and are thus unable to apply it properly to a particular case.[66] Courts tend to be shamefully poor in the application of such data;[67] their track record has been "dreadful."[68] It is not at all clear, though, why courts should have such difficulty here when judges regularly decide complex cases in a wide array of social and scientific contexts.[69]

This dislike and distrust of social science data has led courts to be teleological in their use of this evidence. Social science literature and studies that enable courts to meet predetermined sanist ends are often privileged while data that would require judges to question such ends is frequently rejected.[70] Judges often select certain proferred data that adheres to their preexisting social and political attitudes, and use heuristic reasoning in rationalizing such decisions.[71] Social science data is used pretextually in such cases and is ignored in other cases (especially death penalty cases)[72] to rationalize otherwise baseless judicial decisions.[73]

Courts thus will take the literature out of context,[74] misconstrue the data or evidence being offered,[75] and read such data selectively[76] and/or inconsistently.[77] Other times, courts choose to flatly reject this data or ignore its existence.[78] In other circumstances, courts simply "rewrite" factual records so as to avoid having to deal with social science data that is cognitively dissonant with their view of how the world "ought to be."[79] Even when courts do acknowledge the existence and possible validity of studies that take a contrary position from their decisions, this acknowledgment is frequently little more than mere lip service.

Applying These Principles

Introduction Reliance on heuristics, sanist attitudes, and pretextual and teleological decision making all combines to distort the entire trial and conviction process in death penalty cases involving mentally disabled criminal defendants. In an attempt to make sense of the underlying problems, I will first look at some parallel findings that come from the behavioral and legal insanity defense literature, especially as they assess a defendant's visual appearance. Then I will read the available relevant data on jury behavior and adequacy of counsel in similar factual contexts in an effort to better understand the true dimensions of this issue.

Visual Imagery[80] Although the question under consideration here has not been widely studied,[81] there is an impressive database looking at juror behavior in insanity defense cases that is certainly relevant here. First and foremost, the public has always demanded that mentally ill defendants comport with its popular, concrete, *visual* images of "craziness."[82] Yet the lay public *cannot*, by using its intuitive "common sense," effectively determine who is or is not criminally responsible by whether or not the individual "looks crazy."[83]

In the process of looking for visual cues and clues in determining whether a defendant should be sentenced to death, jurors make their determinations based on their own flawed, prereflective "ordinary common sense"[84] as to whether a defendant looks sufficiently "remorseful."[85] This behavior was noted accurately by Justice Kennedy in his concurrence in *Riggins v. Nevada*,[86] relying on research by William Geimer and Jonathan Amsterdam demonstrating that an assessment of the defendant's level of remorse may be the most determinative factor in the decision as to who will live and who will die.[87]

Thus, cases hinge on witnesses' failure to describe defendants as "raving maniacs," on lay testimony that "there was nothing unusual about defendant's appearance" in the days before the murder, or on police testimony that the same defendant "was neatly dressed and . . . seemed aware and mentally alert,"[88] or on jail or sheriff personnel's testimony that the defendant exhibited no "unusual" behavior.[89] Revealingly, in describing the procedures that must be followed in pretrial psychiatric evaluations, a New York trial court judge set up this juxtaposition:

> If the physician examines the defendant within hours or days of the event, he or she may observe that the defendant was disoriented and agitated or, at the other extreme, composed or feigning symptoms.[90]

Jury studies have shown "pervasive judicial hostility" toward the insanity defense where it was not founded on "flagrant psychotic symptomatology."[91] To the lay person (the juror *or* the judge), the temporarily delirious patient "leaping over chairs and taking the broom-stick to hallucinatory monsters" still *looks* more genuinely psychotic than "a deeply disordered but calm and brittle schizophrenic."[92] In a decision that I can only characterize as bizarre, the New Mexico Supreme Court affirmed a conviction rejecting an insanity defense despite a postverdict statement by a juror that "he could see the devil" in the defendant. Continued the juror:

> I saw in her right away. I saw in her witchcraft. I saw in her rebellion. I saw in her murder. . . . I saw in her all these things because I am a spirited man.[93]

Judges reflect the same vision. Thus, in a "textbook classic" case,[94] a Tennessee intermediate appellate court affirmed a conviction where a jury rejected a defendant's insanity defense in light of *police* testimony that, upon apprehension, the defendant "was sitting with his head down and looked okay," despite the presentation of "overwhelming, even staggering evidence" of an overtly psychotic, paranoid schizophrenic, actively hallucinating defendant.[95] Similarly, the Indiana Supreme Court affirmed a conviction in another rejected-insanity-defense case where the victim's girlfriend testified that, while the defendant was first acting "nervous" with a "'weird' facial expression," she subsequently found his speech and actions "calmer" and testified he did not act "crazy."[96]

Society is also confident that it is *accurate* in its assessment of serious mental illness.[97] This failure to acknowledge "shades of gray" reinforces more subtly our fixed image of "crazy behavior," especially in assessments of criminal responsibility.[98] Beyond this, jurors overascribe validity to clinical opinion expert testimony and tend to trivialize the more accurate actuarial expert testimony.[99] To some extent, this reflects our well-documented tendency to ignore, subordinate, or trivialize behavioral research where such research would be "cognitively dissonant with our intuitive—albeit empirically flawed—views, whereas we, contrarily, give such evidence too *much* weight when it reinforces our previously internalized positions."[100] As John LaFond and Mary Durham have pointed out, in the contexts of civil commitment and the insanity defense, "Neoconservative insanity defense and civil commitment reforms value psychiatric expertise when it contributes to the social control function of law and disparage it when it does not."[101]

Jurors also conflate race and danger in this context, and jurors' racial sentiments are likely to confound the capital sentencing decision.[102] As the Supreme Court noted in *Turner v. Murray*,[103]

> Because of the range of discretion entrusted to a jury in a capital sentencing hearing, there is a unique opportunity for racial prejudice to operate but remain undetected. . . . [A] juror who believes that blacks are violence prone or morally inferior might well be influenced by that belief in deciding whether petitioner's crime involved [such] aggravating factors. . . . Such a juror might also be less favorably inclined toward [a] petitioner's evidence of mental disturbance as a mitigating circumstance. More subtle, less consciously held racial attitudes could also influence a juror's decision. . . . Fear of blacks, which could easily be stirred up by the violent facts of petitioner's crime, might incline a juror to favor the death penalty.[104]

And jurors make their minds up in death penalty cases before they hear all the evidence, in fact before the penalty phase is even reached. A study by the Capital Jury Project, by way of example, found that 50 percent of the jurors interviewed indicated that they had settled in their own mind on the appropriate penalty *prior to the sentencing phase of the trial*.[105] Juror attitudes are also internally inconsistent. Professor Lawrence White has found, by way of example, that mental illness defenses are also ineffective due to juror feelings that (1) mental illness is no excuse,[106] (2) the defendant is faking,[107] and (3) the defendant should have gotten help for his problems.[108] Obviously, if a defendant *is* "faking," the notion of getting help makes utterly no sense at all.[109]

Finally, jurors' use of the "hindsight bias"[110] has been demonstrated to have a confounding effect in death penalty cases. Professor Theodore Eisenberg and his colleagues are clear: in such cases, "the risk of hindsight bias is real."[111] Professors David Wexler and Robert Schopp have written about this bias from a therapeutic jurisprudence perspective in the context of medical malpractice litigation (suggesting bifurcated trials),[112] but there is nothing in the literature about the TJ implications of this bias in death penalty cases. If, though, we have clear evidence that jurors make their minds up in death penalty cases before they hear all the evidence,[113] it should be self-evident that the presence of this hindsight bias leads to decidedly anti-therapeutic results in these cases. If, perhaps, during the voir dire process, this phenomenon was made known to jurors, it might have a stabilizing effect on their deliberation processes in ways that are consistent with TJ values.

Jurors—and judges—come to decisions irrationally in death penalty cases involving persons with mental disabilities. Jurors do this because of their reliance on cognitive simplifying devices, and judges reify these heuristically driven decisions via the use of teleology. As a result, distorted versions of what a "mentally disabled defendant *really* looks like" contaminate decision making and lead to wrong verdicts. The assumption that jurors decide this cohort of cases fairly remains, in the end, baseless.

PROSECUTORIAL MISCONDUCT

Introduction

There is great political incentive for prosecutors to seek the death penalty and for trial judges to impose it. Professor James Liebman makes this crystal clear:

> In all capital-sentencing jurisdictions, but particularly in ones where the political rewards of capital punishment are high and direct (for example, where elections for district attorney and trial judge are frequent and partisan and where voters favor the death penalty) and in ones that believe themselves to be under siege from violent crime, such offenses create incentives to move swiftly and surely from arrest to conviction to capital verdict.[114]

In a footnote, he quotes a newspaper article by Tina Rosenberg about Philadelphia district attorney Lynne Abraham's self-confessedly "passionate" commitment to capital punishment, notwithstanding her doubts whether it deters crime, and her use of it more often per homicide than any other prosecutor in the nation, which follows from her conclusion that it gives citizens "the feeling of control demanded by a city in decay," especially in light of her observation that "[w]e feel our lives are not in our own hands. . . . This is Bosnia").[115] Elsewhere, Liebman underscores how "police, prosecutors, judges, and juries operate with strong incentives to generate as many death sentences as they can—reaping robust psychic, political, and professional rewards—while displacing the costs of their many consequent mistakes onto capital prisoners, post-trial review courts, victims, and the public."[116] Professor J. Amy Dillard is clear: "Prosecutors abuse their discretion when they choose to seek death in order to seat a death-disposed jury."[117]

There is no question that there is always "acute (and ever intensifying) political pressure" on prosecutors "to seek the death penalty."[118] And there is no reason whatsoever to think that this pressure is somehow diminished in the case of a defendant with mental illness, precisely the sort of defendant that most engages a community's fears.[119] And of course, because prosecutors "reap political benefits from being tough on crime but do not typically have to pay for expensive appeals, they have an incentive to seek the death penalty in marginal cases that may be hard to defend on appeal."[120]

In three states (Florida, Alabama, and Delaware), judges have the ability to overturn jury sentences in death penalty cases. According to a report done by the Equal Justice Institute, in Florida (a state where judges are elected), there has not been a single judicial override of a jury-imposed death penalty in twelve years; in Alabama (another judicial election state), 92 percent of judicial overrides are to impose death sentences in cases in which jurors recommended life imprisonment; in Delaware (where judges are appointed), no judge has ever imposed a death sentence via judicial override.[121] Importantly, judges override juries to impose the death penalty more often in a judicial election year.[122]

Both of these phenomena potentially have an especially fatal impact in cases involving defendants with serious mental disabilities.

Outcomes of Misconduct

Reginald Brooks was sentenced to death for the murder of his three sons.[123] Some eighteen years after having been found guilty, a trial judge found he was competent to be executed,[124] noting, however, that the defendant suffered from paranoid schizophrenia and presented with "persecutory delusions that he has been framed for a crime that occurred while he was leaving town."[125] During the litigation process, Brooks' appellate counsel obtained documents, apparently from the trial prosecutor's file, pointing to evidence that in the period leading up to the killings, Reginald Brooks had displayed bizarre, aberrant, and paranoid behavior indicative of deteriorating mental health. Reginald Brooks' trial lawyer has said that none of the documents were disclosed to the defense and that this "secretion of the witness statements totally prevented me from properly and competently representing Mr. Brooks."[126] Brooks was executed on November 15, 2011.[127]

In a study of the thirteen executions that have taken place in California since the death penalty was reinstated in that state in 1977, prosecutorial misconduct was raised as a significant issue in seven of the cases—over half.[128] This cohort of cases includes at least one case in which the prosecutor lied—there is no other word for it—to the jury about the consequences if a "not guilty by reason of insanity" verdict were to be entered,[129] lies that were deemed by the California Supreme Court to be "harmless error."[130]

Professor Angela Davis concludes that "prosecutorial misconduct is widespread and unchecked."[131] Prosecutorial misconduct is the basis for over a fifth of all death penalty reversals.[132] Scholars and critics often describe the "pervasive unfairness" in the modern implementation of the death penalty as including "prosecutorial misconduct . . . [and] the injustice of subjecting . . . persons with serious mental disorders to capital punishment."[133] Capital appeals often include both issues.[134] But what has mostly escaped attention is the way that prosecutorial misconduct festers in the trial of cases involving this cohort of defendants. Professor Alafair Burke and others have raised the question of whether many cases of prosecutorial misconduct may be more attributable to cognitive bias than intentional malfeasance,[135] but, in this context, that attribution, while intellectually interesting, in no way minimizes the harm done by some prosecutors.

The typical approach by courts reviewing claims of prosecutorial misconduct is to determine (1) whether the conduct, objectively considered, violated an established rule of trial practice, and if it did, (2) whether that violation prejudiced the jury's ability to decide the case on the evidence. Under this objective standard, the courts do not consider a prosecutor's intent to violate a trial rule. Thus, if a guilty verdict that is significantly influenced, for example, by a prosecutor's asking prejudicial questions, offering inadmissible evidence, or making improper remarks to a jury is to be reversed, it will be reversed regardless of whether the prosecutor intended to strike a foul blow.[136] To what extent does this happen in the death penalty cases I discuss here?

This leads to a second inquiry: To what extent are prosecutors to blame for the state of affairs discussed in this book?[137] I believe that several global charges can be leveled against members of the prosecutoriate with regard to the specific issue of the misuse and/or exploitation of evidence of mental disability in death penalty cases:

1. Some prosecutors consciously misuse mental disability evidence to play on the fears of, to scare, and to exploit the ignorance of jurors

   Stephen Bright has noted, in the death penalty context, how "most prosecutors and other public officials exploit the victims of crime and the death penalty for political gain by stirring up and pandering to fears of crime."[138] A report by Amnesty International focuses on the questions under consideration in this book by concluding that "US prosecutors can exploit public ignorance or fear regarding mental illness by arguing that the 'flat' or 'unremorseful' demeanor of mentally ill defendants should be considered further grounds for imposing death sentences."[139]

   Earlier in this book, I quoted Jamie Fellner's discussion of prosecutorial conduct in the trials of defendants with mental retardation, noting her criticism of the ways that prosecutors frequently "vigorously challenge the existence of mental retardation, minimize its significance, and suggest that although a capital defendant may 'technically' be considered retarded, he nonetheless has 'street smarts'—and hence should receive the highest penalty."[140] And Professor Evan Mandery has pointed out how prosecutors have systematically opposed legislation that would exclude persons with serious mental illness from being eligible for the death penalty.[141]

2. Some prosecutors consciously seek out expert witnesses who will testify—with total certainty—to a defendant's alleged future dangerousness, knowing that such testimony is baseless.

Previously, I discussed at length the worthless and baseless testimony of Dr. James Grigson on questions of future dangerousness, and how that testimony led inexorably to the inappropriate executions of defendants with mental disabilities.[142] Dr. Grigson was decertified by the American Psychiatric Association and the Texas Society of Psychiatric Physicians in 1995,[143] but he continued to testify in death penalty proceedings for years after that.[144] A simple Westlaw search reveals thirty-three such cases.[145] To the best of my knowledge, there have been no sanctions brought against any of the prosecutors who retained Dr. Grigson to testify in this cohort of cases.

3. Some prosecutors suppress exculpatory psychiatric evidence.[146]

Over the years, there have been multiple examples of cases in which prosecutors have concealed psychiatric evidence that might have made trial impossible, that might have cast doubt on the veracity of state's witnesses, that created doubt as to the voluntariness of the state's witnesses, and that created doubt as to the voluntariness of the defendant's confession.[147]

There has been little activity on the part of prosecutors' associations to sanction those who violate the law and the spirit of justice in such cases. A startling exception to this global indifference came in the form of a Supreme Court *amicus* brief filed by six former Tennessee prosecutors, arguing that the behavior of the trial prosecutor in the case of Abu-Ali Abdur'Rahman had crossed a line that, in doing so, had "taint[ed] all members of the Tennessee bar."[148] But this is a lonely exception.

Judicial sanction is rare as well. In a study of 707 cases in which California courts explicitly found prosecutorial misconduct, the offending prosecutors were "almost never discipline[d]."[149] In his exhaustive study of cases involving prosecutorial misconduct in jury argument, Professor Bennett Gershman (a former prosecutor) was able to find only one decision in which such conduct resulted in discipline.[150] Perhaps this should not be surprising as, remarkably, the legal profession has never addressed the unique ethical issues that arise in death penalty cases.[151]

In short, prosecutors have virtually carte blanche authority to misinform jurors, to play to irrational and sanist fears, and to employ unscrupulous experts. And there are virtually no voices raised in opposition.[152]

ROLE OF JUDGES

As noted earlier in this chapter, Professor James Liebman has written about the political rewards available to judges who impose the death penalty.[153] There is important self-deception at play here. Notes Ronald Tabak, "[T]he self-image of judges is that they do not pay attention to election returns—even though many of them obviously have done so, particularly in dealing with capital punishment cases."[154] Amanda Frost's research reveals that elected judges issue longer sentences and are more likely to impose the death penalty as elections approach, "presumably because they fear being labeled 'soft on crime' by their opponent in the next election."[155] Indeed, a blue-ribbon panel of researchers has concluded that Delaware's change to sentencing by judges in death penalty cases was motivated by the desire for "greater harshness."[156]

This is not news and has even been noted by Justice Stevens in a dissent in a death penalty case: "Not surprisingly, given the political pressures they face, judges are far more likely than juries to impose the death penalty. This has long been the case, and the recent experience of judicial overrides confirms it."[157] This bias is not limited to states in which judges are elected. By way of example, in Tennessee, Governor Don Sundquist proclaimed before a 1996 judicial election that he would appoint only death penalty supporters to be criminal-court judges.[158] These political rewards further warp the system and mock those Supreme Court cases that seek to ensure that only the "worst of the worst"[159] be subjected to execution.

CONCLUSION

We consciously blind ourselves to the ways that jurors, prosecutors, and judges frequently behave in death penalty cases. We do this in spite of an overwhelming body of empirical evidence that tells us that, in practice, the death penalty is sought in ways that trivialize the Supreme Court's mitigation jurisprudence,[160] its competency-to-be-executed jurisprudence,[161] and reliable assessments of dangerousness.[162] As I discuss in the next chapter, this is all exacerbated by the woeful level of counsel made available to the cohort of defendants discussed in this work.

• *10* •

The Death Penalty, Mental Disability, and Adequacy of Counsel

INTRODUCTION[1]

𝒯he common wisdom is that death penalty cases play out on a landscape that pits the forces of retribution and punishment against the forces of abolition and rehabilitation. Supporters, or so the simplified version goes, applaud the death penalty for ensuring that the perpetrators of the most wanton and vilest murders receive the ultimate penalty. Opponents, again oversimplifying, argue both that the penalty is immoral (that the state does not have the moral authority to take the life of another, no matter how depraved the crime) and inherently inequitable (that because of a combination of racial, class, and political biases, it is impossible to create a system in which only the truly worst-of-the-worst capital defendants are subject to a death sentence).

Arguments, both pro and con, vacillate between high-end theory and street anecdote. The pro-death-penalty literature often appears to combine Immanuel Kant and the *New York Post*; the anti–literature substitutes Albert Camus and the *Village Voice* circa the 1970s. When the death penalty is being debated in state legislatures, much of the tone of the debate tracks these philosophical and anecdotal arguments. Yet, when the inevitable parade of death-eligible defendants comes before the trial courts, one issue—never mentioned by supporters, and rarely cited by opponents—often has the most significant impact on who is to be executed and who is not: the adequacy of counsel provided to individuals facing the death penalty. Because this issue is so rarely discussed in public fora, the public has little sense of counsel's significance to ultimate death decision making.

This chapter will proceed in the following manner. First, I will provide a brief overview of what we know about the adequacy of counsel in death penalty cases involving defendants with mental disabilities. Next, I will consider recent case law and policy developments that consider this issue. Then, as I have done in other chapters, I will contextualize both of these variables through the jurisprudential filters of sanism, of pretextuality, and of therapeutic jurisprudence.

THE PROVISION OF COUNSEL

Introduction

An examination of the full range of death penalty cases that have been litigated in the past thirty-five years since the United States Supreme Court's decision in *Gregg v. Georgia*,[2] holding that the death penalty was not necessarily a violation of the Eighth Amendment's ban on cruel and unusual punishment,[3] suggests one undeniable truth: in an amazingly high number of cases, the most critical issue in determining whether a defendant lives or dies is the quality of counsel.[4] As suggested by one veteran death penalty litigator, "[t]he death penalty will too often be punishment not for committing the worst crime, but for being assigned the worst lawyer."[5]

The responsibilities of lawyers in death penalty cases are legion. The attorney must develop a meaningful relationship with a client who is likely the target of public and media animosity and whose unpopularity may taint the quality of that relationship; thus, she must find a way to "humanize" her client.[6] She must investigate for mitigating evidence,[7] obtain expert defense witnesses,[8] investigate to rebut aggravating evidence,[9] and attempt to negotiate a plea bargain where appropriate.[10] If a guilty verdict is rendered, she must be prepared to make informed strategic decisions about the penalty phase.[11]

Look at cases randomly. Or choose a group that involves, say, felony murder, or potentially biased jurors, or a tainted confession, or any other sorting device. If these cases are read carefully (in some cases not very much care is needed, to be sure), the significance of counsel leaps off the page.[12] No one has seriously contradicted Professor Welsh White that "[t]he *single* greatest problem with our system of capital punishment is the quality of representation afforded capital defendants,"[13] nor has anyone seriously questioned the accuracy of Justice Ruth Bader Ginsburg's observation: "I have yet to see a death case among the dozens coming to the Supreme Court on eve-of-execution stay applications in which the defendant was well represented at trial."[14]

A *Harvard Law Review* survey article is blunt: "The utter inadequacy of trial and appellate lawyers for capital defendants has been widely recognized as the single most spectacular failure in the administration of capital punishment."[15] This inadequacy is so pervasive, the survey concludes, as to by itself make the death penalty "unconstitutionally arbitrary."[16] Professor Bruce Green, relying on similar data, also reasons that—in reality—many of the defendants who have been tried, convicted, and sentenced to death have been deprived of their constitutional right to counsel.[17]

Why is this? Many reasons have been offered, but one starting point is Douglas Vick's analysis, one that has lost none of its resonance over the seventeen years since it was written:

> The literature is replete with impressionistic, anecdotal, and empirical evidence that indigent capital defendants are routinely denied assistance of counsel adequate to put into practice the protections that on paper make the death penalty constitutional. This crisis in capital representation is caused by funding systems that discourage experienced and competent criminal attorneys from taking appointments in death penalty cases and prevent even the most talented attorneys from preparing an adequate defense, particularly for the penalty phase.[18]

Capital defendants are typically represented by "the bottom of the bar."[19] As of the late 1980s/early 1990s, 10 percent of death row prisoners in Alabama were represented by trial lawyers subsequently disbarred or disciplined.[20] Almost 13 percent of such inmates in Louisiana were represented by similar counsel;[21] almost 25 percent of Kentucky's death row inmates were represented by lawyers since disbarred or suspended.[22] An appointed counsel in a death case told the press, "I despise [being appointed], I'd rather take a whipping."[23] An American Bar Association (ABA) report on the representation of Georgia defendants facing the death penalty concluded,

> [The state's] recent experience with capital punishment has been marred by examples of inadequate representation ranging from virtually no representation at all by counsel, to representation by inexperienced counsel, to failures to investigate basic threshold questions, to lack of knowledge of governing law, to lack of advocacy on the issue of guilt, to failure to present a case for life at the penalty phase.[24]

And one often gets what one pays for. Professor Robert Weisberg, an appellate defense counsel in death cases, has mordantly noted, "The fees [at trial] were infamously low. The second capital appeal I worked on was a case where the defense lawyer was paid $150 for the entire case, and, believe me, he earned every penny of it."[25] Vick thus concludes on this point:

> In sum, every shortcoming in the quality of capital defense—the disproportionate number of incompetent attorneys assigned to death cases, the lack of experience and expertise of defense counsel, the repeated failure of defense attorneys to investigate and present available mitigating evidence—is ultimately rooted in society's unwillingness to pay for a meaningful defense in death penalty cases.[26]

And the situation is worse—far worse—for defendants with mental disabilities. As I noted earlier, nearly thirty-five years ago, when surveying the availability of counsel to mentally disabled litigants, President Carter's Commission on Mental Health noted the frequently substandard level of representation made available to mentally disabled criminal defendants.[27] Nothing that has happened in the intervening decades has been a palliative for this problem; if anything, it is compounded by the myth that adequate counsel is available to represent both criminal defendants in general, and mentally disabled litigants in particular.[28] And, as the importance of the construction of "mitigating" and "aggravating" evidence grows,[29] so does the need for counsel to be able to understand and utilize this mental disability evidence. As Mental Health America (formerly, the National Mental Health Association) has observed, "The process of determining guilt and imposing sentence is necessarily more complex for individuals with mental health conditions. A high standard of care is essential with regard to legal representation as well as psychological and psychiatric evaluation for individuals with mental health conditions involved in death penalty cases."[30] Thus, the *Commentary to the ABA Guidelines for the Appointment and Performance of Defense Counsel in Death Penalty Cases*[31] requires the use of mitigation experts who have "the clinical skills to recognize . . . congenital, mental and neurological conditions, to understand how these conditions may have affected the defendant's development and behavior."[32]

Writing about this issue, Professor Laura Jochnowitz recently underscored the dilemma in the context of *juror* misconceptions. I believe the phrase "defense counsel" could be substituted for the word "juror" each time in the following excerpt:

> Death row inmates are often afflicted with severe psychological problems and/or below average intelligence, as well as with some related disabling factors like head injuries, drug and childhood abuse histories. Yet claims by capital defendants of extenuating mental impairments may sometimes be investigated poorly or strategically omitted, and even when the claims are presented, they are not well understood by jurors. Defendants' history of mental impairments may be perceived by jurors as stigmatizing, threatening, or not believable. Jurors respond differently and more punitively to some types of mental illness and addiction, than to cognitive impairments. Their personal attributes and criminal justice attitudes may affect their receptivity. Jurors' exposure to mental health and other issues early in the case, at voir dire or the guilt phase of a bifurcated capital trial, may affect whether they pre-judge its significance at the penalty phase. Yet, jurors' exposure to long guilt phase prosecution evidence and bloody crime scene photos, without evidence foreshadowing diminished capacity or reduced culpability may desensitize jurors, before they hear penalty phase evidence.[33]

To what extent do death penalty lawyers "get this"? How do they learn of it? What do they make of it? What sanist heuristics do they use in constructing it?[34]

Consider some of the specific "added" abilities counsel need in cases involving the representation of defendants with serious disabilities facing the death penalty. The *Commentary to the ABA Guidelines for the Appointment and Performance of Defense Counsel in Death Penalty Cases* focuses on the special problems related to the issue of trust in the representation of the defendant with a mental disability or from a different cultural background than the lawyer:

> Many capital defendants are . . . severely impaired in ways that make effective communication difficult: they may have mental illnesses or personality disorders that make them highly distrustful or impair their reasoning and perception of reality; they may be mentally retarded or have other cognitive impairments that affect their judgment and understanding; they may be depressed and even suicidal; or they may be in complete denial in the face of overwhelming evidence. In fact, the prevalence of mental illness and impaired reasoning is so high in the capital defendant population that "It must be assumed that the client is emotionally and intellectually impaired." There will also often be significant cultural and/or language barriers between the client and his lawyers. In many cases, a mitigation specialist, social worker or other mental health expert can help identify and overcome these barriers, and assist counsel in establishing a rapport with the client.[35]

Think about the "bottom of the bar" lawyers described earlier[36] and then try to assess their actual competency in representing this cohort of defendants. Consider the thoughts of Professor John Blume and his colleagues on this issue:

> Many individuals with mental retardation deny their disability and hide behind what has been called a "cloak of competence." This is a defense mechanism often deliberately employed to prevent exposure of a perceivably shameful condition, though sometimes resulting from limited awareness of the extent of the disability. In such cases, the lawyer may not be aware of the individual's disability. If the client is defensive about his disability, the lawyer may think that his client is just being uncooperative. This information gap is obviously detrimental to building an appropriate defense, as well as to preparing for trial. Unfortunately, even if counsel knows of the client's intellectual disability, he may lack the experience necessary to understand his client's cognitive limitations and to know how to best communicate with his client.

Even if counsel ascertains the useful information possessed by a defendant with mental retardation, his client's limited ability to understand questions, instructions, and directions may make it very difficult to prepare him to testify. An additional impediment to effective testimony arises from the difficulty many individuals with mental retardation have with attention span, focus, and communication skills; if called to testify, they may not be able to maintain focus for a long period of time or understand the nature of questioning during cross-examination. They may not be able to understand subtle questions or the gravity of responding precisely. Easily tricked and confused, a person with mental retardation may not be able to verbalize his thoughts coherently; or worse, he may be nonresponsive on the stand. Counsel who understand their clients' limitations will avoid those risks—but often at the cost of foregoing their clients' testimony, even when the client does not have a criminal record. That decision, however, may lead the jury to conclude that the reason the defendant is not testifying is because he is guilty.[37]

Many defendants of ordinary intelligence do not contribute much help to their attorneys in extracting pertinent mitigating information.[38] This is certainly "exacerbated in the situation of a [defendant with mental retardation], who may not even understand what type of information her attorney needs, let alone begin to know how to provide it."[39] The *Atkins* Court stressed the difficulties that persons with mental retardation may have in being able to give meaningful assistance to their counsel, their status as "typically poor witnesses," and the ways that their demeanor "may create an unwarranted impression of lack of remorse for their crimes."[40] This is an extremely important issue to which scant attention has been paid, and it is one that is intensified by the reality that state criminal justice systems are ill equipped to deal with mentally ill or retarded defendants unable to aid their defense attorneys.[41]

Surveys of case law underscore the inability of criminal defendants with mental disabilities to aid their counsel, even in cases in which no violation of Supreme Court precedent related to competency to stand trial has been found.[42] This issue must be reexamined carefully in the post-*Atkins* generation of death penalty cases.

There are other examples as well. In a recent thoughtful and comprehensive article, John Blume and Emily Paavola discuss the need for defense counsel to be competent in the use (and nonuse) of neuroimaging in capital cases.[43] To what extent will occasionally appointed, underfunded counsel "get" the significance of this potential evidence?[44] Also, what about the use (and misuse) of antipsychotic medication on death-penalty-eligible defendants? I wrote the following eighteen years ago, and there is no evidence available that suggests the dilemma has gone away, nor is there any evidence to suggest that occasionally appointed counsel understands these issues any better than do random jurors:

> Jurors miscomprehend the impact of antipsychotic medication on defendants. Medication side-effects often lead them to attribute negative personality traits such as apathy or lack of remorse—exactly those traits

that make it more likely that a death penalty verdict will be returned—to such defendants.[45]

Evidence reveals the enormity of this problem. A review of eighty death sentences issued in Georgia, Mississippi, Alabama, and Virginia between 1997 and 2004 found that "[i]n 73 of the 80 cases, defense lawyers gave jurors little or no evidence to help them decide whether the accused should live or die. The lawyers routinely missed myriad issues of abuse and mental deficiency, abject poverty and serious psychological problems."[46] Such global incompetency on the part of this cohort of lawyers may have been one of the motivators for Liliana Lyra Jubilut's recommendation that there be "a *mandatory* psychiatric evaluation in all capital cases (due to the fact that the disease may be of such a type that the defendant or his or her defense counsel do not recognize the fact that he or she is sick)".[47]

John Blume and Pamela Blume Leonard have made the significance of these errors—and their potential fatal outcome—crystal clear:

> To address mental health issues competently and effectively, defense counsel must understand the wide range of mental health issues relevant to criminal cases, recognize and identify the multitude of symptoms that may be exhibited by our clients, and be familiar with how mental health experts arrive at diagnoses and determine how the client's mental illness influenced his behavior at the time of the offense. Without this knowledge, it is impossible to advocate effectively for a mentally ill client or to overcome jurors' cynicism about mental health issues. We believe juror skepticism often reflects inadequate development and ineffective presentation rather than a biased refusal to appreciate the tragic consequences of mental illness.[48]

The Meaning of Strickland

It does not appear that there is any relief in sight. Since 1983, when the Supreme Court established a pallid, nearly-impossible-to-violate adequacy standard in *Strickland v. Washington*[49] (requiring simply that counsel's efforts be "reasonable" under the circumstances), courts have become less and less interested in the question at hand, and little evidence disputes the failure of *Strickland* to ensure that capital defendants truly receive adequate assistance of counsel.[50]

Per *Strickland*,[51] the benchmark for judging an ineffectiveness claim is "whether counsel's conduct so undermined the proper function of the adversarial process that the trial court cannot be relied on as having produced a just result."[52] To determine whether counsel's assistance was "so defective as to require reversal,"[53] the Court established a two-part test:

> First, the defendant must show that counsel's performance was deficient. This requires showing that counsel made errors so serious that counsel was

not functioning as the "counsel" guaranteed the defendant by the Sixth Amendment. Second, the defendant must show that the deficient performance prejudiced the defense. This requires showing that counsel's errors were so serious as to deprive the defendant of a fair trial, a trial whose result is reliable. Unless a defendant makes both showings, it cannot be said that the conviction or death sentence resulted from a breakdown in the adversary process that renders the result unreliable.[54]

The Court adopted an "objective," "reasonably effective assistance" standard, to be measured by "simple reasonableness under prevailing professional norms."[55] In assessing claims, the Court will "indulge a strong presumption that counsel's conduct falls within the wide range of reasonable professional assistance."[56]

In looking at the case before it, the Court found that counsel had a duty to "make reasonable investigations or to make a reasonable decision that makes particular investigations unnecessary."[57] However, even a "professionally unreasonable"[58] error will not result in reversal if it "had no effect on the judgment."[59] Prejudice—measured by the showing of "a reasonable probability that, but for counsel's unprofessional errors, the result . . . would have been different"[60]—must be shown.[61]

In a sharply worded dissent,[62] Justice Marshall criticized the majority opinion of adoption of a performance standard "that is so malleable that, in practice, it will either have no grip at all or will yield excessive variation in the manner in which the Sixth Amendment is interpreted."[63] By the vagueness of its holding, he charged, the Court has "not only abdicated its own responsibility to interpret the Constitution, but also impaired the ability of the lower courts to exercise theirs."[64]

Individual post-*Strickland* cases are striking. In one case, counsel was found to be effective even though he had failed to introduce ballistics evidence showing that the gun taken from the defendant was not the murder weapon.[65] In another case, an attorney was found constitutionally adequate to provide representation to a death-eligible defendant notwithstanding the fact that he had been admitted to the bar for only six months and had never tried a jury case.[66] Another lawyer was found constitutionally adequate even where during the middle of the trial he appeared in court intoxicated and spent a night in jail.[67] In a pre-*Strickland* case, defense counsel was not even aware that separate sentencing proceedings were to be held in death penalty cases.[68] There is little evidence to contradict Welsh White's conclusion that "[l]ower courts' application of *Strickland* has produced appalling results."[69]

The first comprehensive analysis of *Strickland*—written by the chairperson of the Competency Committee of the ABA Section on Criminal Justice—called it "unfortunate and misguided," charging that it "failed to meet its obligation to help ensure that criminal defendants receive competent representation,"[70] and that it was drafted "to ensure that the review test will produce the same results as the old farce and mockery-due process test."[71] By its own terms, the test's application to *Strickland's* facts "underscores this return to the status quo ante."[72] *Strickland* is thus viewed as "a clear signal that [the Supreme Court] is not at all disturbed with inadequate performance by criminal defense lawyers";[73] its message is that "the problem of competency, at least in criminal cases, should be taken off the agenda."[74] The effectiveness of counsel also, in large measure, may depend on a lawyer's *cultural* competency. As I noted in an earlier article, discussing *Strickland*, "If . . . defendants are also from other cultures, the obligations on the defense team are even greater and the stakes are even higher."[75]

Subsequently, the Supreme Court has been overwhelmingly ambivalent in its reconsiderations of the *Strickland* doctrine. In *Alvord v. Wainwright*,[76] the Court denied *certiorari* in a case where defense counsel accepted his client's refusal to rely on the insanity defense with no independent investigation of his client's mental or criminal history, despite the fact that the record demonstrated unequivocally that the defendant had a history of mental illness and had been acquitted on insanity grounds six years prior to his indictment in the current case.[77] Justice Marshall concluded in his dissent from the *certiorari* denial:

> The lower court has countenanced a view of counsel's constitutional duty that is blind to the ability of the individual defendant to understand his situation and usefully to assist in his defense. The result is to deny to the persons who are most in need of it the educated counsel of an attorney.[78]

In later years, the Supreme Court has returned to this question again, demonstrating, in some instances, more sensitivity to the issues at hand.[79] In *Williams v. Taylor*, it found that a death penalty petitioner had been denied his constitutionally guaranteed right to effective assistance of counsel when his lawyers failed to develop, investigate, and present substantial mitigating evidence during the sentencing phase of his capital trial,[80] a position it adhered to in subsequent cases.[81] But then, in *Schriro v. Landrigan*,[82] a case involving a defendant who had a history of "recurring placements in . . . a psychiatric ward,"[83] the Court reversed a habeas grant, finding that "defense counsel's failure to present mitigating evidence during sentencing phase did not deprive petitioner of effective assistance of counsel."[84]

An examination of an array of reported post-*Strickland* decisions involving findings of deficiency in death penalty cases in which defendants' history of serious mental disability was ignored by counsel clearly calls into question one of the core assumptions of the *Strickland* case: that counsel does exercise substantial professional judgment in providing representation.[85] This is especially critical in cases where counsel completely "misses" what might be seen as mitigating evidence.[86] Consider these cases in which counsel was found to be deficient:

- In *Douglas v. Woodford*,[87] defense counsel performed deficiently, in particular by failing to discover reports from a psychologist that found defendant might have been incompetent to stand trial, with possible brain damage and head injuries.

- In *Summerlin v. Schriro*,[88] defense counsel failed to investigate defendant's social or mental health background, failed to find reports determining defendant to be mentally retarded, and disclosed defendant's diagnosis of paranoid schizophrenia.

- In *Daniels v. Woodford*,[89] defense counsel performed deficiently by relying on one sole inexperienced psychologist who conducted only a cursory evaluation of the defendant, failed to follow up when that evaluation suggested that the defendant was mentally ill, failed to investigate a family history that presented a detailed picture of serious mental illness, and failed to investigate whether the medications prescribed to the defendant or the illegal substances he was taking at the time of the crime had any effect on his mental state, either separately or as combined.[90]

- In *Hovey v. Ayers*,[91] counsel failed to give an expert witness documentation about defendant's mental illness and evidence of defendant's conduct at the time of the crime.

- In *Frierson v. Woodford*,[92] counsel failed to read the record of defendant's prior trials and thus failed to learn that defendant potentially suffered from brain damage (and then when made aware, failed to consult a neurologist), and failed to sufficiently investigate defendant's background so as to learn of his very low IQ scores.[93]

- In *Correll v. Ryan*,[94] counsel failed to investigate and present mitigating evidence about defendant's potential brain damage and his heavy drug use.

- In *Lambright v. Schriro*,[95] the sentence was reversed after the court held that counsel failed to conduct a basic investigation of mitigating factors including suicide attempts, psychiatric hospitalization, traumatic experiences in the Vietnam War, a diagnosis of personality disorder, and a history of major drug problems.

But these examples should not be taken as evidence that the *Strickland* standard has proven to be an effective palliative for the problems at hand. Interpretative cases in both federal and state courts have been wildly inconsistent.[96] Although many appellate cases have reversed convictions or granted writs of habeas corpus based on findings of ineffectiveness,[97] the vast majority have affirmed convictions or the denial of habeas writs, concluding that counsel's performance was adequate under the *Strickland v. Washington* standard.[98] Consideration of a grouping of cases—those construing *Panetti v. Quarterman*[99] and a defendant's right to neurological testing[100]—reveals a series of *Strickland*-based decisions that make a mockery out of the notion of a constitutionally based standard.[101]

Other examples are striking.

- In *Bailey v. True*,[102] counsel's acceptance of a mental health professional's diagnosis of the petitioner did not support a claim of ineffective assistance of counsel, and the state supreme court's finding that medication was not responsible for petitioner's emotionless demeanor at trial was not an unreasonable determination of the facts and did not support habeas relief, despite evidence that jury members had stated that the lack of emotion at trial—likely caused by his medication—contributed to their decision to sentence him to death.[103]

- In *Johnson v. Luebbers*,[104] the defendant, a Vietnam War veteran who suffered from posttraumatic stress disorder, unsuccessfully alleged ineffective assistance of counsel on appeal because his trial lawyer both failed to interview prosecution witnesses and presented inaccurate evidence, which destroyed the credibility of Johnson's PTSD defense.[105]

- In *In re Crew*,[106] a capital defendant failed to establish prejudice from any deficient performance in his trial counsel's failure to discover mitigating evidence that the defendant had "a family history fraught with incest, abuse, dysfunction, mental illness and substance abuse," and thus failed to establish ineffective assistance of counsel in his attorneys' failure to realize that there might be a penalty phase until after the prosecution rested in the guilt phase of the defendant's trial for the murder of his wife.

- In *Berget v. Gibson*,[107] where defendant unsuccessfully sought to withdraw his guilty plea, the evidence showed that he had suffered a severe head injury at the age of fourteen, had been diagnosed with bipolar disorder, and had attempted suicide shortly before his sentencing hearing; nonetheless, his lawyer failed to present evidence of his mental illness, saying, "I simply did not understand the importance of mental health evidence to present a full picture . . . this entire area was left uninvestigated."[108]

- In *Messer v. Kemp*,[109] even though severe mental impairment was important to issues of mitigation at both the guilt and penalty phases, the lawyer was unable to present any evidence of it because he failed to make an adequate showing to the judge that he needed a mental health expert.[110]

ABA Supplemental Guideline 5.1 discusses the needed skill sets—including cultural competency, knowledge of mental health signs and symptoms, and skills required in interviewing and record gathering—required in the provision of adequate counsel.[111] The Court's clear disinclination to carefully assess counsel's performance in providing criminal defense services is reflected squarely in its failure to insist that defense counsel comply with this guideline.[112] On balance, then, *Strickland* is a nonstandard that provides few safeguards for criminal defendants with mental disabilities. In many death penalty cases, *Strickland* is little more than an empty shell. Witnesses before an ABA task force characterized counsel's performance variously as "'scandalous,' 'shameful,' 'abysmal,' 'pathetic,' [and] 'deplorable.'"[113] In the words of one commentator, *Strickland* serves merely as a "gatepost[] on the road to legal condemnation."[114]

SOME JURISPRUDENTIAL FILTERS

Sanism[115]

In discussing the impact of sanism on the criminal justice system, John Parry focuses on its pernicious impact on judges and jurors: "Stigma affects the law in at least two interrelated ways: (1) negative effects on the liberty interests of the person with a mental disability, who is the subject of a legal proceeding, and (2) potential bias, due to sanism, that judges and other courtroom participants may demonstrate towards that person."[116] I believe that this same bias permeates the representation of death penalty defendants as well.[117]

Sanism permeates the legal representation process both in cases in which mental capacity is a central issue and those in which such capacity is a collateral question. Sanist lawyers (1) distrust their mentally disabled clients, (2) trivialize their complaints, (3) fail to forge authentic attorney-client relationships with such clients and reject their clients' potential contributions to case strategizing, and (4) take less seriously case outcomes that are adverse to their clients.[118]

In an earlier article about the right to refuse treatment in the civil commitment context, I said that "the failure to assign adequate counsel bespeaks sanism and pretextuality."[119] The problems are multiplied tenfold (at least) in death penalty cases. In this environment, it is easy to see how inadequate counsel can lead evidence of mental illness that was ostensibly introduced for mitigating purposes[120] to be construed by judges as aggravating instead.[121] In a Florida case discussed earlier, a trial judge concluded that because of the defendant's mental disability (paranoid schizophrenia manifested by hallucinations in which he "saw" others in a "yellow haze"), "the only assurance society can receive that this man never again commits to another human being what he did to [the brutally murdered decedent] is that the ultimate sentence of death be imposed."[122] And of course "[j]udicial complicity in the assignment and performance of inadequate counsel evidences sanism."[123]

To a great extent, sanism in the death penalty decision-making process mirrors sanism in the context of insanity defense decision making.[124] Such decision making is often irrational, rejecting empiricism, science, psychology, and philosophy, and substituting in its place myth, stereotype, bias, and distortion. It resists educational correction, demands punishment regardless of responsibility, and reifies medievalist concepts based on fixed and absolute notions of good and evil and of right and wrong.[125]

Myths similar to those that infect the insanity defense process apply when a mentally disabled defendant is being prosecuted in a capital case. And to confound matters, "enormous pressures" will often be placed on defense counsel to play into the hands of these myths and paint an exaggerated picture of a "totally crazy" defendant to assuage jurors whose "ordinary common sense"[126] demands an all-or-nothing representation of mental illness.[127] The importance of competent, trained, specialized counsel to identify and rebut these sanist myths should be clear on its face.

Pretextuality[128]

The presence of frequently inadequate counsel exacerbates this problem even more and heightens the pretextuality of the entire capital punishment process. Refusal by courts to acknowledge the regularly substandard job done by counsel in this most demanding area of the law is simply pretextual.[129]

If the Supreme Court is remotely serious when it says "death is different,"[130] and if we are to at all adhere to the notion of "super due process" in death penalty cases,[131] it is truly a "farce and mockery"[132] to perpetuate a system in which grossly unqualified lawyers are appointed to represent defendants facing the death penalty, especially those with mental disabilities. Amy Murphy's conclusion that "all that really matters in [ineffective assistance of counsel] claims is the appellate court's view of the case"[133] is a reflection of pretextuality at its most pernicious. Courts' sanctioning of behavior on the part of trial counsel that ignores the ABA guidelines is similarly pretextual. A trial lawyer's failure to even read a prior trial record—a record that would have taught him that his client may have suffered from brain damage warranting a neurological consultation[134]—suggests that it is pretextual to even pretend that there is an authentic and meaningful right to counsel in some death penalty cases involving defendants with mental disabilities.

Therapeutic Jurisprudence[135]

In recent years, scholars have begun to turn their attention more to questions of criminal law, procedure, and the rights of prisoners;[136] however, there has been little attention paid in the TJ literature to death penalty questions.[137]

If therapeutic jurisprudence principles are applied to the questions raised in this chapter, several inquiries immediately surface. First, if mental disability evidence can be seen as aggravating rather than mitigating,[138] what a powerful incentive this may be for mentally disabled criminal defendants to deny their mental illness and simultaneously refuse to seek ameliorative treatment. If jurors, especially, turn "empathy" evidence into evidence of aggravating circumstances, how will that affect the already compromised relationship between counsel and the mentally disabled client? And, for the purposes of this chapter, to what extent is counsel even *aware of* these findings?

In 1993, the Supreme Court held in *Godinez v. Moran*[139] that the standard for waiving counsel or for pleading guilty was to be no more stringent than the standard for competence to stand trial.[140] If *Godinez* allows more severely mentally disabled defendants to plead guilty in life-or-death cases without the aid of counsel, what will the impact be on penal settings (especially death row settings) if there is a significant influx of additional mentally ill prisoners?[141] Even if considered from the perspective of victims, there are therapeutic jurisprudence issues. Representatives of victims' rights organizations have testified before an ABA task force that adequate representation at all stages of the death penalty trial and appellate process was in the best interests of their constituencies.[142]

There is no question that counsel has a heavy burden in cases such as the ones discussed here, but it should no longer be a puzzle or surprise to counsel when faced with such a case. Although not written from an explicitly TJ perspective, Rebecca Covarrubias's recitation of counsel's duties in this context is a perfect primer for the TJ-focused death penalty defense lawyer:

> To avoid falling into the trap of the cloak of competency and making significant errors in judgment, counsel must first realize that their defendant may be mentally ill or mentally retarded. To make this realization, counsel should educate themselves on the signs, symptoms and stereotypes of mental retardation. To learn about the symptoms of mental illness and retardation, counsel should consult the DSM-IV and the AAIDD's [American Association on Intellectual and Developmental Disabilities] definitions. In educating themselves about the stereotypes of mental illnesses, counsel should realize that for both mentally ill and mentally retarded capital defendants, it will not always be physically apparent that the defendant suffers from one of these conditions. By learning about this stereotype, defense counsel can be alert to the fact that they will need to do investigation into their client's history; counsel will also know to ask questions to their client to elicit answers that may indicate if he or she has a mental illness or mental retardation.
>
> Next, defense counsel should gather as much information as possible about the defendant's history including police reports, medical records, birth records, pediatric records and hospital records. In gathering evidence, counsel should also consult with family members and investigate about the defendant's possible history of mental retardation or mental illness. Finally, counsel should request a competency hearing whenever they have a good faith doubt about the defendant's mental health status and espe-

cially when the capital defendant requests to represent himself or herself without using counsel.

Overall, counsel has a heavy burden when representing mentally ill and mentally retarded defendants. And, it is a burden that should not be taken lightly. It is up to defense counsel to recognize the defendant's mental health status, conduct an investigation into the defendant's mental health history and request the vital mental health evaluation that could save the defendant's life.[143]

In her article considering the death penalty process from a TJ perspective, Cynthia Adcock—a law professor who spent thirteen years representing death penalty defendants—listed those affected by the process: lawyers, prosecutors, experts, jurors, trial judges and court staff, family members, friends, prison employees, the governor, ministers, witnesses to the execution, and "finally, the inevitable scores who stand outside the prison gates and elsewhere in protest of the execution and others who just mourn the death of another prisoner killed by their government,"[144] and concluded that there was evidence of "psychological devastation caused by the death penalty on those who the lawmakers do not intend to be the target of death penalty laws."[145] What is clear is the evidence that ineffective trial counsel, which in many cases has led to (improper) death penalty verdicts, is part and parcel of the perpetuation of this entire cycle of trauma and pain. Nothing could be more anti-therapeutic.

In short, any death penalty system that provides inadequate counsel and that, at least as a partial result of that inadequacy, fails to ensure that mental disability evidence is adequately considered and contextualized by death penalty decision makers, fails miserably from a therapeutic jurisprudence perspective.[146]

CONCLUSION

In an article aimed at death penalty defense lawyers, John Blume and a colleague laid out in clear and explicit detail the duties that such lawyers have toward their clients, tasking lawyers with being *credible, comprehensive, consistent,* and *comprehensible.*[147] In their conclusion, they note that "archaic definitions, burden-shifting, and cultural bias against mentally ill persons are only a few of the formidable challenges an attorney faces when defending a client with a mental disability. . . . To shortchange any of [the key principles of representation] is to squander your client's compelling mental health issues. Worst of all, you are more likely to arouse anger and vengeance against the defendant rather than to foster the compassion and mercy you seek on his behalf."[148] Their recommendations are a blueprint to both rebut sanism and pretextuality and to best achieve therapeutic jurisprudential ends.[149]

In a recent article that I wrote—titled *"Too Stubborn to Ever Be Governed by Enforced Insanity": Some Therapeutic Jurisprudence Dilemmas in the Representation of Criminal Defendants in Incompetency and Insanity Cases*[150]—I discussed the therapeutic jurisprudence implications of the representation of defendants pleading the insanity defense, or in cases in which the incompetency-to-stand-trial status is raised. I concluded this way:

> I self-consciously used the word "dilemmas" in the title of this paper, because I think that these are important dilemmas for the entire criminal justice system: for the defendants with mental disabilities who are subject to the court process, for lawyers representing them, for other "players" in the trial process, and for the public. There has been a remarkable explosion of TJ literature in recent years, but painfully little of it has to do with the questions that I am discussing here. I believe—and this is an intuition that is shaped to some extent by my 38 year career of representing and writing about and thinking about criminal defendants with mental disabilities— that the pervasive sanism of the entire justice system is, in large part, the reason why little attention has been paid to this topic.[151]

I believe the same issues that I sought to address in this article are present in cases dealing with defendants with mental disabilities facing the death penalty, but perhaps even more so. Unless and until we openly confront the problems raised by inadequate counsel in such cases, we will continue to willfully blind ourselves to the shams (and shame) that are so many death penalty cases.

The Death Penalty and International Human Rights Law

INTRODUCTION

$\mathcal{T}$o this point, virtually all of the discussion in this book has focused on domestic law. But the inquiry I have undertaken would be incomplete if I did not also look seriously at the impact of international human rights law on the question of the imposition of the death penalty.[1] As discussed earlier,[2] the United States Supreme Court has—over vigorous dissents—turned to human rights law in support of its holding in *Atkins v. Virginia*,[3] that execution of persons with mental retardation violates the Eighth Amendment.[4] There are, however, other issues of concern that go beyond the *Atkins* and *Roper* holdings. In this chapter, I will explore some of those issues.[5]

First, I will consider the important international human rights documents that support the argument that the death penalty violates international human rights law. Then I will return to the topic of dignity that I discussed previously[6] and will consider how that concept is to be constructed in the international human rights context. After that, I will examine how the interplay between the death penalty and international human rights law must be specifically examined in the context of mental disability. I follow this by looking at the role of counsel in this specific context, a topic I examine extensively elsewhere in this work,[7] and then I examine the impact of the UN Convention on the Rights of Persons with Disabilities on these issues. I then conclude by applying a therapeutic jurisprudence lens[8] to this entire question.

INTERNATIONAL HUMAN RIGHTS LAW DOCUMENTS

For over forty years, scholars and advocates have argued that the retention of the death penalty in the United States violates international human rights law.[9] In 1971, the United Nations General Assembly declared that the main objective of Article 3 of the Universal Declaration of Human Rights was to progressively restrict the use of the death penalty, "with a view to . . . abolishing this punishment in all countries."[10] In 1982, the Council of Europe adopted Protocol No. 6 to the European Convention on Human Rights, the first international agreement to provide for complete abolition of capital punishment.[11] In 1984, the UN Economic and Social Council adopted a resolution calling for safeguards in the administration of the death penalty and its use for only the most serious crimes.[12] The UN General Assembly took the final step in its evolution toward an abolitionist stance on the death penalty in 1989, when it adopted and proclaimed the Second Optional Protocol to the International Covenant on Civil and Political Rights, Aiming at the Abolition of the Death Penalty ("Second Optional Protocol"), committing signatory states to abolishing the death penalty.[13] This protocol "reflects the intentional trend toward disfavoring the use of capital punishment and clearly states the UN's support of abolition of the death penalty."[14] Ninety-three countries have abolished the death penalty for all crimes, nine have abolished it for ordinary crimes only, and an additional thirty-six have abolished it in practice.[15]

The Charter of Fundamental Rights of the European Union, adopted in 2000, holds that no person "shall be condemned to the death penalty, or executed."[16] The International Criminal Court expressly forbids the death penalty as a punishment in any matter.[17] As recently as February 2008, a UN General Assembly Resolution declared that the use of the death penalty "undermines human dignity" and called on all states for a moratorium on the use of the death penalty.[18]

Other nations have responded to this call. By way of example, the South African Constitutional Court abolished the death penalty in 1995,[19] a judgment later confirmed in the new Constitution of South Africa.[20] Subsequently, the Constitutional Court[21] has made "frequent and regular reference to international law on the subject of the death penalty, to the decisions of the Human Rights Committee of the United Nations,[22] to the various international legal instruments, and to the judgments of the European Court of Human Rights," and, according to Professor William Schabas, "It is clear that in coming to its conclusion that the death penalty violates the right to life and violates the prohibition of cruel, inhuman, and degrading treatment or punishment, the South African Constitutional Court was enormously influenced by international law on the subject of the death penalty."[23] According to one commentator, "The argument could persuasively be made that that abolition of the death penalty has become part of customary international law."[24]

By retaining the death penalty, the United States aligns itself with such nations as Afghanistan, Belarus, China, the Democratic Republic of the Congo, Equatorial Guinea, Ethiopia, Guatemala, Iran, Iraq, Libya, Saudi Arabia, Somalia, South Sudan, Sudan, Syria, and Zimbabwe.[25] Most agree that "the death penalty practice of the United States is out of step with nearly every other democratic nation and the international human rights community,"[26] and, because of this, retains the reputation of being isolated from international human rights law.[27]

THE ROLE OF DIGNITY[28]

Human rights are necessary for all individuals—human rights violations occur when persons are treated as objects or as a means to others' ends.[29] All citizens—including ones who are institutionalized—have enforceable human rights.[30] International law recognizes that inherent dignity and inalienable rights of all individuals are the foundation of freedom, justice, and peace.[31] Through global covenants, individual rights of offenders are safeguarded against cruel, inhuman, or degrading treatment or punishment;[32] prisoners are to be treated with humanity and dignity, and provided with reformation and social rehabilitation;[33] individuals are guaranteed the right to the highest attainable standard of physical and mental health;[34] individuals are guaranteed respect for human rights and fundamental freedoms in forensic and correctional systems;[35] and prisoners should be treated in a humane manner and with dignity.[36] By way of example, European Human Rights Courts have held that due process rights, criminal procedure protections, prohibitions against cruel punishments, and privacy interests are all supported by an underlying right to dignity.[37] According to Professor Rex Glensy, "this infusion of the right to dignity throughout the European Convention has led the [European Court on Human Rights] to proclaim that human dignity underpins the *entirety* of the document as a general principle of law."[38] By way of example, Switzerland abolished the death penalty because it constituted "a flagrant violation of the right to life and dignity."[39]

What has gone largely uncommented upon is the way that the US Supreme Court's acceptance of the American death penalty—as being fundamentally consistent with fundamental constitutional rights—"has precluded American acceptance of a human rights frame for the issue of capital punishment."[40] Notes Professor Carol Steiker: "It is striking that even in successful abolitionist movements within the United States—like those that led to the recent legislative abolitions in New Jersey, New Mexico, and Illinois—arguments to the effect that capital punishment violates a fundamental human right (to life or dignity) are virtually absent."[41] Elsewhere she has noted, in the same vein, "It is hard for American political leaders to articulate, or for members of the American public to accept, that our much vaunted constitution could validate something that constituted a violation of international human rights."[42]

THE SPECIFIC DILEMMA OF MENTAL DISABILITY

This issue becomes more vexing and complex when we consider the death penalty subtopic that is the focus of this book: its application to persons with mental disabilities. International human rights norms condemn the death penalty for defendants with severe mental illness.[43] In 1984, nine UN safeguards were adopted by the Economic and Social Council and embraced by the General Assembly. Among other goals, the UN safeguards aim to exempt from the death penalty those who are or have become "insane." A 1989 revision of one of these safeguards expanded this exemption to include people "suffering from mental retardation or extremely limited mental competence, whether at the sentencing stage or at execution."[44]

Also, the UN Commission on Human Rights, for example, has adopted a resolution urging all countries that still maintain capital punishment "[n]ot to impose the death penalty on a person suffering from any form of mental disorder."[45] The European Union (EU) has specifically spoken out against inflicting the death penalty on any person with a serious mental illness.[46] Again, the argument can persuasively be made that customary international law prohibits the execution of prisoners who are "insane."[47] Other retentionist nations seek to limit or to ban the use of the death penalty in cases involving persons with serious mental disabilities.[48]

In her discussion of the significance of *Atkins v. Virginia*,[49] Professor Arlene Kanter stresses that that case raises "important issues not only about the label of 'mental retardation' but also about . . . international human rights, and death penalty jurisprudence generally."[50] In his exhaustive analysis of the Supreme Court's death penalty jurisprudence in the context of mental disability, the late Professor Bruce Winick argues that these same principles should authorize a similar ban on the imposition of capital punishment on individuals with severe mental illness.[51] Liliana Lyra Jubilut focuses further on the rights to due process and fair trial in this context: "If more concern for the proper application of due process protections and fair trial were present, more people who suffer from mental illness would be protected from the death penalty."[52]

There may be a ray of hope, however. Professor Margaret E. McGuinness has noted that, even as the United States seeks to "limit[] its obligations under the central human rights regimes . . . and . . . become[s] more confident in its rejection of other multilateral regimes," US courts have "moved closer to the international standards in the one area where it has steadfastly rejected international influence: the death penalty."[53] Consider here how the Supreme Court *has*, in recent years, turned more frequently to international law norms in deciding death penalty cases, most notably in *Atkins* and in *Roper v. Simmons*,[54] abolishing the juvenile death penalty. As noted above, Justice Kennedy explained in *Atkins*, "Within the world community, the imposition of the death penalty for crimes committed by mentally retarded offenders is overwhelmingly disapproved."[55] He fleshed out these views more comprehensively several years later in *Roper*:

> Our determination that the death penalty is disproportionate punishment for offenders under 18 finds confirmation in the stark reality that the United States is the only country in the world that continues to give official sanction to the juvenile death penalty. This reality does not become controlling, for the task of interpreting the Eighth Amendment remains our responsibility. Yet at least from the time of the Court's decision in [*Trop v. Dulles*, 356 U.S. 86 (1958)], the Court has referred to the laws of other countries and to international authorities as instructive for its interpretation of the Eighth Amendment's prohibition of "cruel and unusual punishments." 356 U.S., at 102–103 . . . (plurality opinion) ("The civilized nations of the world are in virtual unanimity that statelessness is not to be imposed as punishment for crime"); see also *Atkins*, *supra*, at 317, n. 21, (recognizing that "within the world community, the imposition of the death penalty for crimes committed by mentally retarded offenders is overwhelmingly disapproved"); *Thompson* [*v. Oklahoma*, 487 U.S. 815], 830–831, and n. 31 (1988) (plurality opinion) (noting the abolition of the juvenile death penalty "by other nations that share our Anglo-American heritage, and by the leading members of the Western European community," and observing that "[w]e have previously recognized the relevance of the views of the international community in determining whether a punishment is cruel and unusual").[56]

THE SIGNIFICANCE OF COUNSEL

As I discussed extensively in an earlier chapter,[57] the pallid effectiveness-of-counsel standard articulated by the Supreme Court in *Strickland v. Washington*[58] has contributed significantly to the conviction and execution of persons with serious mental disabilities. How do international human rights construe this issue?

The right of meaningful access to the courts is recognized in every major human rights instrument,[59] and international tribunals have observed that the right to effective recourse to a competent court "constitutes one of the basic pillars . . . of the very rule of law in a democratic society," and must be more than a mere formality.[60] Certainly, in many instances, the *Strickland* standard has resulted in little more than "the mere formal existence of this important remedy."[61]

THE IMPACT OF THE UN CONVENTION ON THE RIGHTS OF PERSONS WITH DISABILITIES[62]

I turn now to the most important international human rights document—ever—that recognizes the rights of persons with disabilities: the UN Convention on the Rights of Persons with Disabilities (CRPD).[63] In late 2001, the United Nations General Assembly established an ad hoc committee "to consider proposals for a comprehensive and integral international convention to promote and protect the rights and dignity of persons with disabilities."[64] The Ad Hoc Committee drafted a document over the course of five years and eight sessions, and the new CRPD was adopted in December 2006 and opened for signature in March 2007.[65] It entered into force—thus becoming legally binding on state parties—on May 3, 2008, thirty days after the twentieth ratification.[66] One of the hallmarks of the process that led to the publication of the UN Convention was the participation of persons with disabilities and the clarion cry, "Nothing about us, without us."[67] This has led commentators to conclude that the Convention "is regarded as having finally empowered the 'world's largest minority' to claim their rights, and to participate in international and national affairs on an equal basis with others who have achieved specific treaty recognition and protection."[68]

This Convention is the most revolutionary international human rights document ever created that applies to persons with disabilities.[69] The Disability Convention furthers the human rights approach to disability and recognizes the right of people with disabilities to equality in most aspects of life.[70] It clearly and directly repudiates the medical model that traditionally was part and parcel of mental disability law.[71] It furthers the human rights approach to disability and recognizes the right of people with disabilities to equality in most aspects of life. "The Convention responds to traditional models and situates disability within a social model framework[72] and sketches the full range of human rights that apply to all human beings, all with a particular application to the lives of persons with disabilities."[73] It provides a framework for ensuring that mental health laws "fully recognize the rights of those with mental illness."[74]

The CRPD categorically affirms the social model of disability[75] by describing it as a condition arising from "interaction with various barriers [that] may hinder their full and effective participation in society on an equal basis with others" instead of inherent limitations,[76] reconceptualizes mental health rights as disability rights,[77] and extends existing human rights to take into account the specific rights experiences of persons with disabilities.[78] To this end, it calls for "respect for inherent dignity"[79] and "non-discrimination."[80] Subsequent articles declare "freedom from torture or cruel, inhuman or degrading treatment or punishment,"[81] "freedom from exploitation, violence and abuse,"[82] and a right to protection of the "integrity of the person."[83]

The CRPD is unique because it is the first legally binding instrument devoted to the comprehensive protection of the rights of persons with disabilities. It not only clarifies that states should not discriminate against persons with disabilities, but also sets out explicitly the many steps that states must take to create an enabling environment so that persons with disabilities can enjoy authentic equality in society.[84] One of the most critical issues in seeking to bring life to international human rights law in a mental disability law context is the right to adequate and dedicated counsel. The CRPD mandates that "States Parties shall take appropriate measures to provide access by persons with disabilities to the support they may require in exercising their legal capacity"[85] Elsewhere, the convention commands:

> States Parties shall ensure effective access to justice for persons with disabilities on an equal basis with others, including through the provision of procedural and age appropriate accommodations, in order to facilitate their effective role as direct and indirect participants, including as witnesses, in all legal proceedings, including at investigative and other preliminary stages.[86]

"The extent to which this Article is honored in signatory nations will have a major impact on the extent to which this entire Convention affects persons with mental disabilities."[87] If, and only if, there is a mechanism for the appointment of dedicated counsel[88] can this dream become a reality.

The ratification of the CRPD marks the most important development ever seen in institutional human rights law for persons with mental disabilities. The CRPD is detailed, comprehensive, integrated, and the result of a careful drafting process. It seeks to reverse the results of centuries of oppressive behavior and attitudes that have stigmatized persons with disabilities. Its goal is clear: to promote, protect, and ensure the full and equal enjoyment of all human rights and fundamental freedoms of all persons with disabilities, and to promote respect for their inherent dignity.[89] Whether this will actually happen is still far from a settled matter.

It is critical, in the context of this chapter, to take a close look at the Convention's mentions of "dignity," and the commentary about those mentions. As noted above, as ratified, the Convention calls for "respect for inherent dignity."[90] The Preamble characterizes "discrimination against any person on the basis of disability [as] a violation of the inherent dignity and worth of the human person."[91] And these provisions are consistent with the entire Convention's "rights-based approach focusing on individual dignity,"[92] placing the responsibility on the state "to tackle socially created obstacles in order to ensure full respect for the dignity and equal rights of all persons"[93] Professor Michael Stein puts it well this way: A "dignitary perspective compels societies to acknowledge that persons with disabilities are valuable because of their inherent human worth."[94] In Professor Cees Maris' summary: "The Convention's object is to ensure disabled persons enjoy all human rights with dignity."[95]

In his testimony in support of the UN Convention, Eric Rosenthal, the director of Mental Disability Rights International, shared with Congress his observations of the treatment of institutionalized persons with mental disabilities in Central and Eastern European nations: "When governments deny their citizens basic human dignity and autonomy, when they subject them to extremes of suffering, when they segregate them from society—we call these violations of fundamental human rights."[96]

As I discussed in an earlier chapter,[97] Professor Christopher McCrudden— in his review of a variety of international human rights cases—found multiple categories of cases in which "dignity" had been relied on as a basis for a court's judgment:

- Cases involving prohibition of inhuman treatment, humiliation, or degradation by one person over another;
- Cases involving individual choice and the conditions for self-fulfillment, autonomy, and self-realization;
- Cases involving protection of group identity and culture; and
- Cases involving the creation of necessary conditions for individuals to have essential needs satisfied.[98]

Having said this, McCrudden's reading of the case law has led him to the conclusion that "the use of the concept of human dignity has not given rise to a detailed universal interpretation."[99] Notwithstanding this insight, however, he determined that the concept of dignity can provide "a language in which judges can appear to justify how they deal with issues such as the weight of rights, the domestication and contextualization of rights, and the generation of new or more extensive rights."[100]

Consider some of the articles of the CRPD that can easily be read to speak to the question of the imposition of the death penalty on persons with serious mental disabilities: "freedom from torture or cruel, inhuman or degrading treatment or punishment";[101] "freedom from exploitation, violence and abuse";[102] and a right to protection of the "integrity of the person."[103] The United States has signed but not yet ratified the Convention.[104] However, since it has also ratified the Vienna Convention on the Law of Treaties, it is thus obligated to "refrain from acts which would defeat [the CRPD's] object and purpose."[105]

Strikingly, in a comprehensive article on the impact of the CRPD on the use of so-called "supermax" solitary confinement,[106] Kathryn DeMarco carefully and thoughtfully considers the implications of such confinement and concludes that it "runs counter to international human rights law," undercutting, as it does, that body of law's "fundamental aim of 'preserving the right to human dignity,'"[107] arguing that "the time to begin bringing U.S. practice into conformity with the CRPD is now."[108] Her arguments are equally applicable—perhaps, given the finality of a carried-out death sentence, even more so—to the death penalty as it is used in the United States.

THE APPLICATION OF THERAPEUTIC JURISPRUDENCE PRINCIPLES[109]

Earlier in this work, I discussed the overarching principles of therapeutic jurisprudence[110] and sought to apply these principles to the substantive death penalty issues that I discuss throughout this book. However, there has been very little literature that has considered the intersection between therapeutic jurisprudence and human rights,[111] and virtually no literature at all on this intersection in the context of the death penalty.[112]

There have been significant TJ developments in many aspects of international law. Michael King catalogs these,[113] making reference to, inter alia,

- Allan and Allan's study of the therapeutic aspects of South Africa's Truth and Reconciliation Commission,[114]
- Cooper's consideration of the implications of therapeutic jurisprudence for the human right of self-determination in international law,[115]
- King and Guthrie's suggestion that the Northern Territory Emergency Response legislation in Australia is anti-therapeutic, hindering the legislation's objective of the well-being of the relevant Northern Territory communities,[116]
- Olowu's evaluation of TJ as a means of humanizing criminal justice in Africa,[117]
- Nicholson's examination of the anti-therapeutic effects of child labor laws in South Africa,[118] and
- Munir's study of therapeutic jurisprudence in relation to juvenile justice in Pakistan.[119]

Clearly, none of these considers the death penalty. But if, however, we think about, by way of example, the issue of medicating incompetent death row prisoners so as to make them competent to be executed,[120] the connection emerges. This use of state-sanctioned psychiatry violates dignity and also delegitimizes the process involved, making that process anti-therapeutic not solely for those incompetent persons facing death, but for all subject to the same penalty.

Consider also the issues related to adequacy of counsel.[121] As stated flatly by Judge Juan Ramirez and Professor Amy Ronner, "the right to counsel is . . . the core of therapeutic jurisprudence."[122] If counsel in death penalty cases fails to meet the standards articulated in the CRPD—as well as constitutional minima—it strains credulity to argue that such a practice might comport with TJ principles. TJ is the perfect mechanism "to expose [the law's] pretextuality";[123] this pretextuality is clear in the death penalty context.

Further, it is crystal clear that the conditions of prison facilities around the world are textbook examples of anti-therapeutic conditions.[124] Astrid Birgden argues forcefully that "applying therapeutic jurisprudence can assist forensic psychologists in actively addressing human rights in general, as well as prisoners and detainees with mental disabilities in particular."[125] The sorts of "shock-the-conscience" conditions in death rows[126] scream out for an in-depth TJ analysis, to demonstrate their destructiveness and their negative impact on the mental health of those unlucky enough to be housed in such facilities.

The Convention on the Rights of Persons with Disabilities is a document that resonates with TJ values, and "look[s] at law as it actually impacts people's lives."[127] Its bans on "torture or cruel, inhuman or degrading treatment or punishment"[128] and on "exploitation, violence and abuse"[129] must be considered from the perspective of persons with serious mental disabilities facing the death penalty. I believe that the time is right for scholars to engage in a close and careful reading of the TJ literature in this specific context and then apply their findings to questions related to the implementation of this Convention.

The lynchpin for effective and meaningful CRPD enforcement is the presence of dedicated, advocacy-focused counsel available to represent persons with CRPD complaints or grievances.[130] "The failure to assign adequate counsel bespeaks sanism and pretextuality[131] and a failure to consider the implications of therapeutic jurisprudence."[132]

In an earlier analysis of the quality of counsel in death penalty cases, I reasoned that any system offering inadequate counsel would lead to a failure to ensure that mental disability evidence is adequately considered and contextualized by death penalty decision makers, and that such a system "fails miserably from a therapeutic jurisprudence perspective."[133] The CRPD's mandate of access to counsel reflects TJ values and must be implemented if our death penalty system is to, at the least, meet minimal international human rights standards.[134]

In short, therapeutic jurisprudence values—coupled with developments in international human rights law (especially the ratification of the CRPD)—clearly support the abolition of the death penalty, at the very least, as it applies to defendants with mental disabilities. If the penalty is not abolished, then TJ demands a top-to-bottom overhaul of the way that counsel is appointed.

· *12* ·

Conclusion

A decade ago, I began an article about *Atkins v. Virginia*[1] in this manner:

> Anyone who has spent any time in the criminal justice system—as a defense lawyer, as a district attorney, or as a judge—knows that our treatment of criminal defendants with mental disabilities has been, forever, a scandal. Such defendants receive substandard counsel, are treated poorly in prison, receive disparately longer sentences, and are regularly coerced into confessing to crimes (many of which they did not commit). And those of us who know about this system know that it is a scandal of little interest to most lawyers, most citizens, and most judges. . . .

This is not news and has not been so for decades. We remain content to "bury our heads in the sand" and ignore the ramifications of the morally corrupt system that we have created.[2]

This "morally corrupt system" is at its most corrupt when it comes to questions of the death penalty. The Supreme Court's decisions about the application of the death penalty to this population are stupefyingly incoherent, and, perhaps worse, have been applied utterly inconsistently (in some cases, they have been simply ignored in toto) by state courts and by other federal courts. I believe some of these patterns of behavior can be attributed to the ravaging forces of sanism and pretextuality that continue to dominate this area of law and policy.

At the outset, it is uncontestable that mental disability may lead to factually innocent defendants making false confessions.[3] As noted above,[4] of the first 130 exonerations that the New York–based Innocence Project obtained via DNA evidence,[5] 85 involved people who were convicted after confessing falsely.[6] Here, jurors' refuge in false "ordinary common sense"[7] ("Why would someone confess to a crime he didn't commit?") coupled with observational heuristics[8] ("He doesn't look like an innocent person; he seems so complacent") combine to create an environment in which a significant number of innocent persons with mental disabilities have been convicted and sentenced to death. And there is no question in my mind that the prosecutorial apparat is, in many jurisdictions, compliant with this violation of law and ethics.[9]

An examination of all other aspects of the death penalty process reveals a similar sorry picture. Sanism leads jurors to ascribe future dangerousness to virtually all persons with mental disabilities,[10] an ascription made possible by the Supreme Court's pretextual decision in *Barefoot v. Estelle*.[11] Similarly, sanism leads jurors to misinterpret mitigating evidence as aggravating evidence,[12] a blunder abetted by trial judges who seek—in spite of a series of Supreme Court decisions to the contrary—to pretextually limit the introduction of the full range of mitigating evidence envisioned by *Lockett v. Ohio*,[13] *Eddings v. Oklahoma*,[14] *Penry v. Lynaugh*,[15] and *Tennard v. Dretke*.[16]

It is fatuous to search for doctrinal consistency between *Barefoot v. Estelle*,[17] countenancing the most speculative and unreliable expert testimony on the question most likely to pave the way, improperly, for execution, scoffing at the argument that jurors will not be able to accurately assess the value of such testimony, and *Ake v. Oklahoma*,[18] recognizing the need for indigent defendants to have access to independent expertise in cases in which the insanity defense is the defendant's only possible strategy through which she can avoid the imposition of the death penalty.

Notwithstanding the Supreme Court's decision in *Atkins v. Virginia*,[19] individuals with intellectual disabilities continue to be sentenced to death, and those sentences are often upheld on appeal.[20] There is no dispute that many severely mentally ill offenders have been executed after courts have determined that, despite the profundity of their disability, they are nonetheless "competent" to be executed.[21] Notwithstanding the Supreme Court's decisions in *Ford v. Wainwright*[22] and *Panetti v. Quarterman*,[23] individuals with severe mental disabilities continue to be sentenced to death, and those sentences continue to be upheld on appeal.[24] There can be no doubt that the death penalty system does not treat persons with mental disabilities with even the slightest modicum of dignity. The execution of Ricky Rector—who "famously told the officers who took him to his death that he had put the dessert from his last meal aside in order to have it later"[25]—is just one example of many that reflects this dismal reality. It defies credulity that, in the twenty years following the Court's decision in *Ford*—barring execution of the "currently insane"—not a *single* petition for relief under *Ford* was granted in a universe of over 360 cases.[26] These jaw-dropping statistics are testament to the ways that the sanism of jurors and the pretextuality of judges have combined to create a perfect storm to ensure that, in spite of Supreme Court case law to the contrary, defendants with severe mental disabilities continue to be sentenced to death.

The penurious interpretations by lower courts of the pallid effectiveness-of-counsel standard set out in *Strickland v. Wainwright*[27]—affirming death penalty convictions in cases involving a staggering range of inept lawyer performances[28]—are virtually impossible to believe, all in spite of post-*Strickland* decisions such as *Wiggins v. Smith*[29] in which the Court *appeared*[30] to "get" the need for counsel in death penalty cases to be substantially more than what has derisively been called "a warm body with a legal pedigree."[31] But *Strickland* allows us to pretextually countenance the conviction and execution of individuals, not because they committed the worst crime, but because they had the worst lawyer.[32]

Juror behavior, in all its manifestations, reflects the power of sanist myth and prejudice.[33] A depressing record of prosecutorial misconduct, abetted by judges slavishly pandering to "be-tough-on-crime" cries from the electorate,[34] adds to the morass. Our ambivalence about—and frequent rejection of—core international human rights law principles contributes to this state of affairs.[35] We reject a half century of United Nations covenants, conventions, treaties, and declarations, and in doing so align ourselves with some of the most authoritarian regimes in the world. Until this point in time, this rejection has affected all those facing the death penalty roughly equally. However, since the ratification of the UN Convention on the Rights of Persons with Disabilities,[36] it places persons with mental disabilities in an even more fragile position and makes rejection of these international law principles even more problematic.[37]

This panoply of decisions and behaviors is irrational—stunningly irrational—and it can only be explained away by taking seriously the corrosive malignity of sanism and pretextuality. These biases infect every aspect of the death penalty process, and often do so utterly invisibly.[38]

Of course, this book should not lead the reader to conclude that error—egregious error—happens only in cases involving defendants with mental disabilities. Faulty eyewitness identification testimony, botched scientific testimony, flagrant *Brady* violations,[39] and perjured testimony (suborned or not) all account for significant percentages of death row exonerations.[40] The focus here on issues of mental disability should not obscure the enormity of the problem. But I believe that what goes on in the cohort of cases involving defendants under consideration here is largely hidden,[41] and the victims of misadministration of justice are disproportionately silenced.[42] And that is why I have chosen to focus on them.

Is there any remedy on which we can draw? My personal opinion—as should be clear from this book—is that the death penalty should be abolished, but I am realistic enough to acknowledge that this will not likely happen in the United States during my lifetime.[43] Short of that, however, I believe that, if we embrace the teachings and precepts of therapeutic jurisprudence,[44] it will provide the most likely way to minimize damage and harm, and to ensure that the death penalty system operates in such a way as to minimize sanist and pretextual decisions.[45] The death penalty system can never replicate the "ethic of care" that is at the heart of therapeutic jurisprudence.[46] But it can be restructured so as to provide at least a minimal amount of dignity to the participants. Discussing the Supreme Court's *Panetti* decision, Professor Richard Bonnie has noted, "Courts trivialize mental illness, disserve the important principle of autonomy, and compromise the dignity of the law when they allow defendants as disturbed as Panetti to represent themselves in criminal trials."[47] The South African Constitutional Court had the good judgment and sense to rule that the death penalty violated the rights to life and human dignity.[48] We should hold ourselves up to at least this high a standard.

Is the situation hopeless? I do not think so. If we are to have any hope of remediation, however, we must fully and consciously acknowledge the ubiquity and the pernicious powers of sanism and pretextuality, especially in death penalty cases. Once we come to grips with that, I believe there are at least four major remedial steps we can take to, at least partially, ameliorate the situation:

1. We must reexamine the Supreme Court's pallid effectiveness-of-counsel decision of *Strickland v. Washington*,[49] in an effort to finally ameliorate the situation—discussed extensively earlier in this work—of lawyers whose advocacy work falls far below any rational standard of adequacy.[50]

   There is no question that the banal standard that became the law in *Strickland v. Washington* is standardless, that it has given lower courts full impunity to close their eyes to shocking behavior by counsel in countless death cases, and that it has led to the execution of defendants with serious mental disabilities. Although the Supreme Court appeared to understand the gravity of its error two decades after *Strickland* in *Wiggins v. Smith*,[51] the inescapable fact is that the extent to which the death system is broken can, in large measure, be traced to *Strickland*. And it is a brokenness that has a disparate impact on defendants with mental disabilities (since it is far more likely that ineffective, inadequate counsel will not have "gotten" the extent of their clients' disabilities,[52] and will not have been able to effectively present evidence to the jury, both at the mitigation stage and during the trial itself).[53]

   I do not believe that the Supreme Court, as currently constituted, is likely to restructure the *Strickland* standard in the foreseeable future. This leaves, I believe, three potentially successful strategies to employ:

   - The drafting of federal legislation to "overrule" *Strickland*[54] and to create a new standard such as the one crafted by the Fifth Circuit that was vacated in the Supreme Court's opinion in that case: that counsel would be deemed ineffective if the petitioner "suffered actual and substantial detriment to the conduct of his defense," where such detriment was not harmless beyond a reasonable doubt.[55] Such a standard would make it far less likely that the inaction of ineffective counsel would lead to death.

- The adoption of state-by-state legislative strategies to define effectiveness of counsel in accordance with these values.[56]
- The adoption of state-by-state litigation strategies to seek the declaration—under state constitutional law[57]—that a more stringent effectiveness standard is constitutionally required.[58]

2. It is necessary to engage in a serious reevaluation of the roles of expert witnesses in testifying to "future dangerousness" in death penalty cases.

   The death of Dr. Grigson[59] has not ended the problem of expert witnesses testifying as to future dangerousness in death penalty cases in ways that run afoul of guidelines promulgated by the American Psychiatric Association and the American Psychological Association.[60] These groups have been largely silent about this ongoing scandal, one which has led to—and continues to lead to—a disproportionate number of persons with mental disabilities being executed.

   It is time for these organizations to enforce sanctions against such individuals, and for bar associations to similarly sanction prosecutors who continue to use such baseless, false, and potentially fatal testimony.[61]

3. It is time for a new set of standards and guidelines to be employed in cases involving a defendant's competency to be executed.

   Atkins and *Ford/Panetti* have failed to prevent the execution of persons with serious mental disabilities.[62] Although the American Bar Association's Supplemental Guidelines on competency of *counsel* have been engrafted into Supreme Court case law,[63] there are no parallel guidelines on determinations of competency of *defendants*. The pretextual refusal on the part of courts to actually and meaningfully implement these cases means that the bar will have to shoulder this burden in an effort to finally "reach" the Supreme Court in the same way that the Supplementary Guidelines "reached" the Court in *Wiggins*.[64]

4. It is essential that strategies be adopted that would lead to a greater role for international human rights in this entire inquiry (especially the recently ratified United Nations Convention on the Rights of Persons with Mental Disabilities),[65] including a "readers' guide" as to how this body of law can and should be used in domestic death penalty cases.

5. International human rights law is unanimous in its opposition to the death penalty. The United States is one of only three democracies in the world to sanction the death penalty,[66] and one of two that carries it out.[67] Although the United States has not yet ratified the Convention on the Rights of Persons with Disabilities,[68] the fact that we have ratified the Vienna Convention means that, in the period of time prior to Senate ratification, that treaty must be "interpreted in good faith . . . in light of its object and purpose."[69] What that means is, at the least, that the United States must end the application of the death penalty to persons with serious mental disabilities.

Let me turn now to the ways that the application of therapeutic jurisprudence principles may integrate all of these potential ameliorative strategies.

- I have written frequently about how TJ demands that lawyers representing persons with mental disabilities provide authentically effective advocacy-focused representation.[70] In death penalty cases, where the stakes are, intuitively, so much higher than in other cases, this need is even more pressing. As I wrote over fifteen years ago: "Any death penalty system that provides inadequate counsel and that, at least as a partial result of that inadequacy, fails to insure that mental disability evidence is adequately considered and contextualized by death penalty decision-makers, fails miserably from a therapeutic jurisprudence perspective."[71] The jettisoning of the *Strickland* standard would be a major TJ advance.
- A colleague and I have written elsewhere about the ethical principles that constrain forensic psychologists working in institutional and correctional settings, and how these principles are consonant with the tenets of therapeutic jurisprudence.[72] These principles apply equally to the question of the ethics of seeking and admitting into evidence the sort of baseless testimony often offered in death penalty cases. Scholars have written about the similarly baseless presumptions made about the dangerousness of persons with mental disabilities in *civil* commitment actions;[73] again, the stakes are so much higher—and deadlier—in a death penalty case, and testimony such as that offered regularly by Grigson and his acolytes fails any possible TJ test.
- There is already some literature that applies TJ principles to the question of determining competency to be executed, as it applies both to persons with mental retardation[74] and mental disabilities.[75] Scholarship such as this should be relied upon in the crafting of guidelines to ensure that this cohort of individuals will not be put to death in the future.

- Finally, the CRPD is a document that "resonates with TJ values."[76] For a decade, scholars have been urging a fusion of TJ principles and international human rights values.[77] This fusion has become all the more necessary and inevitable after ratification of the CRPD. Last year, in a book about the relationship between international human rights and mental disability law in general, I argued that scholars "need to carefully consider the TJ implications of [the pretextual] 'charade' [created by the presence of inadequate counsel] from an international human rights law perspective"[78] in death penalty cases.[79] Previously, I have argued that the CRPD demands cultural competence on the part of expert witnesses at all stages of the criminal process,[80] a demand that self-evidently includes death penalty cases. Death penalty decisionmakers must familiarize themselves with this convention.

Again, I believe that the concepts of sanism and pretextuality go a long way toward explaining why we continue to subject persons with serious mental disabilities to the death penalty, robbing them, the process, and all of us of the dignity that the legal system should demand. The Supreme Court's ambivalence about all of this is reflected in the incoherence of its case law. The task ahead of us is daunting, but I believe that the application of therapeutic jurisprudence principles, as discussed in this chapter, is our best hope for ameliorating the current state of affairs.

I subtitled this book "The Shame of the States" to call attention to the ways that our legal, political, and social systems are complicit—at all levels—in the ways that the death penalty system mistreats persons with serious mental disabilities. I hope that if the corrective steps suggested in this volume are taken seriously and adopted, we will finally be able to cleanse ourselves of the stain of this shame.

Notes

PREFACE

1. State v. Funicello, 286 A.2d 55 (N.J. 1972). The last execution in New Jersey had taken place in 1963. See Lyn Suzanne Entzeroth, *The End of the Beginning: The Politics of Death and the American Death Penalty Regime in the Twenty-First Century*, 90 OR. L. REV. 797, 827 (2012).

2. 408 U.S. 238 (1972).

3. 428 U.S. 153 (1976).

4. See Stephen F. Smith, *The Supreme Court and the Politics of Death*, 94 VA. L. REV. 283, 298 n. 54 (2008) ("Even during the nationwide stampede to reinstate the death penalty after *Furman*, New Jersey was very slow to act"). Between the time of reenactment and the penalty's abolition in 2007, sixty individuals were sentenced to death, fifty-two of those individuals had their sentences reversed by the courts, and no one was executed. See Entzeroth, *supra* note 1, at 827. For a careful study of this entire period of time, see Jessica Henry, *New Jersey's Road to Abolition*, 29 JUST. SYS. J. 408 (2008).

5. *Hearings on S. 1479 before the N.J. Senate Judiciary Comm.* 13 (1984) (testimony of Joseph H. Rodriguez).

6. Joseph H. Rodriguez, Michael L. Perlin, & John M. Apicella, *Proportionality Review in New Jersey: An Indispensable Safeguard in the Capital Sentencing Process*, 15 RUTGERS L. J. 399 (1984).

7. 466 U.S. 668 (1984) (establishing effectiveness-of-counsel standard; see *infra* chapter 10).

8. 470 U.S. 68 (1985).

9. *Id.* at 83. In this case, we represented *amicus* Coalition for the Fundamental Rights and Equality of Ex-Patients.

10. See e.g., Michael L. Perlin, *The Supreme Court, the Mentally Disabled Criminal Defendant, Psychiatric Testimony in Death Penalty Cases, and the Power of Symbolism: Dulling the Ake in Barefoot's Achilles Heel*, 3 N.Y. L. SCH. HUMAN RTS. ANN. 91 (1985) (Perlin, *Barefoot and Ake*); Michael L. Perlin, *The Supreme Court, the Mentally Disabled Criminal Defendant, and Symbolic Values: Random Decisions, Hidden Rationales, or Doctrinal Abyss?* 29 ARIZ. L. REV. 1 (1987); Michael L. Perlin, *The Sanist Lives of Jurors in Death Penalty Cases: The Puzzling Role of Mitigating Mental Disability Evidence*, 8 NOTRE DAME J. L., ETHICS & PUB. POL. 239 (1994); Michael L. Perlin, *"The Executioner's Face Is Always Well-Hidden": The Role of Counsel and the Courts in Determining Who Dies*, 41 N.Y. L. SCH. L. REV. 201 (1996) (Perlin, *Executioner's Face*); Michael

L. Perlin, *"Life Is In Mirrors, Death Disappears": Giving Life to* Atkins, 33 N. Mex. L. Rev. 315 (2003); Michael L. Perlin, Mental Disability Law: Civil and Criminal (2d ed. 2002).

11. Stephen Bright, *Death by Lottery—Procedural Bar of Constitutional Claims in Capital Cases Due to Inadequate Representation of Indigent Defendants*, 92 W. Va. L. Rev. 679, 695 (1990).

12. David L. Bazelon, *The Defective Assistance of Counsel*, 42 U. Cin. L. Rev. 1, 2 (1973).

13. "Sanism" is an irrational prejudice of the same quality and character of other irrational prejudices that cause (and are reflected in) prevailing social attitudes of racism, sexism, homophobia, and ethnic bigotry. See *infra* chapter 2; see e.g., Michael L. Perlin, *On "Sanism,"* 46 SMU L. Rev. 373 (1992); Michael L. Perlin, The Hidden Prejudice: Mental Disability on Trial (2000).

14. "Pretextuality" means that courts regularly accept (either implicitly or explicitly) testimonial dishonesty, countenance liberty deprivations in disingenuous ways that bear little or no relationship to case law or to statutes, and engage similarly in dishonest (and frequently meretricious) decision making, specifically where witnesses, especially expert witnesses, show a "high propensity to purposely distort their testimony in order to achieve desired ends." Michael L. Perlin, *Pretexts and Mental Disability Law: The Case of Competency*, 47 U. Miami L. Rev. 625, 627 (1993), quoting Charles Sevila, *The Exclusionary Rule and Police Perjury*, 11 San Diego L. Rev. 839, 840 (1974); Perlin, *supra* note 13, at 60–77; see generally *infra* chapter 2.

15. See e.g., Michael L Perlin, *"Baby, Look Inside Your Mirror": The Legal Profession's Willful and Sanist Blindness to Lawyers with Mental Disabilities*, 69 U. Pitt. L. Rev. 589, 602–3 (2008); Michael L. Perlin, *"Half-Wracked Prejudice Leaped Forth": Sanism, Pretextuality, and Why and How Mental Disability Law Developed as It Did*, 10 J. Contemp. Leg. Iss. 3, 18 (1999).

16. Perlin, *Executioner's Face, supra* note 10, at 227.

17. "Therapeutic jurisprudence" presents a new model for assessing the impact of case law and legislation, recognizing that, as a therapeutic agent, the law can have therapeutic or anti-therapeutic consequences. See *infra* chapter 2; see e.g., Michael L. Perlin, *"His Brain Has Been Mismanaged with Great Skill": How Will Jurors Respond to Neuroimaging Testimony in Insanity Defense Cases?*, 42 Akron L. Rev. 885, 912 (2009). The ultimate aim of therapeutic jurisprudence is to determine whether legal rules, procedures, and lawyer roles can or should be reshaped to enhance their therapeutic potential while not subordinating due process principles. See e.g., Michael L. Perlin, *"And My Best Friend, My Doctor, Won't Even Say What It Is I've Got": The Role and Significance of Counsel in Right to Refuse Treatment Cases*, 42 San Diego L. Rev. 735 (2005).

18. See Perlin, *supra* note 13, at 301; see generally, Michael L. Perlin, et al., *Therapeutic Jurisprudence and the Civil Rights of Institutionalized Mentally Disabled Persons: Hopeless Oxymoron or Path to Redemption?* 1 Psychol. Pub. Pol'y & L. 80 (1995).

19. See *infra* chapter 2.

20. See *infra* chapter 11; see generally, Michael L. Perlin, International Human Rights and Mental Disability Law: When the Silenced Are Heard (2011).

21. See e.g., Michael L. Perlin, *"A Change Is Gonna Come": The Implications of the United Nations Convention on the Rights of Persons with Disabilities for the Domestic Practice of Constitutional Mental Disability Law*, 29 No. Ill. U. L. Rev. 483 (2009); Perlin, *supra* note 20. The United States is a signatory to the Convention but has not yet ratified it. At the time of the submission of this manuscript, President Obama has just sent the Convention to the Senate for ratification. See e.g., http://www.disabilityscoop.com/2012/05/18/obama-urges-senate-treaty/15654 (Convention submitted May 17, 2012).

22. See *infra* chapter 2.

23. See sources cited *supra* at note 10; see also, Michael L. Perlin, *"Good and Bad, I Defined These Terms, Quite Clear No Doubt Somehow": Neuroimaging and Competency to Be Executed after* Panetti, 28 Behav. Sci. & L. 621 (2010); Michael L. Perlin, *"And I See Through Your Brain": Access to Experts, Competency to Consent, and the Impact of Antipsychotic Medications in Neuroimaging Cases in the Criminal Trial Process*, 2009 Stanford Technol. L. J. 1.

24. See Perlin, *Barefoot and Ake, supra* note 10.

25. I would not be telling the full story if I did not share how proud I am that a case that Alex worked on as a law student—when he was interning with the Mid-Atlantic Innocence Project—just resulted in a death penalty exoneration. See Hash v. Johnson, 2012 WL 628266 (W.D. Va. 2012).

CHAPTER 1

1. For a valuable overview of constitutional developments from Furman v. Georgia, 408 U.S. 238 (1972) (striking down the death penalty as applied as unconstitutional), to Gregg v. Georgia, 428 U.S. 153 (1976) (death penalty did not per se violate the Constitution), to the modern day, see LINDA E. CARTER, ELLEN S. KREITZBERG, & SCOTT W. HOWE, UNDERSTANDING CAPITAL PUNISHMENT LAW 21–33 (2d ed. 2008). For compendia of death penalty literature, see e.g., *Death Penalty Bibliography* (http://walker.cqpress.com/bib5.asp), and *Books on the Death Penalty* (http://deathpenaltyinfo.org/books-death-penalty).

2. Professor Christopher Slobogin's excellent book, MINDING JUSTICE: LAWS THAT DEPRIVE PEOPLE WITH MENTAL DISABILITY OF LIFE AND LIBERTY (2006) includes several chapters on death penalty issues in this context, but has a wider scope of focus. There are also some important works on the questions of the death penalty eligibility of persons with mental retardation (see *infra* chapter 5); see EMILY FABRYCKI REED, THE PENRY PENALTY: CAPITAL PUNISHMENT AND OFFENDERS WITH MENTAL RETARDATION (1993); JAMIE FELLNER, ROSA EHRENREICH, & MICHELLE CALDERA, BEYOND REASON: THE DEATH PENALTY AND OFFENDERS WITH MENTAL RETARDATION (2001), and of persons with serious mental illness (see *infra* chapter 6), see KENT S. MILLER & MICHAEL L. RADELET, EXECUTING THE MENTALLY ILL: THE CRIMINAL JUSTICE SYSTEM AND THE CASE OF ALVIN FORD (1993), but these are just two of many topics that are discussed in this volume.

Among the most important articles focusing on the full range of issues considered here are Bruce J. Winick, *The Supreme Court's Evolving Death Penalty Jurisprudence: Severe Mental Illness as the Next Frontier*, 50 B.C. L. REV. 785 (2009), and Christopher Slobogin, *Mental Illness and the Death Penalty*, 1 CAL. CRIM. L. REV. 3 (2000).

3. See e.g., Carol S. Steiker & Jordan M. Steiker, *Sober Second Thoughts: Reflections on Two Decades of Constitutional Regulation of Capital Punishment*, 109 HARV. L. REV. 355, 359 (1995), and *id.* n. 9, citing, inter alia, REED, *supra* note 2, at 39 (reporting that while persons with mental retardation make up roughly 2 to 3 percent of the population and do not commit crimes or murders at higher rates than others, they constitute an estimated 12 to 20 percent of those under death sentences).

The phrase "intellectual disability" is far preferred to the pejorative and dated phrase "mental retardation." Reluctantly, I sometimes use the latter here as its use persists both in statutory and case law.

4. Michael L. Perlin, *"Life Is in Mirrors, Death Disappears": Giving Life to* Atkins, 33 N.M. L. Rev. 315 (2003); Christopher Slobogin, *What* Atkins *Could Mean for People with Mental Illness*, 33 N.M. L. REV. 293 (2003).

5. Julie D. Cantor, *Of Pills and Needles: Involuntarily Medicating the Psychotic Inmate When Execution Looms*, 2 IND. HEALTH L. REV. 119 (2005) (40–70 percent). See e.g., James M. Doyle, *The Lawyers' Art: "Representation" in Capital Cases*, 8 YALE J. L. & HUMAN, 417, 442 (1996) (50 percent). Notes Cantor: "Given the psychological pressure of waiting for one's execution day to arrive coupled with the miserable conditions in many prisons, it is somewhat astonishing that the fraction of psychotic inmates does not approach one hundred percent"; *Id.* at 126.

6. http://www.deathpenalty.org/article.php?id=53 (accessed May 22, 2012).

7. Welsh S. White, *Effective Assistance of Counsel in Capital Cases: The Evolving Standard of Care*, 1993 U. ILL. L. REV. 323, 339.

8. Mark D. Cunningham & Mark P. Vigen, *Death Row Inmate Characteristics, Adjustment, and Confinement: A Critical Review of the Literature*, 20 BEHAV. SCI. & L. 191, 193, 201 (2002).

9. See *infra* chapters 5 & 6.

10. Seventeen such cases are discussed on the Death Penalty Information Center's website. See http://deathpenaltyinfo.org/mental-illness-and-death-penalty#executions (list "not exhaustive"). Amnesty International estimates that 10 percent of those executed in the United States over the past three decades had mental disabilities. See http://www.amnesty.org/en/library/info/AMR51/003/2006 (accessed May 22, 2012).

11. See *infra* chapters 5 & 6.

12. See http://www.aclu.org/capital-punishment/mentally-retarded-death-row-exonerations.

13. Harold Hongju Koh, *Different But Equal: The Human Rights of Persons with Intellectual Disabilities*, 63 MD. L. REV. 1, 7 (2004).

14. http://www.deathpenaltyinfo.org/documents/122A.pdf (accessed May 22, 2012). See also position statement of Mental Health America, calling upon states to suspend use of the death penalty "until more just, accurate and systematic ways of . . . considering a defendant's mental status are developed." Mental Health America, *Position Statement 54: Death Penalty and People with Mental Illness*, accessible at http://nhma.org/go/position-statements/54 (accessed May 22, 2012).

15. See Dorean M. Koenig, *Mentally Ill Defendants: Systematic Bias in Capital Cases*, 28 ABA HUM. RTS. MAG. 10 (Summer 2001).

16. TENN. CODE ANN. § 39-13-209(c)(3) (2009). Among the commission's main recommendations were the need to train "all actors in the criminal justice system . . . to recognize mental retardation and mental retardation in capital defendants and death row inmates," AMERICAN BAR ASSOCIATION DEATH PENALTY MORATORIUM IMPLEMENTATION PROJECT, EVALUATING FAIRNESS AND ACCURACY IN STATE DEATH PENALTY SYSTEMS: THE TENNESSEE DEATH PENALTY ASSESSMENT REPORT 311, 321 (2007), and the creation of policies to ensure that such persons are represented by attorneys who "fully realize the significance of their clients' mental limitations," *id.* at 312, and mental disabilities, *id.* at 323. For a discussion of this commission, see William Redick, *Is Tennessee Going to Fix Its Death Penalty?* 45 TENN. B. J. 12 (Sept. 2009).

17. See e.g., Leigh B. Bienen, *Capital Punishment in Illinois in the Aftermath of the Ryan Commutations: Reforms, Economic Realities, and a New Saliency for Issues of Cost*, 100 J. CRIM. L. & CRIMINOLOGY 1301, 1354 (2010); see also, Robert J. Smith, *The Geography of the Death Penalty and Its Ramifications*, 92 B.U. L. REV. 227 (2012).

18. See Atkins v. Virginia, 536 U.S. 304 (2002); see generally, Perlin, *supra* note 4.

19. Panetti v. Quarterman, 551 U.S. 930 (2007); see generally, Michael L. Perlin, *"Good and Bad, I Defined These Terms, Quite Clear No Doubt Somehow": Neuroimaging and Competency to Be Executed after Panetti*, 28 BEHAV. SCI. & L. 621 (2010).

20. Michael L. Perlin, *"The Executioner's Face Is Always Well-Hidden": The Role of Counsel and the Courts in Determining Who Dies*, 41 N.Y. L. SCH. L. REV. 201 (1996).

21. See *infra* chapter 4. See generally, Valerie McClain, Elliot Atkins, & Michael L. Perlin, *"Oh, Stop That Cursed Jury": The Role of the Forensic Psychologist in the Mitigation Phase of the Death Penalty Trial*, in HANDBOOK ON FORENSIC PSYCHOLOGY (Mark Goldstein, ed. 2012) (in press).

22. *Id.*

23. Liliana Lyra Jubilut, *Death Penalty and Mental Illness: The Challenge of Reconciling Human Rights, Criminal Law, and Psychiatric Standards*, 6 SEATTLE J. SOC. JUST. 353, 377 (2007).

24. See Michael L. Perlin, *Psychodynamics and the Insanity Defense: "Ordinary Common Sense" and Heuristic Reasoning*, 69 NEB. L. REV. 3, 61–69 (1990). "[O]rdinary common sense" refers to a "self-referential and non-reflective" way of constructing the world: "I see it that way, therefore everyone sees it that way; I see it that way, therefore that's the way it is."

25. See *infra* chapter 3.

26. See *infra* chapter 2; see generally, Michael L. Perlin, *The Sanist Lives of Jurors in Death Penalty Cases: The Puzzling Role of "Mitigating" Mental Disability Evidence*, 8 NOTRE DAME J. L. ETHICS & PUB. POL'Y 239 (1994). On sanism generally, see Michael L. Perlin, THE HIDDEN PREJUDICE: MENTAL DISABILITY ON TRIAL (2000).

27. See *infra* chapter 9; see generally, Welsh White, *Curbing Prosecutorial Misconduct in Capital Cases: Imposing Prohibitions on Improper Penalty Trial Arguments*, 39 AM. CRIM. L. REV. 1147 (2002).

28. Michael L. Perlin, *Morality and Pretextuality, Psychiatry and Law: Of "Ordinary Common Sense," Heuristic Reasoning, and Cognitive Dissonance*, 19 BULL. AM. ACAD. PSYCHIATRY & L. 131, 133 (1991).

29. See *infra* chapter 2; see generally, Michael L. Perlin, *"Half-Wracked Prejudice Leaped Forth": Sanism, Pretextuality, and Why and How Mental Disability Law Developed as It Did*, 10 J. CONTEMP. LEGAL ISSUES 3 (1999).

30. J.C. Phelan & B.G. Link, *The Growing Belief That People with Mental Illnesses Are Violent: The Role of the Dangerousness Criterion for Civil Commitment*, 33 SOC. PSYCHIATRY & PSYCHIATRIC EPIDEMIOLOGY S7 (1998); Amy C. Watson et al., *From Whence Comes Mental Illness Stigma?*, 49 INT'L J. SOC. PSYCHIATRY 142 (2003); Fred Markowitz, *Mental Illness, Crime, and Violence: Risk, Context, and Social Control*, 16 AGGRESSION AND VIOLENT BEHAVIOR 36 (2011); Virginia Hiday & Padraic Burns, *Mental Illness and the Criminal Justice System*, in Teresa L. Scheid & Tony N. Brown, A HANDBOOK FOR THE STUDY OF MENTAL HEALTH: SOCIAL CONTEXTS, THEORIES, AND SYSTEMS 478 (2d ed. 2010).

31. See *infra* chapter 11.

32. See *infra* chapter 2.

33. See *id.*

34. See e.g., Kevin M. Cremin et al., *Ensuring a Fair Hearing for Litigants with Mental Illnesses: The Law and Psychology of Capacity, Admissibility, and Credibility Assessments in Civil Proceedings*, 17 J. L. & POL'Y 455 (2009).

35. See generally, John H. Blume & Sheri Lynn Johnson, *Killing the Non-Willing:* Atkins, *the Volitionally Incapacitated and the Death Penalty*, 55 S.C. L. REV. 93, 122 n. 157 (2003), (on how trial proceedings "render capital punishment unfair to the mentally ill," quoting Am. Psychological Ass'n, RESOLUTION ON THE DEATH PENALTY IN THE UNITED STATES (Aug. 2001), available at http://www.apa.org/pi/deathpenalty.html).

36. See Ronald J. Tabak, *Foreward*, in THE FUTURE OF AMERICA'S DEATH PENALTY: AN AGENDA FOR THE NEXT GENERATION OF CAPITAL PUNISHMENT RESEARCH, xvii, xix (Charles S. Lanier et al., eds. 2009) (THE FUTURE OF AMERICA'S DEATH PENALTY), identifying issues related to mental illness and mental retardation as ones in which there is a "significant need" for more scholarly attention.

37. The Supreme Court continues to be vexed by these issues. Just before the manuscript for this book was submitted to the publisher, the Supreme Court granted *certiorari* in two related cases on the questions of whether capital prisoners possess a "right to competence" in federal habeas proceeding (Tibbals v. Carter, 2012 WL 895971 (2012)) and whether federal habeas legislation entitles a death row inmate to stay the federal habeas proceedings he initiated if he is not competent to assist counsel (Ryan v. Gonzales, 2012 WL 895970 (2012)). See generally, C. Lee Harrington, *Mental Competence and End-of-Life Decision Making: Death Row Volunteering and Euthanasia*, 29 J. HEALTH POL. POL'Y & L. 1109 (2004).

38. *See* Gregg v. Georgia, 428 U.S. 153 (1975).

39. See *infra* text accompanying notes 55–92.

40. See *infra* chapter 2.

41. See *infra* chapter 3.

42. See *infra* chapter 4.

43. See *infra* chapter 5.

44. See *infra* chapter 6.
45. See *infra* chapter 7.
46. See *infra* chapter 8.
47. See *infra* chapter 9.
48. See *id.*
49. See *id.*
50. See *infra* chapter 10.
51. See *infra* chapter 11.
52. 466 U.S. 668 (1984).
53. David L. Bazelon, *The Defective Assistance of Counsel*, 42 U. CIN. L. REV. 1, 2 (1973). I have served on occasion as an expert witness in appeals of death penalty cases in which ineffectiveness of trial counsel has been alleged.
54. G.A. Res. A/61/106 (2006).
55. ALBERT DEUTSCH, THE SHAME OF THE STATES (1948).
56. *Id.* at 15-16.
57. Richard Dieter, *The Future of Innocence*, in THE FUTURE OF AMERICA'S DEATH PENALTY, *supra* note 36, at 225, 225.
58. Actual innocence is, of course, also a problem in death penalty administration in cases in which mental disability is not a central issue. See e.g., Cooper v. Brown, 565 F.3d 581, 581 (9th Cir. 2009), *cert. denied*, Cooper v. Ayers, 130 S.Ct. 749 (2009) (denying petition for rehearing and petition for rehearing en banc over dissenting opinions of several judges including William A. Fletcher, who wrote, "The State of California may be about to execute an innocent man"), as discussed in Elisabeth Semel, *The Honorable John Paul Stevens: Reflections on Justice John Paul Stevens's Concurring Opinion in* Baze v. Rees*: A Fifth Gregg Justice Renounces Capital Punishment*, 43 U.C. DAVIS L. REV. 783, 870 n. 415 (2010). See generally, KENNETH WILLIAMS, MOST DESERVING OF DEATH? AN ANALYSIS OF THE SUPREME COURT'S DEATH PENALTY JURISPRUDENCE 59–94 (2012).
59. http://www.exonerate.org/about-2/causes-of-wrongful-convictions/false-confessions (accessed May 22, 2012). On the attitudes of the public in general to wrongful convictions, see Marvin Zalman, Matthew Larson, & Brad Smith, *Citizens' Attitudes toward Wrongful Convictions*, 37 CRIM. JUST. REV. 51 (2012) (survey respondents now believe wrongful convictions occur frequently enough to justify major criminal justice system reform).
60. Edward A. Polloway et al., *Special Challenges for Persons with Disabilities in the Criminal Justice System: Introduction to the Special Issue*, 19 EXCEPTIONALITY 211, 214–17 (2011).
61. See generally, Richard Leo & Richard Ofshe, *The Consequences of False Confessions: Deprivations of Liberty and Miscarriages of Justice in the Age of Psychological Interrogation*, 88 J. CRIM. L. & CRIMINOLOGY 429 (1998). For excellent overviews, see I. Bruce Frumkin, *Psychological Evaluation in Miranda Waiver and Confession Cases*, in CLINICAL NEUROPSYCHOLOGY IN THE CRIMINAL FORENSIC CONTEXT 135 (R.L. Denney & J.P. Sullivan, eds. 2008); I. Bruce Frumkin, *Evaluations of Competency to Waive Miranda Rights and Coerced or False Confessions: Common Pitfalls in Expert Testimony*, in POLICE INTERROGATIONS AND FALSE CONFESSIONS: CURRENT RESEARCH, PRACTICE, AND POLICY 191 (G. Lassiter & C. Meissner, eds. 2010).
62. William C. Follette, Deborah Davis, & Richard Leo, *Mental Health Status and Vulnerability to Police Interrogation Tactics*, 22 CRIM. JUST. 42, 43 (2007).
63. *Id.*
64. *Id.* at 47.
65. Caroline Everington & Solomon M. Fulero, *Competence to Confess: Measuring Understanding and Suggestibility of Defendants with Mental Retardation*, 37 MENTAL RETARDATION 212 (1999) (finding significant negative correlations between comprehension and suggestibility measures).
66. On how mental retardation increases the likelihood of conviction of and the imposition of the death penalty on a factually innocent criminal defendant, see Aimee Borromeo, *Mental Retardation and the Death Penalty*, 3 LOY. J. PUB. INT. L. 175, 189 (2002), citing to Brief for

Amici, Physicians for Human Rights, McCarver v. North Carolina, 2001 WL 648605; John H. Blume, Sheri L. Johnson, & Susan E. Millor, *Convicting Lennie: Mental Retardation, Wrongful Convictions, and the Right to a Fair Trial*, 56 N.Y. L. SCH. L. REV. 943, 967 (2011–2012) (discussing the "*heightened* risk of [persons with mental retardation] being found guilty of crimes they did not commit") (emphasis in original).

67. Steven A. Krieger, *Why Our Justice System Convicts Innocent People, and the Challenges Faced by Innocence Projects Trying to Exonerate Them*, 14 NEW CRIM. L. REV. 333, 392–93 (2011).

68. See Cynthia E. Jones, *The Right Remedy for the Wrongly Convicted: Judicial Sanctions for Destruction of DNA Evidence*, 77 FORDHAM L. REV. 2893, 2938 n. 255 (2009).

69. See generally, www.aclu.org/print/capital-punishment/mentally-retarded-death-penalty.

70. As of March 13, 2012, there have been 266 exonerations. See http://www.exonerate.org/about-2/causes-of-wrongful-convictions.

71. Tracey Maclin, *A Criminal Procedure Regime Based on Instrumental Values*, 22 CONST. COMMENT. 197, 230 n. 68 (2005).

72. Allison D. Redlich, *Comparing True and False Confessions among Persons with Serious Mental Illness*, 17 PSYCHOL. PUB. POL'Y & L. 394, 398 (2011).

73. Gisli Gudjonsson et al., *Custodial Interrogation, False Confession, and Individual Differences: A National Study among Icelandic Youth*, 41 PERSONALITY & INDIVIDUAL DIFFERENCES 49 (2006); Gisli Gudjonsson et al., *Confessions and Denials and the Relationship with Personality*, 9 LEG. & CRIMINOL. PSYCHOLOGY 121 (2004); Gisli Gudjonsson et al., *Interrogation and False Confession among Adolescents in Seven European Countries: What Background and Psychological Variables Best Discriminate Between False Confessors and Non-False Confessors?* 15 PSYCHOL. CRIME & L. 711 (2009).

74. Atkins v. Virginia, 536 U.S. 304, 318–19 (2002). See generally *infra* chapter 5.

75. See e.g., www.exonerate.org; www.innocenceprojectmidwest.org; www.ip-no.org; www.falseconfessions.org. On the array of factors that bear significant statistical correlation to wrongful convictions, see Talia Harmon, *Predictors of Miscarriages of Justice in Capital Cases*, 18 JUST. Q. 949 (2001), and Talia Harmon & William Lofquist, *Too Late for Luck: A Comparison on Post-Furman Exonerations and Executions of the Innocent*, 51 CRIME & DELINQ. 498 (2005).

76. *Atkins*, 536 U.S. at 321.

77. Saul Kassin et al., *Police-Induced Confessions: Risk Factors and Recommendations*, 34 LAW & HUM. BEHAV. 3, 8 (2010).

78. *Id.* at 9.

79. Steven A. Drizin & Richard A. Leo, *The Problem of False Confessions in the Post-DNA World*, 82 N.C. L. REV. 891, 933–43 (2004).

80. Christopher Sherrin, *Guilty Pleas from the Innocent*, 30 WINDSOR REV. LEGAL & SOC. ISSUES 1, 13 n. 62 (2011).

81. Samuel Gross et al., *Exonerations in the United States 1989 through 2003*, 95 J. CRIM. L. & CRIMINOLOGY 523, 535 (2005).

82. Brandon L. Garrett, *Judging Innocence*, 108 COLUM. L. REV. 55, 119 (2008); Gross et al., *supra* note 81, at 535.

83. *Atkins*, 536 U.S. at 321. See generally, *infra* chapter 5.

84. *Id.* at 318–19, 320–21.

85. 138 P.3d 549 (Okla. Crim. App. 2006).

86. Compare, Michael L. Perlin, *"You Have Discussed Lepers and Crooks": Sanism in Clinical Teaching*, 9 CLINICAL L. REV. 683, 722 (2003) ("like other lawyers, clinical students often complain, in referring to their clients with mental disabilities, that 'the clients could try harder'").

87. *Howell*, 138 P.3d at 563.

88. 2006 Tenn. Crim. App. LEXIS 454 (June 8, 2006), discussed at 232 S.W.3d 1, 12, *appeal after remand*, 232 S.W.3d 1 (Tenn. 2007); see Pramila A. Kamath, *Blinded by the Bright-Line: Problems with Strict Construction of the Criteria for Death Penalty Exemption on the Basis of Mental Retardation—State v. Strode, 232 S.W.3d 1 (Tenn. 2007)*, 77 U. CIN. L. REV. 321 (2008).

89. *Strode*, 2006 Tenn. Crim. App. LEXIS at *11.

90. 135 P.3d 696 (Ariz. 2006), *cert. denied*, 550 U.S. 937 (2007).

91. *Id.* at 702.

92. *Atkins*, 536 U.S. at 321.

93. Blume, Johnson, & Millor, *supra* note 66, at 957, quoting Sarah F. Haavik & Karl A. Menninger II, Sexuality, Law, and the Developmentally Disabled Person 152 (1981).

94. Blume, Johnson, & Millor, *supra* note 66, at 957.

95. *Id.* at 958.

96. On the related question of how accurate assessments of competency to be executed are necessary to protect defendants who are actually innocent, see Christopher Seeds, *The Afterlife of Ford and Panetti: Execution Competence and the Capacity to Assist Counsel*, 53 St. Louis U. L. J. 309, 345 (2009); see generally, *infra* chapter 6.

CHAPTER 2

1. See e.g., Michael L. Perlin et al., Competence in the Law: From Legal Theory to Clinical Application (2008); Michael L. Perlin, The Jurisprudence of the Insanity Defense (1994); Michael L. Perlin, The Hidden Prejudice: Mental Disability on trial (2000) (Perlin, The Hidden Prejudice).

2. See e.g., Michael L. Perlin, *The Sanist Lives of Jurors in Death Penalty Cases: The Puzzling Role of Mitigating Mental Disability Evidence*, 8 Notre Dame J. L., Ethics & Pub. Pol. 239 (1994) (Perlin, *Sanist Lives*); Michael L. Perlin, *"Good and Bad, I Defined These Terms, Quite Clear No Doubt Somehow": Neuroimaging and Competency to Be Executed after* Panetti, 28 Behav. Sci. & L. 621 (2010); Michael L. Perlin, *"The Executioner's Face Is Always Well-Hidden": The Role of Counsel and the Courts in Determining Who Dies*, 41 N.Y. L. Sch. L. Rev. 201 (1996) (Perlin, *Executioner's Face*); Michael L. Perlin, *"Life Is in Mirrors, Death Disappears": Giving Life to* Atkins, 33 N. Mex. L. Rev. 315 (2003) (Perlin, *Death Disappears*); Michael L. Perlin, *The Supreme Court, the Mentally Disabled Criminal Defendant, Psychiatric Testimony in Death Penalty Cases, and the Power of Symbolism: Dulling the* Ake *in* Barefoot's *Achilles Heel*, 3 N.Y. L. Sch. Human Rts. Ann. 91 (1985).

3. See e.g., Michael L. Perlin, *"What's Good Is Bad, What's Bad Is Good, You'll Find Out When You Reach the Top, You're on the Bottom": Are the Americans with Disabilities Act (and Olmstead v. L.C.) Anything More than "Idiot Wind"?*, 35 U. Mich. J. L. Ref. 235, 236–37 (2001–2002); see generally, Michael L. Perlin, *"Half-Wracked Prejudice Leaped Forth": Sanism, Pretextuality, and Why and How Mental Disability Law Developed as It Did*, 10 J. Contemp. Legal Issues 3 (1999) (Perlin, *Half-Wracked*); Michael L. Perlin, *"Where the Winds Hit Heavy on the Borderline": Mental Disability Law, Theory and Practice, "Us" and "Them,"* 31 Loy. L.A. L. Rev. 775 (1998) (Perlin, *Borderline*).

4. See e.g., Michael L. Perlin, *"Dignity Was the First to Leave": Godinez v. Moran, Colin Ferguson, and the Trial of Mentally Disabled Criminal Defendants*, 14 Behav. Sci. & L. 61 (1996) (Perlin, *Dignity*); Michael L. Perlin, International Human Rights and Mental Disability Law: When the Silenced Are Heard (2011); Michael L. Perlin, *A Law of Healing*, 68 U. Cin. L. Rev. 407 (2000) (Perlin, *Healing*).

5. See e.g., Michael L. Perlin, *"Too Stubborn to Ever Be Governed by Enforced Insanity": Some Therapeutic Jurisprudence Dilemmas in the Representation of Criminal Defendants in Incompetency and Insanity Cases*, 33 Int'l J. L. & Psychiatry 475 (2010); Astrid Birgden & Michael L. Perlin, *"Tolling for the Luckless, the Abandoned and Forsaked": Community Safety, Therapeutic Jurisprudence and International Human Rights Law as Applied to Prisoners and Detainees*, 13 Leg. & Criminol. Psychology 231 (2008).

6. Michael L. Perlin, *"Things Have Changed": Looking at Non-institutional Mental Disability Law through the Sanism Filter*, 46 N.Y. L. Sch. L. Rev. 535, 544 (2003).

7. See e.g., Michael L. Perlin, *Therapeutic Jurisprudence: Understanding the Sanist and Pretextual Bases of Mental Disability Law*, 20 N. ENG. J. CRIM. & CIV. CONFINEMENT 369 (1994).

8. See generally, 1 MICHAEL L. PERLIN, MENTAL DISABILITY LAW: CIVIL AND CRIMINAL § 2D-2, at 523–28 (2d ed. 1998).

9. The classic treatment is G. W. ALLPORT, THE NATURE OF PREJUDICE (1954). For an important alternative perspective, see E. YOUNG-BRUEHL, THE ANATOMY OF PREJUDICES (1996). See generally Michael L. Perlin, *On "Sanism*," 46 SMU L. REV. 373 (1992) (Perlin, *Sanism*); PERLIN, THE HIDDEN PREJUDICE, *supra* note 1, at xvii–xvix; Perlin, *Half-Wracked, supra* note 3.)

10. The phrase "sanism" was most likely coined by Dr. Morton Birnbaum. Morton Birnbaum, *The Right to Treatment: Some Comments on Its Development*, in MEDICAL, MORAL AND LEGAL ISSUES IN HEALTH CARE 97, 106–7 (F. J. Ayd, ed. 1974). See Koe v. Califano, 573 F.2d 761, 764 (2d Cir. 1978); Michael L. Perlin, *Competency, Deinstitutionalization, and Homelessness*, 28 HOUS. L. REV. 63, 92–93 (1991) (discussing Birnbaum's insights).

11. See, e.g., Michael L. Perlin, *Morality and Pretextuality, Psychiatry and Law: Of "Ordinary Common Sense," Heuristic Reasoning, and Cognitive Dissonance*, 19 BULL. AM. ACAD. PSYCHIATRY & L. 131 (1991) (Perlin, *Morality*); Perlin, *Sanism, supra* note 9; Michael L. Perlin, *Pretexts and Mental Disability Law: The Case of Competency*, 47 U. MIAMI L. REV. 625 (1993) (Perlin, *Pretexts*); Michael L. Perlin & Deborah A. Dorfman, *Sanism, Social Science, and the Development of Mental Disability Law Jurisprudence*, 11 BEHAV. SCI. & L. 47 (1993); Perlin, *Sanist Lives, supra* note 2; Michael L. Perlin, *"They're an Illusion to Me Now": Forensic Ethics, Sanism and Pretextuality*, in PSYCHOLOGY, CRIME AND LAW: BRIDGING THE GAP 239 (David Canter & Rita Zukauskien, eds. 2008).

12. See generally, MARTHA MINOW, MAKING ALL THE DIFFERENCE: INCLUSION, EXCLUSION, AND AMERICAN LAW (1990); SANDER GILMAN, DIFFERENCE AND PATHOLOGY: STEREOTYPES OF SEXUALITY, RACE AND MADNESS (1985).

13. See e.g., Joseph Goldstein & Jay Katz, *Abolish the "Insanity Defense"—Why Not?*, 72 YALE L. J. 853, 868–69 (1963); Perlin, *supra* note 10, at 108 (on society's fears *of* mentally disabled persons), and *id.* at 93 n. 174 ("[W]hile race and sex are immutable, we all *can* become mentally ill, homeless, or both. Perhaps this illuminates the level of virulence we experience here") (emphasis in original). On the way that public fears about the purported link between mental illness and dangerousness "drive the formal laws and policies governing mental disability jurisprudence," see John Monahan, *Mental Disorder and Violent Behavior: Perceptions and Evidence*, 47 AM. PSYCHOLOGIST 511 (1992); see also, Renee Binder, *Are the Mentally Ill Dangerous?*, 27 J. AM. ACAD. PSYCHIATRY & L. 189 (1999).

14. But see, Michael L. Perlin, *Psychodynamics and the Insanity Defense: "Ordinary Common Sense" and Heuristic Reasoning*, 69 NEB. L. REV. 3 (1990) (Perlin, *"Ordinary Common Sense"*); Perlin, *Unpacking the Myths: The Symbolism Mythology of Insanity Defense Jurisprudence*, 40 CASE W. RES. L. REV. 599 (1989–1990) (Perlin, *Myths*).

15. See e.g., Donald Bersoff & David J. Glass, *The Not-So Weisman: The Supreme Court's Continuing Misuse of Social Science Research*, 2 U. CHI. L. SCH. ROUNDTABLE 279 (1995).

16. See generally, J. Alexander Tanford, *The Limits of a Scientific Jurisprudence: The Supreme Court and Psychology*, 66 IND. L. J. 137 (1990). On the dangers of teleological decision making in this context, see Michael L. Perlin, *"Baby, Look Inside Your Mirror": The Legal Profession's Willful and Sanist Blindness to Lawyers with Mental Disabilities*, 69 U. PITT. L. REV. 589, 599–600 (2008). I discuss such decision making *infra* chapter 9.

17. See e.g., Norman Finkel, *The Insanity Defense: A Comparison of Verdict Schemas*, 15 LAW & HUM. BEHAV. 533, 535 (1991); Richard Rogers, *APA's Position on the Insanity Defense: Empiricism versus Emotionalism*, 42 AM. PSYCHOLOGIST 840 (1987); Richard Rogers, *Assessment of Criminal Responsibility: Empirical Advances and Unanswered Questions*, 17 J. PSYCHIATRY & L. 73 (1987).

18. See generally, John Monahan & Laurens Walker, *Twenty Five Years of Social Science in Law*, 35 LAW & HUM. BEHAV. 72 (2010).

19. John Monahan & Laurens Walker, *Social Authority: Obtaining, Evaluating, and Establishing Social Science in Law*, 134 U. Pa. L. Rev. 477 (1986); Laurens Walker & John Monahan, *Social Facts: Scientific Methodology as Legal Precedent*, 76 Cal. L. Rev. 877 (1988); John Monahan & Laurens Walker, *Judicial Use of Social Science Research*, 15 Law & Hum. Behav. 571 (1991). Similarly illuminating are Gary Melton's and Michael Saks' insights into "psychological jurisprudence" (the study of community and cultural norms through structures that create or sustain social behavior consistent with values that promote human welfare), see e.g., Gary Melton & Michael Saks, *The Law as an Instrument of Socialization and Social Structure*, in 33 Nebraska Symposium on Motivation: The Law as a Behavioral Instrument 235 (G. Melton, ed. 1985); Michael Saks, *Judicial Attention to the Way the World Works*, 75 Iowa L. Rev. 1011 (1990); Gary Melton, *Law, Science, and Humanity: The Normative Foundation of Social Science in Law*, 14 Law & Hum. Behav. 315 (1990).

20. See generally, 2 Perlin, *supra* note 8, §§ 4B-1 et seq. (2d ed. 1999).

21. See generally, 4 Perlin, *supra* note 8, §§ 9C-1 to 9C-7 (2d ed. 2002).

22. Perlin, *supra* note 10, at 106–8; Perlin, *Sanism*, *supra* note 9, at 398–400; Robert Burt, *Constitutional Law and the Teaching of the Parables*, 93 Yale L. J. 455, 462 (1984).

23. See e.g., Jodi English, *The Light between Twilight and Dark: Federal Criminal Law and the Volitional Insanity Defense*, 40 Hastings L. J. 1, 20 (1988); Perlin, *Myths*, *supra* note 14, at 658 n. 256 (federal legislators ignored empirical evidence about the insanity defense in the debate leading to the passage of the Insanity Defense Reform Act of 1984); see generally, 4 Perlin, *supra* note 8, § 9C-5.

24. That is, the ways that the judicial system either accepts or rejects social science evidence depending on whether or not the use of that data meets the system's a priori needs. See e.g., Paul Appelbaum, *The Empirical Jurisprudence of the United States Supreme Court*, 13 Am. J. L. & Med. 335, 341–42 (1987).

25. See Perlin, *"Ordinary Common Sense," supra* note 14, at 60–61; Perlin, *Pretexts*, *supra* note 12, at 668; Paul Appelbaum, *The Empirical Jurisprudence of the United States Supreme Court*, 13 Am. J. L. & Med. 335, 341–42 (1987); David Faigman, *"Normative Constitutional Fact-Finding": Exploring the Empirical Component of Constitutional Interpretation*, 139 U. Pa. L. Rev. 541, 577 (1991); see also, for an excellent and provocative consideration, Ansar Haroun & Grant Morris, *Weaving a Tangled Web: The Deceptions of Psychiatrists*, 10 J. Contemp. Leg. Iss. 227 (1999).

26. Perlin, *supra* note 16, at 599–600, discussing John Q. La Fond & Mary L. Durham, Back to the Asylum: The Future of Mental Health Law and Policy in the United States 156 (1992):

> Judges' refusals to consider the meaning and realities of mental illness cause them to act in what appears, at first blush, to be contradictory and inconsistent ways and, teleologically, to privilege (where that privileging serves what they perceive as a socially-beneficial value) and subordinate (where that subordination serves what they perceive as a similar value) evidence of mental illness.

See also Tanford, *supra* note 16, at 157; Faigman, *supra* note 25, at 581; Donald Bersoff, *Autonomy for Vulnerable Populations: The Supreme Court's Reckless Disregard for Self-Determination and Social Science*, 37 Vill. L. Rev. 1569 (1992); compare John Monahan & Laurens Walker, Social Science in Law: Cases and Materials 28–29 (1985) (discussing critical legal studies scholars' criticisms of social science in law for privileging empirical findings that are the "product of a closed capitalistic cultural system"); Tanford, *supra* note 16, at 151 (discussing criticism that social science "will be used instrumentally . . . to hide the true political/ideological bases for [judicial] decisions").

27. See generally, Perlin, *Sanism*, *supra* note 9. See also e.g., Bruce Winick, *The Side Effects of Incompetency Labeling and the Implications for Mental Health Law*, 1 Psychol., Pub. Pol'y & L. 6, 33 n. 155 (1995); Christopher Slobogin, *Therapeutic Jurisprudence: Five Dilemmas to Ponder*, 1 Psychol. Pub. Pol'y & L. 193, 199–200 n. 35 (1995) (both discussing sanism in a

therapeutic jurisprudence context). For a recent thoughtful consideration of these issues, see Michael Waterstone & Michael Stein, *Disabling Prejudice*, 102 Nw. U. L. Rev. 1351 (2008).

28. Perlin, *Sanism, supra* note 9, at 373–77. On the phobic base of these fears, see generally, Perlin & Dorfman, *supra* note 11.

29. On the ways that judges conceptualize mental disability professionals in forensic testimonial contexts, see Douglas Mossman, *"Hired Guns," "Whores," and "Prostitutes": Case Law References to Clinicians of Ill Repute*, 27 J. Am. Acad. Psychiatry & L. 414 (1999).

30. See e.g., David Wexler, *Justice, Mental Health, and Therapeutic Jurisprudence*, 40 Clev. St. L. Rev. 517 (1992); Therapeutic Jurisprudence: The Law as a Therapeutic Agent (David Wexler ed., 1990) (Therapeutic Agent); see generally *infra* text accompanying notes 62–80. On the public's lack of knowledge about the underlying scientific data, see *U.S. Public Has Limited Knowledge about Brain Disorders, Survey for Neuroscience Group Finds*, 44 Hosp. & Commun. Psychiatry 696 (Jul.-Dec. 1993). On stigma generally in this context, see e.g., Patrick Corrigan et al., *Blame, Shame, and Contamination: The Impact of Mental Illness and Drug Dependence Stigma on Family Members*, 20 J. Fam. Psychol. 239 (2006) (examining stigma associated with family members suffering from mental illness and drug dependence); Patrick Corrigan et al., *An Attribution Model of Public Discrimination towards Persons with Mental Illness*, 44 J. Health & Soc. Behav. 162, 163–64 (2003) (discussing components of stigmatization).

31. Anthony D'Amato, *Harmful Speech and the Culture of Indeterminacy*, 32 Wm. & Mary L. Rev. 329, 332 (1991).

32. Perlin, *Sanism, supra* note 9, at 400–404.

33. *Id.* at 398–406; Keri K. Gould & Michael L. Perlin, *"Johnny's in the Basement/Mixing Up His Medicine": Therapeutic Jurisprudence and Clinical Teaching*, 24 Seattle U. L. Rev. 339, 345 n. 35 (2000); see also, Michael L. Perlin, *Fatal Assumption: A Critical Evaluation of the Role of Counsel in Mental Disability Cases*, 16 Law & Hum. Behav. 39, 45–52 (1992). Sanism and the improper use of heuristics (see *infra* chapter 9; see generally, Perlin, *Ordinary Common Sense, supra* note 14) often overlap here. Thus, legislators in one state estimated that, during a specified time period, 4,400 defendants pled insanity and 1,800 of those pleas were successful; in reality, only 102 defendants asserted the defense, and just one was successful. See 4 Perlin, *supra* note 8, § 9C-3.1, at 331 n. 34, discussing findings reported in Richard Pasewark & Mark Pantle, *Insanity Plea: Legislators' View*, 136 Am. J. Psychiatry 222–23 (1979). The defense is raised in less than 1 percent of all cases, and is successful just about one-fourth of the time. See Lisa Callahan et al., *The Volume and Characteristics of Insanity Defense Pleas: An Eight-State Study*, 19 Bull. Am. Acad. Psychiatry & L. 331 (1991). On the *public's* misunderstanding of insanity defense use and success, see generally, Valerie Hans, *An Analysis of Public Attitudes toward the Insanity Defense*, 24 Criminology 393 (1986).

34. See e.g., John Parry, *The Death Penalty and Persons with Mental Disabilities: A Lethal Dose of Stigma, Sanism, Fear of Violence, and Faulty Predictions of Dangerousness*, 29 Mental & Physical Disability L. Rep. 667 (2005); Perlin, *Sanist Lives, supra* note 2.

35. Perlin, *Morality, supra* note 11, at 133. See also, Charles Sevilla, *The Exclusionary Rule and Police Perjury*, 11 San Diego L. Rev. 839, 840 (1974) (discussing fabricated police testimony).

36. Perlin, The Hidden Prejudice, *supra* note 1, at 67.

37. Faigman, *supra* note 25, at 577.

38. *Id.* at 581.

39. Katheryn Katz, *Majoritarian Morality and Parental Rights*, 52 Alb. L. Rev. 405, 461 (1988) (on court's reading of impact of parents' homosexuality in child custody decisions); Tanford, *supra* note 16, at 153–54. See e.g., Holbrook v. Flynn, 475 U.S. 560, 571 n. 4 (1986) (defendant's right to fair trial not denied where uniformed state troopers sat in front of spectator section in courtroom; court rejected contrary empirical study and based decision on its own "experience and common sense").

40. See e.g., Thomas Hafemeister & Gary Melton, *The Impact of Social Science Research on the Judiciary*, in Reforming the Law: Impact of Child Development Research 27 (Gary

Melton, ed. 1987); Peter W. Sperlich, *The Evidence on Evidence: Science and Law in Conflict and Cooperation*, in THE PSYCHOLOGY OF EVIDENCE AND TRIAL PROCEDURE 325 (Saul Kassin & Lawrence S. Wrightsman, eds. 1985); Craig Haney, *Data and Decisions: Judicial Reform and the Use of Social Science*, in THE ANALYSIS OF JUDICIAL REFORM 43 (Philip L. Du Bois, ed. 1982).

41. See e.g., Barefoot v. Estelle, 463 U.S. 880, 897–902 (1983), discussed extensively *infra* chapter 3; Faigman, *supra* note 25, at 584 (discussing Parham v. J.R., 442 U.S. 584 (1979)); see also Watkins v. Sowders, 449 U.S. 341 (1981) (refusal of courts to acknowledge social science research on ways that jurors evaluate and misevaluate eyewitness testimony).

42. The classic example is Chief Justice Burger's opinion for the court in *Parham*, 442 U.S. at 605–10 (approving more relaxed involuntary civil commitment procedures for juveniles than for adults). See e.g., Gail Perry & Gary Melton, *Precedential Value of Judicial Notice of Social Facts:* Parham *as an Example*, 22 J. FAM. L. 633 (1984):

> The *Parham* case is an example of the Supreme Court's taking advantage of the free rein on social facts to promulgate a dozen or so of its own by employing one tentacle of the judicial notice doctrine. The Court's opinion is filled with social facts of questionable veracity, accompanied by the authority to propel these facts into subsequent case law and, therefore, a spiral of less than rational legal policy making.

Id. at 645; see also Winsor Schmidt, *Considerations of Social Science in a Reconsideration of* Parham v. J.R. *and the Commitment of Children to Public Mental Institutions*, 13 J. PSYCHIATRY & L. 339 (1985) (same). On the Supreme Court's special propensity in mental health cases to base opinions on "simply unsupportable" factual assumptions, see Stephen Morse, *Treating Crazy People Less Specially*, 90 W. VA. L. REV. 353, 382 n. 64 (1987).

43. See e.g., Washington v. Harper, 494 U.S. 210, 229–30 (1990) (prisoners retain limited liberty interest in right to refuse forcible administration of antipsychotic medications), in which the majority acknowledges, and emphasizes in response to the dissent, the harmful, and perhaps fatal, side effects of the drugs. The court also stressed the "deference that is owed to medical professionals . . . who possess . . . the requisite knowledge and expertise to determine whether the drugs should be used." *Id.* at 230 n. 12. *Cf. id.* at 247–49 (Stevens, J., concurring in part & dissenting in part) (suggesting that the majority's side effects acknowledgement is largely illusory), discussed in 2 PERLIN, *supra* note 8, § 3B-8.2 (2d ed. 1999). See generally, Perlin, *Sanist Lives, supra* note 2, at 264–65.

44. See e.g., Perlin, *Executioner's Face, supra* note 2; Perlin, *Death Disappears, supra* note 2.

45. 477 U.S. 399 (1986).

46. See *infra* chapter 6.

47. *Ford*, 477 U.S. at 506, citing Coker v. Georgia, 433 U.S. 584, 597 (1977) (plurality opinion). See also e.g., Irvin v. Dowd, 366 U.S. 717, 721 (1961) (Clark, J.): "England, from whom the Western World has largely taken its concepts of individual liberty and of the dignity and worth of every man, has bequeathed to us safeguards for their preservation" (on right to jury trial).

48. Carol Sanger, *Decisional Dignity: Teenage Abortion, Bypass Hearings, and the Misuse of Law*, 18 COLUM. J. GENDER & L. 409, 415 (2009).

49. Tamar R. Birckhead, *Toward a Theory of Procedural Justice for Juveniles*, 57 BUFF. L. REV. 1447, 1474 (2009).

50. Katherine Kruse, *The Human Dignity of Clients*, 93 CORNELL L. REV. 1343, 1353 (2008).

51. Eric Miller, *Embracing Addiction: Drug Courts and the False Promise of Judicial Interventionism*, 65 OHIO ST. L. J. 1479, 1569 n. 473 (2004).

52. On how a lack of lawyers available to litigants in social justice cases can lead to a lack of dignity in the judicial process, see Frans Viljoen, *A Human Rights Court for Africa, and Africans*, 30 BROOK J. INT'L L. 1, 20 (2004), discussing (in the context of the African Court on Human Rights) how a lack of lawyers can make reliance on the law "fanciful."

53. In re Mental Health of K.G.F., 29 P.3d 485, 493–94 (Mont. 2001), see generally, Michael L. Perlin, *"I Might Need a Good Lawyer, Could Be Your Funeral, My Trial": A Global*

Perspective on the Right to Counsel in Civil Commitment Cases, and Its Implications for Clinical Legal Education, 28 WASH. U. J. L. & SOC'L POL'Y 241, 246–49 (2008).

54. Tom R. Tyler, *The Psychological Consequences of Judicial Procedures: Implications for Civil Commitment Hearings*, 46 SMU L. REV. 433, 443 (1992).

55. On the connection between dignity and humiliation, see Daniel Statman, *Humiliation, Dignity and Self-Respect*, 13 PHIL. PSYCHOL. 523 (2000). The relationship between dignity and humiliation has developed into an important field of study. See http://humiliationstudies.org/index.php.

56. Christopher McCrudden, *Human Dignity and the Judicial Interpretation of Human Rights*, 19 EUR. J. INT'L L. 655, 686–94 (2008).

57. See South Africa v. Makwanyane 1995 (3) SA 391 (CC) at 434 para. 95 (S. Afr.).

58. Hugo Adam Bedau, *The Eighth Amendment, Human Dignity, and the Death Penalty*, in THE CONSTITUTION OF RIGHTS: HUMAN DIGNITY AND AMERICAN VALUES 145, 145 (Michael J. Meyer & William A. Parent, eds. 1992).

59. 408 U.S. 238, 270 (1972) (Brennan, J., concurring).

60. See Eva S. Nilsen, *Decency, Dignity, and Desert: Restoring Ideals of Humane Punishment to Constitutional Discourse*, 41 U.C. DAVIS L. REV. 111, 116 (2007) (discussing how the Supreme Court's "narrow and formalistic reading of the Eighth Amendment" violates basic concepts of human dignity). Collateral to the central issues considered in this book is the question of the extent to which dehumanizing death row conditions further rob death row defendants—and the entire criminal justice process—of dignity. See e.g., Meghan J. Ryan, *Remedying Wrongful Execution*, 45 U. MICH. J. L. REFORM 261, 284–87 (2012); ROBERT JOHNSON, DEATH WORK: A STUDY OF THE MODERN EXECUTION PROCESS 218–19 (2d ed. 2006). On how this specifically exacerbates mental conditions, see Kate McMahon, *Dead Man Waiting: Death Row Delays, the Eighth Amendment, and What Courts and Legislatures Can Do*, 25 BUFF. PUB. INT. L. J. 43, 51–52 (2006–2007), discussing Knight v. Florida, 528 U.S. 990, 994 (1999) (Breyer, J., dissenting from denial of writ of *certiorari*).

61. See generally, Perlin, *supra* note 5; Michael L. Perlin, *"Justice's Beautiful Face": Bob Sadoff and the Redemptive Promise of Therapeutic Jurisprudence*, 40 J. PSYCHIATRY & L. 265 (2012); Michael L. Perlin, *"There Are No Trials Inside the Gates of Eden": Mental Health Courts, the Convention on the Rights of Persons with Disabilities, Dignity, and the Promise of Therapeutic Jurisprudence*, in COERCIVE CARE: LAW AND POLICY (Bernadette McSherry & Penelope Weller, eds. 2012) (in press).

62. See e.g., DAVID B. WEXLER, THERAPEUTIC JURISPRUDENCE: THE LAW AS A THERAPEUTIC AGENT (1990); DAVID B. WEXLER & BRUCE J. WINICK, LAW IN A THERAPEUTIC KEY: RECENT DEVELOPMENTS IN THERAPEUTIC JURISPRUDENCE (1996); BRUCE J. WINICK, CIVIL COMMITMENT: A THERAPEUTIC JURISPRUDENCE MODEL (2005); David B. Wexler, *Two Decades of Therapeutic Jurisprudence*, 24 TOURO L. REV. 17 (2008); 1 PERLIN, *supra* note 8, § 2D-3, at 534–41 (2d ed. 1998). Wexler first used the term in a paper he presented to the National Institute of Mental Health in 1987. See David B. Wexler, *Putting Mental Health into Mental Health Law: Therapeutic Jurisprudence*, 16 L. & HUM. BEHAV. 27, 32–33 (1992); David B. Wexler & Bruce J. Winick, *Therapeutic Jurisprudence as a New Approach to Mental Health Law Policy Analysis and Research*, 45 U. MIAMI L. REV. 979 (1991).

63. *See* Michael L. Perlin, *"His Brain Has Been Mismanaged with Great Skill": How Will Jurors Respond to Neuroimaging Testimony in Insanity Defense Cases?*, 42 AKRON L. REV. 885, 912 (2009); see Kate Diesfeld & Ian Freckelton, *Mental Health Law and Therapeutic Jurisprudence*, in DISPUTES AND DILEMMAS IN HEALTH LAW 91 (I. Freckelton & K. Peterson, eds. 2006) (for a transnational perspective).

64. Michael L. Perlin, *"You Have Discussed Lepers and Crooks": Sanism in Clinical Teaching*, 9 CLINICAL L. REV. 683 (2003); Michael L. Perlin, *"And My Best Friend, My Doctor / Won't Even Say What It Is I've Got": The Role and Significance of Counsel in Right to Refuse Treatment Cases*, 42 SAN DIEGO L. REV. 735 (2005); Michael L. Perlin, *"Everybody Is Making Love / Or Else Expecting Rain": Considering the Sexual Autonomy Rights of Persons Institutionalized Because of Mental Disability in Forensic Hospitals and in Asia*, 83 U. WASH. L. REV. 481 (2008).

65. David B. Wexler, *Therapeutic Jurisprudence and Changing Concepts of Legal Scholarship*, 11 BEHAV. SCI. & L. 17, 21 (1993).

66. Perlin, *Healing, supra* note 4, at 412; Perlin, *Borderline, supra* note 3, at 782.

67. Bruce J. Winick, *Foreword: Therapeutic Jurisprudence Perspectives on Dealing with Victims of Crime*, 33 NOVA L. REV. 535, 535 (2009).

68. David B. Wexler, *Practicing Therapeutic Jurisprudence: Psychological Soft Spots and Strategies*, in DANIEL P. STOLLE, DAVID B. WEXLER, & BRUCE J. WINICK, PRACTICING THERAPEUTIC JURISPRUDENCE: LAW AS A HELPING PROFESSION 45 (2000) (STOLLE et al).

69. Bruce Winick, *A Therapeutic Jurisprudence Model for Civil Commitment*, in INVOLUNTARY DETENTION AND THERAPEUTIC JURISPRUDENCE: INTERNATIONAL PERSPECTIVE ON CIVIL COMMITMENT, 23, 26 (Kate Diesfeld & Ian Freckelton, eds. 2003).

70. Claire B. Steinberger, *Persistence and Change in the Life of the Law: Can Therapeutic Jurisprudence Make A Difference?* 27 LAW & PSYCHOL. REV. 55, 65 (2003). The most thoughtful sympathetic critique of TJ remains Slobogin, *supra* note 27.

71. Perlin, *supra* note 6.

72. Ian Freckelton, *Therapeutic Jurisprudence Misunderstood and Misrepresented: The Price and Risks of Influence*, 30 T. JEFFERSON L. REV. 575, 582 (2008).

73. Susan Daicoff, *The Role of Therapeutic Jurisprudence within the Comprehensive Law Movement*, in STOLLE et al., *supra* note 68, at 365.

74. Warren Brookbanks, *Therapeutic Jurisprudence: Conceiving an Ethical Framework*, 8 J. L. & MED. 328, 329–30 (2001).

75. See e.g., Bruce J. Winick & David B. Wexler, *The Use of Therapeutic Jurisprudence in Law School Clinical Education: Transforming the Criminal Law Clinic*, 13 CLINICAL L. REV. 605, 605–7 (2006); David B. Wexler, *Not Such a Party Pooper: An Attempt to Accommodate (Many of) Professor Quinn's Concerns about Therapeutic Jurisprudence Criminal Defense Lawyering*, 48 B.C. L. REV. 597, 599 (2007); Brookbanks, *supra* note 74; Gregory Baker, *Do You Hear the Knocking at the Door? A "Therapeutic" Approach to Enriching Clinical Legal Education Comes Calling*, 28 WHITTIER L. REV. 379, 385 (2006). On how the use of therapeutic jurisprudence can lead to "emotionally intelligent" justice, see Michael S. King, *Restorative Justice, Therapeutic Jurisprudence and the Rise of Emotionally Intelligent Justice*, 32 MELB. U. L. REV. 1096 (2008).

76. Amy D. Ronner, *The Learned-Helpless Lawyer: Clinical Legal Education and Therapeutic Jurisprudence as Antidotes to Bartleby Syndrome*, 24 TOURO L. REV. 601, 627 (2008).

77. Amy D. Ronner, *Songs of Validation, Voice, and Voluntary Participation: Therapeutic Jurisprudence, Miranda and Juveniles*, 71 U. CIN. L. REV. 89, 94–95 (2002); see generally, AMY D. RONNER, LAW, LITERATURE AND THERAPEUTIC JURISPRUDENCE (2010).

78. See e.g., DAVID WEXLER, REHABILITATING LAWYERS: PRINCIPLES OF THERAPEUTIC JURISPRUDENCE FOR CRIMINAL LAW PRACTICE (2008); Astrid Birgden & Michael L. Perlin, *"Where the Home in the Valley Meets the Damp Dirty Prison": A Human Rights Perspective on Therapeutic Jurisprudence and the Role of Forensic Psychologists in Correctional Settings*, 14 AGGRESSION & VIOLENT BEHAVIOR 256 (2009); Birgden & Perlin, *supra* note 5. In a recent article, Professor Wexler calls for a state-by-state look at all of criminal procedure from a TJ perspective. See David Wexler, *New Wine in New Bottles: The Need to Sketch a Therapeutic Jurisprudence "Code" of Proposed Criminal Processes and Practices*, accessible at http://papers.ssrn.com/sol3/papers.cfm?abstract_id=2065454.

79. See e.g., Bruce Winick, *The Supreme Court's Evolving Death Penalty Jurisprudence: Severe Mental Illness as the Next Frontier*, 50 B.C. L. REV. 785, 801 (2009); Cynthia F. Adcock, *The Collateral Anti-Therapeutic Effects of the Death Penalty*, 11 FLA. COASTAL L. REV. 289 (2010); Bruce J. Winick, *Competency for Execution*, in BRUCE J. WINICK, THERAPEUTIC JURISPRUDENCE APPLIED: ESSAYS ON MENTAL HEALTH LAW 289 (1997); David B. Wexler & Bruce J. Winick, *Therapeutic Jurisprudence and Criminal Justice Mental Health Issues*, 16 MENTAL & PHYSICAL DISABILITY L. REP. 225, 225 (1992). See also, Perlin, *Executioner's Face, supra* note 2, at 235:

[A]ny death penalty system that provides inadequate counsel and that, at least as a partial result of that inadequacy, fails to insure that mental disability evidence is adequately considered and contextualized by death penalty decision-makers, fails miserably from a therapeutic jurisprudence perspective.

CHAPTER 3

1. Lindsey S. Vann, *History Repeats Itself: The Post-Furman Return to Arbitrariness in Capital Punishment*, 45 U. RICH. L. REV. 1255, 1272 (2011), and see *id.* at n. 135 (listing representative statutes).

2. 463 U.S. 880 (1983).

3. See Michael L. Perlin, *Myths, Realities, and the Political World: The Anthropology of Insanity Defense Attitudes*, 24 BULL. AM. ACAD. PSYCHIATRY & L. 5, 22 (1996), quoting Deborah C. Scott et al., *Monitoring Insanity Acquittees: Connecticut's Psychiatric Security Review Board*, 41 HOSP. & COMMUNITY PSYCHIATRY 980, 982 (1990) (persons with mental disabilities are "the most despised and feared group in society").

4. 428 U.S. 262 (1976).

5. See James Liebman & Michael J. Shepard, *Guiding Capital Sentencing Discretion beyond One "Boiler Plate": Mental Disorder as a Mitigating Factor*, 66 GEO. L. J. 757, 759 n. 15 (1978).

6. See 4 MICHAEL L. PERLIN, MENTAL DISABILITY LAW: CIVIL AND CRIMINAL § 12-2, at 477–78 (2d ed. 2002).

7. TEX. CRIM. PROC. ART. § 37.071 (2)(b) (1). Professor Charles Black has suggested that the concept of a "probability 'beyond a reasonable doubt' is and can only be puzzling—even mind-boggling—to a jury or to anybody." Charles Black, *Due Process for Death:* Jurek v. Texas, 26 CATH. U.L. REV. 1 (1976).

8. See *Jurek*, 428 U.S. at 264.

9. For a consideration of the elusiveness in defining "dangerousness" in another context, see 1 PERLIN, *supra* note 6, § 2A-4.1 (2d ed. 1998).

10. Examples suggested in the opinion included decisions involving admission to bail, sentencing, and parole releases. *Jurek*, 428 U.S. at 275.

11. *Id.* at 274–76. For a subsequent case dealing with this question, see e.g., O'Dell v. Netherland, 95 F.3d 1214 (4th Cir. 1996), *aff'd on other gds.*, 521 U.S. 151 (1997).

12. Black, *supra* note 7, at 8.

13. 428 U.S. 153 (1976).

14. *The Supreme Court, 1975 Term*, 90 HARV. L. REV. 58, 63, 71 (1976).

15. See Giles R. Scofield, *Due Process in the United States Supreme Court and the Death of the Texas Capital Murder Statute*, 8 AM. J. CRIM. L. 1 (1980).

16. William Green, *Capital Punishment, Psychiatric Experts, and Predictions of Dangerousness*, 13 CAP. U. L. REV. 533, 540–42 (1984).

17. 550 U.S. 233, 250 n. 12 (2007) ("To the extent that *Jurek* implied at the time it was decided that all that was required by the Constitution was that the defense be authorized to introduce all relevant mitigating circumstances, and that such information merely be before the jury, it has become clear from our later cases that the mere ability to present evidence is not sufficient").

18. *Id.* at 252 n. 13, citing, inter alia, Lockett v. Ohio, 438 U.S. 586 (1978), and Eddings v. Oklahoma, 455 US. 104 (1982). For an earlier state case, see First v. State, 846 S.W.2d 836 (Tex. Crim. App. 1992) (death sentence reversed and remanded because state sentencing scheme improperly failed to allow the sentencing court to consider mitigating circumstances before sentencing).

19. Stephen Kanter, *Sleeping Beauty Wide Awake: State Constitutions as Important Independent Sources of Individual Rights*, 15 LEWIS & CLARK L. REV. 799, 807 n. 35 (2011).

20. Carissa Byrne Hessick & F. Andrew Hessick, *Recognizing Constitutional Rights at Sentencing*, 99 CAL. L. REV. 47, 73 (2011).

There are issues of race to consider as well. It is well known that an all-white jury is significantly more likely to impose death than is a racially mixed jury, and a black defendant/white victim case is much more likely to result in a death sentence when the jury is heavily white, William J. Bowers et al., *Death Sentencing in Black and White: An Empirical Analysis of the Role of Jurors' Race and Jury Racial Composition*, 3 U. PA. J. CONST. L. 171, 191–96 (2001); however, in this context it needs to be stressed that the race of the defendant also influences jurors' perceptions of future dangerousness, see John H. Blume et al., *When Lightning Strikes Back: South Carolina's Return to the Unconstitutional Standardless Capital Sentencing Regime of the Pre-Furman Era*, 4 CHARLESTON L. REV. 479, 520 n. 184 (2010), reporting on the research relied upon in Stephen P. Garvey, *Aggravation and Mitigation in Capital Cases: What Do Jurors Think?*, 98 COLUM. L. REV. 1538, 1559 (1998).

21. See 4 PERLIN, *supra* note 6, § 12-2.1, at 479–86; see generally, Michael L. Perlin, *The Supreme Court, the Mentally Disabled Criminal Defendant, and Symbolic Values: Random Decisions, Hidden Rationales, or Doctrinal Abyss?* 29 ARIZ. L. REV. 1 (1987).

22. 463 U.S. 880 (1983). For a critical, pre-*Barefoot* analysis of the administration of death penalty cases in Texas, see George Dix, *Administration of the Texas Death Penalty Statutes: Constitutional Infirmities Related to the Prediction of Dangerousness*, 55 TEX. L. REV. 1343, 1396, 1399 (1977) (failure of majority of Texas Supreme Court to "scrutinize more diligently" expert psychiatric testimony on dangerousness issue in similar cases was "discouraging"; trial courts use expert testimony in "woefully inadequate" way at penalty phase).

23. One of the psychiatrists testifying on the state's behalf, Dr. James Grigson, subsequently became known as "Dr. Death." See e.g., Charles Ewing, *"Dr. Death" and the Case for an Ethical Ban on Psychological Predictions of Dangerousness in Capital Sentencing Proceedings*, 8 AM. J. L. & MED. 407, 410 (1983); see also, Brock Mehler, *The Supreme Court and State Psychiatric Examinations of Capital Defendants: Stuck Inside of Jurek with the Barefoot Blues Again*, 59 UMKC L. REV. 107, 114–15 (1990) (discussing how Grigson's skills "have helped send more than 100 persons to death row"). For other cases involving Dr. Grigson, see e.g., Fuller v. State, 829 S.W.2d 191 (Tex. Crim. App. 1992), *reh'g denied* (1992), *cert. denied*, 508 U.S. 941 (1993), *further proceedings sub nom.* Fuller v. Johnson, 114 F.3d 491 (5th Cir.), *cert. denied*, 522 U.S. 963 (1997); Redmen v. State, 828 P.2d 395 (Nev. 1992), *cert. denied*, 506 U.S. 880 (1992), *overruled on other grounds by* Alford v. State, 906 P.2d 714 (Nev. 1995); Cook v. State, 821 S.W.2d 600 (Tex. Crim. App.), *reh'g denied* (1991), *cert. denied*, 503 U.S. 998 (1992); Bennett v. State, 766 S.W.2d 227 (Tex. Crim. App.), *cert. denied*, 492 U.S. 911 (1989); Mines v. Quarterman, 267 Fed. Appdx. 356 (5th Cir. 2008), *cert. denied*, 555 U.S. 938 (2008) (reversing, in part, Mines v. Cockrell, 2003 WL 21982190 (N.D. Tex. 2003) (counsel not ineffective in failing to object to future dangerousness testimony by the "notorious" Dr. Grigson and was in fact effective in getting concessions on cross-examination).

For an analysis of cases in which Dr. Grigson has participated, see George Dix, *Participation by Mental Health Professionals in Capital Murder Sentencing*, 1 INT'L J. L. & PSYCHIATRY 283 (1978) (*Professional Participation*); George Dix, *Expert Prediction Testimony in Capital Sentencing Evidentiary and Constitutional Considerations*, 19 AM. CRIM. L. REV. 47 (1981) (*Expert Prediction*). Professor Dix has suggested that Dr. Grigson operated "at the brink of quackery." George Dix, *The Death Penalty, "Dangerousness," Psychiatric Testimony, and Professional Ethics*, 5 AM. J. CRIM. L. 151, 172 (1977) (*Professional Ethics*). Grigson was reprimanded twice in the early 1980s by the American Psychiatric Association, then expelled from the group in 1995 because it found his testimony unethical and untrustworthy, William R. Montross Jr. & Patrick Mulvaney, *Virtue and Vice: Who Will Report on the Failings of the American Criminal Justice System?* 61 STAN. L. REV. 1429, 1438 n. 29 (2009), and for indicating, while testifying in court as an expert witness, "that he could predict with 100 [percent] certainty that the individuals would engage in future violent acts," Daniel Shuman & Stuart Greenberg, *The Role of Ethical Norms in the Admissibility of Expert*

Testimony, 37 JUDGES' J. 4, 6 (Winter 1998), citing American Psychiatric Association, *News Release* No. 95-25, July 20, 1995. See generally, Gardner v. Johnson, 247 F.3d 551, 556 (5th Cir. 2001); RON ROSENBAUM, TRAVELS WITH DR. DEATH AND OTHER UNUSUAL INVESTIGATIONS (1991), and see Lisa Dennis, *Constitutionality, Accuracy, Admissibility: Assessing Expert Predictions of Future Violence in Capital Sentencing Proceedings*, 10 VA. J. SOC. POL'Y & L. 292, 301 (2002): "For critics of the *Barefoot* decision, Dr. James Grigson represents the epitome of their deepest fears." Dr. Grigson has effectively countered attacks on his credibility "by unflappably informing conservative Texas jurors that he is the preeminent mental health expert on the criminal mind and that the APA's [American Psychiatric Association's] position simply reflects a visceral reaction of East Coast liberals who oppose the death penalty." Brent E. Newton, *A Case Study in Systemic Unfairness: The Texas Death Penalty, 1973–1994*, 1 TEX. F. ON C. L. & C. R. 1, 23 (1994). See also, Meghan Shapiro, *An Overdose of Dangerousness: How "Future Dangerousness" Catches the Least Culpable Capital Defendants and Undermines the Rationale for the Executions It Supports*, 35 AM. J. CRIM. L. 145, 163 n. 82 (2008): "Grigson attacked the decision and the APA [American Psychiatric Association], calling the organization a bunch of liberals who think queers are normal," quoting, in part, Texas Defender Service, *A State of Denial: Texas Justice and the Death Penalty*, 30, available at http://02f2fd4.netsolhost.com/tds/images/publications/Chap3.pdf.

Grigson was not the only psychiatrist to so testify. See Thomas Regnier, *Barefoot in Quicksand: The Future of "Future Dangerousness" Predictions in Death Penalty Sentencing in the World of Daubert and Kumho*, 37 AKRON L. REV. 469, 496 (2004), quoting, in part, Jonathan Sorensen & James Marquart, *Prosecutorial and Jury Decision-Making in Post-Furman Texas Capital Cases*, 18 N.Y.U. REV. L. & SOC'L CHANGE 743, 749 (1990–1991) (Grigson "has spawned a 'growing entourage of Grigson-like psychiatrists acting as hired guns for the state'").

24. Neither doctor examined the defendant prior to testifying. *Barefoot*, 463 U.S. at 885. According to Dr. Paul Appelbaum, the decision to pose hypothetical questions to experts who did not personally examine the defendant may have resulted from the Supreme Court's opinion in Estelle v. Smith, 451 U.S. 484 (1981), which held that it was a constitutional violation not to warn a defendant at the outset of such a pretrial psychiatric examination that the information he revealed might be used against him, Paul Appelbaum, *Hypotheticals, Psychiatric Testimony, and the Death Sentence*, 12 BULL. AM. ACAD. PSYCHIATRY & L. 169, 170–71 (1984) (*Hypotheticals*).

25. See TEX. CRIM. PROC. CODE ANN. § 37.071 (Vernon 1981).

26. *Barefoot*, 463 U.S. at 884.

27. Under then-operative Texas procedures, special questions are submitted to the jury as part of the penalty phase. *Id.* at 883–84.

28. *Id.* at 884–85.

29. *Id.* at 885.

30. 697 F.2d 593 (5th Cir. 1983). *See Barefoot*, 463 U.S. at 885–87, for the full procedural history below.

31. 459 U.S. 1169 (1983).

32. *Barefoot*, 463 U.S. at 896.

33. *Id.*

34. *Id.* On this point, the Court relied heavily upon its opinion in *Jurek*, rejecting the claim that it was impossible to predict future behavior and that dangerousness was thus an invalid consideration in death penalty imposition decision making. *Id.*

35. *Barefoot*, 463 U.S. at 898. On this point, the Court relied on O'Connor v. Donaldson, 422 U.S. 563, 576 (1975) (nondangerous mentally ill person could not be institutionalized against his will), and Addington v. Texas, 441 U.S. 418, 429 (1979) (commitment determination turns on "*meaning* of the facts which must be interpreted by expert[s]") (emphasis in original).

Also, under the rules of evidence, such testimony is ordinarily admitted, with the fact finder—who would have the benefit of cross-examination and contrary evidence by the opposing party (*Barefoot*, 463 U.S. at 898)—determining the appropriate weight to be allocated. *Barefoot*, 463

U.S. at 898. While such evidence may be opposed as erroneous on either a case-by-case or global basis, *id.*, the jury should have the benefit of all of the available evidence. *Id.* at 898–99.

The Court stressed that no evidence was offered by the defendant at trial to contradict the testimony in question. *Id.* at 899 n. 5. See also *id.* at n. 7 (no contradiction of state's expert testimony that psychiatrists could predict future dangerousness of individuals "if given enough information"). But see *Hypotheticals*, *supra* note 24, at 173–75 (experts in *Barefoot* had "inadequate information" and were "[lacking] crucial data" needed in order to appropriately make the diagnoses offered). For subsequent research, see Mark Cunningham & Thomas Reidy, *Integrating Base Rate Data in Violence Risk Assessments at Capital Sentencing*, 16 BEHAV. SCI. & L. 71 (1998).

Recommendations for improving the accuracy of violence risk assessments at capital sentencing have specified that these estimates should be anchored to context-relevant violence base rate data that are conservatively particularized with empirically demonstrated factors. See Mark Cunningham & Jon R. Sorensen, *Capital Offenders in Texas Prisons: Rates, Correlates, and an Actuarial Analysis of Violent Misconduct*, 31 LAW & HUM. BEHAV. 553, 555 (2007).That, of course, was not done in this case. See Daniel A. Krauss & Bruce D. Sales, *The Effects of Clinical and Scientific Expert Testimony on Juror Decision Making in Capital Sentencing*, 7 PSYCHOL. PUB. POL. & L. 267, 267, 305 (2001) (concluding that "jurors are more influenced by clinical opinion expert testimony than by actuarial expert testimony" and that the adversarial process fails to counter this bias).

36. *Amicus* Brief of American Psychiatric Association, Barefoot v. Estelle, 463 U.S. 880 (1983), at 14.

37. *Id.* See *Barefoot*, 463 U.S. at 916, 920–23 (Blackmun, J., dissenting), sources cited at nn. 1–5.

See generally 1 PERLIN, *supra* note 6, § 2A-4.3c; Norval Miller & Marc Morris, *Predictions of Dangerousness: Ethical Concerns and Proposed Limits*, 2 NOTRE DAME J. L. ETHICS & PUB. POL. 393 (1986). Professor John Monahan continues to remain the most significant thinker in this area of law and behavior. See JOHN MONAHAN, PREDICTING VIOLENT BEHAVIOR: AN ASSESSMENT OF CLINICAL TECHNIQUES (1981), reprinted as THE CLINICAL PREDICTION OF VIOLENT BEHAVIOR (1981); for subsequent work, see e.g., John Monahan, *Violence Prediction: The Past Twenty Years and the Next Twenty Years*, 23 CRIM. JUST. & BEHAV. 107 (1996); John Monahan, *Mental Disorder and Violent Behavior*, 47 AM. PSYCHOLOGIST 511–21 (1992); John Monahan, *Clinical and Actuarial Predictions of Violence*, in MODERN SCIENTIFIC EVIDENCE: THE LAW AND SCIENCE OF EXPERT TESTIMONY 281, 308 (David L. Faigman et al., eds. 1997); John Monahan, *Jurisprudence of Risk Assessment: Forecasting Harm among Prisoners, Predators, and Patients*, 92 VA. L. REV. 391 (2006); Jennifer L. Skeem & John Monahan, *Current Directions in Violence Risk Assessment*, 20 CURRENT DIRECTIONS PSYCHOL. SCI. 38, 39–41 (2011); John Monahan, *Structured Risk Assessment of Violence*, in TEXTBOOK OF VIOLENCE ASSESSMENT AND MANAGEMENT 17, 19–27 (Robert I. Simon & Kenneth Tardiff, eds. 2008); John Monahan & Lauren Walker, *Twenty-Five Years of Social Science in Law*, 35 LAW & HUM. BEHAV. 72 (2011).

38. 451 U.S. 454 (1981) (*Miranda* applies to statements given to psychiatric expert witnesses called by the state to testify either as to a defendant's sanity or the appropriate penalty to be imposed following conviction). See generally 4 PERLIN, *supra* note 6, § 10- 2.1; Perlin, *supra* note 6, at 23–28.

39. *Estelle*, 451 U.S. at 473, quoted in *Barefoot*, 463 U.S. at 898. The Court was unpersuaded that the American Psychiatric Association (APA), as *amicus*, sought to bar such expert testimony:

The *amicus* does not suggest that there are not other views held by members of the Association or of the profession in general. Indeed, as this case and others indicate, there are doctors who are quite willing to testify at the sentencing hearing; who think, and will say, that they know what they are talking about, and who expressly disagree with the Association's point of view.

Id. at 399. But see *Professional Ethics, supra* note 23, at 172 (*Barefoot* witness Grigson operated "at the brink of quackery"); see also e.g., Shapiro, *supra* note 23, at 165: "Jurors understandably are likely to opt for the expert who can help them in the dangerousness prediction they are forced by law to make, who takes some of the onus of the decision off their shoulders, and who offers an escape route from the potential consequences of an incorrect non-dangerousness prediction."

Further, the APA added that it was "unconvinced . . . that the adversary process cannot be trusted to sort out the reliable from the unreliable evidence and opinions about future dangerousness," *Barefoot,* 463 U.S. at 901, adding that this was so "particularly when the convicted felon has the opportunity to present his own side of the case." *Id. Cf.* Ake v. Oklahoma, 470 U.S. 68 (1985) (indigent criminal defendant who makes a threshold showing that insanity is likely to be a significant factor at trial is constitutionally entitled to a psychiatrist's assistance), discussed in, inter alia, Michael L. Perlin, *"And I See through Your Brain": Access to Experts, Competency to Consent, and the Impact of Antipsychotic Medications in Neuroimaging Cases in the Criminal Trial,* 2009 STAN. TECH. L. REV. 4, *14, and see *infra* chapter 8. The APA specifically rejected what it characterized as Justice Blackmun's charge in his dissenting opinion, see *Barefoot,* 463 U.S. at 920–23 (Blackmun, J., dissenting), that a jury would not be able to separate "the wheat from the chaff," *id.* at 899–900, answering that "[w]e do not share in this low evaluation of the adversary process," *id.,* discussing *infra* text accompanying note 92.

40. *Barefoot,* 463 U.S. at 903. See Pamela Wilkins, *Rethinking Categorical Prohibitions on Capital Punishment,* 40 U. MEM. L. REV. 423, 480 (2009); "From *Jurek v. Texas* to *Barefoot v. Estelle* to *Simmons v. South Carolina* [512 U.S. 154 (1994)] and its progeny, the Court consistently has refused to condemn jurors' consideration of future dangerousness."

41. *Id.* at 904 (quoting *Barefoot,* 596 S.W.2d at 887). See generally, on this point, Michael L. Perlin, *The Supreme Court, the Mentally Disabled Criminal Defendant, Psychiatric Testimony in Death Penalty Cases, and the Power of Symbolism: Dulling the* Ake *in* Barefoot's *Achilles Heel,* 3 N.Y. L. SCH. HUMAN RTS. ANN. 91, 118 (1985) (*Barefoot's Ake*), and *id.,* text accompanying nn. 156–60). See also Raymond A. Bonner, *Death Penalty,* 1984 ANN. SURVEY AM. L. 493, 507–8: "Expert testimony predicated on hypotheticals and speculation has no place in a death sentencing system that claims to value fairness and reliability." *Cf. Hypotheticals, supra* note 24, at 176 (while hypotheticals ought not necessarily to be entirely excluded from the capital sentencing process, "they ought to be inadmissible as the *sole* basis for a psychiatric opinion") (emphasis in original).

On the application of these rules to the case before it, the Court concluded that there was no error, noting that the defendant could have put forth his *own* hypothetical (*Barefoot,* 463 U.S. at 905 n. 10), and that, when an expert witness is as positive about his predictions as were the witnesses in *Barefoot* (Dr. Grigson, for instance, asserted that he was "100% sure" that an individual with the characteristics described in the hypothetical would commit violent acts in the future, *id.* at n. 11; for the full colloquy on this point, see *Hypotheticals, supra* note 24, at 169), the easier it should be to impeach them, *Barefoot,* 463 U.S. at 905 n. 11. Noted the Court: "Dr. Fason [defendant's witness] testified at the habeas hearing that if a doctor claimed to be 100% sure of something without examining the patient, 'we would kick him off the staff of the hospital for his arrogance.' H. Tr. 48. Similar testimony could have been presented at Barefoot's trial, but was not." *Id.*

Compare State v. Pennington, 575 A.2d 816, 832–35 (N.J. 1990) (improper for prosecutor to cross-examine defense psychiatric experts on medical reports upon which they did not rely); Beagel v. State, 813 P.2d 699 (Alaska App. 1991) (abuse of discretion for trial court to exclude expert opinion that defendant's statements claiming responsibility for fatal shooting were the product of psychogenic amnesia and confabulation). For more recent cases, see e.g., State v. King, 387 N.J. Super. 522 (N.J. App. Div. 2006); Sundstrom v. Frank, 630 F. Supp. 2d 974 (E.D. Wis. 2007).

42. *Barefoot,* 463 U.S. at 916 (Blackmun, J., dissenting). Justices Brennan and Marshall would have vacated the death penalty as violative of the cruel and unusual punishment clause, *id.* (Marshall, J., dissenting); Justice Blackmun, on the other hand, would have vacated and remanded "for further proceedings." *Id.* at 938 (Blackmun, J., dissenting).

Justice Stevens concurred, *id.* at 906, reasoning that, while he agreed with that aspect of Justice Marshall's dissent which found "serious procedural error" in the way the Fifth Circuit handled the case, *id.*, he agreed with the majority's ultimate conclusion that the District Court's judgment should be affirmed. *Id.*

Justice Marshall dissented (for himself and Justice Brennan), *id.*, arguing that (1) the procedures followed by the Court of Appeals were inconsistent with prior Supreme Court case law (*id.*, and see *id.* at 908–12, discussing Garrison v. Patterson, 391 U.S. 464 (1968); Carafas v. LaVallee, 391 U.S. 234 (1968), and Nowakowski v. Maroney, 386 U.S. 542 (1967)), and (2) the Court's adoption of summary procedures was "grossly improper." *Barefoot*, 463 U.S. at 915 (Marshall, J., dissenting).

43. *Cf. Addington*, 441 U.S. at 423 (rejecting preponderance of evidence standard—used in the "typical civil case involving a monetary dispute between private parties"—because the person facing such commitment "should not be asked to share equally with society the risk of error when the possible injury to the individual is significantly greater than any possible harm to the state," *id.* at 427).

44. *Barefoot*, 463 U.S. at 916 (Blackmun, J., dissenting).

45. *Id.* at 917.

46. *Id.*

47. *Id.*

48. *Id.* at 919.

49. *Id.*

50. *Id.* (quoting Paul Gianelli, *The Inadmissibility of Novel Scientific Evidence: Frye v. United States, a Half-Century Later*, 80 COLUM. L. REV. 1197, 1237 (1980)). See generally, sources cited in *Barefoot*, 463 U.S. at 919 n. 8 (Blackmun, J., dissenting); Note, *People v. Murtishaw: Applying the Frye Test to Psychiatric Predictions of Dangerousness in Capital Cases*, 70 CALIF. L. REV. 1069, 1075–77 (1982) (hereinafter *Murtishaw* Note) (on prejudicial impact of expert predictions of dangerousness). But see Wendy Brickell, *Is It the CSI Effect or Do We Just Distrust Juries?* 23 CRIM. JUST. 10 (Summer 2008) (questioning the empirical evidence for the proposition that jurors inappropriately defer to forensic experts).

51. *Barefoot*, 463 U.S. at 919.

52. *Id.* at 924. *Cf.* Note, *Estelle v. Smith and Psychiatric Testimony: New Limits on Predicting Future Dangerousness*, 33 BAYLOR L. REV. 1015, 1033 (1981) ("When the decision of whether a criminal defendant shall live or die is put to the jury, only the *most credible* evidence should be used in the determination") (emphasis added).

53. *See* 4 PERLIN, *supra* note 6, § 12-2.2, at 486–88.

54. *Professional Participation*, *supra* note 23, at 289. Professor Dix used this phrase, of course, five years *prior* to the *Barefoot* decision.

55. See, e.g. Paul Appelbaum, *Death, the Expert Witness, and the Dangers of Going Barefoot*, 34 HOSP. & COMMUN. PSYCHIATRY 1003 (1983); *Hypotheticals*, *supra* note 24; Paul Appelbaum, *The Supreme Court Looks at Psychiatry*, 141 AM. J. PSYCHIATRY 827 (1984); Murray Levine, *The Adversary Process and Social Science in the Courts: Barefoot v. Estelle*, 12 J. PSYCHIATRY & L. 147, 170 (1984); *The Supreme Court, 1982 Term*, 97 HARV. L. REV. 70, 121 n. 28, 127 (1983); C. Richard Showalter & Richard Bonnie, *Psychiatrists and Capital Sentencing: Risks and Responsibilities in a Unique Legal Setting*, 12 BULL. AM. ACAD. PSYCHIATRY & L. 159, 176 (1984); Thomas Grisso & Paul Appelbaum, *Is It Unethical to Offer Predictions of Future Violence?*, 16 LAW & HUM. BEHAV. 621 (1992); Daniel Shuman & Stuart Greenberg, *The Role of Ethical Norms in the Admissibility of Expert Testimony*, 37 JUDGES' J. 5 (Winter 1998); Regnier, *supra* note 23, at 469–70. Earlier criticisms are catalogued in Ira P. Robbins, *Toward a More Just and Effective System of Review in State Death Penalty Cases*, 40 AM. U. L. REV. 1, 149 n. 508 (1990).

For the most "blistering" critique (see *Barefoot's Ake*, *supra* note 41, at 118 n. 155), see William Geimer, *Death at Any Cost: A Critique of the Supreme Court's Recent Retreat from Its Death Penalty Standards*, 12 FLA. ST. U. L. REV. 737, 760–66 (1985), characterizing *Barefoot* as a "gross retreat" from the Court's commitment to reliability in death penalty sentencing, *id.* at 760; as a "bad faith abandonment" of established fairness standards, *id.* at 764; and as a reflection of the "little desire on the part of the majority to be bothered with facts at all," *id.* at 763. See generally, Steven Smith, *Mental Health Expert Witnesses: Of Science and Crystal Balls*, 7 Behav. Sci. & L. 145 (1980); Mehler, *supra* note 23. Professor C. Michael Risinger and his colleagues conclude, "We have yet to find a single word of praise for, or in defense of, *Barefoot* in the literature of either science or law." C. Michael Risinger et al., *Exorcism of Ignorance as a Proxy for Rational Knowledge: The Lessons of Handwriting Identification "Expertise,"* 137 U. Pa. L. Rev. 731, 780–81 n. 215 (1989).

56. See e.g., Richard Bonnie, *Psychiatry and the Death Penalty: Emerging Problems in Virginia*, 66 Va. L. Rev. 167, 177–78 (1980); Showalter & Bonnie, *supra* note 55, at 166–67; George Dix, *Clinical Evaluation of the "Dangerousness" of "Normal" Criminal Defendants*, 66 Va. L. Rev. 525, 575 (1980) (mental health professional should be prohibited from expressing any predictive opinion more specific than that "the subject poses a *greater risk than the average person* of engaging in future assaultive or otherwise criminal conduct") (footnote omitted) (emphasis added).

57. Mark D. Cunningham et al., *Capital Jury Decision-Making: The Limitations of Predictions of Future Violence*, 15 Psychol. Pub. Pol'y & L. 223, 248 (2009).

58. James W. Marquart et al., *Gazing into the Crystal Ball: Can Jurors Accurately Predict Dangerousness in Capital Cases?*, 23 Law & Soc'y Rev. 449, 462–64 (1989). For the most recent assessment in the *civil* context, see Nicholas Scurich & Richard John, *The Normative Threshold for Psychiatric Civil Commitment*, 50 Jurimetrics J. 425 (2010) (using decision theory, and concluding that involuntary commitment of "only the highest risk individuals" is justified). On the way that *Barefoot* simply rejected empiricism and social science, see Jordan M. Steiker, *The Role of Constitutional Facts and Social Science Research in Capital Litigation: Is "Proof" of Arbitrariness or Inaccuracy Relevant to the Constitutional Regulation of the American Death Penalty?* in The Future of America's Death Penalty: An Agenda for the Next Generation of Capital Punishment Research 23, 29–31 (Charles S. Lanier et al., eds. 2009).

59. Bonnie, *supra* note 56, at 188. On how psychological evaluations at capital sentencing are "fraught with complex considerations of personal, professional, logistical, parameter and procedural factors," see Mark Cunningham, *Informed Consent in Capital Sentencing Evaluations: Targets and Content*, 37 Prof'l Psychology: Res. & Prac. 452, 458 (2006).

Writing three years prior to the Court's decision in *Barefoot*, Professor Bonnie set out three suggestions to guide forensic mental health witnesses:

1. An expert witness should decline to offer any opinion on the dangerousness issue unless he has conducted a comprehensive examination of the defendant, with extensive attention to developmental and behavioral history, directed specifically at the probability of future violence. Under no circumstances should an examination focused on competency to stand trial, or even on the defendant's mental state at the time of the offense, be used as a basis for formulation of an opinion on dangerousness.
2. An expert witness should not express an opinion on a defendant's dangerousness unless he has special training and experience in conducting such evaluations, unless he is fully familiar with the developing clinical literature on this subject, and unless he qualifies his opinions with the observation that clinical predictions of future violence currently lack empirical validation.
3. An expert witness asked to express an opinion on a defendant's dangerousness should do so only if the opinion derives from a generally accepted diagnostic or psychodynamic framework.

Bonnie, *supra* note 56, at 177 (footnotes omitted).

60. O. Carter Snead, *Neuroimaging and the "Complexity" of Capital Punishment*, 82 N.Y.U. L. Rev. 1265, 1339 (2007). See also, John F. Edens et al., *Predictions of Future Dangerousness in Capital Murder Trials: Is It Time to "Disinvent the Wheel?"* 29 Law & Human Behav. 55, 81 (2005) (on how poor expert testimony is obscured by the "guise of science").

61. Cunningham et al., *supra* note 57, at 226.

62. Jurek v. Texas, 428 U.S. 262 (1976). See *supra* text accompanying notes 6–16.

63. *Barefoot*, 463 U.S. at 898. *Cf.* Comment, *Crystal-Balling Death*, 30 BAYLOR L. REV. 35, 54 (1978) (pointing out that *Jurek* "did not deal at all with the specific problem of psychiatric judgments which purport to predict future dangerousness"). See e.g., Lyle G. v. Harlem Valley Psychiatric Center, 521 N.Y.S.2d 94 (A.D. 1987) (rejecting, on the basis of *Barefoot*, challenges to psychiatric expertise to predict dangerousness) (non–death penalty case).

64. Addington v. Texas, 441 U.S. 418, 429 (1979) 441 U.S. 418, 429 (1979).

65. Project, *Civil Commitment of the Mentally Ill*, 14 UCLA L. REV. 822, 829 n. 35 (1967).

66. *Barefoot's Ake*, *supra* note 41, at 111 (emphasis in original; footnote omitted). On the question of the need for extra reliability in capital punishment decision making, see Woodson v. North Carolina, 428 U.S. 280, 305 (1976) (opinion of Stewart, Powell, Stevens, J.). See also Ford v. Wainwright, 477 U.S. 399 (1986), discussed extensively *infra* chapter 6.

67. On the meager follow-up litigation on this aspect of *Barefoot*, see *infra* notes 68–70.

See, however, State v. Davis, 477 A.2d 308 (N.J. 1984), sanctioning the admissibility of statistical evidence by a defendant at the penalty phase of a capital case relating to empirical studies pertaining to the defendant's rehabilitory potential in a case where the defendant raised his character as a mitigating factor (*id.* at 310–12; see N.J. STAT. ANN. § 2C:11-3c(5)(h) (1982)), relying on Justice Blackmun's dissent to buttress its position, 477 A.2d at 311, and discussed extensively in *Barefoot's Ake*, *supra* note 41, at 119–21; State v. Daniels, 446 S.E.2d 298 (N.C. 1994), *cert. denied*, 513 U.S. 1135 (1995) (expert testimony in capital case could be based on review of records of other doctors and discussions with the defendant's friends and family, even if expert conducted no in-person tests or evaluations of defendant), discussed in John Christopher Johnson, *State v. Daniels: Chief Justice Exum's Quantum Theory of Psychiatric Testimony*, 73 N.C. L. REV. 2326 (1995).

68. But see *Davis*, 477 A. 2d at 312, 314. *Cf.* Deveau v. United States, 483 A.2d 307, 315–16 (D.C. App. 1984) (quoting Justice Blackmun's dissent on unreliability of psychiatric predictions of future dangerousness), and *id.* at 316 ("If the trial court has reason to reject the opinions of the experts on the issue of dangerousness, it may also do so even though they are unanimous").

69. Streetman v. State, 698 S.W.2d 132, 137 (Tex. Crim. App. 1985)Streetman v. State, 698 S.W.2d 132, 137 (Tex. Crim. App. 1985); Nethery v. State, 692 S.W.2d 686, 708–9 (Tex. Crim. App. 1985) (a Dr. Grigson case); Holloway v. State, 691 S.W.2d 608, 616–17 (Tex. Crim. App. 1984); Smith v. State, 683 S.W.2d 393, 409 (Tex. Crim. App. 1984). But see Brown v. State, 689 S.W.2d 219, 221 (Tex. Crim. App. 1984) (Teague, J., dissenting from denial of defendant's motion for rehearing) (*Barefoot* distinguishable in case where defendant sought unsuccessfully to introduce testimony "to assist jurors in judging or evaluating eyewitness identification testimony").

70. See e.g., State v. Gates, 503 A.2d 163, 166 (Conn. 1986); State v. Plath, 313 S.E.2d 619, 627 (S.C. 1984); Edmonds v. Commonwealth, 329 S.E.2d 807, 813 (Va. 1985); Woomer v. Aiken, 856 F.2d 677 (4th Cir.), *reh'g & reh'g en banc denied* (1988); Lagrone v. State, 942 S.W.2d 602 (Tex. App. 1997), *reh'g denied* (1997), *cert. denied*, 522 U.S. 917 (1997); Moody v. Johnson, 139 F.3d 477 (5th Cir. 1998), *cert. denied*, 525 U.S. 940 (1998). See also, In re L.R., 497 A.2d 753, 755 (Vt. 1985) (hypothetical question permissible at involuntary civil commitment proceeding under authority of *Barefoot*). But see Thomas v. State, 378 S.E.2d 686, 687 (Ga. 1989) (exclusion of court-appointed psychiatrist's testimony on grounds of "irrelevancy and questionable scientific reliability" proper); Buttrum v. Black, 721 F. Supp. 1268, 1310–11 (N.D. Ga. 1989), *aff'd*, 908 F.2d 695 (1th Cir. 1990) (error under *Barefoot* and Ake v. Oklahoma, 470 U.S. 68 (1985), to fail to provide defendant with funds for psychological assistance so as to oppose prosecution witness's opinion evidence as to defendant's future dangerousness); Hanson v. State, 72 P.3d 40 (Okla. App. 2003) (defendant entitled to *Daubert* hearing where prosecutor sought to exclude as unreliable defendant's proffered testimony about his future nondangerousness). *Daubert* is discussed in this context *infra* at text accompanying notes 71–81.

Compare People v. Mattson, 268 Cal. Rptr. 802, 837–38 (1990), *cert. denied*, 498 U.S. 1017 (1990), *superseded by statute on other grounds as stated in* People v. Jennings, 807 P.2d 1009, 1043 n. 13 (Cal. 1991), *reh'g denied* (1991), *cert. denied*, 502 U.S. 969 (1991) (notwithstanding decision in People v. Murtishaw, 175 Cal. Rptr. 738 (1981), prohibiting psychiatric predictions of future dangerousness at sentencing phase in capital cases, no error committed when prosecutor questioned expert witnesses as to defendant's potential future dangerousness where defendant had initially raised issue of his likely future nondangerousness). For other relevant cases, see e.g., Soria v. State, 933 S.W.2d 46 (Tex. Crim. App. 1996), *reh'g denied* (1996), *cert. denied*, 520 U.S. 1253 (1997); Savino v. Murray, 82 F.3d 593 (4th Cir. 1996), *cert. denied*, 518 U.S. 1036 (1997).

For an analysis of the interplay between *Barefoot* and the Supreme Court case of Satterwhite v. Texas, 486 U.S. 249 (1988) (harmless error rule applies to admission of psychiatric testimony in violation of Sixth Amendment right to counsel at psychiatric exam), see 4 PERLIN, *supra* note 6, § 10-2.3b. Compare Marla L. Mitchell, *The Wizardry of Harmless Error: Brain, Heart, Courage Required When Reviewing Capital Sentences*, 4 KAN. J. L. & PUB. POL'Y 51 (1994) (harmless error analysis has no place in capital sentence jurisprudence due to the quality of death in relation to other punishments).

71. Daubert v. Merrill Dow Pharmaceuticals Inc., 509 U.S. 579 (1993) (allowing jurors to hear evidence and weigh facts from experts whose testimony included novel scientific theories, if the case warranted—even if those theories had not gained "general acceptance" in the scientific community—as long as the testimony was "relevant" and "reliable"). For cases applying *Daubert* to criminal procedure questions, see e.g., United States v. Hall, 93 F.3d 1337 (7th Cir. 1996), *reh'g denied* (1996), *cert. denied*, 511 U.S. 1085 (1994) (remanding where trial court used incorrect standard in excluding expert testimony on a defendant's susceptibility to giving a false confession); Moore v. Ashland Chem. Co., 151 F.3d 269 (5th Cir. 1998), *cert. denied*, 526 U.S. 1064 (1999) (clinical medical testimony on causation must pass *Daubert* test); Hanson v. State, 72 P.3d 40 (Okla. App. 2003), appeal after new sentencing hearing, 206 P.3d 1020 (Ola. 2009), *cert. denied*, 130 S. Ct. 808 (2009) (error for trial court to exclude, on *Daubert* grounds, defense expert's testimony about risk assessment and probability proffered to rebut continuing threat testimony, without holding a *Daubert* hearing), and United States v. Nichols, 169 F.3d 1255 (10th Cir.), *cert. denied*, 528 U.S. 934 (1999) (Oklahoma courthouse bombing case). On *Daubert* in this context, see JOHN PARRY & ERIC DROGIN, CRIMINAL LAW HANDBOOK ON PSYCHIATRIC AND PSYCHOLOGICAL EVIDENCE AND TESTIMONY 20–22 (2000); Daniel Krauss & Bruce Sales, *The Effects of Clinical and Scientific Expert Testimony on Juror Decisionmaking in Capital Sentencing*, 7 PSYCHOLOGY, PUB. POL'Y & L. 267 (2001); Teneille Brown & Emily Murphy, *Through a Scanner Darkly: Functional Neuroimaging as Evidence of a Criminal Defendant's Past Mental States*, 62 STAN. L. REV. 1119 (2010); compare Steven Erickson, *Blaming the Brain*, 11 MINN. J. L. SCI. & TECH. 27 (2010).

72. Kumho Tire Co. v. Carmichael, 526 U.S. 137 (1999) (applying *Daubert* to nonscientific expert testimony).

73. On the application of *Daubert* to cases involving neuroimaging evidence, see *infra* chapter 8.

74. Edens et al., *supra* note 60, at 57 (emphasis added). The "disinvent the wheel" phrase comes directly from *Barefoot*: see 463 U.S. at 896: "The suggestion that no psychiatrist's testimony may be presented with respect to a defendant's future dangerousness is somewhat like asking us to disinvent the wheel."

75. See *Flores v. Johnson*, 210 F.3d 456, 464–65 (5th Cir.), *cert. denied*, 531 U.S. 987 (2000).

76. See Roberts v. Thaler, 2011 WL 5433982, *15 (E.D. Tex. 2011).

77. 330 S.W.3d 253 (Tex. Crim. App. 2010).

78. *Id.* at 275–77.

79. *Id.* at 275 n. 54.

80. *Id.* at 286–87.

81. Edens et al., *supra* note 60; Eric F. Citron, *Sudden Death: The Legislative History of Future Dangerousness and the Texas Death Penalty*, 25 YALE L. & POL'Y REV. 143 (2006); Graham

Baker, *Defining and Determining Retardation in Texas Capital Murder Defendants: A Proposal to the Texas Legislature*, 9 Scholar 237 (2007).

82. Perlin, *supra* note 39, at *23 n. 83, citing Paul Giannelli, *Forensic Science under the Microscope*, 34 Ohio N. U. L. Rev. 315, 317 & n. 22 (2008); see generally, Deirdre Dwyer, *(Why) Are Civil and Criminal Expert Evidence Different?*, 43 Tulsa L. Rev. 381, 382–84 (2007).

83. Michael L. Perlin, *"His Brain Has Been Mismanaged with Great Skill": How Will Jurors Respond to Neuroimaging Testimony in Insanity Defense Cases?*, 42 Akron L. Rev. 885, 906–7 & 907 n. 139 (2009), citing D. Michael Risinger, *Navigating Expert Reliability: Are Criminal Standards of Certainty Being Left on the Dock?*, 64 Alb. L. Rev. 99, 105–8 (2000). Dwyer, *supra* note 82, at 382–84. Professor Susan Rozelle is blunter: "The game of scientific evidence looks fixed." Susan Rozelle, *Daubert, Schmaubert: Criminal Defendants and the Short End of the Science Stick*, 43 Tulsa L. Rev. 597, 598 (2007).

84. Paul Giannelli, *Daubert: Interpreting the Federal Rules of Evidence*, 15 Cardozo L. Rev. 1999, 2021 (1994).

85. See Regnier, *supra* note 23, at 506–7.

86. For cases affirming criminal convictions in the face of *Daubert* challenges, see e.g., Brewer v. State, 2011 Tex. Crim. App. Unpub. LEXIS 888 (Tex. Crim. App. 2011); Perez v. State, 113 S.W.3d 819 (Tex. App. Austin 2003); In re *Zamora*, 2007 Tex. App. LEXIS 5852 (Tex. App. Beaumont 2007); In re *Detention of Pederson*, 2000 Wash. App. LEXIS 629 (Wash. Ct. App. 2000); *Commonwealth v. Bradway*, 816 N.E.2d 152 (Mass. App. Ct. 2004); R.K. v. Kanaskie, 2007 U.S. Dist. LEXIS 50361 (S.D. Fla. 2007).

87. Michael Gottesman, *From Barefoot to Daubert to Joiner: Triple Play or Double Error?* 40 Ariz. L. Rev. 753, 756 (1998); Paul Gianelli, *Daubert: Interpreting the Federal Rules of Evidence*, 15 Cardozo L. Rev. 1999, 2020–21 (1994) (same).

88. See *infra* chapter 10.

89. On the relationship between *Barefoot* and effectiveness of counsel, see *Barefoot's Ake*, *supra* note 41.

90. *Barefoot*, 463 U.S. at 898.

91. See Mehler, *supra* note 23, at 123 ("Counsel should acquire enough understanding of psychology to . . . effectively cross-examine Dr. Death"). See also generally, Krauss & Sales, *supra* note 35. Compare Mark Cunningham et al., *Life and Death in the Lone Star State: Three Decades of Violence Predictions by Capital Juries*, 29 Behav. Sci. & L. 1, 1 (2011) (confidence of legislators and courts in the violence prediction capabilities of capital jurors is "misplaced"); Mark Cunningham, Thomas Reidy, & Jan Sorensen, *Assertions of "Future Dangerousness" at Federal Capital Sentencing: Rates and Correlates of Subsequent Prison Misconduct and Violence*, 32 Law & Hum. Behav. 46, 61 (2008) (error rate of "future dangerousness" assertions is "sobering").

92. See *infra* chapter 9 (on role of jurors).

93. *Barefoot*, 463 U.S. at 901 n. 7.

94. Jessica M. Tanner, *"Continuing Threat" to Whom?: Risk Assessment in Virginia Capital Sentencing Hearings*, 17 Cap. Def. J. 381, 399 (2005).

See generally, Mark D. Cunningham & Thomas J. Reidy, *Don't Confuse Me with the Facts: Common Errors in Violence Risk Assessment at Capital Sentencing*, 26 Crim. Just. & Behav. 20 (1999) (criticizing prevailing methodologies for inadequately relying on base rates, for failing to consider context, for being susceptible to illusory correlations, for failing to define the severity of projected future violence, for overreliance on clinical interviews, for misapplying psychological testing, for making faulty implications about antisocial personality disorders and psychopathy, for ignoring the effects of aging, for misusing patterns of behavior, for neglecting the potentiality of preventive measures, for depending on insufficient data, and for failing to express risk estimates in probabilistic terms).

95. William Berry III, *Ending Death by Dangerousness: A Path to the De Facto Abolition of the Death Penalty*, 52 Ariz. L. Rev. 889, 907 (2010).

96. Rabindranath Ramana, *Living and Dying with a Double-Edged Sword: Mental Health Evidence in the Tenth Circuit's Capital Cases*, 88 DENV. U. L. REV. 339, 369–70 (2011).

97. See John H. Blume, Stephen P. Garvey, & Sheri Lynn Johnson, *Future Dangerousness in Capital Cases: Always "At Issue,"* 86 CORNELL L. REV. 397, 404 (2001). Compare J.W. Looney, *Neuroscience's New Techniques for Evaluating Future Dangerousness: Are We Returning to Lombroso's Biological Criminality?* 32 U. ARK. LITTLE ROCK L. REV. 301, 314 (2010): "The second most powerful aggravating factor (next to the crime itself) for juries in death penalty cases is evidence of future dangerousness" (author a sitting circuit judge in Arkansas).

98. Vann, *supra* note 1, at 1273, citing Cunningham et al., *supra* note 57, at 240, 246.

99. Christopher Slobogin, *A Jurisprudence of Dangerousness*, 98 NW. U. L. REV. 1, 53 (2003).

100. Mark D. Cunningham & Thomas J. Reidy, *Violence Risk Assessment at Federal Capital Sentencing*, 29 CRIM. JUST. & BEHAV. 512, 532–33 (2002).

101. Vann, *supra* note 1, at 1274 n. 141, citing Cunningham et al., *supra* note 57, at 225, 244.

102. Shapiro, *supra* note 23, at 147; see Edens et al., *supra* note 60, at 81 ("it is evident that courts continue to allow unreliable expert opinions of violence risk").

103. Berry, *supra* note 95, at 889.

104. MICHAEL L. PERLIN, THE JURISPRUDENCE OF THE INSANITY DEFENSE 295–96 (1994).

105. See *supra* notes 23 & 41.

106. Michael L. Perlin, *"Half-Wracked Prejudice Leaped Forth": Sanism, Pretextuality, and Why and How Mental Disability Law Developed as It Did*, 10 J. CONTEMP. LEGAL ISSUES 3, 27–28 (1999).

107. A "false negative" is a prediction (or a decision based upon a belief) that an actually violent person will not be violent. See Henry J. Steadman, *The Right Not to Be a False Positive: Problems in the Application of the Dangerousness Standard*, 52 PSYCHIATRIC Q. 84, 85–86 (1980).

108. Peter Margulies, *Judging Myopia in Hindsight: Bivens Actions, National Security Decisions, and the Rule of Law*, 96 IOWA L. REV. 195, 211 n. 70 (2011), relying on Christopher Slobogin, *Dangerousness and Expertise Redux*, 56 EMORY L. J. 275, 311–16 (2006). In this context, on the question of "how fears about how a mistake would look in retrospect" to fact finders, see Douglas Mossman, *Dangerousness Decisions: An Essay on the Mathematics of Clinical Violence Predictions and Involuntary Hospitalization*, 2 U. CHI. L. SCH. ROUNDTABLE 95, 134 (1995).

109. 850 F.2d 231 (5th Cir 1988).

110. *Id.* at 234.

111. John Parry, *The Death Penalty and Persons with Mental Disabilities: A Lethal Dose of Stigma, Sanism, Fear of Violence, and Faulty Predictions of Dangerousness*, 29 MENTAL & PHYSICAL DISABILITY L. REP. 667, 667 (2005) (footnote omitted).

112. See generally, William Brooks, *The Tail Still Wags the Dog: The Pervasive and Inappropriate Influence by the Psychiatric Profession on the Civil Commitment Process*, 86 N.D. L. REV. 259, 259 (2010) ("the nebulous nature of the concept of dangerousness enables doctors to make pretextual assessments of danger").

113. *Barefoot*, 463 U.S. at 902.

114. *Id.* at 901 n. 7.

115. *Id.* at 898–901.

116. See *infra* chapter 10 (on global inadequacy of counsel).

117. On *Barefoot* and pretextuality, see Michael L. Perlin, *Pretexts and Mental Disability Law: The Case of Competency*, 47 U. MIAMI L. REV. 625, 668 (1993).

118. See e.g., Cunningham & Reidy, *supra* note 35; Cunningham & Sorensen, *supra* note 35; Cunningham et al., *supra* note 57; Cunningham et al., *supra* note 57. In one of the first therapeutic jurisprudence scholarly articles, Deborah Dorfman—a mental disability law litigator and professor—noted that "[W]e often presume that all mentally disabled individuals are dangerous by virtue of their mentally ill status, regardless of their actual condition and despite the fact that few of them

are actually dangerous." Deborah A. Dorfman, *Through a Therapeutic Jurisprudence Filter: Fear and Pretextuality in Mental Disability Law*, 10 N.Y. L. Sch. J. Hum. Rts. 805, 808 (1993).

119. Bruce J. Winick, *Sex Offender Law in the 1990s: A Therapeutic Jurisprudence Analysis*, 4 Psychol. Pub. Pol'y. & L. 505, 561 (1998).

120. *Id.*

121. Michael L. Perlin et al., *Therapeutic Jurisprudence and the Civil Rights of Institutionalized Mentally Disabled Persons: Hopeless Oxymoron or Path to Redemption?* 1 Psychol. Pub. Pol'y & L. 80, 87 (1995) (citations omitted).

122. Cunningham & Reidy, *supra* note 100, at 21.

123. Cunningham et al., *supra* note 57, at 251–52.

CHAPTER 4

1. Portions of the first through third sections of this chapter are adapted from Michael L. Perlin, *"The Executioner's Face Is Always Well-Hidden": The Role of Counsel and the Courts in Determining Who Dies*, 41 N.Y. L. Sch. L. Rev. 201 (1996).

2. See *Mental Health and Human Rights: Report of the Task Panel on Legal and Ethical Issues*, 20 Ariz. L. Rev. 49, 62 (1978), discussed in Michael L. Perlin, *Unpacking the Myths: The Symbolism Mythology of Insanity Defense Jurisprudence*, 40 Case W. Res. L. Rev. 599, 654 (1989–1990).

3. See e.g., Melody Martin, *Defending the Mentally Ill Client in Criminal Matters: Ethics, Advocacy, and Responsibility*, 52 U. Toronto Fac. L. Rev. 73 (1993) (discussing ethical issues facing counsel in cases involving mentally disabled criminal defendants); Kenneth B. Nunn, *The Trial as Text: Allegory, Myth, and Symbols in the Adversarial Criminal Process: A Critique of the Role of the Public Defender and a Proposal for Reform*, 32 Am. Crim. L. Rev. 743 (1995) (discussing myth in criminal cases); Michael L. Perlin, *Fatal Assumption: A Critical Evaluation of the Role of Counsel in Mental Disability Cases*, 16 Law & Hum. Behav. 39 (1992) (discussing myth in mental disability cases); Douglas W. Vick, *Poorhouse Justice: Underfunded Indigent Defense Services and Arbitrary Death Sentences*, 43 Buff. L. Rev. 329, 397–98 (1995) (discussing myth in criminal cases).

4. See generally, Jeffrey L. Kirchmeier, *Aggravating and Mitigating Factors: The Paradox of Today's Arbitrary and Mandatory Capital Punishment Scheme*, 6 Wm. & Mary Bill Rts. J. 345 (1998); see also, Valerie McClain, Elliot Atkins, & Michael L. Perlin, *"Oh, Stop That Cursed Jury": The Role of the Forensic Psychologist in the Mitigation Phase of the Death Penalty Trial*, in Handbook on Forensic Psychology (Mark Goldstein, ed. 2012) (in press). These findings have been required since the Supreme Court developed its mitigation jurisprudence in Eddings v. Oklahoma, 455 U.S. 104, 114 (1982), and Lockett v. Ohio, 438 U.S. 586, 604 (1978); see generally, 4 Michael L. Perlin, Mental Disability Law: Civil and Criminal § 12-3.3, at 493–95 (2d ed. 2002) (discussing *Eddings* and *Lockett*).

5. On the proliferation of aggravating factors in capital sentencing statutes, see Chelsea Creo Sharon, *The "Most Deserving" of Death: The Narrowing Requirement and the Proliferation of Aggravating Factors in Capital Sentencing Statutes*, 46 Harv. C.R.-C.L. L. Rev. 223 (2011).

6. See Evan J. Mandery, *Federalism and the Death Penalty*, 66 Albany L. Rev. 809, 810 (2003).

7. See e.g., Robert J. Smith, *The Geography of the Death Penalty and Its Ramifications*, 92 B.U. L. Rev. 227, 249 (2012): "The death penalty must be reserved for those who commit the worst of the worst offenses, but even among that limited group of offenders, the death penalty is only permissible for the most culpable offenders." But see Kevin Doyle, *Lethal Crapshoot: The Fatal Unreliability of the Penalty Phase*, 14 U. Pa. J. L. & Soc'l Change 275, 323 (2007–2008) ("All too often, a penalty phase will be a constitutionally unreliable determination waiting to happen").

8. 42 Pa. C.S.A. § 9711 (d).

9. 42 Pa. C.S.A. § 9711 (e).

10. 42 Pᴀ. C.S.A. § 9711 (e)(2).

11. 42 Pᴀ. C.S.A. § 9711 (e)(3).

12. 42 Pᴀ. C.S.A. § 9711 (c)(1)(iii).

13. 42 Pᴀ. C.S.A. § 9711 (c)(4).

14. See State v. Biegenwald, 524 A.2d 130, 155–56 (N.J. 1987). At the time that the *Biegenwald* case was decided, New Jersey's death penalty statute (see N.J. Sᴛᴀᴛ. Aɴɴ. § 2C:11-3 et seq.) was substantially similar to the Pennsylvania law. That penalty was abolished in New Jersey in 2007. See State v. Kenney, 2010 WL 3075642, *8 (N.J. Super. App. Div. 2010). For a candid discussion about abolition and about county-by-county practice in New Jersey during the years that the death penalty was operative, see W. Michael Murphy et al., *Panel I: The Struggle in the Courtroom*, 33 Sᴇᴛᴏɴ Hᴀʟʟ Lᴇɢɪs. J. 69 (2008).

15. Welsh S. White, *Capital Punishment's Future*, 91 Mɪᴄʜ. L. Rᴇᴠ. 1429, 1434 (1993) (reviewing Rᴀʏᴍᴏɴᴅ Pᴀᴛᴇʀɴᴏsᴛᴇʀ, Cᴀᴘɪᴛᴀʟ Pᴜɴɪsʜᴍᴇɴᴛ ɪɴ Aᴍᴇʀɪᴄᴀ (1991)); see also, Welsh S. White, *Effective Assistance of Counsel in Capital Cases: The Evolving Standard of Care*, 1993 U. Iʟʟ. L. Rᴇᴠ. 323, 338 (1993) (quoting a leading capital defense lawyer as stating, "[I]t's a rare case in which the capital defendant has no mental problems").

16. Russell Stetler, *The Mystery of Mitigation: What Jurors Need to Make a Reasoned Moral Response in Capital Sentencing*, 11 U. Pᴀ. J. L. & Sᴏᴄ. Cʜᴀɴɢᴇ 237, 237 (2007–2008). For a study of both mock jurors and actual jurors, see Marla Sandys et al., *Aggravation and Mitigation: Findings and Implications*, 37 J. Psʏᴄʜɪᴀᴛʀʏ & L. 189 (2009).

17. On the question of whether a defendant may *prevent* his lawyer from introducing mitigation evidence at the penalty phase, see Kamela Nelan, *Restricting Waivers of the Presentation of Mitigating Evidence by Incompetent Death Penalty "Volunteers,"* 27 Dᴇᴠ. Mᴇɴᴛᴀʟ Hᴇᴀʟᴛʜ L. 24 (Jan. 2008), and see *infra* note 65. This was an issue in Moran v. Godinez, 972 F.2d 263, 265 (9th Cir. 1992), *rev'd*, 509 U.S. 389 (1993) (establishing a unitary standard for competency to stand trial and competency to waive counsel and plead guilty) (defendant sought to plead guilty so as to avoid the presentation of evidence that could prevent imposition of the death penalty).

18. See Eddings v. Oklahoma, 455 U.S. 104, 114 (1982); Lockett v. Ohio, 438 U.S. 586, 604 (1978); see generally, 4 Pᴇʀʟɪɴ, *supra* note 4, § 12-3.3, at 493–95. Earlier statutes are collected in Ellen Fels Berkman, M*ental Illness as an Aggravating Circumstance in Capital Sentencing*, 89 Cᴏʟᴜᴍ. L. Rᴇᴠ. 291, 296–98 (1989). See *infra* text accompanying notes 104–5.

On how key terms in mitigation statutes are often "poorly defined and poorly understood by jurors," see Elizabeth S. Varkessian, *Dangerously Biased: How the Texas Capital Sentencing Statute Encourages Jurors to Be Unreceptive to Mitigation Evidence*, 29 Qᴜɪɴɴɪᴘɪᴀᴄ L. Rᴇᴠ. 237, 250 (2011), citing, inter alia, Cʀᴀɪɢ Hᴀɴᴇʏ, Dᴇᴀᴛʜ ʙʏ Dᴇsɪɢɴ: Cᴀᴘɪᴛᴀʟ Pᴜɴɪsʜᴍᴇɴᴛ ᴀs ᴀ Sᴏᴄɪᴀʟ Psʏᴄʜᴏʟᴏɢɪᴄᴀʟ Sʏsᴛᴇᴍ 143 (2005); James Luginbuhl & Julie Howe, *Discretion in Capital Sentencing Instructions: Guided or Misguided?*, 70 Iɴᴅ. L. J. 1161, 1181 (1995); on the Texas system in general, see Eric Citron, *Sudden Death: The Legislative History of Future Dangerousness and the Texas Death Penalty*, 25 Yᴀʟᴇ L. & Pᴏʟ'ʏ Rᴇᴠ. 143 (2006).

19. 428 U.S. 153 (1976). See generally, McClain, Atkins, & Perlin, *supra* note 4.

20. See James S. Liebman & Michael J. Shepard, *Guiding Capital Sentencing Discretion beyond the "Boiler Plate": Mental Disorder as a Mitigating Factor*, 66 Gᴇᴏ. L. J. 757, 759–60 n. 17 (1978) (discussing the Court's decisions in *Gregg*; Jurek v. Texas, 428 U.S. 262 (1976); Profitt v. Florida, 428 U.S. 242 (1976); Roberts v. Louisiana, 428 U.S. 325 (1976), and Woodson v. North Carolina, 428 U.S. 280 (1976)). On the ways that jury instructions affect decision making in this context, see Susie Cho, *Capital Confusion: The Effect of Jury Instructions on the Decision to Impose Death*, 85 J. Cʀɪᴍ. L. & Cʀɪᴍɪɴᴏʟᴏɢʏ 532, 561 (1994) (criticizing the Supreme Court for relying on "intuitive assumptions of juror infallibility").

On the parallel (but often closely related) question of the factors that influence jurors in insanity defense cases, see Karen Whittemore & James R.P. Ogloff, *Factors That Influence Jury Decision Making: Disposition Instructions and Mental State at the Time of the Trial*, 19 Lᴀᴡ &

HUM. BEHAV. 283 (1995); Carmen Cirincione & Charles Jacobs, *Identifying Insanity Acquittals: Is It Any Easier?* 23 LAW & HUM. BEHAV. 487 (1999); Randy Borum & Sol Fulero, *Empirical Research on the Insanity Defense and Attempted Reforms: Evidence toward Informed Policy*, 23 LAW & HUM. BEHAV. 375 (1999); Tarika Daftury-Kapur et al., *Measuring Knowledge of the Insanity Defense: Scale Construction and Validation*, 29 BEHAV. SCI. & L. 40 (2011).

21. 4 PERLIN, *supra* note 4, § 12-3.2, at 493 (quoting Liebman & Shepard, *supra* note 20, at 818).

22. Doyle, *supra* note 7, at 323.

23. Material accompanying notes 24–34 is partially adapted from MICHAEL L. PERLIN, LAW AND MENTAL DISABILITY § 4.47(C), at 642–43 (1994).

24. 438 U.S. 586 (1978).

25. *Id.* at 604. For a thoughtful contemporaneous analysis of *Lockett*'s place on the Supreme Court's jurisprudential death penalty continuum, see Margaret Jane Radin, *Cruel Punishment and Respect for Persons: Super Due Process for Death*, 53 S. CAL. L. REV. 1143 (1980).

26. 455 U.S. 104 (1982).

27. *Id.* at 114.

28. *Id.* at 107–8.

29. *Id.* at 107.

30. *Id.* at 107–8.

31. See *id.* at 108–9. The state raised three aggravating circumstances in favor of imposing a death sentence: "that the murder was especially heinous, atrocious or cruel, that the crime was committed for the purpose of avoiding or preventing a lawful arrest, and that there was a probability that defendant would commit criminal acts of violence that would constitute a continuing threat to society." *Id.* at 106–7.

32. *Id.* at 113–17.

33. *Id.* at 115 n. 10.

34. C. Richard Showalter & Richard Bonnie, *Psychiatry and Capital Sentencing: Risks and Responsibilities in a Unique Legal Setting*, 12 BULL. AM. ACAD. PSYCHIATRY & L. 159, 161 (1984) (emphasis added). On the importance of using a qualified expert in uncovering possible mitigation evidence, see John Fabian, *Death Penalty Mitigation and the Role of the Forensic Psychologist*, 27 LAW & PSYCHOL. REV. 73 (2003). For subsequent cases, see e.g., Lackey v. State, 819 S.W.2d 111 (Tex. Crim. App. 1989), *reh'g overruled* (1991), *cert. denied*, 513 U.S. 1086 (1995); State v. Fierro, 804 P.2d 72 (Ariz. 1990), *reconsideration denied* (1991); State v. Gibbs, 436 S.E.2d 321 (N.C. 1993), *cert. denied*, 512 U.S. 1246 (1994); Webb v. Warden 2011 WL 724774 (Conn. Super. 2011); Miller v. State, 2010 WL 129708 (Ark. 2010); State v. Frawley, 172 P.3d 144 (N.M. 2007).

35. 130 S. Ct. 447 (2009).

36. *Id.* at 455. The military service was also relevant to a mitigation inquiry because of "the intense stress and mental and emotional toll that combat took." *Id.* See also, Sears v. Upton, 130 S. Ct. 3259 (2010) (state postconviction court failed to apply proper prejudice inquiry in determining that counsel's facially inadequate mitigation investigation did not prejudice defendant).

37. This section is largely adapted from PERLIN, *supra* note 23, § 4.47(C), at 643.

38. 492 U.S. 302 (1989). See e.g., Bigby v. Dretke, 402 F.3d 551 (5th Cir. 2005), *cert. den.*, 546 U.S. 900 (2005) (sentencing instruction failed to allow jury to give effect to mitigating evidence and stripped it of vehicle for expressing its reasoned moral response to appropriateness of death penalty, in violation of Eighth Amendment).

39. *Penry*, 492 U.S. at 321 (quoting Franklin v. Lynaugh, 487 U.S. 164, 185 (1988)). The defendant in Penry was mentally retarded. See *id.* at 307. See generally 4 PERLIN, *supra* note 4, § 12-3.3, at 495–97, discussing *Penry*. On the traditional role of clemency in such cases, see Daniel T. Kobil, *The Quality of Mercy Strained: Wresting the Pardoning Power from the King*, 69 TEX. L. REV. 569, 624–27 (1991). On *Penry*'s failure to prevent the execution of persons with mental retardation, see *infra* chapter 5.

40. See *Penry*, 492 U.S. at 322.

41. *Id.*

42. *Id.* at 322–26. See also e.g., Bigby v. Dretke 402 F.3d 551 (5th Cir. 2005) (striking jury instructions in death penalty cases that fail to ask about mitigating factors including a consideration of the defendant's social, medical, and psychological history, saying that the jury must be instructed to consider mitigating factors even when answering unrelated questions).

43. See *id.* at 328; see also e.g., Kwan Fai Mak v. Blodgett, 754 F. Supp. 1490 (W.D. Wash. 1991) (holding that ineffective assistance of counsel was demonstrated where lawyer failed to adduce mitigating evidence regarding severe assimilation difficulties experienced by adolescents from Far Eastern cultures when they relocate to the United States).

44. Penry v. Johnson, 532 U.S. 782, 786 (2001). See generally 4 Perlin, *supra* note 4, § 12-3.3, at 498–500, discussing *Penry II*.

45. *Id.* at 796.

46. *Id.* at 797.

47. *Id.* at 800. For commentary on *Penry II*, see David Barron, *I Did Not Want to Kill Him But Thought I Had To: In Light of* Penry II's *Interpretation of* Blystone, *Why the Constitution Requires Jury Instructions on How to Give Effect to Relevant Mitigating Evidence in Capital Cases*, 11 J. L. & Pol'y 207 (2002).

48. 542 U.S. 274 (2004).

49. *Id.* at 281.

50. *Id.* at 283.

51. Compare Atkins v. Virginia, 536 U.S. 304 (2002) (Eighth Amendment bars the execution of persons with mental retardation). See *infra* chapter 5.

52. *Tennard*, 542 U.S. at 284.

53. *Id.* at 285.

54. *Id.*, citing McKoy v. North Carolina, 494 U.S. 433 (1990).

55. *Id.* at 276, citing Boyde v. California, 494 U.S. 370 (1990).

56. *Id.* at 281. On how failure to investigate such potentially mitigating evidence may give rise to a claim for ineffectiveness of counsel under Strickland v. Washington, 466 U.S. 668 (1984), see *infra* chapter 10; see Rompilla v. Beard, 545 U.S. 374 (2005).

57. *Tennard*, 542 U.S. at 287, *citing* Atkins v. Virginia, 536 U.S. 304 (2002). See generally, Michael L. Perlin, *"Life Is in Mirrors, Death Disappears": Giving Life to* Atkins, 33 N. Mex. L. Rev. 315 (2003).

58. *Tennard*, 542 U.S. at 289. See Smith v. Texas, 543 U.S. 37 (2004) (state death penalty systems must allow the sentencer to give full consideration to all mitigating circumstances); see also e.g., Bigby v. Dretke, 402 F.3d 551 (5th Cir. 2005).

59. Portions of this section are generally adapted from Perlin, *supra* note 23, § 4.47(D), at 644–45.

60. See Porter v. McCollum, 130 S. Ct. 447 (2009); see also e.g., Moody v. State, 418 So. 2d 989 (Fla. 1982); Smith v. Mullin, 379 F.3d 919 (10th Cir. 2004) (court's rejection of claimed *Penry II* error in capital murder trial was not contrary to or an unreasonable application of federal law, where general mitigation instruction allowing consideration of all evidence, when coupled with additional instruction listing particular mitigating factors which did not include mental retardation, did not prevent jury from giving effect to evidence of petitioner's impaired cognitive functioning).

61. See Spivey v. Zant, 661 F.2d 464, 472 (5th Cir. 1981). The Capital Jury Project has found that 45 percent of jurors failed to understand that they were allowed to consider *any* mitigating evidence during the sentencing phase of the trial, not solely the factors listed in the instructions. See http://www.capitalpunishmentincontext.org/issues/juryinstruct.

62. See e.g., Morgan v. Zant, 743 F.2d 775 (11th Cir. 1984); Westbrook v. Zant, 704 F.2d 1487 (11th Cir. 1983); Hanson v. State, 72 P.3d 40 (Okla. App. 2003) (prejudicial error where

court refused defendant's proposed list of nine mitigating circumstances supported by evidence and instructed jury that it should consider three mitigating factors on which evidence had been introduced and "any others" that the jury found to exist).

63. See e.g., People v. Devin, 444 N.E.2d 102 (Ill. 1982); State v. Brogdon, 457 So. 2d 616 (La. 1984); State v. Woomer, 299 S.E.2d 317 (S.C. 1982). See generally, Christopher Slobogin, *Mental Illness and the Death Penalty*, 1 CAL. CRIM. L. REV. 3 (2000).

64. See e.g., State v. Smith, 638 P.2d 696 (Ariz. 1981).

65. State v. Ashworth, 706 N.E.2d 1231, *reconsideration den.*, 709 N.E.2d 173 (Ohio 1999), *cert. denied*, 528 U.S. 908 (1999) (trial court obligated to inquire into whether waiver is knowing and voluntary); Wilkins v. Bowersox, 145 F.3d 1006 (8th Cir. 1998), *reh'g & suggestion for reh'g en banc denied* (1998), *cert. den.*, 525 U.S. 1094 (1999) (waiver not knowing, intelligent, and voluntary); Ocha v. State, 826 So. 2d 956 (Fla. 2002) (defendant's waiver was voluntary, court conducted adequate investigation of its own and did not abuse discretion by failing to order further testing of defendant); see also *id.* at 966 (arguing for adopting a procedure for the appointment of special counsel to present available mitigation for the benefit of the jury, trial court, and appellate court reviewing for proportionality) (Pariente, J., concurring).

See *Porter*, 130 S. Ct. at 453 (although defendant was "fatalistic and uncooperative, . . . that does not obviate the need for defense counsel to conduct *some* sort of mitigation investigation") (emphasis in original). On the complex legal issues that relate to the waiver of the presentation of mitigation testimony, see Justin Marceau, *Exploring the Intersection of Effectiveness and Autonomy in Capital Sentencing*, 42 CAL. W. L. REV. 183 (2008).

66. State v. Reid, 981 S.W.2d 1676 (Tenn. 1998) (pretrial notice must be filed).

67. See Wood v. Allen, 130 S. Ct. 841 (2010), discussed *infra* note 83.

68. Sears v. Upton, 130 S. Ct. 3259 (2010) (state postconviction court failed to apply proper prejudice inquiry in determining that counsel's facially inadequate mitigation investigation did not prejudice defendant). In *Sears*, counsel had presented evidence describing the defendant's childhood as "stable, loving, and essentially without incident," *id.* at 3261, in an effort to "portray the adverse impact of [his] execution on his family and loved ones," a strategy that backfired as the prosecutor "used the evidence of [petitioner's] purportedly stable and advantaged upbringing against him during the State's closing argument," *id.* at 3262. Rather than being "privileged in every way," as the state argued, defendant had suffered sexual abuse from a male cousin, was demeaned by his mother who referred to him and his brothers as "little mother fuckers," and his father who was "verbally abusive" and disciplined him "with age-inappropriate military-style drills," *id.*

69. See Simmons v. State, 419 So. 2d 316, 317 (Fla. 1982) (noting that at sentencing, the defendant presented testimony of an examining psychiatrist who concluded that, while the defendant was neither psychotic nor neurotic, while he knew right from wrong, and while he was of normal intelligence, he suffered from a character disorder and extreme emotional immaturity); see also State v. English, 367 So. 2d 815, 819 (La. 1979) (holding that at the penalty phase, even where the insanity defense is rejected, "another dimension of mental condition comes into play").

70. Compare *Simmons*, 419 So. 2d at 320 (stating that the potential for rehabilitation is an element of character and thus may not be excluded from consideration as a potentially mitigating factor), with Volle v. State, 474 So. 2d 796, 804 (Fla. 1985) (distinguishing *Simmons*, where proffered testimony of corrections consultants and prison psychiatrists that defendant—if given life sentence rather than death—would be a "model prisoner," was characterized as irrelevant to sentencing inquiry).

71. See People v. Moseley, 281 N.Y.S.2d 762, 765 (1967) (finding that defendant was not attempting to relitigate the issue of his legal insanity or criminal responsibility; instead, he was properly endeavoring to persuade the jury that, while his mental illness was not a defense to the crime, it may have rendered it impossible for him to exercise any self-control and should, therefore, be considered in mitigation); see also Mines v. State, 390 So. 2d 332, 337 (Fla. 1980) (finding of sanity does not eliminate consideration of statutory mitigating factors concerning mental condition).

72. See Washington v. Commonwealth, 323 S.E.2d 577, 586 (Va. 1984); see also, Bigby v. Dretke, 402 F.3d 551 (5th Cir. 2005) (defendant's mental disorder must be considered as a mitigating factor in sentencing in a death penalty case, even if mental illness was not brought up in the trial).

73. See generally, 4 PERLIN, *supra* note 4, § 12-3.5, at 505.

74. George Dix, *Psychological Abnormality and Capital Sentencing: The New "Diminished Responsibility,"* 7 INT'L J. L. & PSYCHIATRY 249, 264 (1984); see also, Ronald J. Tabak, *Executing People with Mental Disabilities: How We Can Mitigate an Aggravating Situation*, 25 ST. LOUIS U. PUB. L. REV. 283 (2006); see e.g., State v. Smith, 292 S.E.2d 264, 272, 276–77 (N.C. 1982), *cert. denied*, 459 U.S. 1056 (1982) (evidence of emotional disturbance as result of antisocial personality insufficient to mitigate in case of "agonizing and humiliating torture" of "wanton, brutal murder"). Compare *Smith*, 459 U.S. at 1056–58 (separate opinion of Stevens, J., respecting denial of *certiorari*), suggesting, *id.* at 1056, a "serious question of compliance," with Lockett v. Ohio, 438 U.S. 586 (1978).

For subsequent research, see e.g., John F. Edens et al., *The Impact of Mental Health Evidence on Support for Capital Punishment: Are Defendants Labeled Psychopathic Considered More Deserving of Death?*, 23 BEHAV. SCI. & L. 603 (2005); Michelle E. Barnett et al., *When Mitigation Evidence Makes a Difference: Effects of Psychological Mitigating Evidence on Sentencing Decisions in Capital Trials*, 22 BEHAV. SCI. & L. 751 (2004); Sandys et al., *supra* note 16, at 194; Paul Litton, *Responsibility Status of the Psychopath: On Moral Reasoning and Rational Self-Governance*, 39 RUTGERS L. J. 349, 350 (2008); Melody Dickson, *Dismantling the Free Will Fairytale: The Importance of Demonstrating the Inability to Overcome in Death Penalty Narratives*, 77 UMKC L. REV. 1123 (2009).

At least one case has considered—in the course of an opinion which sheds important light on the role of counsel and client in decision making in this aspect of the trial process—the right of the defendant to proffer mitigating evidence at the guilt phase of a capital trial over his lawyer's objections. See People v. Frierson, 705 P.2d 396 (Cal. 1985). There, the defendant's lawyer essentially took the position that the presentation of a mitigation defense would backfire and lead to the imposition of the death penalty. *Id.*, 705 P.2d at 400. The case is couched in "diminished capacity" terminology. See generally, 4 PERLIN, *supra* note 4, § 9A-3.6. In reversing the penalty judgment, the California Supreme Court held that, given the "fundamental importance" of the issue, *Frierson*, 705 P.2d at 405, counsel could not "properly refuse to honor defendant's clearly expressed desire to present a defense at that stage," *Id.* at 403. *Cf.* People v. Robertson, 767 P.2d 1109 (Cal. 1989), *cert. denied*, 493 U.S. 985 (1989) (capital defendant could waive right to be present at sentence modification hearing).

75. Christopher Seeds, *Strategery's Refuge*, 99 J. CRIM. L. & CRIMINOL. 987, 990 (2009).

76. See e.g., Stephen P. Garvey, *Aggravation and Mitigation in Capital Cases: What Do Jurors Think?*, 98 COLUM. L. REV. 1538, 1559 (1998) (44.3 percent of jurors reported that they were much less likely to vote for the death penalty in cases involving defendants with mental retardation; 26.7 percent of responding jurors stated that they would be much less likely to return a death sentence if the defendant had a history of mental illness). Garvey's findings are discussed carefully in Rabindranath Ramana, *Living and Dying with a Double-Edged Sword: Mental Health Evidence in the Tenth Circuit's Capital Cases*, 88 DENV. U. L. REV. 339, 350 (2011).

77. American Psychiatric Association, *Diminished Responsibility in Capital Sentencing*, 2004, as referred to in http://www.aclu.org/capital-punishment/mental-illness-and-death-penalty. On the difficulties inherent in overcoming juror "cynicism" about mental illness, see Russell Stetler, *Mental Disabilities and Mitigation*, 23 CHAMPION 49 (1999).

78. Sandys et al., *supra* note 16. And see *id.* (on the other hand, defendants who experienced a traumatic life event *out of their control* are more likely to receive a life sentence).

79. See e.g., Gary Kowaluk, *Defense Strategy in Capital Cases: The Denial Defense Trap*, 47 CRIM. L. BULL. 893, 920 (2011).

80. *Id.* at 923.

81. http://www.newyorker.com/reporting/2011/05/09/110509fa_fact_toobin. See also *id.* (quoting Recer): "Someone who is a beloved brother and husband and father and son can also commit a terrible act. Those two things are not mutually exclusive. It's not the way human nature works. And that could be a reason to spare his life."

82. Jesse Cheng, *Frontloading Mitigation: The "Legal" and the "Human" in Death Penalty Defense*, 35 LAW & SOC'L INQUIRY 39, 39–40 (2010). See also e.g., Sean D. O'Brien, *When Life Depends on It: Supplementary Guidelines for the Mitigation Function of Defense Teams in Death Penalty Cases*, 36 HOFSTRA L. REV. 693, 732 (2008) ("A successful capital defense investigation, therefore, is one that leaves no stone unturned in examining a wide range of evidence from a broad set of sources to discover and communicate the humanizing events and conditions that exist in the life of every capital client"); John Matthew Fabian, *Mitigating Murder at Capital Sentencing: An Empirical and Practical Psycho-legal Strategy*, 9 J. FORENS. PSYCHOL. PRAC. 1 (2009) (investigation and preparation of mitigation testimony critical to penalty phase of case); Craig Haney, *Condemning the Other in Death Penalty Trials: Biographical Racism, Structural Mitigation, and the Empathic Divide*, 53 DEPAUL L. REV. 1557, 1581 (2004) ("evidence that provides a humanizing narrative account of the defendant's life and prior actions is essential to a case in mitigation because it helps capital jurors understand how forces beyond the defendant's control shaped the direction of his life and the adaptive nature of many of the actions in which he engaged").

83. See Wood v. Allen, 130 S. Ct. 841 (2010), holding that state court's factual determination that defense counsel made a strategic decision not to pursue or present evidence of defendant's mental deficiencies was not unreasonable in light of the evidence presented; compare *id.* at 853 (Stevens, J., dissenting):

> A decision cannot be fairly characterized as "strategic" unless it is a conscious choice between two legitimate and rational alternatives. It must be borne of deliberation and not happenstance, inattention, or neglect. See *Wiggins*, . . . (concluding that counsel's "failure to investigate thoroughly resulted from inattention, not reasoned strategic judgment"); *Strickland*, . . . Moreover, "a cursory investigation" does not "automatically justif[y] a tactical decision with respect to sentencing strategy." *Wiggins*, . . . Although we afford deference to counsel's strategic decisions, *Strickland*, . . . for this deference to apply there must be some evidence that the decision was just that: strategic.

84. Leona D. Jochnowitz, *How Capital Jurors Respond to Mitigating Evidence of Defendant's Mental Illness, Retardation, and Situational Impairments: An Analysis of the Legal and Social Science Literature*, 47 CRIM. L. BULL. 839, 840 (2011). Professor Seeds points out the depth of the split in cases reviewing the question of counsel's effectiveness at this stage. See Seeds, *supra* note 75, at 1020, reporting that nearly 60 percent (32 of 54) of the Sixth Circuit's decisions on the effectiveness of capital counsel's mitigation investigation and presentation come with a dissent or involve some disagreement on the application of Sixth Amendment law to the facts of the case. See also Wiggins v. Smith, 539 U.S. 510, 527 (2003) (holding that when considering the effectiveness of counsel's presentation of mitigation evidence in a death penalty case, "a court must consider not only the quantum of evidence already known to counsel, but also whether the known evidence would lead a reasonable attorney to investigate further"), discussed at greater length *infra* text accompanying notes 93–94.

85. See *infra* chapter 10. The defense lawyer's role in this enterprise is set out carefully and comprehensively in John H. Blume & Pamela Blume Leonard, *Principles of Developing and Presenting Mental Health Evidence in Criminal Cases*, 30 CHAMPION 63 (Nov. 2000).

86. Seeds, *supra* note 75, at 992–93.

87. See Kowaluk, *supra* note 79.

88. O'Brien, *supra* note 82, at 706.

89. Leona Jochnowitz, *Missed or Foregone Mitigation: Analyzing Claimed Error in Missouri Capital Clemency Cases*, 46 CRIM. L. BULL. 347, 375 (2010).

90. 539 US 510 (2003).

91. *Id.* at 532–35.

92. *Id.* at 524.

93. American Bar Association, *Guidelines for the Appointment and Performance of Defense Counsel in Death Penalty Cases*, 31 Hofstra L. Rev. 913, 919 (2003) (*Guidelines*), as discussed in Emily Hughes, *Arbitrary Death: An Empirical Study of Mitigation*, 89 Wash. U. L. Rev. 581, 629 (2012).

94. *Guidelines*, *supra* note 93, at 959.

95. *Id.* For a thoughtful inquiry into the role of the mitigation specialist, see Emily Hughes, *Mitigating Death*, 18 Cornell J. L. & Pub. Pol'y 337 (2009). On the diverse set of skills needed to engage in fact investigation, see Russell Stetler, *Mitigation Investigation: A Duty That Demands Expert Help But Can't Be Delegated*, 31 The Champion 61 (Mar. 2007).

96. O'Brien, *supra* note 82, at 695.

97. Seeds, *supra* note 75, at 999. But see Jochnowitz, *supra* note 84, at 374–75 (presentation of potentially mitigating family/social history omitted in nearly a quarter of all cases studied).

98. See O'Brien, *supra* note 82, at 722–24 (on humanizing the client).

99. On the significance of *nonverbal cues* in judicial perceptions of remorse, see Emily Corwin et al., *Defendant Remorse, Need for Affect, and Juror Sentencing Decisions*, 40 J. Am. Acad. Psychiatry & L. 41 (2012). This insight raises profoundly important issues in cases involving defendants from non-Western cultures. See Tracy Novinger, Intercultural Communication: A Practical Guide 21 (2001):

> Many people from Asian and Latin American cultures avoid eye contact as a sign of respect. This is also true of many African Americans, particularly in the southern United States. Many North American employers, teachers and similar "authority" figures interpret avoidance of eye contact as a sign of disrespect or deviousness.

On the need for cultural competence in forensic evaluations in general, see Michael L. Perlin & Valerie McClain, *"Where Souls Are Forgotten": Cultural Competencies, Forensic Evaluations and International Human Rights*, 15 Psychol., Pub. Pol'y & L 257 (2009).

100. Elliot Atkins et al., *Forensic Psychological Consultation in US Death Penalty Cases in State and Federal Courts* (presentation to American College of Forensic Psychology, San Francisco, CA (Aug. 2006) (copy on file with author)). See generally, Blume & Leonard, *supra* note 85.

As I will explore subsequently, see *infra* chapter 8, the potential availability of relatively new evaluative techniques—including neuroimaging—needs to be weighed by defense lawyers as part of their work at this stage of the death penalty case. See e.g., John H. Blume & Emily C. Paavola, *Life, Death, and Neuroimaging: The Advantages and Disadvantages of the Defense's Use of Neuroimages in Capital Cases—Lessons from the Front*, 62 Mercer L. Rev. 909 (2011); Michael L. Perlin & Valerie R. McClain, *Unasked (and Unanswered) Questions about the Role of Neuroimaging in the Criminal Trial Process*, 28 Am. J. Forensic Psychology 5 (2010); O. Carter Snead, *Neuroimaging and the "Complexity" of Capital Punishment*, 82 N.Y.U. L. Rev. 1265 (2007); Peggy Sasso, *Implementing the Death Penalty: The Moral Implications of Recent Advances in Neuropsychology*, 29 Cardozo L. Rev. 765 (2007).

101. On the specific relationship perceived by the public on the relationship between mental illness and evil, see Michael L. Perlin, *"What's Good Is Bad, What's Bad Is Good, You'll Find out When You Reach the Top, You're on the Bottom": Are the Americans with Disabilities Act (and Olmstead v. L.C.) Anything More than "Idiot Wind"?*, 35 U. Mich. J. L. Ref. 235, 239 n. 30 (2001–2002); Michael L. Perlin, *"There Are No Trials Inside the Gates of Eden": Mental Health Courts, the Convention on the Rights of Persons with Disabilities, Dignity, and the Promise of Therapeutic Jurisprudence*, in Coercive Care: Law and Policy (Bernadette McSherry & Penelope Weller, eds. 2012) (in press) (Perlin, *Gates of Eden*).

102. McClain, Atkins, & Perlin, *supra* note 4, manuscript at 36–37.

103. See *supra* chapter 2 for a full discussion.

104. See Berkman, *supra* note 18, at 299–300; Holman v. Gilmore, 126 F.3d 876, 873 (7th Cir. 1997): "What little scientific data we possess implies that trying to persuade the jury

that the accused is mentally ill is worse than no defense at all." For case studies in which juries used serious mental illness as an aggravator, see Laurie T. Izutsu, *Applying Atkins v. Virginia to Capital Defendants with Severe Mental Illness*, 70 BROOK. L. REV. 995 (2005). Compare Seeds, *supra* note 75, at 1033: "Whether jurors perceive double-edged life history evidence as more mitigating than aggravating or vice versa may depend on more than the nature of the evidence. It may also depend on how the evidence is presented."

105. Miller v. State, 373 So. 2d 882, 885 (Fla. 1979) (vacating death sentence). See *Upholding Law and Order*, HARTSVILLE MESSENGER, June 24, 1997, at 5B col. 1, cited in Lyn Entzeroth, *Putting the Mentally Retarded Criminal Defendant to Death: Charting the Development of a National Consensus to Exempt the Mentally Retarded from the Death Penalty*, 52 ALA. L. REV. 911, 927 n. 158 (2011) ("[t]here is all the more reason to execute a killer if he is also insane or retarded . . . an insane or retarded killer is more to be feared than a sane or normal killer"). See also, Scott Sundby, *The Jury as Critic: An Empirical Look at How Capital Juries Perceive Expert and Lay Testimony*, 83 VA. L. REV. 1109, 1165–67 (1997) (describing a case where some jurors' concern that defendant's mental illness would make him dangerous in the future overrode the mitigating evidence that he was a person with paranoid schizophrenia).

106. See MICHAEL L. PERLIN, THE JURISPRUDENCE OF THE INSANITY DEFENSE 387–92 (1994).

107. Michael L. Perlin, *The Sanist Lives of Jurors in Death Penalty Cases: The Puzzling Role of Mitigating Mental Disability Evidence*, 8 NOTRE DAME J. L., ETHICS & PUB. POL. 239, 265 (1994).

108. See Seth Branham, *Criminal Law: Oklahoma's New Standard of Proof in Competency Proceedings: Due Process, State Interests, and a Murderer Named Cooper*, 51 OKLA. L. REV. 135, 151 (1998), relying on Perlin, *supra* note 107, at 265–70.

109. See Michael L. Perlin, *Psychodynamics and the Insanity Defense: "Ordinary Common Sense" and Heuristic Reasoning*, 69 NEB. L. REV. 3, 61–69 (1990).

110. See James M. Doyle, *The Lawyers' Art: "Representation" in Capital Cases*, 8 YALE J. L. & HUMAN. 417, 445 (1996) ("[T]here will be enormous pressures to craft a representation that earns the defendant membership in a preexisting, stereotypical category of 'acute' or 'extreme' illness, and to show that he fits into that category all of the time—that he is all sickness, no function").

111. See Michael L. Perlin & Keri K. Gould, *Rashomon and the Criminal Law: Mental Disability Law and the Federal Sentencing Guidelines*, 22 AM. J. CRIM. L. 431, 452–55 (1995).

112. United States v. Harpst, 949 F.2d 860, 863 (6th Cir. 1991).

113. United States v. Daly, 883 F.2d 313, 319 (4th Cir. 1989).

114. On our "culture of blame," see e.g., Neil R. Feigenson, *Sympathy and Legal Judgment: A Psychological Analysis*, 65 TENN. L. REV. 1, 60 & n. 258 (1997); Perlin, *Gates of Eden, supra* note 101. On our "culture of harm," see Craig Haney, *A Culture of Harm: Taming the Dynamics of Cruelty in Supermax Prisons*, 35 CRIM. JUST & BEHAV. 956 (2008). On the attribution of blame in the context of the aggravation/mitigation stage in specific, see Katherine Polzer & Kimberly Kempf-Leonard, *Social Construction of Aggravating and Mitigating Factors: How Capital Jurors Attribute Blame*, 45 CRIM. L. BULL. 982 (2009).

For contrasting examples as to how blame is contextualized in death penalty cases of defendants with major mental disabilities, compare http://www.internationaljusticeproject.org/illnessjbrown.cfm (accessed May 22, 2012), discussing the case of James Willie Brown (death row inmate diagnosed on seventeen occasions as having paranoid schizophrenia, but sentenced to death based on expert testimony that hallucinogenic flashbacks from the use of LSD years before the killing caused his mental illness), to Kristin Parke & John Tote, *A Better Law for North Carolina* (Mar. 27, 2010), http://www.newsobserver.com/2010/03/28/408647/a-better-law-for-north-carolina.html (last accessed May 12, 2012), discussing the case of Abdullah El-Amin Shareef, who was sentenced to life imprisonment instead of death, apparently in large part because just before the murder, the defendant had been turned away from a mental health program where he had sought treatment).

115. See generally Michael L. Perlin, *Pretexts and Mental Disability Law: The Case of Competency*, 47 U. Miami L. Rev. 625, 670–72 (1993).

116. See generally, Bernard Weiner, *On Sin Versus Sickness: A Theory of Perceived Responsibility and Social Motivation*, 48 Am. Psychologist 957 (1993).

117. Perlin, *supra* note 115, at 671.

118. Perlin, *supra* note 107, at 277.

119. See *supra* chapter 2 for a full discussion.

120. See Michael L. Perlin, *Unpacking the Myths: The Symbolism Mythology of Insanity Defense Jurisprudence*, 40 Case W. Res. L. Rev. 599, 648–55 (1989–1990). For representative case examples, see People v. Seuffer, 582 N.E.2d 71, 79 (Ill. 1991); State v. Papasavvas, 790 A.2d 798 (N.J. 2002); ex parte Trawick, 698 So.2d 162 (Ala. 1997), *cert. den.*, 522 U.S. 1000 (1997).

121. See Michael L. Perlin, *"The Borderline Which Separated You from Me": The Insanity Defense, the Authoritarian Spirit, the Fear of Faking, and the Culture of Punishment*, 82 Iowa L. Rev. 1375, 1390, 1412 (1997) (reporting on the research of, inter alia, Dorothy Otnow Lewis et al., *Neuropsychiatric, Psychoeducational, and Family Characteristics of 14 Juveniles Condemned to Death in the United States*, 145 Am. J. Psychiatry 584, 588 (1988) (Lewis, *Condemned to Death*); Dorothy Otnow Lewis et al., *Psychiatric, Neurological, and Psychoeducational Characteristics of 15 Death Row Inmates in the United States*, 143 Am. J. Psychiatry 838, 841 (1986); P.J. Taylor, *Motives for Offending among Violent and Psychotic Men*, 147 Brit. J. Psychiatry 491, 496–97 (1985).

122. See James R.P. Ogloff, *The Juvenile Death Penalty: A Frustrated Society's Attempt for Control*, 5 Behav. Sci. & L. 447 (1987) (discussing the scenario preceding Vermont's elimination of a minimum age for prosecuting children as adults in murder cases).

123. See James W. Marquart et al., *Gazing into the Crystal Ball: Can Jurors Accurately Predict Dangerousness in Capital Cases?*, 23 L. & Soc'y Rev. 449, 466 (1989). On the ways that jurors may equate mental illness with future dangerousness, see John Bessler, *Revisiting Beccaria's Vision: The Enlightenment, America's Death Penalty, and the Abolition Movement*, 4 NW J. L. & Soc. Pol'y 195, *166 n. 812 (2009). See generally *supra* chapter 3.

124. Phoebe C. Ellsworth et al., *The Death-Qualified Jury and the Defense of Insanity*, 8 Law & Hum. Behav. 81, 90 (1984).

125. Perlin, *supra* note 121, at 1399 (citing, inter alia, Neil Vidmar & Dale T. Miller, *Social-psychological Processes Underlying Attitudes toward Legal Punishment*, 14 L. & Soc'y Rev. 565, 591 (1980)). On the ways that death penalty supporters are motivated by "vindictive revenge," see Robert M. Bohm, *Retribution and Capital Punishment: Toward a Better Understanding of Death Penalty Opinion*, 20 J. Crim. Just. 227 (1992). On the relationship between religious belief and support for the death penalty, see Harold G. Grasmick et al., *Religious Beliefs and Public Support for the Death Penalty for Juveniles and Adults*, 16 J. Crime & Just. 59 (1993) (stating that adherence to a literal interpretation of the Bible is predictive of support for the death penalty). For a more recent reconsideration, see James F. Hooper, *The Insanity Defense: History and Problems*. 25 St. Louis U. Pub. L. Rev. 409 (2006).

126. See Shari Seidman Diamond, *Instructing on Death: Psychologists, Juries, and Judges*, 48 Am. Psychologist 423, 429–30 (1993).

127. See Robert Hayman, *Beyond Penry: The Remedial Use of the Mental Retardation Label in Death Penalty Sentencing*, 59 UMKC L. Rev. 17, 47–48 (1990) (noting that "[t]ragically, the full range of stereotypes victimizes the mentally retarded defendant at the capital sentencing stage").

128. *Id.* (relying on Hans Toch & Kenneth Adams, The Disturbed Violent Offender 18–19 (1989)).

129. 597 So. 2d 776 (Fla. 1992).

130. *Id.* at 780.

131. Eddings v. Oklahoma, 455 U.S. 104 (1982).

132. Lockett v. Ohio, 438 U.S. 586 (1978).

133. Penry v. Lynaugh, 492 U.S. 302 (1989).

134. Tennard v. Dretke, 542 U.S. 274 (2004).

135. See Peter Meijes Tiersma, *Dictionaries and Death: Do Capital Jurors Understand Mitigation?*, 1995 Utah L. Rev. 1, 10–23 (1995); see also e.g., Valerie P. Hans, *Death by Jury*, in Challenging Capital Punishment: Legal and Social Science Approaches 149, 168–71 (Kenneth C. Haas & James A. Inciardi, eds. 1988) (discussing jury understanding of mitigating and aggravating evidence); Stephen P. Garvey, *Aggravation and Mitigation in Capital Cases: What Do Jurors Think?*, 98 Colum. L. Rev. 1538 (1998); Julie Schroeder et al., *Mitigating Circumstances in Death Penalty Decisions: Using Evidence-Based Research to Inform Social Work Practice in Capital Trials*, 51 Soc. Work 361 (2006).

136. For relevant cases, see 4 Perlin, *supra* note 4, § 12-3.4, at 500–505, and Michael L. Perlin & Heather E. Cucolo, Mental Disability Law: Civil and Criminal (2012 Cum. Supp.), § 12-3.4 at 136. Compare e.g., Cunningham v. Zant, 928 F.2d 1006 (11th Cir. 1991) (stating that counsel was not ineffective for failing to investigate the defendant's mental retardation as a mitigating factor); Doyle v. Dugger, 922 F.2d 646 (11th Cir. 1991) (stating same involving extreme emotional disturbance); Francis v. Dugger, 908 F.2d 696 (11th Cir. 1990) (stating same involving fetal alcohol syndrome); McCoy v. Lynaugh, 874 F.2d 954 (5th Cir. 1989) (stating same involving mental illness evidence); Prejean v. Smith, 889 F.2d 1391 (5th Cir. 1989) (stating same involving organic brain syndrome evidence); Romero v. Lynaugh, 884 F.2d 871 (5th Cir. 1989) (stating same involving intoxication evidence); Laws v. Armontrout, 863 F.2d 1377 (8th Cir. 1988) (stating same involving mental illness evidence); Thomas v. State, 511 So. 2d 248 (Ala. Crim. App. 1987) (stating same involving mental illness evidence); and King v. State, 503 So. 2d 271 (Miss. 1987) (stating same involving low intelligence), with Loyd v. Smith, 899 F.2d 1416 (5th Cir. 1990) (stating that the attorney's failure to explore mitigating psychiatric evidence prejudiced the defendant); Evans v. Lewis, 855 F.2d 631 (9th Cir. 1988) (stating same); and Middleton v. Dugger, 849 F.2d 491 (11th Cir. 1988) (stating same). The Supreme Court has returned to this issue frequently. Compare Wood v. Allen, 130 S. Ct. 841, 843 (2010) (state court's factual determination that defense counsel made strategic decision not to pursue or present evidence of defendant's mental deficiencies was not unreasonable in light of the evidence presented); Smith v. Spisak, 130 S. Ct. 676 (2010) (assuming counsel performed deficiently in making a penalty-phase closing argument that allegedly understated the facts upon which defense experts based their mental illness conclusions, defendant was not prejudiced, as element of ineffective assistance of counsel); and Cullen v. Pinholster, 131 S. Ct. 1388 (2011) (state Supreme Court could have reasonably concluded that petitioner was not prejudiced by counsel's allegedly deficient performance) to Sears v. Upton, 130 S. Ct. 3259 (2010) (state postconviction court failed to apply proper prejudice inquiry in determining that counsel's facially inadequate mitigation investigation did not prejudice defendant).

137. See Berkman, *supra* note 18, at 299–300; Hayman, *supra* note 127, at 47–48.

138. William S. Geimer, *Law and Reality in the Capital Penalty Trial*, 18 N.Y.U. Rev. L. & Soc. Change 273, 286 (1990–1991).

139. Beyond the scope of this book are the questions raised by defendants who elect to be executed (known as "voluntary executions," see Christy Chandler, *Voluntary Executions*, 50 Stan. L. Rev. 1897 (1998), and see Rees v. Peyton, 384 U.S. 312, 313–14 (1966) (per curiam) (defendant's mental competence was the most significant consideration in determining whether the defendant would be allowed to withdraw a *certiorari* petition relating to his death sentence). The therapeutic jurisprudence implications of this process are considered thoughtfully in C. Lee Harrington, *Mental Competence and End-of-Life Decision Making: Death Row Volunteering and Euthanasia*, 29 J. Health Pol. Pol'y & L. 1109, 1141–42 (2004).

140. See generally *supra* chapter 2.

141. Compare Perlin, *supra* note 57, at 342, noting Dr. Dorothy Lewis's documentation that juveniles imprisoned on death row were quick to tell her and her associates, "I'm not crazy," or "I'm not a retard" (see Lewis et al., *Condemned to Death*, *supra* note 121, at 588, and see generally, Lewis et al, *supra* note 121).

142. On the therapeutic jurisprudence implications of the varying ways that fact finders may construe mental disability evidence in death penalty cases, see Ramana, *supra* note 76, at 372–74.

143. See *infra* chapter 10.

144. See Cait Clarke & James Neuhard, *Making the Case: Therapeutic Jurisprudence and Problem Solving Practices Positively Impact Clients, Justice Systems and Communities They Serve,* 17 ST. THOMAS L. REV. 781, 788 (2005).

145. See e.g., Bruce Winick, *Redefining the Role of the Criminal Defense Lawyer at Plea Bargaining and Sentencing: A Therapeutic Jurisprudence/Preventive Law Model,* 5 PSYCHOL. PUB. POL'Y & L. 1034 (1999); DAVID B. WEXLER, REHABILITATING LAWYERS: PRINCIPLES OF THERAPEUTIC JURISPRUDENCE FOR CRIMINAL LAW PRACTICE (2008); David B. Wexler, *A Tripartite Framework for Incorporating Therapeutic Jurisprudence in Criminal Law, Research, and Practice,* 7 FLA. COASTAL L. REV. 95 (2005) (compare Mae C. Quinn, *An RSVP to Professor Wexler's Warm Therapeutic Jurisprudence Invitation to the Criminal Defense Bar: Unable to Join You, Already (Somewhat Similarly) Engaged,* 48 B.C. L. REV. 539 (2007)).

146. See Atkins et al., *supra* note 100, and text *supra* accompanying notes 98–100.

147. David Wexler, *Therapeutic Jurisprudence: An Overview,* 17 T.M. COOLEY L. REV. 125, 125 (2000).

148. DAVID B. WEXLER & BRUCE J. WINICK, LAW IN A THERAPEUTIC KEY: DEVELOPMENTS IN THERAPEUTIC JURISPRUDENCE XVII (1996). See e.g., Porter v. McCollum, 130 S. Ct. 447 (2009), discussed *supra* text accompanying notes 35–36.

149. See Perlin & McClain, *supra* note 99, at 265–66.

150. See *id.* at 260; O'Brien, *supra* note 82, at 754–55; Eric Freedman, *Re-stating the Standard of Practice of Death Penalty Counsel: The Supplementary Guidelines for the Mitigation Function of Defense Teams in Death Penalty Cases,* 36 HOFSTRA L. REV. 663 (2008).

151. See Michael L. Perlin, *"Too Stubborn to Ever Be Governed by Enforced Insanity": Some Therapeutic Jurisprudence Dilemmas in the Representation of Criminal Defendants in Incompetency and Insanity Cases,* 33 INT'L J. L. & PSYCHIATRY 475 (2010).

152. See Ray Moses, *Persuading the Sentencing Body Not to Return a Death Verdict,* 20 CHAMPION 52 (Nov. 1996).

153. See http://www.dpa.state.ky.us/library/manuals/mental/Ch04.html#13. Research on the factors that influence capital jurors in the sentencing phase repeatedly has found that mental health issues are extremely significant. When jurors are convinced that a defendant was acting under an extreme mental condition or emotional disturbance or has significant mental limitations, they are more inclined to grant mercy. . . . According to death penalty specialists, Professor John and Pamela Blume Leonard, Esq., "Make the mental illness real to the jury so they can comprehend its devastating and disastrous effect on your client." John Blume & Pamela Blume Leonard, *Capital Cases,* 23 THE CHAMPION 63 (2000).

154. See Craig Haney, *The Social Context of Capital Murder: Social Histories and the Logic of Mitigation,* 35 SANTA CLARA L. REV. 547, 560–61 (1995): "Social histories, in this context, . . . are not excuses, they are explanations."

155. See *supra* note 81 (quoting veteran defense lawyer Danalynn Recer):

The shooting of the officer was "a freak circumstance," not part of any pattern in Quintero's life, Recer said. His brain injury, along with alcoholism, the fact that he suffered abuse at the hands of his father, and his history of depression and anxiety had all combined to cause him to snap in a way that he never would again. "The State wants you to think he is the bad guy that shot Officer Johnson or he's someone who has a deep faith and is a great brother and is a great husband, father—but it has to be one or the other. And that's not the case. We know from human nature that's not the case," Recer said. Quintero was both. "Someone who is a beloved brother and husband and father and son can also commit a terrible act. Those two things are not mutually exclusive. It's not the way human nature works. And that could be a reason to spare his life."

156. See e.g., in the context of incompetency and insanity cases, Perlin, *supra* note 151.

CHAPTER 5

1. This section is largely adapted from Michael L. Perlin, *"Life Is in Mirrors, Death Disappears": Giving Life to* Atkins, 33 N. Mex. L. Rev. 315 (2003).

2. See e.g., David L. Bazelon, *The Defective Assistance of Counsel*, 42 U. Cin. L. Rev. 1, 2 (1973) (referring to such lawyers as "walking violations of the Sixth Amendment").

3. See e.g., Coleman v. Wilson, 912 F. Supp. 1282, 1320 (E.D. Cal. 1995).

4. See e.g., Thomas Hafemeister & John Petrila, *Treating the Mentally Disordered Offender: Society's Uncertain, Conflicted, and Changing Views*, 21 Fla. St. U. L. Rev. 729, 754 n. 91 (1994) (citing cases).

5. This path is traced explicitly in Justice Brennan's dissent in Colorado v. Connelly, 479 U.S. 157, 178 n. 2 (1986). On false confessions in this context, see generally C.K. Sigelman et al., *When in Doubt Say Yes: Acquiescence in Interview with Mentally Retarded Persons*, 19 Mental Retardation 53, 53–58 (1981).

6. See generally Michael L. Perlin, The Hidden Prejudice: Mental Disability on Trial (2000).

7. 536 U.S. 304 (2002).

8. The phrase "mental retardation" is atavistic and should be avoided in conversation, in litigation, and in scholarship. I use it here (instead of the more appropriate and accurate "intellectual disabilities")—with a heavy heart—because that is the phrase that is used in virtually every case ever decided in this area. See *supra* chapter 1, note 3.

9. *Atkins*, 536 U.S. at 321.

10. 477 U.S. 399 (1986). See *infra* chapter 6.

11. *Id.* at 431.

12. 492 U.S. 302 (1989).

13. 532 U.S. 782 (2001).

14. 477 U.S. 399 (1986). See *infra* chapter 6.

15. *Id.* at 405–10.

16. 339 U.S. 9 (1950).

17. *Ford*, 477 U.S. at 405.

18. *Id.* at 405–6 (citing, inter alia, Solem v. Helm, 463 U.S. 277, 285–86 (1983) (Burger, C.J., dissenting)).

19. *Id.* at 406 (citing Trop v. Dulles, 356 U.S. 86, 101 (1958) (plurality opinion)).

20. *Id.* (citing Coker v. Georgia, 433 U.S. 584, 597 (1977) (plurality opinion)).

21. See *infra* chapter 6.

22. 551 U.S. 930 (2007).

23. *Panetti*, 551 U.S. at 956.

24. See Pamela A. Wilkins, *Competency for Execution: the Implications of a Communicative Model of Retribution*, 76 Tenn. L. Rev. 713, 742 (2009): "The good news from *Panetti* is that the Court finally articulated a specific justification for the Eighth Amendment ban: the execution of an incompetent inmate lacks retributive value." See generally, Bruce Winick, *The Supreme Court's Evolving Death Penalty Jurisprudence: Severe Mental Illness as the Next Frontier*, 50 B.C. L. Rev. 785 (2009); Jeffrey Kirchmeier, *The Undiscovered Country: Execution Competency & Comprehending Death*, 98 Ky. L. Rev. 263 (2009–2010); Michael L. Perlin, *"Good and Bad, I Defined These Terms, Quite Clear No Doubt Somehow": Neuroimaging and Competency to Be Executed after* Panetti, 28 Behav. Sci. & L. 671 (2010).

25. 492 U.S. 302 (1989). For the Supreme Court's subsequent decision in *Penry*, see Penry v. Johnson, 532 U.S. 782 (2001), discussed in 4 Michael L. Perlin, Mental Disability Law: Civil and Criminal §§ 10-2.3e, 12-3.3 (2d ed. 2002). In the latter decision, the Supreme Court again remanded because of errors in the trial court's charge on the issue of mitigation. See *Penry*, 532 U.S. at 797–801.

26. For representative pre-*Penry* cases dealing with this population, see e.g., Bell v. Lynaugh, 858 F.2d 978 (5th Cir. 1988), *cert. denied*, 492 U.S. 925 (1989) (individuals with mental retardation subject to death penalty); State v. Jones, 378 S.E.2d 594 (S.C. 1989), *cert. denied*, 494 U.S. 1060 (1990) (same outcome); Brogdon v. Butler, 824 F.2d 338 (5th Cir. 1987) (same outcome).

27. *Penry*, 492 U.S. at 307–8.

28. *Id.* at 333.

29. *Id.* On the failure of the insanity defense to provide protection to this population, see Perlin, *supra* note 1, at 324–25 (footnotes omitted):

> Justice O'Connor's bald assertion that the insanity defense serves as a bulwark to protect against the conviction and punishment of persons with severe mental disabilities stands in stark opposition to the track record of counsel in the representation of such individuals in this area and ignores the post-Hinckley political reality that the insanity defense has been severely truncated in many jurisdictions and has been "abolished" in others.

30. *Penry*, 492 U.S. at 333.

31. *Id.* at 334. See generally V. Stephen Cohen, *Exempting the Mentally Retarded from the Death Penalty: A Comment on Florida's Proposed Legislation*, 19 FLA. ST. U. L. REV. 457 (1991).

32. No other member of the court joined in this aspect of Justice O'Connor's opinion. The remainder of the opinion reflected a majority.

33. *Penry*, 492 U.S. at 336.

34. *Id.* at 338–39.

35. *Id.* at 338–40. This assertion of Justice O'Connor has been used to buttress a decision upholding the admissibility of a confession of a person with mental retardation (see generally 4 PERLIN, *supra* note 25, §§ 10-3-10 to 3.3d). See United States v. Macklin, 900 F.2d 948, 952–53 (6th Cir. 1990).

36. *Penry*, 492 U.S. at 340.

37. *Id.* at 341. Justices Brennan and Marshall joined in those aspects of the majority's opinion that dealt with the question of mitigation. Justice Stevens also partially dissented (for himself and Justice Blackmun), concluding that executions of persons with mental retardation are unconstitutional.

38. *Id.* at 346.

39. *Id.* at 346–48. Even if mental retardation were not always associated with the requisite lack of culpability, Justice Brennan argued that he would still find capital punishment unconstitutional for such individuals, since there is no assurance that an adequate individualized assessment of whether the death penalty is a proportionate punishment will be made at the conclusion of each death penalty trial as the relationship between degree of culpability and status of mental retardation is not "isolated" as a factor that "determinatively bars a death sentence." *Id.*

40. *Id.* at 348 (quoting Enmund v. Florida, 458 U.S. 782, 801 (1982)).

41. *Penry*, 492 U.S. at 348–49.

42. *Id.* at 350–51 (Scalia, J., concurring in part and dissenting in part). If a punishment is not "unusual," he explained, then it is not unconstitutional, "even if out of accord with the theories of penology favored by the Justices of this Court."

43. Note, *The Supreme Court-Leading Cases*, 103 HARV. L. REV. 137, 153 (1989).

44. *Penry*, 492 U.S. at 153–54.

45. *Id.* at 154. See also *id.* at 154–55 (noting that, in other death penalty rulings, the court has considered public opinion polls in weighing consensus questions). Compare Michael L. Perlin, *Psychodynamics and the Insanity Defense: "Ordinary Common Sense" and Heuristic Reasoning*, 69 NEB. L. REV. 3, 32–35 (1990) (discussing role of "imperfect public opinion" in death penalty and insanity defense jurisprudence).

46. Compare, e.g., LAWRENCE KOHLBERG, THE PHILOSOPHY OF MORAL DEVELOPMENT (1981) to CAROL GILLIGAN, IN A DIFFERENT VOICE (1982); see Charles Thomas & Samuel

Foster, *A Sociological Perspective on Public Support of Capital Punishment*, 45 Am. J. Orthopsychiatry 641 (1975).

47. Compare Fleming v. Zant, 386 S.E.2d 339 (Ga. 1989) (executing mentally retarded persons constitutes cruel and unusual punishment under the Georgia constitution; defendant must present evidence at habeas hearing so that the court can determine whether there is a genuine issue of fact as to his retardation), to Buttrum v. Black, 721 F. Supp. 1268, 1307 (N.D. Ga. 1989), *aff'd*, 908 F.2d 695 (11th Cir. 1990) (noting that *Penry* "forecloses" defendant's argument that death penalty was unconstitutionally applied to her because she was "emotionally 12 or 13 at the time of the crime"). See also Richardson v. State, 598 A.2d 1 (Md. Spec. App. 1991), *aff'd*, 630 A.2d 238 (Md. 1993) (issue of whether defendant's mental retardation was bar to capital punishment should be determined by trier of fact at sentencing stage, not at pretrial proceeding); Ex parte Williams, 833 S.W.2d 150 (Tex. Crim. App. 1992) (defendant entitled to charge that jury could consider and give mitigating effect to evidence of mental retardation in sentencing phase; writ of habeas corpus granted, sentence vacated); State v. Patillo, 417 S.E.2d 139 (Ga. 1992) (barring execution of mentally retarded persons under Georgia statute, the jury should not be informed of the effect of a finding of mental retardation in a death penalty case).

48. Michael L. Perlin, *"The Executioner's Face Is Always Well-Hidden": The Role of Counsel and the Courts in Determining Who Dies*, 41 N.Y. L. Sch. L. Rev. 201, 216 (1996).

49. The Supreme Court had granted *certiorari* on the same issue the previous year, but then dismissed that petition as moot after the North Carolina state legislature enacted a ban on the execution of offenders with mental retardation. McCarver v. North Carolina, 533 U.S. 975 (2001).

50. *Atkins*, 536 U.S. at 306.

51. *Id.* at 308.

52. *Id.*

53. *Id.* at 309.

54. *Id.*

55. *Id.*

56. *Id.* at 310 (quoting State v. Atkins, 534 S.E.2d 312, 323–24 (2000)).

57. *Atkins*, 536 U.S. at 311.

58. For the most recent thoughts about proportionality in a death penalty context, see William Berry III, *Promulgating Proportionality*, 46 Ga. L. Rev. 69 (2011).

59. *Atkins*, 536 U.S.at 312 (quoting Penry, 492 U.S. at 331).

60. *Id.* at 314–15.

61. *Id.* at 315–16.

62. *Id.* at 317.

63. *Id.*

64. *Id.* at 118.

65. *Id.*

66. See 428 U.S. 153, 183 (1976).

67. *Atkins*, 536 U.S. at 319 (quoting, in part, *Enmund*, 458 U.S. at 798). On the implications of treating all persons with mental retardation as a group for these purposes, see Christopher Slobogin, *Is Atkins the Antithesis or Apotheosis of Anti-Discrimination Principles? Sorting Out the Group-Wide Effects of Exempting People with Mental Retardation from the Death Penalty*, 55 Ala. L. Rev. 1101 (2004).

68. See e.g., *Godfrey v. Georgia*, 446 U.S. 420, 433 (1980) (vacating death sentence because petitioner's crimes did not reflect "a consciousness materially more 'depraved' than that of any person guilty of murder").

69. *Atkins*, 536 U.S. at 319.

70. *Enmund*, 458 U.S. at 799. For a comprehensive overview of the relationship between the death penalty and deterrence in general, see Carol S. Steiker, *No, Capital Punishment Is Not Morally Required: Deterrence, Deontology, and the Death Penalty*, 58 Stan. L. Rev. 751 (2005).

71. *Atkins*, 536 U.S. at 320. Again, on its implications for treating all persons with mental retardation as a group for these purposes, see Slobogin, *supra* note 67.

72. *Atkins*, 536 U.S. at 320.

73. *Id.*

74. *Id.* at 321.

75. *Id.*

76. *Id.*

77. *Id.* (quoting, in part, *Ford*, 477 U.S. at 405). On this question, see generally, Susan Raeker-Jordan, *Parsing Personal Predilections: A Fresh Look at the Supreme Court's Cruel and Unusual Punishment Jurisprudence*, 58 Me. L. Rev. 99 (2006).

The decision in *Atkins* has left Japan as the only industrialized nation in the world to not prohibit the execution of persons with mental retardation. See Simon H. Fisherow, *Follow the Leader?: Japan Should Formally Abolish the Execution of the Mentally Retarded in the Wake of Atkins v. Virginia*, 14 Pac. Rim L. & Pol'y J. 455 (2005).

78. *Atkins*, 536 U.S. at 316 n. 21.

79. *Id.* at 324 (Rehnquist, C.J., dissenting).

80. *Id.* at 338 (Scalia, J., dissenting).

81. *Id.* at 338–39.

82. *Id.* at 342.

83. *Id.* at 348.

84. *Id.* at 348–49 (quoting, in part, Thompson v. Oklahoma, 487 U.S. 815, 873 (1988) (Scalia, J., dissenting)).

85. *Id.* at 349.

86. *Id.* at 351.

87. *Id.*

88. *Id.* at 352.

89. *Id.*

90. *Id.* at 353. Justice Scalia contrasted this, curiously, with a reference to the feigning insanity defense pleader who then "risks commitment to a mental institution until he can be cured (and then tried and executed)." *Id.* How a defendant who feigns insanity can be cured is, to be honest, beyond me. See generally, Michael L. Perlin, *"The Borderline Which Separated You from Me": The Insanity Defense, the Authoritarian Spirit, the Fear of Faking, and the Culture of Punishment*, 82 Iowa L. Rev. 1375, 1408–16 (1997).

91. *Atkins*, 536 U.S. at 354 (quoting 1 Hale, Pleas of the Crown 32–33 (1736)).

Following remand from the Supreme Court, prosecutorial misconduct in withholding evidence that impeached the story of Atkins' codefendant came to light, and Atkins was ultimately sentenced to life imprisonment. See In re Virginia, 677 S.E.2d 236 (Va. 2009) (denying writ of mandamus after trial court's decision to commute Atkins' sentence to life imprisonment).

92. In addition to those questions discussed below (and the question of its application to defendants with mental *illness*, see *infra* chapter 6), commentators have addressed the question of *Atkins*' application to noncapital offenses, see Timothy Cone, *Developing the Eighth Amendment for Those "Least Deserving" of Punishment: Statutory Mandatory Minimums for Non-Capital Offenses Can Be "Cruel and Unusual" When Imposed on Mentally Retarded Offenders*, 34 N.M. L. Rev. 35 (2004). For future research agendas, see John Blume, Sheri Lynn Johnson, & Christopher Seeds, *Mental Retardation and the Death Penalty*, in The Future of America's Death Penalty: An Agenda for the Next Generation of Capital Punishment Research 241, 255–56 (Charles S. Lanier et al., eds. 2009).

93. The states' track record in the wake of the parallel case of Ford v. Wainwright, 477 U.S. 399 (1986), has been spotty, to say the least. See 4 Perlin, *supra* note 25, § 12-4.1e, at 543 (noting that post-*Ford* case law reveals "a continued failure on the part of many courts to

authentically implement the *Ford* decision"). On changes in the *Ford* methodology as mandated by Panetti v. Quarterman 551 U.S. 930 (2007), *see infra* chapter 6.

On the need for legislatures to adopt "*Atkins* procedures," see e.g., Graham Baker, *Defining and Determining Retardation in Texas Capital Murder Defendants: A Proposal to the Texas Legislature*, 9 Scholar 237 (2007); Brooke Amos, *Atkins v, Virginia: Analyzing the Correct Standard and Examination Practices to Use When Determining Mental Retardation*, 14 J. Gender Race & Just. 469 (2011). On the deficiencies in Texas' implementation of such procedures in ex parte Briseno, 135 S.W.3d 1, 5 n. 7 (Tex. Crim. App. 2004), see Peggy M. Tobolowsky, *A Different Path Taken: Texas Capital Offenders' Post-Atkins Claims of Mental Retardation*, 39 Hastings Const. L. Q. 1, 45–64 (2011). On how the *Briseno* factors were simply "made up," see Doug Lieb, *Can Section 1983 Help to Prevent the Execution of Mentally Retarded Prisoners?*, 121 Yale L. J. 1571 (2012).

94. See Douglas Mossman, *Atkins v. Virginia: A Psychiatric Can of Worms*, 33 N.M. L. Rev. 255 (2003). For a survey of state responses to *Atkins*, concluding that it is not clear that a majority of states are effectuating the case's intent, see David DeMatteo et al., *A National Survey of State Legislation Defining Mental Retardation: Implications for Policy and Practice after Atkins*, 25 Behav. Sci. & L. 781 (2007); Holly T. Sharp, *Determining Mental Retardation in Capital Defendants: Using a Strict IQ Cut-off Number Will Allow the Execution of Many That Atkins Intended to Spare*, 12 Jones L. Rev. 227 (2008). For a survey of such cases, see Richard J. Bonnie & Katherine Gustafson, *The Challenge of Implementing Atkins v. Virginia: How Legislatures and Courts Can Promote Accurate Assessments and Adjudications of Mental Retardation in Death Penalty Cases*, 41 U. Rich. L. Rev. 811, 818 n. 25 (2007).

On the difficulties posed by reliance on a numerical IQ score in this context, see John Matthew Fabian et al., *Life, Death, and IQ: It's Much More Than Just a Score: Understanding and Utilizing Forensic Psychological and Neuropsychological Evaluations in Atkins Intellectual Disability/ Mental Retardation Cases*, 59 Clev. St. L. Rev. 399 (2011); see also, Robert Sanger, *Close Test Scores and Epigenetics in* Atkins *Cases*, 39 CACJ Forum 27 (Apr. 2012).

95. See Bobby v. Bies, 129 S. Ct. 2145 (2009) (holding a hearing on whether defendant qualified under *Atkins* did not violate the issue preclusion doctrine of the Double Jeopardy Clause).

96. Compare e.g., Larry P. v. Riles, 793 F.2d 969 (9th Cir. 1984) (discussing the discriminatory impact of IQ tests in school placements). For more recent cases, see e.g., Ortiz v. United States, 664 F.3d 1151 (8th Cir. 2011); United States v. Martinez-Haro, 645 F.3d 1228 (10th Cir. 2011); Khanh Van Vo v. Astrue, 2011 WL 5900961 (D. Kan. 2011); Hernandez v. Thaler, 2011 WL 4437091 (W.D. Tex. 2011).

97. See Christopher Slobogin, *What Atkins Could Mean for People with Mental Illness*, 33 N.M. L. Rev. 293 (2003). For recent cases, see e.g., Hill v. Humphrey, 662 F.3d 1335 (11th Cir. 2011); Chester v. Thaler, 666 F.3d 340 (5th Cir. 2011); Black v. Bell, 664 F.3d 81 (6th Cir. 2011).

98. See e.g., Smith v. State, 2002 WL 126985, at *57 (Ala. Crim. App. 2002) (listing defendant Willie Smith's "verbal IQ of 75, classified as the borderline range between mild retardation and low-average intelligence" as a "properly found" mitigating factor) (decided prior to *Atkins*). See also e.g., ex parte Clemons, 55 So.3d 348 (Ala. 2007); State v. Waddy, 2006 WL 1530117 (Ohio App. 2006).

99. Compare Apprendi v. New Jersey, 530 U.S. 466 (2000) (enhancing jury role in determination of factors increasing defendant's potential punishment), with Ring v. Arizona, 536 U.S. 584 (2002) (holding that an Arizona statute authorizing trial judge to determine the presence or absence of the aggravating factors in a death penalty case violates the Sixth Amendment right to a jury trial in capital prosecutions.

100. Harper v. Virginia Dep't of Taxation, 509 U.S. 86 (1993) (explaining methodology for determining application of retroactivity doctrine). See also e.g., In re Turner, 637 F.3d 1200 (11th Cir. 2011); Allen v. Buss, 558 F.3d 657 (7th Cir. 2009); In re Mathis, 483 F.3d 395 (5th Cir. 2007).

101. See Carol Steiker & Jordan Steiker, *Sober Second Thoughts: Reflections on Two Decades of Constitutional Regulation of Capital Punishment*, 109 HARV. L. REV. 355, 426 (1995):

> On the other hand, if the Court remains committed to addressing in some significant sense the concerns that originally animated it in *Furman* and *Gregg*, it is hard to see why the Court has not attempted to flesh out the ideas for alternative regulatory regimes that we have sketched. It is difficult to imagine a body of doctrine that is much worse—either in its costs of implementation or in its negligible returns—than the one we have now.

See also Judith Resnik, *Managerial Judges*, 96 HARV. L. REV. 374, 433 (1982) ("The mere existence of rules does not automatically result in their enforcement, and the costs of implementation can be high").

102. See generally *infra* chapter 10 (on counsel issues in general).

103. 466 U.S. 668 (1984). See *infra* chapter 10.

104. See *infra* chapter 9. On the need for public education in this specific context, see Ronald Tabak, *Mental Disability and Capital Punishment: A More Rational Approach to a Disturbing Subject*, 34 HUM. RTS. 5, 15–16 (Spring 2007). On how *Atkins* destigmatizes persons with mental disabilities, see Slobogin, *supra* note 67, at 1007.

105. I discuss this cognitive error—assuming that planfulness bespeaks rationality—*infra* chapter 9, at n. 21.

106. See *supra* chapter 4.

107. Even raising this issue assumes that jurors can determine who is a person with mental retardation. The empirical research suggests that jurors fail at this task regularly. See e.g., Marcus Boccaccini et al., *Jury Pool Members' Beliefs about the Relation between Potential Implications in Functioning and Mental Retardation: Implications for* Atkins-*Type Cases*, 34 LAW & PSYCHOL. 1 (2010).

108. 470 U.S. 68 (1985). See generally, Michael L. Perlin, *The Supreme Court, the Mentally Disabled Criminal Defendant, Psychiatric Testimony in Death Penalty Cases, and the Power of Symbolism: Dulling the* Ake *in* Barefoot's *Achilles Heel*, 3 N.Y. L. SCH. HUMAN RTS. ANN. 91 (1985).

109. See Penny White, *Treated Differently in Life, But Not in Death*, 76 TENN. L. REV. 685, 706 (2009).

110. See e.g., Dorothy Lewis et al., *Neuropsychiatric, Psychoeducational, and Family Characteristics of 14 Juveniles Condemned to Death in the United States*, 145 AM. J. PSYCHIATRY 584 (1988), discussed *supra* chapter 4, at note 121.

111. On counsel issues in general, see *infra* chapter 10.

112. 509 U.S. 389 (1993) (standard for competence to waive counsel or enter a guilty plea is identical to that of competence to stand trial).

113. 554 U.S. 564 (2008) (constitution permits states to insist upon representation by counsel for those who are competent enough to stand trial but who are sufficiently ill to be incompetent to conduct trial proceedings by themselves).

114. See *infra* notes 136, 200–201, 213, discussing Brumfield v. Cain, 2012 WL 602163 (M.D. La. 2012).

115. See generally, Perlin, *supra* note 90.

116. On the failure of the insanity defense to provide protection to this population, see Perlin, *supra* note 1, at 324–25, discussed *supra* note 29.

117. On prosecutorial misconduct in death penalty cases involving persons with mental disabilities, see *infra* chapter 9.

118. See *supra* chapter 1.

119. See *infra* chapter 10.

120. On the public's demand that mentally disabled defendants "look crazy," see generally, Michael L. Perlin, *Unpacking the Myths: The Symbolism Mythology of Insanity Defense Jurispru-*

dence, 40 CASE W. RES. L. REV. 599, 724–27 (1989–1990); Michael L. Perlin, *The Sanist Lives of Jurors in Death Penalty Cases: The Puzzling Role of "Mitigating" Mental Disability Evidence*, 8 NOTRE DAME J. L., ETHICS & PUB. POL'Y 239, 265 (1994) ("[T]he public has always demanded that mentally ill defendants comport with its visual images of 'craziness.'"). See also e.g., JOHN PARRY & ERIC DROGIN, CIVIL LAW HANDBOOK ON PSYCHIATRIC AND PSYCHOLOGICAL EVIDENCE AND TESTIMONY § 1.01, at 1–2 (2001).

121. The vast majority of criminal defense lawyers have had no training in identifying or understanding mental retardation. See e.g., Ruth Luckasson, *The Death Penalty and Those with Mental Retardation*, in AMNESTY INTERNATIONAL USA, THE MACHINERY OF DEATH: A SHOCKING INDICTMENT OF CAPITAL PUNISHMENT IN THE UNITED STATES 93 (1994); Sandra A. Garcia & Holly V. Steele, *Mentally Retarded Offenders in the Criminal Justice and Mental Retardation Services Systems in Florida: Philosophical, Placement, and Treatment Issues*, 41 ARK. L. REV. 809, 820 (1988).

122. See *infra* chapter 10.

123. See generally, James Ellis, *Disability Advocacy and Atkins*, 57 DEPAUL L. REV. 653 (2008) (Ellis was Atkins' appellate counsel).

124. See *supra* chapter 1, at note 17, and see *infra* chapter 9, at text accompanying notes 84–85.

125. 504 U.S. 127 (1992) (discussing the right of competent criminal defendants to refuse the involuntary administration of antipsychotic medications).

126. *Id.* at 144, relying on William Geimer & Jonathan Amsterdam, *Why Jurors Vote Life or Death: Operative Factors in Ten Florida Death Penalty Cases*, 15 AM. J. CRIM. L. 1, 51–53 (1987–1988). On the extent to which fear of persons with mental illness is a key determining factor in jury death penalty decision making, see Stephen Garvey, *The Emotional Economy of Capital Sentencing*, 75 N.Y.U. L. REV. 26 (2000).

127. See generally, Scott E. Sundby, *The Capital Jury and Absolution: The Intersection of Trial Strategy, Remorse, and the Death Penalty*, 83 CORNELL L. REV. 1557 (1998) (examining how juries use defendant's remorse in deciding between the death penalty and a life sentence).

128. See generally, Denis Keyes et al., *Mitigating Mental Retardation in Capital Cases: Finding the "Invisible" Defendant*, 22 MENTAL & PHYSICAL DISABILITY L. REP. 529 (1998).

129. See Joseph A. Nese Jr., *The Fate of Mentally Retarded Criminals: An Examination of the Propriety of Their Execution under the Eighth Amendment*, 40 DUQ. L. REV. 373, 383 (2002) (citing ROSA EHRENREICH & JAMIE FELLNER, BEYOND REASON: THE DEATH PENALTY AND OFFENDERS WITH MENTAL RETARDATION 4 (Malcolm Smart & Cynthia Brown, eds., Human Rights Watch) (2001)).

130. *Id.*

131. Keyes et al., *supra* note 128, at 536 (citing ROBERT EDGERTON, THE CLOAK OF COMPETENCE: STIGMA IN THE LIVES OF THE MENTALLY RETARDED (1967)).

132. 362 U.S. 402, 402 (1960). In *Dusky*, the Court asked whether the defendant "has sufficient present ability to consult with his lawyer with a reasonable degree of rational understanding" and whether he has a "rational as well as factual understanding of the proceedings against him." See Michael L. Perlin, *"For the Misdemeanor Outlaw": The Impact of the ADA on the Institutionalization of Criminal Defendants with Mental Disabilities*, 52 ALA. L. REV. 193, 200 (2000) (criticizing *Dusky* as "confusing and less than helpful").

133. Nese, *supra* note 129, at 383 (citing EHRENREICH & FELLNER, *supra* note 129, at 22).

134. Keyes et al., *supra* note 128, at 536.

135. See Winiviere Sy, *The Right of Institutionalized Disabled Patients to Engage in Consensual Sexual Activity*, 23 WHITTIER L. REV. 545, 563–64 (2001) (discussing State v. Soura, 796 P.2d 109, 115 (Idaho 1990), where the court noted that the victim's "facial expressions consisting of a 'sagging jaw, mouth open' and tendency to 'stare off into space'" were evidence of her mental retardation). For an astonishing report, see Keyes et al., *supra* note 128, at 530 n. 17: "In one recent case, one of the authors learned that the prosecutor's expert, a psychologist,

suggested that because the defendant could wash his own laundry, ride the bus and watch TV on his own, he did not have mental retardation."

136. Brumfield v. Cain, 2012 WL 602163, *26 (M.D. La. 2012). The court continued:

> Even so, because strengths can coexist alongside weaknesses, one or two instances of him exhibiting oral communication skills expected of adults could hardly be said to outweigh the other documented adaptive weaknesses in the conceptual domain. As the diagnostic guidelines state, "adaptive behavior refers to typical and actual functioning and not to capacity or maximum functioning" (citation omitted).

137. Keyes et al., *supra* note 128, at 536 (citing EDGERTON, *supra* note 131).

138. *Atkins*, 536 U.S. at 321.

139. 466 U.S. 668 (1984) (holding that the proper standard for attorney performance is that of reasonably effective assistance).

140. See *infra* chapter 10.

141. See e.g., Louis Bilionis & Richard Rosen, *Lawyers, Arbitrariness, and the Eighth Amendment*, 75 TEX. L. REV. 1301, 1321–22 n. 65 (1997); Shruti S.B. Desai, *Effective Capital Representation of the Mentally Retarded Defendant*, 13 CAP. DEF. J. 251, 253 n. 12 (2001); Jonathan Bing, *Protecting the Mentally Retarded from Capital Punishment: State Efforts since Penry and Recommendations for the Future*, 22 N.Y.U. REV. L. & SOC. CHANGE 59, 84–85 nn. 157–58 (1996); John Blume & David Bruck, *Sentencing the Mentally Retarded to Death: An Eighth Amendment Analysis*, 41 ARK. L. REV. 725 (1988); James Ellis & Ruth A. Luckasson, *Mentally Retarded Criminal Defendants*, 53 GEO. WASH. L. REV. 414 (1985).

142. Perlin, *supra* note 1, at 336; see also e.g., Rebecca Klaren & Irene Rosenberg, *Splitting Hairs in Ineffective Assistance of Counsel Cases: An Essay on How Ineffective Assistance of Counsel Doctrine Undermines the Prohibition against Executing the Mentally Retarded*, 31 AM. J. CRIM. L. 339 (2004).

143. See *infra* chapter 9, text accompanying notes 4–6.

144. See Andrea D. Lyon, *But He Doesn't Look Retarded: Capital Jury Selection for the Mentally Retarded Client Not Excluded after Atkins v. Virginia*, 57 DEPAUL L. REV. 701 (2008). On the research questions that still remain as to how jurors process evidence of mental retardation in death penalty cases, see Leona D. Jochnowitz, *How Capital Jurors Respond to Mitigating Evidence of Defendant's Mental Illness, Retardation, and Situational Impairments: An Analysis of the Legal and Social Science Literature*, 47 CRIM. L. BULL. 839, 844 (2011).

145. Research demonstrates that mental health professionals frequently commit this important error. See e.g., Diane Courselle et al., *Suspects, Defendants, and Offenders with Mental Retardation in Wyoming*, 1 WYO. L. REV. 1, 5 (2001) (relying upon PRESIDENT'S COMMITTEE ON MENTAL RETARDATION, REPORT TO THE PRESIDENT: CITIZENS WITH MENTAL RETARDATION AND THE CRIMINAL JUSTICE SYSTEM 3–22 (1991)); Keyes et al., *supra* note 128, at 530. It defies credulity to suggest that lay jurors are more sophisticated in their determinations.

146. ALAN STONE, MENTAL HEALTH AND LAW: A SYSTEM IN TRANSITION 219 (1976). See also Caton F. Roberts et al., *Implicit Theories of Criminal Responsibility: Decision Making and the Insanity Defense*, 11 LAW & HUM. BEHAV. 207, 226 (1987) (the only defendant who will likely be found universally insane is the "totally mad individual who acts impulsively in response to a glaring psychotic process that is itself tied thematically to a criminal action").

147. James S. Liebman & Michael J. Shepard, *Guiding Sentencer Discretion beyond the "Boilerplate": Mental Disorder as a Mitigating Factor*, 66 GEO. L. J. 757, 825 (1978).

148. Edward Miller, *Executing Minors and the Mentally Retarded: The Retribution and Deterrence Rationales*, 43 RUTGERS L. REV. 15, 50 (1990).

149. See e.g., Murtishaw v. Woodford, 255 F.3d 926 (9th Cir. 2001).

150. Patricia Hagenah, *Imposing the Death Sentence on Mentally Retarded Defendants: The Case of Penry v. Lynaugh*, 59 UMKC L. REV. 135, 151 (1990).

151. See *supra* chapter 4.

152. Perlin, *supra* note 48, at 233.

153. See e.g., Susan Bandes, *Empathy, Narrative, and Victim Impact Statements*, 63 U. CHI. L. REV. 361 (1996); Jeffrey J. Pokorak, *Dead Man Talking: Competing Narratives and Effective Representation in Capital Cases*, 30 ST. MARY'S L. J. 421 (1999).

154. Perlin, *supra* note 48, at 233, quoting, in part, William S. Geimer, *Law and Reality in the Capital Penalty Trial*, 18 N.Y.U. REV. L. & SOC. CHANGE 273, 286 (1990–1991).

155. Richard Sherwin, *Law, Violence, and Illiberal Belief*, 78 GEO. L. J. 1785, 1821 n. 164 (1990). See also e.g., Elizabeth F. Maringer, *Witness for the Prosecution: Prosecutorial Discovery of Information Generated by Non-testifying Defense Psychiatric Experts*, 62 FORDHAM L. REV. 653, 653 n. 3 (1993), discussing attorney who had a psychologist examine his client prior to trial, but "wouldn't allow the doctor to testify. Like many other defense attorneys, he assumed talk of brain disorders, mental retardation or childhood abuse could evoke fear instead of empathy").

156. *Atkins*, 536 U.S. at 321 (citing Penry v. Lynaugh, 492 U.S. at 323–25).

157. *Id.* at 320.

158. See *supra* chapter 4.

159. See Denise Paquette Boots et al., *Death Penalty Support for Special Offender Populations of Legally Convicted Murderers: Juveniles, the Mentally Retarded, and the Mentally Incompetent*, 22 BEHAV. SCI. & L. 223 (2004).

160. Robert L. Hayman Jr., *Beyond Penry: The Remedial Use of the Mentally Retarded Label in Death Penalty Sentencing*, 59 UMKC L. REV. 17, 48 (1990); see *id.* n. 166 (citing Samuel Pillsbury, *Emotional Justice: Moralizing the Passions of Criminal Punishment*, 74 CORNELL L. REV. 655 (1989) (urging that empathy with the offender is crucial to the fairness of the sentencing scheme and must be explicitly mandated to counter "the myth of dispassion")).

161. Francine Banner, *Rewriting History: The Use of Feminist Narratives to Deconstruct the Myth of the Capital Defendant*, 26 N.Y.U. REV. L. & SOC. CHANGE 569, 600 (2000–2001) (citing Eileen McNamara, *Nobody Cared He Was Insane*, BOSTON GLOBE, Nov. 30, 1996, at B1).

162. Banner, *supra* note 161, at 600. See also Welsh S. White, *Effective Assistance of Counsel in Capital Cases: The Evolving Standard of Care*, 1993 U. ILL. L. REV. 323, 362 (citing Deana D. Logan, *Is It Mitigation or Aggravation? Troublesome Areas of Defense Evidence in Capital Sentencing*, CAL. ATT'YS FOR CRIM. JUST. F., Sept./Oct. 1989, at 14 (discussing the possibility that a jury may "glean from evidence relating to defendant's mental problems or background difficulties that the defendant is an 'irreparable monster' who must be put to death to safeguard society")).

163. See Daniel B. Kessler, *Atkins v. Virginia: Suggestions for the Accurate Diagnosis of Mental Retardation*, 43 JURIMETRICS J. 415 (2003); James R. Flynn, *Tethering the Elephant*, 12 PSYCHOL., PUB. POL'Y & L. 170 (2006).

164. See John Fabian, *Death Penalty Mitigation and the Role of the Forensic Psychologist*, 27 LAW & PSYCHOLOGY 73 (2003). On how states routinely deviate from clinical definitions of mental retardation in post-*Atkins* cases, see John Blume, Sheri Johnson, & Christopher Seeds, *Of Atkins and Men: Deviations from Clinical Definitions of Mental Retardation in Death Penalty Cases*, 18 CORNELL J. L. & PUB. POL'Y. 689 (2009).

165. On a defendant's right to an expert, see Ake v. Oklahoma, 470 U.S. 68, 74 (1985), discussed *infra* text accompanying notes 172–77.

166. Keyes et al., *supra* note 128, at 536.

167. Desai, *supra* note 141, at 268.

168. *Id.*

169. *Id.*

170. *Id.* quoting, in part, John H. Blume & Pamela Blume Leonard, *Principles of Developing and Presenting Mental Health Evidence in Criminal Cases*, 23 THE CHAMPION 63, 70 (Nov. 2000):

Thus the testimony of lay witnesses, such as defendant's family, friends, teachers or neighbors, should always be presented to augment the testimony of experts. When testimony regarding the defendant's mental retardation is presented from various sources, defense counsel must interlock the testimonies and other relevant evidence to achieve a comprehensible presentation of the mental retardation issue.

171. See *supra* text accompanying note 135, discussing Keyes et al., *supra* note 128, at 536.

172. 470 U.S. 68 (1985).

173. *Id.* at 83.

174. Compare Jones v. State, 375 S.E.2d 648, 652 (Ga. 1988) (defendant not entitled under *Ake* to appointment of a psychologist), and Hough v. State, 524 N.E.2d 1287 (Ind. 1987) (no right under *Ake* to appointment of social psychologist to help in jury selection), with Funk v. Commonwealth, 379 S.E.2d 371, 371–74 (Va. App. 1989) (court decision to appoint clinical psychologist satisfies *Ake*), and King v. State, 877 S.W.2d 583 (Ark. 1994) (appointment of psychologist sufficient under state statute).

175. See e.g., PARRY & DROGIN, *supra* note 120, § 1.09(e), at 35–37.

176. STEPHEN A. SALTZBURG & DANIEL J. CAPRA, AMERICAN CRIMINAL PROCEDURE 802 (8th ed. 2007). See also David A. Harris, Ake *Revisited: Expert Psychiatric Witnesses Remain beyond Reach for the Indigent*, 68 N.C. L. REV. 763, 783 (1990) ("Lower courts often have interpreted *Ake* less than generously, unduly constricting the availability of the right").

177. Keyes et al., *supra* note 128, at 530. See *supra* text accompanying note 145.

178. On the related question of the application of *Ake* to access to neuroimaging experts, see Michael L. Perlin & Valerie R. McClain, *Unasked (and Unanswered) Questions about the Role of Neuroimaging in the Criminal Trial Process*, 28 AM. J. FORENSIC PSYCHOL. (2009); see *infra* chapter 8.

179. See Perlin, *supra* note 132, at 236: "[T]he fear that defendants will fake the insanity defense to escape punishment continues to paralyze the legal system." See also e.g., Jacqueline Gonzales, *Improving the Handling of Mentally Retarded Defendants in the Criminal Justice System*, 17 TEX. WESLEYAN L. REV. 143, 146 (2011) (some "argue courts should not consider mental retardation because it is too easy for defendants to work the system by faking a disability").

180. See Rebecca J. Covarrubias, *Lives in Defense Counsel's Hands: The Problems and Responsibilities of Defense Counsel Representing Mentally Ill or Mentally Retarded Capital Defendants*, 11 SCHOLAR 413, 464 (2009) (defendants with mental retardation "often try to mask and hide their symptoms so that they can better cope").

181. Perlin, *supra* note 90, at 1412, relying on findings reported in Dorothy Lewis et al., *Neuropsychiatric, Psychoeducational, and Family Characteristics of 14 Juveniles Condemned to Death in the United States*, 145 AM. J. PSYCHIATRY 584, 588 (1988) (stating that death row juveniles "almost uniformly tried to hide evidence of cognitive deficits and psychotic symptoms"), and in Dorothy Otnow Lewis et al., *Psychiatric and Psychoeducational Characteristics of 15 Death Row Inmates in the United States*, 143 AM. J. PSYCHIATRY 838, 841 (1986) (stating that all but one of a sample of death row inmates studied attempted to minimize rather than exaggerate their degree of psychiatric disorders).

182. Nese, *supra* note 129, at 383 (citing EHRENREICH & FELLNER, *supra* note 129, at 4).

183. See e.g., People v. McCleary, 567 N.E.2d 434, 437 (Ill. App. Ct. 1990) (testimony from doctor finding that, in his opinion, defendant was insane and that "defendant did not want to be known as a crazy person and, in fact, was 'malingering sanity'").

184. On the question of whether a defendant may not be sufficiently mentally retarded to be incompetent to stand trial, but sufficiently so that he comes within the *Atkins* doctrine, see State v. McClain, 610 S.E.2d 783 (N.C. App. 2005) (so finding defendant).

185. Michael Mello, *Facing Death Alone: The Post-Conviction Attorney Crisis on Death Row*, 37 Am. U. L. Rev. 513, 550 (1988).

186. Rebecca Dick-Hurwitz, Penry v. Lynaugh: *The Supreme Court Deals a Fatal Blow to Mentally Retarded Capital Defendants*, 51 U. Pitt. L. Rev. 699, 724 (1990).

187. A*tkins*, 536 U.S. at 321.

188. James Liebman, *The Overproduction of Death*, 100 Colum. L. Rev. 2030, 2108 n. 185 (2000).

189. See e.g., Jeffrey Wertkin, *Competency to Stand Trial*, 90 Geo. L. J. 1514, 1515–16 n. 1308 (2002), discussing, inter alia, United States v. Santos, 131 F.3d 16, 20–21 (1st Cir. 1997); United States v. Morrison, 153 F.3d 34, 39–40, 46–47 (2d Cir. 1998); Noland v. French, 134 F.3d 208, 211, 219 (4th Cir. 1998); Moody v. Johnson, 139 F.3d 477, 482 (5th Cir. 1998); United States v. Collins, 949 F.2d 921, 926–27 (7th Cir. 1991); Wise v. Bowersox, 136 F.3d 1197, 1202–5 (8th Cir. 1998); United States. v. Frank, 956 F.2d 872, 874–75 (9th Cir. 1991); Foster v. Ward, 182 F.3d 1177, 1189–91 (10th Cir. 1999).

190. 509 U.S. 389 (1993).

191. *Id.* at 390.

192. *Id.* at 398.

193. *Id.*

194. *Id.* at 400 (quoting Parke v. Raley, 506 U.S. 20, 29 (1992)).

195. *Id.* at 402, citing Medina v. California, 505 U.S. 437 (1992). I criticize *Godinez* in Michael L. Perlin, *"Dignity Was the First to Leave": Godinez v. Moran, Colin Ferguson, and the Trial of Mentally Disabled Criminal Defendants*, 14 Behav. Sci. & L. 61 (1996).

196. 554 U.S. 164, 171–72 (2008). On how intellectual deficits raise "grave concerns" regarding representational competency, see Mark Cunningham & Mark Vigen, *Without Appointed Counsel in Capital Postconviction Proceedings: The Self-Representation Competency of Mississippi Death Row Inmates*, 26 Crim. Just. & Behav. 293, 294 (1999).

197. Michael L. Perlin & Heather E. Cucolo, Mental Disability Law: Civil and Criminal (2012 Cum. Supp.), § 8B-3.1c(1), at 44–51.

198. Jennifer W. Corinis, *A Reasoned Standard for Competency to Waive Counsel after Godinez v. Moran*, 80 B.U. L. Rev. 265, 280 (2000). See generally, Perlin, *supra* note 191. For discussions of the spectacle of Scott Panetti's self-representation—see Panetti v. Quarterman, 551 U.S. 930 (2007), discussed extensively *infra* chapter 6—see e.g., Ashley G. Wilkinson, *The Right of Self-Representation Revisited: A Return to the Star Chamber's Disrespect for Defendant Autonomy?*, 48 Washburn L. J. 465, 465 n. 1 (2009) ("While Scott Panetti represented himself against charges for slaying his ex-wife's family, he donned a purple cowboy suit, revealed his tattoo to the jurors, and tried to subpoena Jesus, the Pope, and JFK").

Many state constitutions mandate dignity values in both civil and criminal contexts. See e.g., Hadi v. Cordero, 955 So. 2d 17, 19 (Fla. Dist. Ct. App. 2006), quoting Fla. Stat. § 916.107; John D. Castiglione, *Human Dignity under the Fourth Amendment*, 2008 Wis. L. Rev. 655, 690 n. 182 (2008) (listing state constitutional provisions).

199. Corinis, *supra* note 198, at 280; see generally Perlin, *supra* note 195.

200. See *supra* chapter 2; see generally, Perlin, *supra* note 6.

201. Michael L. Perlin, *"There's No Success Like Failure/and Failure's No Success at All": Exposing the Pretextuality of Kansas v. Hendricks*, 92 Nw. U. L. Rev. 1247, 1258 (1997), discussing, inter alia, judicial responses to O'Connor v. Donaldson, 422 U.S. 563 (1975) (right to liberty); Jackson v. Indiana, 406 U.S. 715 (1972) (application of Due Process Clause to commitments following incompetency to stand trial findings); Lessard v. Schmidt, 349 F. Supp. 1078 (E.D. Wis. 1972) (application of substantive and procedural Due Process Clauses to involuntary civil commitment process).

202. *Brumfield*, 2012 WL 602163, *33 (M.D. La. 2012).

203. *Id.*

204. Bridget M. Doane & Karen L. Salekin, *Susceptibility of Current Adaptive Behavior Measures in Feigned Deficits*, 33 LAW & HUM. BEHAV. 329 (2009).

205. See generally, Perlin, *supra* note 90.

206. See Perlin, *supra* note 49, at 216.

207. E. Selene Steelman, *A Question of Revenge: Munchausen Syndrome by Proxy and a Proposed Diminished Capacity Defense for Homicidal Mothers*, 8 CARDOZO WOMEN'S L. J. 261, 305 (2002).

208. Bryan Dupler, *The Uncommon Law: Insanity, Executions, and Oklahoma Criminal Procedure*, 55 OKLA. L. REV. 1, 38 n. 208 (2002).

209. Perlin, *supra* note 90, at 1408.

210. See Joseph Tussman & Jacobus tenBroek, *The Equal Protection of the Laws*, 37 CALIF. L. REV. 341, 351–52 (1949).

211. Gilbert Geis & Robert F. Meier, *Abolition of the Insanity Plea in Idaho: A Case Study*, 477 ANNALS 72, 73 (1985) (emphasis added) (explaining that Idaho residents hold the view that persons should not be able to avoid punitive consequences of criminal acts by reliance on "either a real or a faked plea of insanity").

212. See State v. Perry, 610 So. 2d 746, 781 (La. 1992) (Cole, J., dissenting) ("Society has the right to protect itself from those who would commit murder and seek to avoid their legitimate punishment by a subsequently contracted, *or* feigned, insanity") (emphasis added).

213. *Atkins*, 536 U.S. at 353.

214. Michael L. Perlin, *Pretexts and Mental Disability Law: The Case of Competency*, 47 U. MIAMI L. REV. 625, 678–79 (1993); see also Perlin, *supra* note 90, at 1405:

> Perhaps the oldest of the insanity defense myths is that criminal defendants who plead insanity are usually faking, a myth that has bedeviled American jurisprudence since the mid-nineteenth century. Of the 141 individuals found NGRI [not guilty by reason of insanity] in one jurisdiction over an eight year period, there was no dispute that 115 were schizophrenic and in only three cases was the diagnostician unwilling or unable to specify the nature of the patient's mental illness.

Compare Robert Wettstein & Edward Mulvey, *Disposition of Insanity Acquittees in Illinois*, 16 BULL. AM. ACAD. PSYCHIATRY & L. 11, 15 (1988) (one of 137 insanity acquittees seen as malingering).

215. It was, no doubt, the prevalence of this attitude that led Judge Brady to point out, in the habeas corpus grant in *Brumfield*, 2012 WL 602163, at *33:

> It bears repeating that the remedy granted here is a limited one. While ineligible for execution, Brumfield will remain incarcerated in Angola for the rest of his life. This ruling does not "let him off easy" on some convoluted procedural technicality. It merely seeks to fairly apply the law as written.

216. Perlin, *supra* note 132, at 235–36; Perlin, *supra* note 214, at 680.

217. See e.g., David Baldus et al., *Racial Discrimination and the Death Penalty in the Post-Furman Era: An Empirical and Legal Overview with Recent Findings from Philadelphia*, 83 COR-NELL L. REV. 1638, 1688–89, tbl. 6 (1998).

218. See *infra* chapter 9.

219. But see Mark Alan Ozimek, *The Case for a More Workable Standard in Death Penalty Jurisprudence: Atkins v. Virginia and Categorical Exemptions under the Imprudent "Evolving Standards of Decency" Doctrine*, 34 U. TOL. L. REV. 651, 677 n. 290 (2003), quoting Petitioner's Brief at 34 in Atkins v. Virginia (No. 00-8452) (Atkins argued that there are "factors that heighten the risk that the death penalty may be imposed" such as "jurors' lack of experience with, and faulty stereotypes regarding, persons with mental retardation, coupled with the potential for prosecutors to exploit such ignorance or stereotypes").

220. Jamie Fellner, *Beyond Reason: Executing Persons with Mental Retardation*, 28 HUM. RTS. 9, 12 (2002).

221. See *infra* chapter 9 (discussing prosecutorial misconduct in death penalty cases involving defendants with mental disabilities).

222. See, for empirical assessments, R. Gregg Dwyer & Richard L. Frierson, *The Presence of Low IQ and Mental Retardation among Murder Defendants Referred for Pretrial Evaluation*, 51 J. FORENSIC SCI. 678 (2006); John H. Blume, Sheri Lynn Johnson, & Christopher Seeds, *An Empirical Look at Atkins v. Virginia and Its Application in Capital Cases*, 76 TENN. L. REV. 625 (2009).

223. Clive A. Stafford Smith & Remy Voisin Starns, *Folly by Fiat: Pretending That Death Row Inmates Can Represent Themselves in Post-conviction Proceedings*, 45 LOY. L. REV. 55, 70 n. 92 (1999). See *supra* chapter 1.

224. Timothy Hall, *Legal Fictions and Moral Reasoning: Capital Punishment and the Mentally Retarded Defendant after Penry v. Johnson*, 35 AKRON L. REV. 327, 327 (2002), and *id.* nn. 2–3, citing, inter alia, Joan Petersilia, *Justice for All? Offenders with Mental Retardation and the California Corrections System*, Dec. 1, 1997 PRISON J. 358, 380; Randall Coyne & Lyn Entzeroth, *Report Regarding Implementation of the American Bar Association's Recommendations and Resolutions Concerning the Death Penalty and Calling for a Moratorium on Executions*, 4 GEO. J. ON FIGHTING POVERTY 3, 40 (1996) (between 12 and 20 percent).

225. Jonathan L. Bing, *Protecting the Mentally Retarded from Capital Punishment: State Efforts since Penry and Recommendations for the Future*, 22 N.Y.U. REV. L. & SOC. CHANGE 59, 62–63 (1996).

226. 224 S.W.3d 577 (Ky. 2006).

227. 543 U.S. 551 (2005) (execution of juvenile violates the Eighth Amendment). See Jamie Hughes, *For Mice or Men or Children? Will the Expansion of the Eighth Amendment in Atkins v. Virginia Force the Supreme Court to Re-Examine the Minimum Age for the Death Penalty?*, 93 J. CRIM. L. & CRIMINOLOGY 973 (2003).

228. 2006 WL 1900630 (W.D. Tex. 2006).

229. *Id.* at *11. Compare State v. Anderson, 996 So. 2d 973 (La. 2008) (statutory exemption concerning age-eighteen requirement did not violate equal protection clause; death sentence upheld).

230. 453 F.3d 690 (6th Cir. 2006).

231. *Id.* at 698.

232. 138 P.3d 549 (Okla. Crim. App. 2006).

233. Compare, Michael L. Perlin, *"You Have Discussed Lepers and Crooks": Sanism in Clinical Teaching*, 9 CLINICAL L. REV. 683, 722 (2003) ("like other lawyers, clinical students often complain, in referring to their clients with mental disabilities, that 'the clients could try harder'").

234. *Howell*, 138 P.3d at 563.

235. 2006 Tenn. Crim. App. LEXIS 454 (June 8, 2006), discussed at 232 S.W.3d 1, 12, *appeal after remand*, 232 S.W.3d 1 (Tenn. 2007); see Pramila A. Kamath, *Blinded by the Bright-Line: Problems with Strict Construction of the Criteria for Death Penalty Exemption on the Basis of Mental Retardation—State v. Strode, 232 S.W.3d 1 (Tenn. 2007)*, 77 U. CIN. L. REV. 321 (2008).

236. *Strode*, 2006 Tenn. Crim. App. at *11.

237. 212 Ariz. 516, 135 P.3d 696 (Ariz. 2006), *cert. denied*, 550 U.S. 937 (2007).

238. *Id.* at 702.

239. 664 F.3d 81 (6th Cir. 2011).

240. *Id.* at 99.

241. See JOHN PARRY & ERIC DROGIN, CRIMINAL LAW HANDBOOK ON PSYCHIATRIC AND PSYCHOLOGICAL EVIDENCE AND TESTIMONY (2000).

242. See *infra* chapter 9.

243. E.g., People v. Kelley, 142 Cal. Rptr. 457, 467 (Cal. Ct. App. 1977) (stating that a prosecutor is held to a higher standard because of his or her unique role in exercising sovereign state power); State v. Ferrone, 113 A. 452, 455 (Conn. 1921) (stating that a prosecutor is a high public officer charged to seek impartial justice).

244. Bryan Dupler, *Capital Cases Involving Mental Retardation*, 93 Am. Jur. Trials 1, § 26 (2011).

245. See Winick, *supra* note 24, at 849–51, sketching out the application of these principles to *Atkins*-type cases.

246. *Id.* at 849, and see *id.* at 853–54, discussing the TJ benefit of determining who is mentally retarded for *Atkins* purposes at an early stage in the proceedings.

247. Amy D. Ronner, *The Learned-Helpless Lawyer: Clinical Legal Education and Therapeutic Jurisprudence as Antidotes to Bartleby Syndrome*, 24 Touro L. Rev. 601, 627 (2008).

CHAPTER 6

1. This section is largely adapted from 4 Michael L. Perlin, Mental Disability Law: Civil and Criminal §§ 12-4.1 to 1e (2d ed. 2002).

2. Paul Appelbaum, *Competence to be Executed: Another Conundrum for Mental Health Professionals*, 37 Hosp. & Commun. Psychiatry 682 (1986).

3. 477 U.S. 399 (1986).

4. 551 U.S. 930 (2007).

5. Appelbaum, *supra* note 2, at 682.

6. 536 U.S. 304 (2002).

7. On the question of the competency of persons with mental *retardation* to be executed, see Michael L. Perlin et al., Competence in the Law: From Legal Theory to Clinical Application 115–23 (2008), and see *infra* chapter 5 discussing *Atkins*, *supra*.

8. For a helpful overview, see Jonathan Entin, *Psychiatry, Insanity, and the Death Penalty: A Note on Implementing Supreme Court Decisions*, 79 J. Crim. L. & Criminology 218 (1988).

9. Geoffrey Hazard & David Louisell, *Death, the State, and the Insane: Stay of Execution*, 9 UCLA L. Rev. 381 (1962).

10. *Id.* at 383–84 (citing Blackstone, Commentaries *395–*396 (13th ed. 1800)).

11. Hazard & Louisell, *supra* note 9, at 383 (citing 1 Hale, Pleas of the Crown 34–35 (1736)).

12. Hazard & Louisell, *supra* note 9, at 384–85 (citing Coke, Third Institute 6 (1797)).

13. Hazard & Louisell, *supra* note 9, at 387 (citing Aquinas, Summa Theologica, First Part, *Treatise on the Angels*, ques. 64, art. 2, objection, reply to second objection; Aquinas, Summa Contra Gentiles, bk. 3, ch. 146).

14. Hazard & Louisell, *supra* note 9 at 387–88 (citing and quoting Shakespeare, *Hamlet*, act. III, sc. iii, lines 72–96).

15. See also Barbara Ward, *Competency for Execution: Problems in Law and Psychiatry*, 14 Fla. St. U. L. Rev. 35, 49–57 (1986). Traditional arguments are collected in Solesbee v. Balkcom, 339 U.S. 9, 17–19 (1950) (Frankfurter, J., dissenting).

16. William White, Insanity and the Criminal Law 245 (1923) (da Capo 1981 reprint).

17. *Solesbee*, 339 U.S. at 9. In 1897, the Court had held that a pre-execution competency hearing was not necessary. See Nobles v. Georgia, 168 U.S. 399, 399 (1897), discussed in this context in Bruce Arrigo & Jeffrey Tasca, *Right to Refuse Treatment, Competency to be Executed, and Therapeutic Jurisprudence: Toward a Systematic Analysis*, 24 L. & Psychol. Rev. 1, 14 (1999).

18. Trop v. Dulles, 356 U.S. 86 (1958). See also Robinson v. California, 370 U.S. 660 (1962).

19. See Michael L. Perlin, *The Supreme Court, the Mentally Disabled Criminal Defendant, Psychiatric Testimony in Death Penalty Cases, and the Power of Symbolism: Dulling the* Ake *in* Barefoot's *Achilles Heel*, 3 N.Y. L. Sch. J. Human Rts. 91, 97 (1985). See generally, Hans Adam Bedeau, The Death Penalty in America 3–95 (3d ed. 1982).

20. Appelbaum, *supra* note 2, at 682.

21. A poll from January 7, 2004, reported that 69 percent of adults support the death penalty. However, when Americans were asked how they felt about the execution of mentally ill inmates, only 25 percent said they support executing mentally ill persons. See Angela Kimber, *Psychotic Journeys of the Green Mile*, 22 T.M. Cooley L. Rev. 27, 27 (2005) (relying on The Gallup Poll, May 6–9, 2002, available at http:// www.pollingreport.com/crime.htm, and Humphrey Taylor, *The Harris Poll, More Than Two-Thirds of Americans Continue to Support the Death Penalty* (Jan. 7, 2004), at http:// www.harrisinteractive.com/harris_poll/index.asp?PID=431).

22. See, for a survey, Henry Steadman, et al., *Mentally Disordered Offenders: A National Survey of Patients and Facilities*, 6 L. & Hum. Behav. 31 (1982).

23. See, on the health problems of prisoners, Eric Neisser, *Is There a Doctor in the Joint? The Search for Constitutional Standards for Prison Health Care*, 63 Va. L. Rev. 921 (1977). On the specific problems of mentally ill prisoners, see B. James George, *The American Bar Association's Mental Health Standards: An Overview*, 53 Geo. Wash. L. Rev. 338, 371–74 (1985). See generally 4 Perlin, *supra* note 1, at § 11-4.3

24. It has been estimated that "as many as fifty percent of Florida's death row inmates become intermittently insane." Ward, *supra* note 15, at 42. See generally, Dorothy Otnow Lewis et al., *Psychiatric and Psychoeducational Characteristics of 15 Death Row Inmates in the United States*, 143 Am. J. Psychiatry 838 (1986). See also Louis Jolyon West, *Psychiatric Reflections on the Death Penalty*, 45 Am. J. Orthopsychiatry 689, 694 (1975). On the human rights implications of lengthy death row stays, see Richard Dieter, *The Death Penalty and Human Rights: U.S. Death Penalty and International Law*, 30–33 (2003), accessible at http://www. deathpenaltyinfo.org/Oxfordpaper.pdf.

25. The general ethical issues relating to medical participation in execution by lethal injection were raised twenty-five years ago by Dr. William Curran and an associate who argued that such involvement—"by intentional, careful, skillful injection of a medically prepared substance into the veins of the prisoner," William Curran & Ward Casscells, *The Ethics of Medical Participation in Capital Punishment by Intravenous Drug Injection*, 302 New Eng. J. Med. 226, 228 (1980)— seemed to constitute a "grievous expansion of medical condonation of and participation in capital punishment." *Id.* See also *Strange Bedfellows: Death Penalty and Medicine*, 248 J.A.M.A. 518 (1982).

Drawing on declarations of the international Conference for the Abolition of Torture, *id.*, citing *Final Report, Amnesty International Conference for the Abolition of Torture* (Paris, France), Dec. 10–11, 1973, and the Twenty-Ninth World Medical Assembly of the World Medical Association (the so-called Declaration of Tokyo) (Curran & Cascells, *supra*, at 228, citing 22 World Med. J. 87 (1975)), the authors concluded that a medical professional who "orders or prepares a chemical substance to kill a prisoner under sentence of death would be in direct violation," Curran & Cascells, *supra*, at 229, of these accords. Similarly, they suggested that it would be ethically improper for physicians to monitor the condemned prisoner's condition during the drug administration and to carry on this action to pronounce his death when heartbeat and respiration were found to be absent. Curran & Cascells, *supra*, at 229.

They concluded by urging that medical professionals should "examine seriously the issues presented by this new method of capital punishment." *Id.* at 230: "The line should be drawn here. The medical profession in the United States should formally condemn all forms of medical participation in this method of capital punishment." *Id.*

See generally, Bruce Arrigo & Jeffrey Tasca, *Right to Refuse Treatment, Competency to be Executed, and Therapeutic Jurisprudence: Toward a Systematic Analysis*, 24 L. & Psychol. Rev. 1 (1999); Alfred Freedman & Abraham Halpern, *The Psychiatrist's Dilemma: A Conflict of Roles in Legal Executions*, 33 Australian & N.Z. J. Psychiatry 629 (1999); Alfred M. Freedman & Abraham L. Halpern, *The Erosion of Ethics and Morality in Medicine: Physician Participation in Legal Executions in the United States*, 41 N.Y. L. Sch. L. Rev. 169 (1996); Richard Showalter, *Psychiatric Participation in Capital Sentencing Procedures*, 13 Int'l J. L. & Psychiatry 261 (1990); Douglas Mossman, *Assessing and Restoring Competency to Be Executed: Should Psychiatrists Participate?*, 5 Behav. Sci. & L. 397 (1987); Richard Bonnie, *Dilemmas in Administering the Death Penalty: Conscientious Abstention, Professional Ethics, and the Needs of the Legal System,* 14 LAW & HUM. BEHAV. 67 (1990); Stanley Brodsky, *Professional Ethics and Professional Morality in the Assessment of Competence for Execution: A Reply to Bonnie,* 14 LAW & HUM. BEHAV. 91 (1990); Richard Bonnie, *Grounds for Professional Abstention in Capital Cases: A Reply to Brodsky,* 14 LAW & HUM. BEHAV. 99 (1990).

26. Ward, *supra* note 15, at 100. See also Note, *Medical Ethics and Competency to Be Executed,* 96 YALE L. J. 167, 173–79 (1986) (hereinafter Yale Note). See *id.* at 184 (characterizing dilemma as "insoluble").

27. Michael Radelet & George Barnard, *Ethics and the Psychiatric Determination of Competency to Be Executed,* 14 BULL. AM. ACAD. PSYCHIATRY & L. 37, 43 (1986).

28. Radelet & Barnard, *supra* note 28, at 43.

29. FLA. STAT. ANN § 922.07 (1985).

30. See Ward, *supra* note 15, at 75 n. 231. For a survey of all state laws, see *id.* at 101–7 (appendix).

31. Ford v. State, 374 So. 2d 496, 497 (Fla. 1979), Ford v. State, 374 So. 2d 496, 497 (Fla. 1979), *cert. denied,* 445 U.S. 972 (1980).

32. *Ford,* 477 U.S. at 401.

33. *Id.* at 402.

34. *Id.*

35. "Delusions" are false beliefs or wrong judgments held with convictions despite incontrovertible evidence to the contrary.

36. "Hallucinations" are the apparent, often strong, subjective perception of an object or event when no such situation is present.

37. *Ford,* 477 U.S. at 402.

38. *Id.*:

He believed that the prison guards, part of the conspiracy, had been killing people and putting the bodies in the concrete enclosures used for beds. Later, he began to believe that his women relatives were being tortured and sexually abused somewhere in the prison. This notion developed into a delusion that the people who were tormenting him at the prison had taken members of Ford's family hostage. The hostage delusion took firm hold and expanded, until Ford was reporting that 135 of his friends and family were being held hostage in the prison, and that only he could help them. By "day 287" of the "hostage crisis," the list of hostages had expanded to include "senators, Senator Kennedy, and many other leaders." App., 53. In a letter to the Attorney General of Florida, written in 1983, Ford appeared to assume authority for the "crisis," claiming to have fired a number of prison officials. He began to refer to himself as "Pope John Paul, III," and reported having appointed nine new justices to the Florida Supreme Court. *Id.* at 59.

Id.

39. *Id.*

40. *Id.* at 402–3. Ford subsequently refused to see the psychiatrist again, believing that he had now joined the conspiracy against him. *Id.* at 403. Later, Ford "regressed further into nearly complete incomprehensibility, speaking only in a code characterized by intermittent use of the word 'one,' making statements such as 'Hands one, face one. Mafia one. God one, father one. Pope one. Pope one, leader one." [App.] at 72. *Ford,* 477 U.S. at 403.

41. FLA. STAT. ANN § 922.07 (1985).

42. FLA. STAT. ANN § 922.07 (2) (1985).

43. *Ford,* 477 U.S. at 404. One psychiatrist diagnosed Ford as suffering from "psychosis with paranoia," a second as "psychotic," and a third as having a "severe adaptational disorder." *Id.* All three, however, found that he had enough "cognitive" functioning to know "fully well what can happen to him." *Id.*

44. *Id.*

45. *Id.*

46. *Id.*

47. *Id.* After the district court denied the petition without a hearing, the Eleventh Circuit granted a certificate of probable cause and stayed the defendant's execution, Ford v. Strickland, 734 F.2d 538 (11th Cir. 1984), and the Supreme Court rejected the state's application to vacate the stay, Wainwright v. Ford, 467 U.S. 1220 (1984). A divided panel of the Eleventh Circuit affirmed the district court's denial of the writ, 752 F.2d 526 (11th Cir. 1985), and the Supreme Court granted *certiorari* "to resolve the important issue whether the Eighth Amendment prohibits the execution of the insane and, if so, whether the District Court should have held a hearing on [defendant's] claim." *Ford*, 477 U.S. at 405.

48. On the question of what procedures were appropriate to satisfy the Constitution, three other Justices joined Justice Marshall. *Ford*, 477 U.S. at 401. Justice Powell concurred on that issue, and wrote separately. *Id.* at 418. Justice O'Connor (for herself and Justice White) concurred in part and dissented in part. *Id.* at 427. Justice Rehnquist (for himself and the chief justice) dissented. *Id.* at 431. See *infra* text accompanying notes 63–66.

49. *Id.* at 405–10.

50. 339 U.S. 9 (1950).

51. *Ford*, 477 U.S. at 405.

52. *Id.* at 405–6 (citing, inter alia, Solem v. Helm, 463 U.S. 277, 285–86 (1983) (Burger, C.J., dissenting)).

53. *Ford*, 477 U.S. at 406 (citing Trop v. Dulles, 356 U.S. 86, 101 (1958) (plurality opinion)).

54. *Ford*, 477 U.S. at 406 (citing Coker v. Georgia, 433 U.S. 584, 597 (1977) (plurality opinion)).

55. *Ford*, 477 U.S. at 406–7.

56. *Ford*, 477 U.S. at 408 (quoting Hawles, *Remarks on the Trial of Mr. Charles Bateman*, 11 How. St. Tr. 474, 477 (1685)).

57. *Ford*, 477 U.S. at 408.

58. *Id.*: "[I]t was early observed that 'the judge is bound' to stay the execution upon insanity of the prisoner." *Id.* (citing 1 CHITTY, A PRACTICAL TREATISE ON THE CRIMINAL LAW *761 (5th Am. ed. 1847), and 1 WHARTON, A TREATISE ON CRIMINAL LAW § 59 (8th ed. 1880)).

59. *Ford*, 477 U.S. at 408.

60. *Id.* See *id.* at 408–9 n. 2 (listing statutes).

61. *Id.* at 409.

62. *Id.* at 409–10.

63. *Id.* at 312–13.

64. 28 U.S.C. § 2254(d)(2).

65. 28 U.S.C. § 2254(d)(3).

66. 28 U.S.C. § 2254(d)(6).

67. *Ford*, 477 U.S. at 411.

68. *Id.* at 411–12.

69. *Solesbee*, 339 U.S. at 23 (Frankfurter, J., dissenting). See also, O'Connor v. Donaldson, 422 U.S. 563, 584 (1975) (Burger, C.J., concurring) ("there are many forms of mental illness that are not understood"); Addington v. Texas, 441 U.S. 418, 429 (1979) ("Given the lack of certainty and the fallibility of psychiatric diagnosis, there is a serious question as to whether a state could ever prove beyond a reasonable doubt that an individual is both mentally ill and likely to be dangerous").

70. *Ford*, 477 U.S. at 412.

71. The Governor's office had refused to inform the defendant's counsel whether his submission of written materials (including psychiatric reports of experts who examined Ford "at great length") would be considered. *Id.* at 413.

72. *Id.* In Townsend v. Sain, 372 U.S. 293, 312 (1953), the Court held that "where an applicant for a writ of habeas corpus alleges facts which, if proved, would entitle him to relief,

the federal court to which the application is made has the power to receive evidence and try the facts anew."

73. *Ford*, 477 U.S. at 413.
74. *Id.* (quoting Jurek v. Texas, 428 U.S. 262, 276 (1976) (plurality opinion)).
75. *Ford*, 477 U.S. at 414.
76. *Id.* at 415:

"[C]ross-examination . . . is beyond any doubt the greatest legal engine ever invented for the discovery of the truth." 5 J. Wigmore, *Evidence* § 1367 (Chadbourn rev. 1974). Cross-examination of the psychiatrists, or perhaps a less formal equivalent, would contribute markedly to the process of seeking truth in sanity disputes by bringing to light the bases for each expert's beliefs, the precise factors underlying those beliefs, any history of error or caprice of the examiner, any personal bias with respect to the issue of capital punishment, the expert's degree of certainty about his or her own conclusions, and the precise meaning of ambiguous words used in the report.

77. *Id.* See also *id.* at n. 3:

The adequacy of the factfinding procedures is further called into question by the cursory nature of the underlying psychiatric examination itself. While this Court does not purport to set substantive guidelines for the development of expert psychiatric opinion, *cf.* Barefoot v. Estelle, 463 U.S. 880, 903 (1983) (parallel citations omitted), we can say that the goal of reliability is unlikely to be served by a single group interview, with no provisions for the exercise of the psychiatrists' professional judgment regarding the possible need for different or more comprehensive evaluative techniques. The inconsistency and vagueness of the conclusions reached by the three examining psychiatrists in this case attest to the dubious value of such an examination.

78. See FLA. STAT. ANN. § 922.07 (West 1985).
On the issue of dual loyalties in general, see Jerome Shestack, *Psychiatry and the Dilemma of Dual Loyalties*, in MEDICAL, MORAL AND LEGAL ISSUES IN MENTAL HEALTH CARE 7 (Frank J. Ayd Jr., ed. 1974); Loren Roth, *To Respect Persons, Families, and Communities: Some Problems in the Ethics of Mental Health Care*, 40 PSYCHIATRY DIGEST 17 (1979); Michael L. Perlin, *Power Imbalances in Therapeutic and Forensic Relationships*, 9 BEHAV. SCI. & L. 111 (1991). On this issue in the context of other competency inquiries, see PERLIN ET AL., *supra* note 7, chapter 2C.
79. *Ford*, 477 U.S. at 416.
80. *Id.*
81. *Id.* at 416–17. See also *id.* at 417 n. 4.
82. *Id.* at 416.
83. *Id.* at 417.
84. *Id.* at 417–18.
85. *Ford*, 477 U.S. at 418 (Powell, J., concurring).
86. *Id.*
87. *Id.* at 427 (O'Connor, J., concurring in part and dissenting in part).
88. *Id.*
89. *Id.*
90. *Id.*
91. *Id.* at 427–28.
92. *Id.* at 431 (Rehnquist, J., dissenting).
93. *Id.*
94. *Id.*
95. *Id.* at 432.
96. *Id.* at 434.
97. *Id.* at 435.

98. *Id.*:

A claim of insanity may be made at any time before sentence, and, once rejected, may be used again; a prisoner found sane two days before execution might claim to have lost his sanity the next day thus necessitating another judicial determination of his sanity and presumably another stay of execution.

99. *Ford*, 477 U.S. at 429 (O'Connor, J., concurring in part and dissenting in part).

100. *Id.* at 435 (Rehnquist, J., dissenting).

101. *See* Ingo Keilitz & Junius Fulton, The Insanity Defense and Its Alternatives: A Guide for Policymakers (1984).

102. See generally, Michael L. Perlin, The Jurisprudence of the Insanity Defense (1994); Michael L. Perlin, "*The Borderline Which Separated You from Me*": *The Insanity Defense, the Authoritarian Spirit, the Fear of Faking, and the Culture of Punishment*, 82 Iowa L. Rev. 1375 (1997).

103. Michael L. Perlin, *"Life Is in Mirrors, Death Disappears": Giving Life to Atkins*, 33 N.M. L. Rev. 315, 321 (2003).

104. Isaac Ray, A Treatise on the Medical Jurisprudence of Insanity § 247, at 243 (Overholser, ed. 1962).

105. Appelbaum, *supra* note 2, at 683. See also Yale Note, *supra* note 26, at 186:

The states have enacted and implemented competency to be executed statutes that pose an irreconcilable ethical conflict for the medical profession. Based on an analysis of the relevant medical ethics and state interests, this Note contends that the state must accommodate the ethical integrity of the medical profession. This proposal is not revolutionary. The state has traditionally respected and upheld the ethical integrity of various professions. It must now do so in the context of medical treatment of the insane condemned, because to do so otherwise results in the anathema of making "one learned profession the very agent of an attack upon the ethical foundations of another."

(footnotes omitted) (quoting, in part, Derr, *Why Food and Fluids Can Never Be Denied*, 16 Hastings Center Rep. 28, 30 (Feb. 1986)).

106. See Michael Radelet & Kent Miller, *The Aftermath of Ford v. Wainwright*, 10 Behav. Sci. & L. 339 (1992).

107. For a retrospective review of *Ford* in light of *Panetti*, see Michael Mello, *Executing the Mentally Ill: When Is Someone Sane Enough to Die?* 22 Crim. Just. 30 (Fall 2007).

108. See 4 Perlin, *supra* note 1, § 12-4.1e, at 542–43 n. 457 (citing cases).

109. See Boggs v. State, 667 So. 2d 765, 766 n. 3 (Fla. 1996) (discussing press report of trial judge's beliefs that defendant was "faking mental illness to avoid execution"). On the significance of this position to Justice Scalia's opinion in *Atkins*, see *supra* chapter 5. See generally, on this question, Perlin, *supra* note 102. It is more likely that persons with mental illness try to "mask or hide their symptoms." See Rebecca J. Covarubias, *Lives in Defense Counsel's Hands: The Problems and Responsibilities of Defense Counsel Representing Mentally Ill or Mentally Retarded Capital Defendants*, 11 Scholar 413, 465 (2009).

110. See 4 Perlin, *supra* note 1, § 12.4.1e, at 544:

Ford reflects the depth of the split on the question of the standards to be employed in determining one's competency to be executed. Further, the perplexing inconsistencies between the positions taken by several of the Justices and their opinions in other mental disability cases probably result from the grave difficulties the Justices face in resolving these questions. Unfortunately, the fact that the procedural aspect of *Ford* is "controlled" by a plurality opinion will make it far more difficult for legislators in those states with statutes similar to Florida's to draft new laws that are constitutionally sound.

See e.g., Cuevas v. Collins, 932 F.2d 1078, 1084 (5th Cir. 1991) (hearing not required unless defendant is "so deranged that he is unaware that he is about to be put to death"); Garrett v. Collins, 951 F.2d 57 (5th Cir. 1992) (holding that defendant's belief that his dead aunt would protect him from effects of toxic agents used during execution did not preclude imposition of death penalty on grounds of incompetency); for subsequent cases, see e.g., Heidnik v. Horn, 960 F. Supp. 74 (E.D. Pa. 1997); Walton v. Johnson, 440 F.3d 160 (4th Cir. 2006); Bedford v. Bobby, 645 F.3d 372 (6th Cir. 2011); Baird v. State, 833 N.E.2d 28 (Ind. 2005); Coe v. State, 17 S.W.3d 193 (Tenn. 2000) (all denying *Ford* applications).

Perhaps the most famous case is that of Ricky Rector (who told the officers who took him to his death "that he had put the dessert from his last meal aside in order to have it later." See Albert Alschuler, *Bill Clinton's Parting Pardon Party*, 100 J. CRIM. L. & CRIMINOLOGY 1131, 1133 (2010); Laura Mansnerus, *Damaged Brains and the Death Penalty*, N.Y. TIMES (July 21, 2001). See *infra* chapter 12, text accompanying note 25.

See also Shaw v. Delo, 762 F. Supp. 853 (E.D. Mo. 1991) (holding that funds for investigative and expert services to support incompetency claim were not necessary). On the question of whether a trial court can exclude the death penalty as a possible punishment because of a defendant's mental illness, see Commonwealth v. Ryan, 5 S.W.3d 113 (Ky. 1999) (finding that court lacked authority to do so).

111. *Panetti*, 448 F.3d, at 819; see also *id.* at 818 (discussing *Ford*, 477 U.S., at 421–22 (Powell, J., concurring in part and concurring in judgment)).

112. See Nina Farahany, *Cruel and Unusual Punishments*, 86 WASH. U. L. REV. 859, 913–14 (2009), discussing the "near quarter century of mayhem the Court produced between its decisions in *Ford* and *Panetti*." See generally, Michael L. Perlin, *"Good and Bad, I Defined These Terms, Quite Clear No Doubt Somehow": Neuroimaging and Competency to Be Executed after Panetti*, 28 BEHAV. SCI. & L. 621 (2010).

113. *Panetti*, 551 U.S. at 936.

114. *Id.*; see Perlin, *supra* note 112. While representing himself, Panetti wore a purple cowboy costume, rambled incoherently, gestured threateningly at jurors, went into trances, nodded off, and tried to subpoena people like Jesus Christ and John F. Kennedy. See Covarrubias, *supra* note 109, at 463–64 nn. 292–93, relying upon Todd J. Gillman & Diane Jennings, *Justices Block Execution of Texas Killer: Death for Schizophrenic Is Cruel and Unusual, Supreme Court Rules*, DALLAS MORNING NEWS, June 29, 2007, at A12, and Ralph Blumenthal, *Insanity Issue Lingers as Texas Execution Is Set*, N.Y. TIMES, Feb. 4, 2004, at A12.

115. *Panetti*, 551 U.S. at 935.

116. *Id.*

117. *Id.*

118. Panetti v. Dretke, 401 F. Supp. 705, 711 (W.D. Tex. 2004).

119. Panetti v. Dretke, 448 F.3d 815 (5th Cir. 2006).

120. Panetti v. Quarterman, 549 U.S. 1106 (2007).

121. In a jurisdictional ruling of great importance to death penalty litigation, the Court also found that the defendant's claim was not barred by federal legislation that generally prohibited "successive" habeas corpus applications. See Panetti v. Quarterman, 551 U.S. 930, 942 (2007). The significance of this portion of the opinion is beyond the scope of this chapter.

122. See Amanda M. Brown, *Panetti v. Quarterman: Due Process for Mentally Ill Defendants Facing the Death Penalty*, 9 LOY. J. PUB. INT. L 273, 286 (2008), arguing that the expansion of *Ford* in *Panetti* was "inadvertent."

123. *Panetti*, 551 U.S. at 951.

124. *Id.* at 952. See Wood v. Thaler, 787 F. Supp. 2d 458, 487 (W.D. Tex. 2011) (once a petitioner has made a threshold showing of insanity, "it was incumbent upon the state habeas trial court to accord petitioner an opportunity to be heard").

125. *Panetti*, 551 U.S. at 954, quoting, in part, *Ford*, 477 U.S., at 423–24 (Powell, J., concurring in part and concurring in judgment) (internal quotation marks omitted).

126. *Panetti*, 551 U.S. at 954. See *id*:

> Four expert witnesses testified on petitioner's behalf in the District Court proceedings. One explained that petitioner's mental problems are indicative of "schizo-affective disorder," resulting in a "genuine delusion" involving his understanding of the reason for his execution. According to the expert, this delusion has recast petitioner's execution as "part of spiritual warfare . . . between the demons and the forces of the darkness and God and the angels and the forces of light." As a result, the expert explained, although petitioner claims to understand "that the state is saying that [it wishes] to execute him for [his] murder[s]," he believes in earnest that the stated reason is a "sham" and the State in truth wants to execute him "to stop him from preaching." Petitioner's other expert witnesses reached similar conclusions concerning the strength and sincerity of this "fixed delusion."

(citations to record omitted).

127. *Id.* at 955.

128. *Id.* at 956. Compare Overstreet v. State, 877 N.E.2d 144, 173 (Ind. 2007): "However, fatal to Overstreet's federal constitutional claim is that there was no evidence presented to the post-conviction court one way or the other on whether Overstreet is aware of the punishment he is about to suffer and why he is to suffer it"); State v. Irick, 320 S.W.3d 284, 295 (Tenn. 2010): "Under *Panetti*, execution is not forbidden so long as the evidence shows that the prisoner does not question the reality of the crime or the reality of his punishment by the State for the crime committed."

129. *Panetti*, 551 U.S. at 956, quoting *Panetti*, 448 F.3d at 819.

130. *Panetti*, 448 F.3d at 817–18.

131. *Panetti*, 551 U.S. at 956–57.

132. *Panetti*, 448 F.3d at 817–18.

133. *Id.*

134. *Id.*

135. 477 U.S. at 407–8.

136. *Id.* at 408.

137. *Panetti*, 551 U.S. at 959.

138. *Id.*

139. *Id.* at 960.

140. *Id.*

141. *Id.* at 962.

142. *Id.*

On remand, the habeas court held a new *Ford* hearing, and again denied Panetti's claim, finding he was competent to be executed, concluding that his delusions "do not prevent his rational understanding of the causal connection between those murders and his death sentence, and he in fact has such an understanding." Panetti v. Quarterman, 2008 WL 2338498, *36 (W.D. Tex. 2008). The court recognized that Panetti "was mentally ill when he committed his crime and continues to be mentally ill today, *id.* at *37, but nonetheless determined that he "has both a factual and rational understanding of his crime, his impending death, and the causal retributive connection between the two. Therefore, if any mentally ill person is competent to be executed for his crimes, this record establishes it is Scott Panetti." *Id.* See e.g., Lyn Entzeroth, *The Challenge and Dilemma of Charting a Course to Constitutionally Protect the Severely Mentally Ill Capital Defendant from the Death Penalty*, 44 Akron L. Rev. 529, 557 n. 152 (2011).

Panetti appealed the decision to the Fifth Circuit Court of Appeals; however, before it issued an opinion, the Fifth Circuit stayed and abated the proceedings so that Panetti could return to the state court to raise a claim, based on the Supreme Court's then-recently issued decision in Indiana v. Edwards, 554 U.S. 164 (2008), establishing limits on the right to self-representation. See Panetti v. Quarterman, No. 08-70015 (5th Cir., Dec. 17, 2008). That claim was dismissed, see ex parte, *Panetti*, WR-37, 145-02 (Tex. Crim. App. 2009), and Panetti subsequently sought, and was granted, a motion to stay and abate until the *Edwards* claim could be resolved on appeal. See Panetti v. Thaler, 2010 WL 2640336 (W.D. Tex. 2010). Panetti's *Edwards* application was subsequently rejected, over dissent, in state court, see ex parte, *Panetti*, 326 S.W.3d 615 (Tex. Crim. App. 2010), *cert. den.*, 131 S. Ct. 3027 (2011). Panetti's subsequent habeas corpus petition was rejected because (1) *Edwards* did not retroactively apply to collateral attacks, and (2) because Panetti was found not incompetent to represent himself under *Edwards*. Panetti v. Thaler, 2012 WL 290115 (W.D. Tex. 2012).

143. *Panetti*, 551 U.S. at 952. See Hatfield v. Parsons, 2011 WL 5822122, *20 n. 27 (S.D. W. Va. 2011) (emphasis added):

> *Panetti*'s analysis of *Ford* is relevant to the present case because it confirms by analogy *the ines-capable conclusion* that prohibiting a defendant from responding to the state's evidence (through testimony, the introduction of evidence, or cross-examination) violates the defendant's due process rights as established in *Pate*, *Drope*, and *Medina*.

144. *Panetti*, 551 U.S. at 959.

145. See Pamela A. Wilkins, *Competency for Execution: The Implications of a Communicative Model of Retribution*, 76 Tenn. L. Rev. 713, 742 (2009): "The good news from *Panetti* is that the Court finally articulated a specific justification for the Eighth Amendment ban: the execution of an incompetent inmate lacks retributive value." See generally, Bruce Winick, *The Supreme Court's Evolving Death Penalty Jurisprudence: Severe Mental Illness as the Next Frontier*, 50 B.C. L. Rev. 785 (2009); Jeffrey Kirchmeier, *The Undiscovered Country: Execution Competency & Comprehending Death*, 98 Ky. L. Rev. 263 (2009–2010); Perlin, *supra* note 112.

146. Courts are urged to "look outside the narrow framework of competency to be executed [to other areas of legal competencies ... for purposes of analyzing what criteria are relevant to a substantive competency test," in Gary R. Studen, *Panetti v. Quarterman: Solving the Competency Dilemma by Broadening the Concept of Rational Understanding in Competency-To-Be-Executed Determinations*, 39 Seton Hall L. Rev. 163, 190 (2009). Compare Simon v. Epps, 2012 WL 669433, *8 (5th Cir. 2012), relying on *Ford* and *Panetti* in holding that procedures that allowed the *state* to present expert evaluations while Simon was prevented from presenting countervailing expert evaluations "violated fundamental fairness and due process."

147. Christopher Seeds, *The Afterlife of Ford and Panetti: Execution Competence and the Capacity to Assist Counsel*, 53 St. Louis U. L. J. 309, 338 (2009). See *id.* at 310, arguing that, since *Ford*, "the capacity to assist counsel has been viewed as a dispensable relic."

148. 477 U.S. at 418–29 (Powell, J., concurring).

149. Seeds, *supra* note 147, at 310.

150. *Id.* at 339.

151. J. Amy Dillard, *And Death Shall Have No Dominion: How to Achieve the Categorical Exemption of Mentally Retarded Defendants from Execution*, 45 U. Rich. L. Rev. 961, 984 (2011).

152. For a pre-*Panetti* case, see e.g., Walton v. Johnson, 440 F.3d 160, 172 (4th Cir. 2006) ("We conclude that there is no Constitutional requirement under *Ford* that Walton be able to assist counsel to be deemed competent to be executed"). A Westlaw search of < "assist counsel" /250 Panetti> reveals no decided cases on this point (search last performed May 28, 2012).

Note that soon before the manuscript for this book was submitted, the Supreme Court granted *certiorari* in two related cases on the questions of whether capital prisoners possess a "right to competence" in federal habeas proceedings (Tibbals v. Carter, 2012 WL 895971 (2012)) and whether federal habeas legislation entitles a death row inmate to stay the federal habeas proceedings he initiated if he is not competent to assist counsel (Ryan v. Gonzales, 2012 WL 895970 (2012)). See *supra* chapter 1.

153. See e.g., Thompson v. Bell, 580 F.3d 423, 434–35 (6th Cir. 2009) (noting that *Panetti* "clarifie[d]" *Ford*, and that the state court's decision rejecting the defendant's claim was "unreasonable" under *Panetti*).

154. 536 U.S. 304 (2002) (defendant's mental retardation barred the imposition of the death penalty); see Rivera v. Quarterman, 505 F.3d 349, 358 (5th Cir. 2007) ("The lesson we draw from *Panetti* is that, where a petitioner has made a prima facie showing of retardation as Rivera did, the state court's failure to provide him with the opportunity to develop his claim deprives the state court's decision of the deference normally due"); see also e.g., Hearn v. Quarterman, 2008 WL 679030, *3 (N.D. Tex. 2008):

> Although the court finds that Hearn's counsel, through the exercise of due diligence and reasonable competence, could have concluded earlier than he did that evidence of Hearn's neuropsychological deficits and fetal alcohol syndrome might satisfy the "significant limitations in intellectual functioning" element of the mental retardation definition, and that his counsel could have secured supporting expert testimony before responding to the state's summary judgment motion, this factor is outweighed by the importance of the new evidence and the fact that the state is unlikely to suffer unfair prejudice as a result of granting the requested relief.

Hearn was subsequently supplemented in Hearn v. Quarterman, 2008 WL 3362041, *7 (N.D. Tex. 2008), finding that Hearn's prima facie showing of mental retardation supported his conclusion that an *Atkins* claim was "potentially meritorious."

155. See e.g., United States v. Wolfson, 616 F. Supp. 2d 398, 420 (S.D.N.Y. 2008):

> The principles that the Court explained in *Panetti* spring from the Court's interpretation of "rational understanding" as applied to an execution for purposes of the Eighth Amendment. The same requirement of "rational understanding" applies to the determination of competence under the due process clause.

156. See Brooks v. Bobby, 458 Fed.Appx. 416, 418 (6th Cir. 2011) ("States need not give prisoners unlimited opportunities to prove they are incompetent to be executed").

157. See *infra* chapter 7.

158. *Panetti*, 551 U.S. at 952.

159. *Id.* at 959.

160. Panetti v. Quarterman, 2006 WL 3880284, *26 (2006) (appellant's petition for *certiorari*).

161. See Michael L. Perlin, *Pretexts and Mental Disability Law: The Case of Competency*, 47 U. Miami L. Rev. 625, 634 (1993), discussing Fuentes v. Shevin, 407 U.S. 67, 85 n. 14 (1972) (provision of a discovery mechanism not invoked by a single defendant in a 442-case sample).

162. See *Panetti*, 2008 WL 2338498, at *30 (noting a number of states that do not define competency to be executed); see e.g., Ala. Code § 15-16-23 (LexisNexis 1995); Cal. Penal Code § 3701 (West 2000); Conn. Gen. Stat. Ann. § 54-101 (West 2009); Del. Code Ann. tit. 11, § 406 (2007); Ind. Code Ann. § 11-10-4-2 (LexisNexis 2003); Kan. Stat. Ann. § 22-4006 (2007); Mass. Ann. Laws ch. 279, § 62 (LexisNexis 2002); Neb. Rev. Stat. § 29-2537 (2008); Nev. Rev. Stat. § 176.425 (2007); S.C. Code Ann. § 44-23-220 (2002); S.D. Codified Laws § 23A-27A-22 (2008); Va. Code Ann. § 19.2-177.1 (2008), as discussed in Kirchmeier, *supra* note 145, at 283 n. 137.

163. *Panetti*, 551 U.S. at 960.

164. Compare e.g., United States v. Salava, 978 F.2d 320 (7th Cir. 1992) (rejecting a government argument that expert testimony on the insanity defense should be excluded because the diagnosis did not qualify as "severe" for purposes of 18 U.S.C. § 17; instead accepting the expert's opinion that the defendant's diagnosis of antisocial and paranoid personality disorder were severe), to Beiswenger v. Psychiatric Sec. Review Bd., 84 P.3d 180 (Or. Ct. App. 2004) (because legislature intended to exclude personality disorders such as sexual conduct disorders and substance abuse from the definition of "mental disease or defect" under the insanity defense, personality disorders also should not be treated as mental diseases or defects when considering the continued commitment of insanity acquittees). See generally, Bruce Winick, *Ambiguities in the Legal Meaning and Significance of Mental Illness*, 1 Psychol. Pub. Pol'y & L. 534 (1995)

(discussing the implications of Foucha v. Louisiana, 504 U.S. 71 (1992), on this question (in *Foucha*, the Supreme Court ruled that due process barred the retention of a non-mentally ill insanity acquittee in a mental hospital).

165. *Panetti*, 551 U.S. at 959.

166. D.G. Maxted, *Panetti v. Quarterman: Raising the Bar against Executing the Incompetent*, 4 Duke J. Const. L. & Pub. Pol'y Sidebar 99, 113–14 (2008).

167. 536 U.S. 304 (2002). See *supra* chapter 5.

168. Christopher Slobogin, *Mental Illness and the Death Penalty*, 1 Cal. Crim. L. Rev. 3, *39 (2000).

169. *Id.* In his essay, Slobogin uses the term "mental illness" "to refer primarily to the psychoses." *Id.*, at *4. See Kirchmeier, *supra* note 145, at 299 ("Humans do not wish to believe they are cruel, and there is something cruel about killing people who cannot appreciate the reasons why they are being killed—or even appreciate that they are being killed").

170. In City of Cleburne, Texas v. Cleburne Living Center, 473 U.S. 432 (1985) (mental retardation not a suspect classification for equal protection analysis purposes), the Court nonetheless determined that a zoning permit requirement banning group homes for persons with mental retardation violated the Equal Protection Clause because it rested on "an irrational prejudice against the mentally retarded," *id.* at 450.

171. Christopher Slobogin, *What* Atkins *Could Mean for Persons with Mental Illness*, 33 N.M. L. Rev. 298, 313 (2003) (Slobogin, *What* Atkins *Could Mean*). The discussion of "juvenile murderers" referred to the Court's then-recent decision in Thompson v. Oklahoma, 487 U.S. 815 (1988), which "intimates that the Court will eventually prohibit execution of children in their mid-teens and below." *Id.* at 294. The Court subsequently did rule that the execution of juveniles violated the Eighth Amendment. See Roper v. Simmons, 543 U.S. 551 (2005). See also, Christopher Slobogin, *Is* Atkins *the Antithesis or Apotheosis of Anti-Discrimination Principles?: Sorting Out the Groupwide Effects of Exempting People with Mental Retardation from the Death Penalty*, 55 Ala. L. Rev. 1101 (2004) (making similar arguments).

172. Slobogin, *What* Atkins *Could Mean*, *supra* note 171, at 314.

173. See *id.* at 305 n. 91: "Another reason why people with mental illness may be sentenced to death is because they do not 'look' ill to jurors." See generally, Perlin, *supra* note 103; Michael L. Perlin, *The Sanist Lives of Jurors in Death Penalty Cases: The Puzzling Role of "Mitigating" Mental Disability Evidence*, 8 Notre Dame J. L. Ethics & Pub. Pol'y 239 (1994). On the need, in this context, for a robust public information campaign to "inform the public, legislature, and players in the criminal justice system . . . to encourage incorporation of the realities of schizophrenia, and other mental illness, into the decision-making processes of legislative bodies," see Bethany Bryant, *Expanding* Atkins *and* Roper: *A Diagnostic Approach to Excluding the Death Penalty as Punishment for Schizophrenic Offenders*, 78 Miss. L. J. 905, 936 (2009).

174. Richard Bonnie, *Panetti v. Quarterman: Mental Illness, the Death Penalty, and Human Dignity*, 5 Ohio St. J. Crim. L. 257, 262 (2007).

175. *Recommendations of the American Bar Association Section of Individual Rights and Responsibilities Task Force on Mental Disability and the Death Penalty*, 54 Cath. U. L. Rev. 1115, § 2 (2005).

176. See *Atkins*, 536 U.S. at 318–20.

177. Christopher Slobogin, *Mental Disorder as an Exemption from the Death Penalty: The ABA-IRR Task Force Recommendations*, 54 Cath. U. L. Rev. 1133, 1150 (2005), citing Michael L. Perlin, *On "Sanism,"* 46 SMU L. Rev. 373, 374 (1992).

178. Saby Ghoshray, *Tracing the Moral Contours of the Evolving Standards of Decency: The Supreme Court's Capital Jurisprudence Post-Roper*, 45 J. Cath. Legal Studies 561, 619 (2007) ("I would argue the Supreme Court must now step forward to lay another layer of prohibitions against death penalty sentences for the mentally ill, including those diagnosed with mental illness anytime during the process between the commission of a crime and execution").

179. Ronald J. Tabak, *Executing People with Mental Disabilities: How We Can Mitigate an Aggravating Situation*, 25 St. Louis U. Pub. L. Rev. 283, 306 (2006) ("We need to address the

practice of executing people for crimes that likely would not have occurred but for their serious mental disabilities").

180. Helen Shin, *Is the Death of the Death Penalty Near? The Impact of* Atkins *and* Roper *on the Future of Capital Punishment for Mentally Ill Defendants*, 76 FORDHAM L. REV. 465, 515–16 (2007) ("nearly all of the same arguments that were offered and accepted by the Supreme Court regarding the diminished culpability of juveniles and mentally retarded persons, and the deterrent and retributive effects of imposing the death penalty on such defendants in *Roper* and *Atkins*, can also be made convincingly about the severely mentally ill").

181. Pamela A. Wilkins, *Rethinking Categorical Prohibitions on Capital Punishment: How the Current Test Fails Mentally Ill Offenders and What to Do about It*, 40 U. MEM. L. REV. 423, 430 (2009). See also, Entzeroth, *supra* note 142, at 531 n. 6, citing John Parry, *The Death Penalty and Persons with Mental Disabilities: A Lethal Dose of Stigma, Sanism, Fear of Violence, and Faulty Predictions of Dangerousness*, 29 MENTAL & PHYSICAL DISABILITY L. REP. 667 (2005), in support of the position that there should be a categorical exemption for persons with serious mental illness.

On how the Court's decisions in this area have "heightened the risk of unjust executions," see KENNETH WILLIAMS, MOST DESERVING OF DEATH? AN ANALYSIS OF THE SUPREME COURT'S DEATH PENALTY JURISPRUDENCE 110 (2012).

182. See e.g., Bonnie, *supra* note 174, at 282 (characterizing Panetti's trial as reflecting an "appalling failure" of the criminal justice system), and see *id.* at 261 ("To anyone who has any understanding of the debilitating effects of severe mental illness and any respect for the dignity of the judicial process, this must have been a painful and distressing spectacle.").

On the related question of whether a person found guilty but mentally ill (GBMI)—see 4 PERLIN, *supra* note 1, § 9A-3.7, at 169–79—should be subject to capital punishment, see Anne S. Emanuel, *Guilty but Mentally Ill Verdicts and the Death Penalty: An Eighth Amendment Analysis*, 68 N.C. L. REV. 37, 38 (1989) ("a guilty but mentally ill verdict establishes that the defendant, because of mental illness, bears diminished responsibility for his crime, and that such a verdict renders society's most severe sanction, the death penalty, disproportionate as a matter of law"). Prior to Connecticut's recent abolition of the death penalty—see http://articles.cnn.com/2012-04-25/justice/justice_connecticut-death-penalty-law-repealed_1_capital-punishment-death-penalty-information-center-death-sentences?_s=PM:JUSTICE (April 25, 2012)—that state had banned the execution of persons with serious mental illness via statutory language that sounded significantly similar to GBMI laws. See CONN. GEN. STAT. ANN. § 53a-46a(h)(3):

> The court shall not impose the sentence of death on the defendant if the jury or, if there is no jury, the court finds by a special verdict, as provided in subsection (e), that at the time of the offense . . . (3) the defendant's mental capacity was significantly impaired or the defendant's ability to conform the defendant's conduct to the requirements of law was significantly impaired but not so impaired in either case as to constitute a defense to prosecution.

183. *Id.* at 277, citing Trop v. Dulles, 356 U.S. 86, 100 (1958). The issue, according to Professor Christopher Seeds, remains "open," "unsettled," "recurring," and "important." Seeds, *supra* note 147, at 371, quoting Rector v. Bryant, 501 U.S. 1239, 1243 (1991) (Marshall, J., dissenting from denial of *certiorari*).

184. See generally, William W. Berry, *Promulgating Proportionality*, 46 GA. L. REV. 69 (2011).

185. Winick, *supra* note 145, at 855. See also, Robert Batey, *Categorical Bars to Execution: Civilizing the Death Penalty*, 45 HOUS. L. REV. 1493, 1527 (2009) ("The Supreme Court should also complement the *Ford-Panetti* ban on executing the seriously mentally ill by holding that severe mental illness at the time of the crime also bars capital punishment"); Corena Larimer, *Equal Protection from Execution: Expanding* Atkins *to Include Mentally Impaired Offenders*, 60 CASE W. RES. L. REV. 925, 949 (2010) (similarly urging expansion of *Atkins*' holding; *Panetti* not cited); Laurie T. Izutsu, *Applying* Atkins v. Virginia *to Capital Defendants with Severe Mental Illness*, 70 BROOK. L. REV. 995 (2005) (same).

186. Winick, *supra* note 145, at 856. For examples of state courts finding death sentences disproportionate in cases involving defendants with serious mental illness, see Entzeroth, *supra* note 142, at 572–73. Of course, these cases are the exception, not the rule. See *id.* at 573 (discussing cases affirming death penalty).

187. Pamela A. Wilkins, *Competency for Execution: The Implications of a Communicative Model of Retribution*, 76 Tenn. L. Rev. 713, 770 (2009). See also, Wilkins, *supra* note 145, at 483, arguing for an Eighth Amendment ban on the execution of such individuals ("Mentally ill offenders—indeed, all offenders—deserve at least that much"). Compare Dan Markel, *Executing Retributivism: Panetti and the Future of the Eighth Amendment*, 103 Nw. U. L. Rev. 1163, 1222 (2009) ("In what can only be described as a bittersweet irony, Scott Panetti's sad delusions have served as a catalyst, bringing us to a juncture where the hope of a better and more justly applied Eighth Amendment is ahead of us and not far beyond our current grasp").

188. Entzeroth, *supra* note 142, at 581: "My reluctant conclusion is that the Court is going to engage in an isolated, narrow approach to constitutional construction on this issue, and while *Atkins* and *Roper* may be useful, they will not be determinative." See also, John H. Blume & Sheri Lynn Johnson, *Killing the Non-Willing:* Atkins, *the Volitionally Incapacitated and the Death Penalty*, 55 S.C. L. Rev. 93, 143 (2003) (arguing that *Atkins* should apply to cases involving defendants who are mentally ill, but concluding that an "inviolate" standard is likely to be "unrealized," thus urging application of *Atkins* to defendants with "major mental illnesses."

189. Wilkins, *supra* note 145, at 483.

190. On the possible application of Ring v. Arizona 536 U.S. 584, 601, 609 (2002) (aggravating factors must be treated as akin to essential elements of a crime because, absent aggravating factors, the defendant cannot be sentenced to death) to *Panetti*, see Danielle N. Devens, *Competency for Execution in the Wake of Panetti: Shifting the Burden to the Government*, 82 Temp. L. Rev. 1335 (2010) (arguing that *Ring* demands that sanity should be considered an essential element of an offense, and thus must be proven beyond a reasonable doubt in a competence-for-execution proceeding).

191. See *supra* chapter 2.

192. John D. Castiglione, *Qualitative and Quantitative Proportionality: A Specific Critique of Retributivism*, 71 Ohio St. L. J. 71, 111 (2010).

193. Rex D. Glensy, *The Right to Dignity*, 43 Colum. Hum. Rts. L. Rev. 65, 123–24 (2011), citing Ford v. Wainright, 477 U.S. 399, 407 (1986); Bonnie, *supra* note 174, and John F. Stinneford, *Incapacitation through Maiming: Chemical Castration, the Eighth Amendment, and the Denial of Human Dignity*, 3 U. St. Thomas L. J. 559, 566 (2006).

194. On the related question of TJ implications of maintaining separate death rows on prisoners, on staff, and on questions of resource allocation, see Andrea Lyon & Mark Cunningham, *"Reason Not the Need": Does the Lack of Compelling State Interest in Maintaining a Separate Death Row Make It Unlawful?* 33 Am. J. Crim. L. 1, 25–27 (2005) (arguing that segregated, highly restrictive death rows constitute cruel and unusual punishment) (TJ not mentioned specifically in article). On the implications of such institutional settings for dignity inquiries, see *supra* chapter 2, note 61, discussing Meghan J. Ryan, *Remedying Wrongful Execution*, 45 U. Mich. J. L. Reform 261, 284–87 (2012); Robert Johnson, Death Work: A Study of the Modern Execution Process 218–19 (2d ed. 2006). On how these conditions exacerbate mental conditions, see Kate McMahon, *Dead Man Waiting: Death Row Delays, the Eighth Amendment, and What Courts and Legislatures Can Do*, 25 Buff. Pub. Int. L. J. 43, 51–52 (2006–2007), discussing Knight v. Florida, 528 U.S. 990, 994 (1999) (Breyer, J., dissenting from denial of writ of *certiorari*).

195. *Panetti*, 551 U.S. 958.

196. See e.g., Therapeutic Jurisprudence: The Law as a Therapeutic Agent 121, 122 (David Wexler, ed. 1990); Essays in Therapeutic Jurisprudence (David B. Wexler & Bruce J. Winick, eds. 1991); Law in a Therapeutic Key: Recent Developments in Therapeutic Jurisprudence (David B. Wexler & Bruce J. Winick, eds. 1996); Therapeu-

tic Jurisprudence Applied: Essays on Mental Health Law (Bruce J. Winick, ed. 1997); David B. Wexler, *Putting Mental Health Into Mental Health Law: Therapeutic Jurisprudence*, 16 L. & Hum. Behav. 27 (1992).

197. See e.g., David B. Wexler & Bruce J. Winick, *Therapeutic Jurisprudence as a New Approach to Mental Health Law Policy Analysis and Research*, 45 U. Miami L. Rev. 979, 992–97 (1991); Bruce J. Winick, *Competency to Be Executed: A Therapeutic Jurisprudence Perspective*, 10 Behav. Sci. & L. 317, 328–37 (1992); Bruce Arrigo & Jeffrey J. Tasca, *Right to Refuse Treatment, Competency to Be Executed, and Therapeutic Jurisprudence: Toward a Systematic Analysis*, 23 law & Psychol. Rev. 1, 43–46 (1999); Robert L. Sadoff, *Therapeutic Jurisprudence: A View from a Forensic Psychiatrist*, 10 N.Y. L. Sch. J. Hum. Rts. 825, 827 (1993). See also, Michael L. Perlin, *"The Executioner's Face Is Always Well-Hidden": The Role of Counsel and the Courts in Determining Who Dies*, 41 N.Y. L. Sch. L. Rev. 201, 234 (1996); Michael L. Perlin, *A Law of Healing*, 68 U. Cin. L. Rev. 407, 432 (2000).

198. Winick, *supra* note 145, at 856–57.

199. See *infra* chapter 11.

200. Liliana Lyra Jubilut, *Death Penalty and Mental Illness: The Challenge of Reconciling Human Rights, Criminal Law, and Psychiatric Standards*, 6 Seattle J. Soc. Just. 353, 378–79 (2007).

201. See Indiana v. Edwards, 554 U.S. 164 (2008) (Constitution permits states to insist upon representation by counsel for those who are competent enough to stand trial but who are sufficiently ill to be incompetent to conduct trial proceedings by themselves).

202. See e.g., Grant Morris et al., *Competency to Stand Trial on Trial*, 4 Hous. J. Health L. & Pol'y 193 (2004).

203. Michael L. Perlin, *"Everything's a Little Upside Down, as a Matter of Fact the Wheels Have Stopped": The Fraudulence of the Incompetency Evaluation Process*, 4 Houston J. Health L. & Pol'y 239, 252 (2004).

CHAPTER 7

1. This section is generally adapted from 4 Michael L. Perlin, Mental Disability Law: Civil and Criminal, § 12-4.3, at 550–53 (2d ed. 2002).

2. Compare e.g., Alfred Freedman & Abraham Halpern, *The Erosion of Ethics and Morality in Medicine: Physician Participation in Legal Executions in the United States*, 41 N.Y. L. Sch. L. Rev. 169 (1996), to Robert T.M. Phillips, *The Psychiatrist as Evaluator: Conflicts and Conscience*, 41 N.Y. L. Sch. L. Rev. 189 (1996), and compare e.g., Melissa McDonnell & Robert Phillips, *Physicians Should Treat Mentally Ill Death Row Inmates, Even if Treatment Is Refused*, 38 J. L. Med. & Ethics 774 (2010), to Howard Zonana, *Physicians Must Honor Refusal of Treatment to Restore Competency by Non-Dangerous Inmates on Death Row*, 38 J. L. Med. & Ethics 764 (2010). Noted Dr. Phillips in 1996, "In the past decade, nothing has sparked more intense debate among psychiatrists than their role in capital sentencing proceedings." Phillips, *supra* at 189, and see *id.* n. 1 (listing references).

3. Freedman & Halpern, *supra* note 2, at 187. For a discussion of the positions of professional and medical organizations on this issue, see Kursten B. Hensl, *Restored to Health to Be Put to Death: Reconciling the Legal and Ethical Dilemmas of Medicating to Execute in Singleton v. Norris*, 49 Vill. L. Rev. 291, 327–28 (2004); Kacie McCoy Daugherty, *Synthetic Sanity: The Ethics and Legality of Using Psychotropic Medications to Render Death Row Inmates Competent for Execution*, 17 J. Contemp. Health L. & Pol'y 715, 730–32 (2001).

4. Phillips, *supra* note 2, at 193–94. Compare Hensl, *supra* note 3, at 323 (characterizing psychiatric involvement in this process as "treating to kill"). See also e.g., Mental Health America, *Position Statement 54: Death Penalty and People with Mental Illness*, accessible at http://nhma.org/ go/position-statements/54 (accessed May 22, 2012) ("MHA is opposed to the practice of having a

psychiatrist or other mental health professional treat a person in order to restore competency solely to permit the state to execute that person, and MHA opposes the practice of medicating defendants involuntarily in order to make them competent either to stand trial or to be executed").

5. See *infra* text accompanying notes 37–50, discussing Singleton v. Norris, 992 S.W.2d 768 (Ark. 1999), and subsequent litigation in that case.

6. Julie Cantor, *Of Pills and Needles: Involuntarily Medicating the Psychotic Inmate When Execution Looms*, 2 IND. HEALTH L. REV. 117, 169–70 (2005).

7. 477 U.S. 399 (1986). See *supra* chapter 6.

8. 551 U.S. 930 (2007). See *supra* chapter 6.

9. On refusal of medication generally, see 4 PERLIN, *supra* note 1, §§ 12-4.1 to 1e; 2 PERLIN, *supra* note 1, §§ 3B-1 *et seq.* (2d ed. 1999). On prisoners' right to refuse medication, see *id.*, § 3B-8.2; see generally Washington v. Harper, 494 U.S. 210 (1990). See MICHAEL L. PERLIN ET AL., COMPETENCE IN THE LAW: FROM LEGAL THEORY TO CLINICAL APPLICATION 148-66 (2008).

10. See e.g., Michaela P. Sewall, *Pushing Execution over the Constitutional Line: Forcible Medication of Condemned Inmates and the Eighth and Fourteenth Amendments*, 51 B.C. L. REV. 1279, 1281 (2010). On the "little guidance" provided by the *Model Rules*, the *Restatement*, and the common law to attorney representing a defendant in these circumstances, Michael D. Grabo & Michael Sapoznikow, *Current Development Note, The Ethical Dilemma of Involuntary Medication in Death Penalty Cases*, 15 GEO. J. LEGAL ETHICS 795, 808 (2002).

11. 494 U.S. 1015 (1990).

12. 498 U.S. 38 (1990), *reh'g denied*, 498 U.S. 1075 (1991).

13. 494 U.S. 210 (1990).

14. State v. Perry, 502 So. 2d 543, 546 (La. 1986), State v. Perry, 502 So. 2d 543, 546 (La. 1986), *cert. denied*, 484 U.S. 872, *reh'g denied*, 484 U.S. 992 (1987).

15. *Id.* at 547.

16. *Id.* at 545. Following his conviction, Perry was treated on several occasions in the prison's psychiatric unit, where he received an antipsychotic drug (Haldol). Richardson, *Involuntary Medication on Death Row: Is It Cruel and Unusual?*, 1990–1991 ABA PREVIEW 18 (Sept. 28, 1990).

17. *Perry*, 502 So. 2d at 563–64.

18. Perry v. Louisiana, No. 89-5120 (May 24, 1990) Perry v. Louisiana, No. 89-5120 (May 24, 1990), Petitioner's Brief on Merits, J.A. 126–49 (Petitioner's Brief).

19. *Id.*

20. *Id.*

21. *Id.*

22. See *Ford*, 477 U.S. at 522 (Powell, J., concurring), discussed in 4 PERLIN, *supra* note 1, § 12-4.1c, accompanying notes 384–86.

23. Petitioner's Brief, *supra* note 18.

24. *Id.*

25. State v. Perry, 543 So. 2d 487 (La.). State v. Perry, 543 So. 2d 487 (La.), *reh'g denied*, 545 So. 2d 1049 (1989).

26. Perry v. Louisiana, 494 U.S. 1015 (1990).

27. 498 U.S. 38 (1990), *reh'g denied*, 498 U.S. 1075 (1991).

28. 494 U.S. 210; see 2 PERLIN, *supra* note 1, § 3B-8.2 (convicted prisoners' right to refuse treatment). Interestingly, the Supreme Court had decided *Harper* about one week *prior* to its decision to grant *certiorari* in *Perry*.

29. *Supreme Court Sidesteps Issue of Restoring Inmates' Competency to Allow Execution*, PSYCHIATRIC NEWS (Dec. 21, 1990), at 6 (quoting Dr. Paul Appelbaum).

30. See 498 U.S. at 1075.

31. A state can always provide more rights to a criminal defendant under its constitution than are afforded to the defendant under the US constitution, but can never afford fewer. See e.g., ERWIN CHEMERINSKY ET AL., FEDERAL JURISDICTION § 10.5, at 707 (4th ed. 2003) ("State

constitutions can provide more rights than exist under the United States Constitution, but the state court must make it clear that the decision is based on the state constitution").

32. State v. Perry, 610 So. 2d 746 (La. 1992).

33. _Id._ at 747–48.

34. On the right of defendants awaiting trial or at trial to refuse the involuntary administration of antipsychotic medication, see Riggins v. Nevada, 504 U.S. 127 (1992), discussed in 2 Perlin, _supra_ note 1, § 3B-8.3. On the right of incompetent-to-stand-trial defendants to refuse the involuntary administration of antipsychotic medication designed to make them competent to stand trial, see Sell v. United States, 539 U.S. 166 (2003) (holding that defendant has qualified right to refuse to take antipsychotic drugs prescribed solely to render him competent to stand trial; medication over objection is permissible where court finds treatment medically appropriate, substantially unlikely to have side effects that may undermine the fairness of the trial, and, taking account of less intrusive alternatives, necessary significantly to further important governmental trial-related interest); see generally, Michael L. Perlin, _"And My Best Friend, My Doctor / Won't Even Say What It Is I've Got": The Role and Significance of Counsel in Right to Refuse Treatment Cases_, 42 San Diego L. Rev. 735, 736 (2005).

35. The following section draws on Michael L. Perlin & Heather Ellis Cucolo, Mental Disability Law: Civil and Criminal (2010 Cum. Supp.), § 12-4.3, at 164–69, and Michael L. Perlin, _"Insanity Is Smashing Up Against My Soul": Panetti v. Quarterman and Questions That Won't Go Away_ (2008), accessible at http://papers.ssrn.com/sol3/papers.cfm?abstract_id=1130890.

36. Singleton v. State, 437 S.E.2d 53, 60–62 (S.C. 1993).

37. 992 S.W.2d 768 (Ark. 1999).

38. See 528 U.S. 1084 (2000). The _Singleton_ decision from Arkansas is criticized in Kelly Gabos, _The Perils of Singleton v. Norris: Ethics and Beyond_, 32 Am. J. L. & Med. 117 (2006).

39. 319 F.3d 1018 (8th Cir. 2003), _cert. den._, 540 U.S. 832 (2003).

40. 319 F.3d at 1025.

41. _Id._

42. _Id._

43. _Id._

44. _Id._ at 1026.

45. _Id._

46. _Id._ at 1027.

47. 429 U.S. 97, 103 (1976).

48. _Singleton_, 319 F.3d at 1030, citing _Estelle_, 429 U.S. at 103.

49. _Id._, citing Ford. v. Wainwright, 477 U.S. 399, 410 (1986).

50. _Id._ at 1034.

51. _Id._ at 1037.

The US Supreme Court denied _certiorari_, see 540 U.S. 832 (2003), and after more than twenty years on death row, Singleton was executed in January of 2004. _Singleton_ is sharply criticized in Stephanie Zwein, _Executing the Insane: A Look at Death Penalty Schemes in Arkansas, Georgia and Texas_, 12 Suffolk J. Trial & App. Advocacy 93 (2007), Hensl, _supra_ note 3, and in Rebecca A. Miller-Rice, _The "Insane" Contradiction of Singleton v. Norris: Forced Medication in a Death Row Inmate's Medical Interest Which Happens to Facilitate His Execution_, 22 U. Ark. Little Rock L. Rev. 659 (2000). But see Dominic Rupprecht, _Compelling Choice: Forcibly Medicating Death Row Inmates to Determine Whether They Wish to Pursue Collateral Relief_, 114 Penn St. L. Rev. 333 (2009) (supporting _Singleton_'s rationale).

52. For a somewhat muddled decision involving an attempted challenge to ad hoc procedures in Texas for determining competency to be executed, see _Kemp v. Cockrell_, 2003 U.S. Dist. LEXIS 8736 (N.D. Tex. 2003) (due process claims were procedurally barred, petitioner had no right to counsel or _Ake_ expert assistance and issue of competency to be executed was not ripe because no

execution date was pending). For pre-*Panetti* commentary, see e.g., Howard Zonana, *Competency to Be Executed and Forced Medication: Singleton v. Norris*, 31 J. AMER. ACAD. PSYCHIATRY & L. 372 (2003); Gabos, *supra* note 38; Gregory Dolin, *A Healer or an Executioner? The Proper Role of a Psychiatrist in a Criminal Justice System*, 17 J. L. & HEALTH 169 (2002); Cantor, *supra* note 6; Angela Kimber, *Psychotic Journeys of the Green Mile*, 22 T.M. COOLEY L. REV. 27 (2005).

53. 448 F.3d 815 (5th Cir. 2006), *rev'd sub. nom.* Panetti v. Quarterman, 551 U.S. 930 (2007). On why Panetti's trial was "truly a judicial farce, and a mockery of self-representation," see Richard J. Bonnie, Panetti v. Quarterman: *Mental Illness, the Death Penalty, and Human Dignity*, 5 OHIO ST. J. CRIM. L. 257, 261 (2007) (quoting Scott Monroe, Panetti's standby counsel). Panetti was found competent while taking antipsychotic medication, which he stopped taking shortly prior to trial, and did not resume; Panetti represented himself in this unmedicated condition. 551 U.S. at 936–37. See generally, Christopher Seeds, *The Afterlife of Ford and* Panetti*: Execution Competence and the Capacity to Assist Counsel*, 53 ST. LOUIS U. L. J. 309 (2009). On subsequent litigation in the *Panetti* case, see *supra* chapter 6, note 142.

54. *Id.* at 817.

55. Panetti v. Quarterman, 549 U.S. 1106 (2007).

56. Panetti v. Quarterman, 551 U.S. 930 (2007).

57. On why the Supreme Court should not have "evaded" this issue, see Holland Sergent, *Can Death Row Inmates Just Say No?: The Forced Administration of Drugs to Render Inmates Competent for Execution in the United States and Texas*, 35 TEX. TECH. L. REV. 1299, 1323 (2004).

58. See Washington v. Harper, 494 U.S. 210, 236 (1990) (holding that the right to be free of medication must be balanced against the state's duty to treat inmates with mental illness and run a safe prison); Riggins v. Nevada, 504 U.S. 127, 129 (1992) (reversing conviction because trial court enforced administration of antipsychotic drugs during defendant's trial at which he relied on the insanity defense); Sell v. United States, 539 U.S. 166, 179 (2003) (holding that a defendant has qualified right to refuse to take antipsychotic drugs prescribed solely to render him competent to stand trial; medication over objection is permissible where court finds treatment medically appropriate, substantially unlikely to have side effects that may undermine the fairness of the trial, and, taking account of less intrusive alternatives, necessary significantly to further important governmental trial-related interests). But compare e.g., Amir Vonsover, *No Reason for Exemption: Singleton v. Norris and Involuntary Medication of Mentally Ill Capital Murderers for the Purpose of Execution*, 7 U. PA. J. CONST. L. 311 (2004), discussing the potential application of these three cases, and concluding, *id.* at 339, that the involuntary administration of medication to incompetent defendants "comport[s] with the law of *Sell*" and "furthers the retributive and deterrent goals of capital punishment"; Brent W. Stricker, *Seeking an Answer: Questioning the Validity of Forcible Medication to Ensure Mental Competency of Those Condemned to Die*, 32 MCGEORGE L. REV. 317, 339–40 (2000), reading *Harper* to allow involuntary medication in such circumstances.

59. See Lyn Entzeroth, *The Illusion of Sanity: The Constitutional and Moral Danger of Medicating Condemned Prisoners in Order to Execute Them*, 76 TENN. L. REV. 641, 658 (2009).

60. See e.g., MICHAEL L. PERLIN, THE HIDDEN PREJUDICE: MENTAL DISABILITY ON TRIAL 125–56 (2000); Michael L. Perlin & Deborah A. Dorfman, *Is It More Than "Dodging Lions and Wastin' Time"?: Adequacy of Counsel, Questions of Competence, and the Judicial Process in Individual Right to Refuse Treatment Cases*, 2 PSYCHOL. PUB. POL'Y & L. 114, 120 (1996); Perlin, *supra* note 34.

61. Perlin, *supra* note 34, at 738.

62. See *infra* chapter 10.

63. Stricker, *supra* note 58, at 340. See also, Dolin, *supra* note 52, at 214 ("the mere prospect of execution does not make psychiatric help unethical, any more than the fact of incarceration makes such help unethical").

64. Zonana, *supra* note 1, at 773.

65. See *supra* chapter 2.

66. Bruce A. Arrigo & Jeffrey J. Tasca, *Right to Refuse Treatment, Competency to be Executed, and Therapeutic Jurisprudence: Toward a Systematic Analysis*, 23 LAW & PSYCHOL. REV. 1, 43–47 (1999), relying upon, inter alia, BRUCE WINICK, THE RIGHT TO REFUSE MENTAL HEALTH TREATMENT (1997), and Bruce Winick, *The Jurisprudence of Therapeutic Jurisprudence*, 3 PSYCHOL. PUB. POL'Y & L. 184, 185–90 (1997).

67. Bruce Winick, *Competency to Be Executed: A Therapeutic Jurisprudence Perspective*, 10 BEHAV. SCI. & L. 317, 332 (1992).

68. *Id.* at 334.

CHAPTER 8

1. See *supra* chapter 6.

2. The question of future dangerousness is discussed extensively elsewhere. See *supra* chapter 3.

3. See *supra* chapter 2.

4. See *infra* chapter 9.

5. See *supra* chapter 2.

6. 470 U.S. 68, 74 (1985).

7. 551 U.S. 930 (2007).

8. 477 U.S. 399 (1986).

9. This section is generally adapted from Michael L. Perlin, *"His Brain Has Been Mismanaged with Great Skill": How Will Jurors Respond to Neuroimaging Testimony in Insanity Defense Cases?*, 42 AKRON L. REV. 885 (2009).

10. O. Carter Snead, *Neuroimaging and the 'Complexity' of Capital Punishment*, 82 N.Y.U. L. REV. 1265, 1316 (2007).

11. Jonathan H Marks, *Interrogational Neuroimaging in Counterterrorism: A "No-Brainer" or Human Rights Hazard*, 33 AM. J. L. & MED. 483, 492 (2007), quoting WILLIAM UTTAL, THE NEW PHRENOLOGY: THE LIMITS OF LOCALIZING COGNITIVE PROCESSES IN THE BRAIN (2003). On the international implications of this issue, see Dominique Church, *Neuroscience in the Courtroom: An International Concern*, 53 WM. & MARY L. REV. 1825 (2012).

12. David Eagleman, *Neuroscience and the Law*, 45 HOUS. LAWYER 36, 38 (April 2008).

13. Bruce Arrigo, *Punishment, Freedom, and the Culture of Control: The Case of Brain Imaging and the Law*, 33 AM. J. L. & MED. 457, 480 (2007).

14. E.g., Richard Redding, *The Brain-Disordered Defendant: Neuroscience and Legal Insanity in the 21st Century*, 56 AM. U. L. REV. 51, 75–77 (2006).

15. Avram Barth, *A Double-Edged Sword: The Role of Neuroimaging in Federal Capital Sentencing*, 33 AM. J. L. & MED. 501, 521–22 (2007).

16. Judy Illes & Eric Racine, *Imaging or Imagining? A Neuroethics Challenge Informed by Genetics*, AM. J. BIOETHICS, Mar./Apr. 2005, at 5, 7.

17. Donald R. Reeves et al., *Limitations of Brain Imaging in Forensic Psychiatry*, 31 J. AM. ACAD. PSYCHIATRY & L. 89, 89 (2003) (emphasis added).

18. Joseph H. Baskin et al., *Is a Picture Worth a Thousand Words? Neuroimaging in the Courtroom*, 33 AM. J. L. & MED. 239, 247 (2007) (emphasis added).

19. Redding, *supra* note 14, at 101 (emphasis added).

20. Joachim Witzel et al., *Neurophilosophical Perspectives of Neuroimaging in Forensic Psychiatry— Giving Way to a Paradigm Shift?* 26 BEHAV. SCI. & L. 113, 115 (2008).

21. Jurgen Muller et al., *Disturbed Prefrontal and Temporal Brain Function During Emotion and Cognition Interaction in Criminal Psychopathy*, 26 BEHAV. SCI. & L. 131, 131 (2008).

22. Dov Fox, *Brain Imaging and the Bill of Rights: Memory Detection Technologies and American Criminal Justice*, 8 Am. J. Bioethics 34, 36 (2008).

23. Alexandra Roberts, *Everything New Is Old Again: Brain Fingerprinting and Evidentiary Analogy*, 9 Yale J. L. & Tech. 234, 266 n. 155 (2006–2007).

24. Reeves, *supra* note 17, at 90.

25. Timo Vloet et al., *Structural and Functional MRI Findings in Children and Adolescents with Antisocial Behavior*, 26 Behav. Sci. & L. 99, 99 (2008).

26. Amanda Pustilnik, *Violence on the Brain: A Critique of Neuroscience in Criminal Law*, available at http://ssrn.com/abstract=111250, manuscript at 5.

27. Laurence Tancredi & Jonathan Brodie, *The Brain and Behavior: Limitations in the Legal Use of Functional Magnetic Resonance Imaging*, 33 Am. J. L. & Med. 271, 289 (2007).

28. *Id.*

29. Compare Diane Hoffmann & Karen Rothenberg, *Judging Genes: Implications of the Second Generation of Genetic Tests in the Courtroom*, 66 Md. L. Rev. 858 (2007) (DNA tests), to Aimee Logan, *Who Says So? Defining Cruel and Unusual Punishment by Science, Sentiment, and Consensus*, 35 Hastings Const. L. Q. 195 (2008) (IQ tests).

30. Fox, *supra* note 22, at 36.

31. Roberts, *supra* note 23, at 248–49.

32. Jay Aronson, *Brain Imaging, Culpability, and the Juvenile Death Penalty*, 13 Psychol. Pub. Pol'y & L. 115, 128 (2007).

33. See e.g., Sabrina Weber et al., *Structural Brain Abnormalities in Psychopaths—A Review*, 26 Behav. Sci. & L. 7 (2008); Laura Guy & John Edens, *Gender Differences in Attitudes toward Psychopathic Sexual Offenders*, 24 Behav. Sci. & L. 65 (2006); Muller et al., *supra* note 21.

34. See e.g., Marks, *supra* note 11; Sean Thompson, *The Legality of the Use of Psychiatric Neuroimaging in Intelligence Interrogation*, 90 Cornell L. Rev. 1601 (2005).

35. Jennifer Kulynych, *Psychiatric Neuroimaging Evidence: A High-Tech Crystal Ball*, 49 Stan. L. Rev. 1249, 1256 (1997).

36. Jane Moriarty, *Flickering Admissibility: Neuroimaging in the U.S. Courts*, 26 Behav. Sci. & L. 29, 45 n. 133(2008), quoting Marks, *supra* note 11, at 486.

37. Laura Khoshbin & Shahram Khoshbin, *Imaging the Mind, Minding the Image: An Historical Introduction to Brain Imaging and the Law*, 33 Am. J. L. & Med. 171, 182 (2007).

38. *Id.* at 183, 185. See also, Tancredi & Brodie, *supra* note 27, at 289; Khoshbin & Khoshbin, *supra* note 37, at 183; Jennifer Kulynych, *Brain, Mind, and Criminal Behavior: Neuroimaging as Scientific Evidence*, 36 Jurimetrics J. 235, 244 (1996) (all using "seduction" or "seductive" as the descriptor), and *An Overview of the Impact of Neuroscience Evidence in Criminal Law* (2004) (President's Council on Bioethics Staff Working Paper), available at http://www.bioethics.gov/background/neuroscience_evidence.html, at 10 (discussing how jurors can be "dazzled" by MRI displays).

39. Neil Feigenson, *Brain Imaging and Courtroom Evidence: On the Admissibility and Persuasiveness of fMRI*, 2 Int'l J. L. in Context 233, 243 (2006).

40. Moriarty, *supra* note 36, at 48.

41. Michael L. Perlin, *"The Borderline Which Separated You From Me": The Insanity Defense, the Authoritarian Spirit, the Fear of Faking, and the Culture of Punishment*, 82 Iowa L. Rev. 1375, 1417 (1997).

42. Michael L. Perlin, *Competency, Deinstitutionalization, and Homelessness: A Story of Marginalization*, 28 Hous. L. Rev. 63, 89 n. 154 (1991).

43. Feigenson, *supra* note 39, at 248.

44. Perlin, *Borderline, supra* note 41, at 1417.

45. Arrigo, *supra* note 13, at 474. See also, Marks, *supra* note 11, at 492, discussing Tom Buller's critique of "reductionist neuroscience" (citing to Tom Buller, *Brains, Lies and Psychological Explanations*, in Neuroethics: Defining the Issues in Theory, Practice and

POLICY 51 (Judy Illes, ed. 2005)), and Pustilnik, *supra* note 26, manuscript at 7 (discussing "neuroreductionism"), and at 9 (discussing "ontological reductionism").

46. Feigenson, *supra* note 39, at 248, quoting RICHARD NISBETT & LEE ROSS, HUMAN INFERENCE: STRATEGIES AND SHORTCOMINGS OF SOCIAL JUDGMENT (1980).

47. Khoshbin & Khoshbin, *supra* note 37, at 171.

48. See Marks, *supra* note 11; Thompson, *supra* note 34.

49. David L. Faigman et al., *Check Your Crystal Ball at the Courthouse Door, Please: Exploring the Past, Understanding the Present, and Worrying about the Future of Scientific Evidence*, 15 CARDOZO L. REV. 1799, 1834–35 (1994).

50. As of May 28, 2012, a simple Westlaw JLR search for "CSI effect" showed 237 documents in which that phrase was used.

51. According to Wendy Brickell, there are actually *two* effects: One view is that the CSI (crime scene investigation) effect increases the burden on the prosecution by creating a greater expectation that scientific evidence will be presented at trial. The other view is that the CSI effect increases the defense's burden—forcing defense attorneys to overcome jurors' perception that scientific evidence is infallible. Wendy Brickell, *Is It the CSI Effect or Do We Just Distrust Juries?*, 23 CRIM. JUST. 10, 11 (Summer 2008).

52. According to Judge Donald Shelton, "I once heard a juror complain that the prosecution had not done a thorough job because 'they didn't even dust the lawn for fingerprints.'" Donald E. Shelton, *The "CSI Effect": Does It Really Exist?*, available at http://sssrn.com/abstract=1163231, document at 2. Monica Robbers points out that jurors "appear to have no tools to assess the credibility of forensic testing on television shows or in trials." Monica Robbers, *Blinded by Science: The Social Construction of Reality in Forensic Television Shows and Its Effect on Criminal Jury Trials*, 19 CRIM. JUST. POL'Y REV. 84 (2008). See also e.g., Simon A. Cole & Rachel Dioso-Villa, *Investigating the "CSI Effect" Effect: Media and Litigation Crisis in Criminal Law*, 61 STAN. L. REV. 1335 (2009); N.J. Schweitzer & Michael J. Saks, *The CSI Effect: Popular Fiction about Forensic Science Affects the Public's Expectations about Real Forensic Science*, 47 JURIMETRICS 357 (2007); Edward J. Ungvarsky, *The CSI Effect: The True Effect of Crime Scene Television on the Justice System: Remarks on the Use and Misuse of Forensic Science to Lead to False Convictions*, 41 NEW ENG. L. REV. 609 (2007).

53. Donald Shelton et al., *A Study of Juror Expectations and Demands Concerning Scientific Evidence: Does the "CSI Effect" Exist?*, 9 VAND. J. ENT. & TECH. L. 331 (2006).

54. *Id.* at 358. And see *id.* at 362 ("[S]urvey results did not show that the demand for scientific evidence as proof of guilt was related to watching crime related television programs").

55. Khoshbin & Khoshbin, *supra* note 37, at 182.

56. See generally, Perlin, *supra* note 9, at 915.

57. 470 U.S. 68, 74 (1985).

58. *Ake* is also discussed in the context of the competency of defendants with mental retardation to be executed *supra* chapter 5.

59. Publicly financed counsel represented about 66 percent of federal felony defendants in 1998 and 82 percent of felony defendants in the seventy-five most populous counties in 1996. http://www.ojp.usdoj.gov/bjs/id.htm#publications; http://www.ojp.usdoj.gov/bjs/pub/press/iddcpr.htm.

60. For sample fee scales, see e.g., http://www.nhhealthcost.org/uninsuredWizardUser-Input.aspx?procedure=16&procedureName=MRI+-+Brain+(outpatient). See generally, Steve Silberman, *Don't Even Think about Lying: How Brain Scans Are Reinventing the Science of Lie Detection*, WIRED, Jan. 2006, at 147 (available at http://www.wired.com/wired/archive/14.01/lying.html?pg=4&topic=lying&topic_set).

61. 470 U.S. 68, 74 (1985). See generally, 4 MICHAEL L. PERLIN, MENTAL DISABILITY LAW: CIVIL AND CRIMINAL, § 9A-5.1, at 217–27 (2d ed. 2002).

62. *Ake*, 470 U.S. at 75.

63. *Id.*

64. *Id.* at 77.

65. *Id.*

66. *Id.* While such a defendant does not have a right to all the assistance that a wealthier defendant might be able to purchase, he is nonetheless entitled to "an adequate opportunity to present [his] claims fairly within the adversary system." Ross v. Moffitt, 417 U.S. 600, 612 (1974).

67. Britt v. North Carolina, 404 U.S. 226, 227 (1971).

68. *Ake*, 470 U.S. at 77. The Court cited Little v. Streater, 452 U.S. 1 (1982) (indigent's right to blood grouping tests in paternity action); and Mathews v. Eldridge, 424 U.S. 319 (1976), on this point.

69. *Ake*, 470 U.S. at 78.

70. *Id.*

71. *Id.* at 79–80 & nn. 4–6. See e.g., 18 U.S.C. § 3006A(e) (1985).

72. *Ake*, 470 U.S. at 79.

73. *Id.*

74. *Id.* at 80.

75. *Ake*, 470 U.S. at 80–81.

76. *Id.* at 81.

77. *Id.*, quoting, in part, Martin R. Gardner, *The Myth of the Impartial Psychiatric Expert— Some Comments Concerning Criminal Responsibilities and the Decline of the Age of Therapy*, 2 LAW & PSYCHOLOGY REV. 99, 113–14 (1976).

78. *Ake*, 470 U.S. at 82. On the ethical issues involved in the relationship between the lawyer and the mental health expert, see W. Lawrence Fitch et al., *Legal Ethics and the Use of Mental Health Experts in Criminal Cases*, 5 BEHAV. SCI. & L. 105, 109–16 (1987).

79. *Ake*, 470 U.S. at 82.

80. *Id.* at 82–83.

It is in such cases that a defense may be devastated by the absence of a psychiatric examination and testimony; with such assistance, the defendant might have a reasonable chance of success. In such a circumstance, where the potential accuracy of the jury's determination is so dramatically enhanced, and where the interests of the individual and the State in an accurate proceeding are substantial, the State's interest in its fisc must yield.

Id. at 83 (footnote omitted).

On the question of what is a "significant factor," see e.g., Volanty v. Lynaugh, 874 F.2d 243 (5th Cir.), *cert. denied*, 493 U.S. 955 (1989) (defendant's bare assertion that he was heroin addict insufficient basis for *Ake* appointment); Mendoza v. Leapley, 5 F.3d 341 (8th Cir. 1993) (habeas corpus relief denied; failure to appoint expert psychologist did not deprive petitioner of fair trial); Perkins v. State,450 S.E.2d 324 (Ga. App. 1994) (refusal to appoint psychiatrist at trial not error where psychiatrist who had done pretrial evaluation of defendant concluded that he was sane).

For a recent collection of cases, see Theodore Greeley, *The Plight of Indigent Defendants in a Computer-Based Age: Maintaining the Adversarial System by Granting Indigent Defendants Access to Computer Experts*, 16 VA. J. L. & TECH. 400, 417–18 nn. 146–47 (2011).

81. *Ake*, 470 U.S. at 83. The Court emphasized that this did not give the defendant the right to "choose a psychiatrist of his personal liking," *id.*; its concern was simply that an indigent defendant "have access to a competent psychiatrist," *id. Cf.* In re Gannon, 301 A.2d 493 (N.J. Cty. Ct. 1973) (indigent in civil commitment case has no right "to shop around for a psychiatrist who agrees with him"). See generally 1 PERLIN, *supra* note 61, § 2B-13, at 275–76.

82. *Ake*, 470 U.S. at 83–84.

83. *Id.* at 84.

84. STEPHEN A. SALTZBURG & DANIEL J. CAPRA, AMERICAN CRIMINAL PROCEDURE 802 (8th ed. 2007). See also David A. Harris, Ake *Revisited: Expert Psychiatric Witnesses Remain*

Beyond Reach for the Indigent, 68 N.C. L. Rev. 763, 783 (1990) ("Lower courts often have interpreted *Ake* less than generously, unduly constricting the availability of the right."); see also, Comment, *Nonpsychiatric Expert Assistance and the Requisite Showing of Need: A Catch-22 in the Post-*Ake *Criminal Justice System*, 37 Emory L. J. 995 (1988) (arguing *Ake* should be read to encompass nonpsychiatric expert assistance).

See e.g., United States v. Brown, 441 F.3d 1330, 1365 (11th Cir. 2006) (no *Ake* error where defendant cannot show that denial of expert had "substantial and injurious effect or influence in determining the jury's verdict," quoting Conklin v. Schofield, 366 F.3d 1191, 1209 (11th Cir. 2004); Alverson v. Workman, 595 F.3d 1142, 1155 (10th Cir. 2010) (state's allegation of future dangerousness was not based on state-sponsored psychiatric evidence, but rather on defendant's history of "violent criminal conduct"; Hood v. Cockrell, 72 Fed. Appdx. 171 (5th Cir. 2003) (*Ake* denial harmless error); White v. Johnson, 153 F.3d 197 (5th Cir. 1998) (same).

85. Compare Jones v. State, 189 Ga. App. 232, 375 S.E.2d 648 (1988) (rejecting defendant's request for additional psychological evaluation; limiting *Ake* to *psychiatrists*), and Hough v. State, 524 N.E.2d 1287 (Ind. 1987) (no right under *Ake* to appointment of social psychologist to help in jury selection), to Funk v. Commonwealth, 8 Va. App. 91, 379 S.E.2d 371 (1989) (rejecting defendant's argument that psychiatric assistance is *mandated* under *Ake*; no error to appoint clinical *psychologist*), and King v. State, 317 Ark. 293, 877 S.W.2d 583 (1994) (appointment of psychologist sufficient under state statute).

86. Wallace v. State, 553 N.E.2d 456 (Ind. 1990), *cert. denied*, 500 U.S. 948 (1991).

87. Rey v. State, 897 S.W.2d 333 (Tex. Crim. App. 1995).

88. See e.g., Husske v. Commonwealth, 19 Va. App. 30, 448 S.E.2d 331 (1994) (state required to appoint DNA expert under *Ake*), *vacated*, 21 Va. App. 91, 462 S.E.2d 120 (1995) (*Ake* issue not discussed), *aff'd*, 252 Va. 203, 476 S.E.2d 920 (1996), *cert. denied*, 519 U.S. 1154 (1997). For a later consideration of the application of *Ake* to DNA and other nonpsychiatric evidence, see Paul Giannelli, *Ake v. Oklahoma: The Right to Expert Assistance in a Post-Daubert, Post-DNA World*, 89 Cornell L. Rev. 1305, 1418–19 (2004), concluding that "*Ake*'s rationale extends to nonpsychiatric experts."

Beyond the scope of this book is a related, important question: Is neuroimaging evidence— for purposes of assessing validity and reliability of testimony—more like DNA evidence or more like other more traditional forensic evidence (e.g., bite marks, hair comparisons, etc.). See e.g., Dawn McQuiston-Surrett & Michael Saks, *Communicating Opinion Evidence in the Forensic Identification Sciences: Accuracy and Impact*, 59 Hastings L. J. 1159 (2008).

89. Giannelli, *supra* note 88, at 1418.

90. *Jones* is discussed in this context in Kulynych, *supra* note 35, at 1254, and Mark Pettit, *FMRI and BF Meet FRE: Brain Imaging and the Federal Rules of Evidence*, 33 Am. J. L. & Med. 319, 335 (2007).

For post-*Ake* decisions, see Michael L. Perlin & Heather Ellis Cucolo, Mental Disability Law: Civil and Criminal, § 9A-5.1, at 85–86 (2010 Cum. Supp.).

91. 750 So.2d 6, 16–17 (Fla. 1999).

92. 2008 WL 2721155 (Ariz. App. 2008).

93. *Smith* was a challenge based on Atkins v. Virginia, 536 U.S. 304 (2002), arguing that the defendant's mental retardation barred the imposition of the death penalty. Concluded the Court on this issue:

> Thus, while we do not dispute Thompson's testimony that frontal lobe damage can be a cause of mental retardation, Smith has not demonstrated on the facts before us how a current PET scan would be useful in assessing the pivotal question presented in this case-whether his mental functioning was significantly more deficient thirty years ago than today.

Smith, 2008 WL 2721155, at *4.

94. 167 F.3d 1339, 1348–49 (10th Cir.), *cert. denied,* 528 U.S. 987 (1999).

95. See Allen v. Mullin, 368 F.3d 1220, 1236 (10th Cir. 2004) (discussing *Walker*).

96. *Walker,* 167 F.3d at 1348–49.

97. 620 N.Y.S.2d 656, 657 (App. Div. 1994).

98. See Neil Feigenson & Richard Sherwin, *Thinking Beyond the Shown: Implicit Inferences in Evidence and Argument,* 6 Law, Probability & Risk 295, 299–300 (2007), citing Dean Mobbs et al., *Law, Responsibility, and the Brain,* 5 Public Library of Science e103, available at www.plosbiology.org.

99. See Feigenson & Sherwin, *supra* note 98, at 299, quoting Richard Henson, *What Can Functional Neuroimaging Tell the Experimental Psychologist?* A58 Q. J. Experimental Psychology 193 (2005): "There is a real danger that pictures of blobs on brains seduce one into thinking that we can now directly observe psychological constructs." See also, Tancredi & Brodie, *supra* note 27, at 289. Compare Robert Granacher, *Commentary: Applications of Functional Neuroimaging to Civil Litigation of Mild Traumatic Brain Injury,* 36 J. Am. Acad. Psychiatry & L. 323, 323 (2008) ("The overselling of [neuroimaging evidence] by lawyers is a serious potential evidentiary concern in civil litigation").

100. On the dangers of showing "undue deference" to expert witnesses, see e.g., Elaine Sutherland, *Undue Deference to Experts Syndrome?* 16 Ind. Int'l & Comp. L. Rev. 375 (2006). On the dangers of "anecdotal forensics," see e.g., David Faigman, *Anecdotal Forensics, Phrenology, and Other Abject Lessons from the History of Science,* 59 Hastings L. J. 979 (2008).

On the implications of the *Daubert* doctrine on these questions, we know that courts generally "lower the bar" on the resolution of *Daubert* issues in criminal cases. See e.g., Paul Giannelli, *Forensic Science under the Microscope,* 34 Ohio N.U. L. Rev. 315, 317 (2008), and *id.* n. 22 (citing authorities); see generally, Deirdre Dwyer, *(Why) Are Civil and Criminal Expert Evidence Different?,* 43 Tulsa L. Rev. 381, 382–84 (2007). On the question addressed here, see James Merikangas, *Commentary; Functional MRI Lie Detection,* 36 J. Amer. Acad. Psychiatry & L. 499 (2008) (FMRI evidence, for purposes of lie detection, does not meet *Daubert* standards). I discuss *Daubert* in the future dangerousness context *supra* in chapter 3.

101. This section is adapted from Michael L. Perlin, *"Good and Bad, I Defined These Terms, Quite Clear No Doubt Somehow": Neuroimaging and Competency to Be Executed after Panetti,* 28 Behav. Sci. & L. 621 (2010).

102. See *supra* chapter 6.

103. 551 U.S. 930 (2007).

104. 477 U.S. 399 (1986).

105. *Panetti,* 551 U.S. at 956.

106. See Pamela A. Wilkins, *Competency for Execution: The Implications of a Communicative Model of Retribution,* 76 Tenn. L. Rev. 713, 742 (2009): "The good news from *Panetti* is that the Court finally articulated a specific justification for the Eighth Amendment ban: the execution of an incompetent inmate lacks retributive value." See generally, Bruce Winick, *The Supreme Court's Evolving Death Penalty Jurisprudence: Severe Mental Illness as the Next Frontier,* 50 B.C. L. Rev. 785 (2009); Jeffrey Kirchmeier, *The Undiscovered Country: Execution Competency & Comprehending Death,* 98 Ky. L. Rev. 263 (2009–2010).

107. A simple Westlaw ALLCASES search ("panetti v. quarterman" & neuroimaging neuroscience "pet scan" "spect scan" mri fmri) (conducted May 28, 2012) reveals a universe of only twelve cases, none of which raise this specific issue in this context. See Dillbeck v. McNeil, 2010 WL 419401 (N.D. Fla. 2010); Jones v. Ryan, 583 F.3d 626 (9th Cir. 2009); Walls v. McNeil, 2009 WL 3187066 (N.D. Fla. 2009); Sireci v. Secretary, Fla. Dep't of Corrections, 2009 WL 651140 (M.D. Fla. 2009); Kimbrough v. Crosby, 2008 WL 544867 (M.D. Fla. 2008); Woodall v. Simpson, 2008 WL 5666261 (W.D. Ky. 2008); Brumfield v. Cain, 2012 WL 602163 (M.D. La. 2012); Cole v. Workman, 2011 WL 3862143 (N.D. Okla. 2011); Smithers v. Secretary, Dept. of Corrections, 2011 WL 2446576 (M.D. Fla. 2011); Card v. McNeil, 2010 WL

4945419 (N.D. Fla. 2010); Crittenden v. Ayers, 624 F.3d 943 (9th Cir. 2010); Lawrence v. McNeil, 2010 WL 2890576 (N.D. Fla. 2010). Compare Chris Koepke, *Panetti v. Quarterman: Exploring the Unsettled and Unsettling*, 45 Hous. L. Rev. 1383, 1404 (2008) (*Panetti* leaves "a tremendous number of issues for lower courts to resolve").

108. *Panetti*, 551 U.S. at 960.

109. On the specific question of the value of neuroimaging evidence in discovering brain lesions that might affect criminal responsibility, see Shelley Batts, *Brain Lesions and Their Implications in Criminal Responsibility*, 27 Behav. Sci. & L. 261 (2009).

110. See Perlin, *supra* note 9, at 895–98. There have been other locally and regionally high-profile cases involving neuroimaging testimony. See e.g., United States v. Mezvinsky, 206 F. Supp. 2d 661 (E.D. Pa. 2002) (multi-million-dollar fraud case; defendant was former congressman); People v. Goldstein, 786 N.Y.S.2d 428 (A.D. 2004), *rev'd on other gds.*, 843 N.E.2d 727 (N.Y. 2005) (murder case in which victim was Kendra Webdale, after whom New York State's assisted outpatient treatment law was named).

111. Moriarty, *supra* note 36, at 39; see also, Snead, *supra* note 10, at 1298; Amanda Pustilnik, *Violence on the Brain: A Critique of Neuroscience in Criminal Law*, 44 Wake Forest L. Rev. 183, 185 n. 9 (2009) (listing cases where such testimony has been offered by defendants at the mitigation stage of a death penalty case). See e.g., United States v. Williams, 2009 WL 424583, **5–6 (D. Hawai'i 2009) (discussing the debate as to the reliability of fMRI scans, and citing, inter alia, to Laura Khoshbin & Shahram Khoshbin, *Imaging the Mind, Minding the Image: An Historical Introduction to Brain Imaging and the Law*, 33 Am. J. L. & Med. 171 (2007) (discussed *infra* text accompanying notes 111–12).

112. Moriarty, *supra* note 36, at 44.

113. *Id.* at 45; Snead, *supra* note 10, at 1308 n. 215. See e.g., State v. Holmes, 5 So. 3d 42 (La. 2008).

114. John H. Blume & Emily C. Paavola, *Life, Death and Neuroimaging: The Advantages and Disadvantages of the Defense's Use of Neuroimages in Capital Cases-Lessons from the Front*, 62 Mercer L. Rev. 909, 910–11 (2011).

115. See Michael L. Perlin, *"Life Is in Mirrors, Death Disappears": Giving Life to* Atkins, 33 N. Mex. L. Rev. 315, 335 (2003) (Perlin, *Death Disappears*) ("The quality of counsel in providing legal representation to mentally disabled criminal defendants is a disgrace"); see also generally, Michael L. Perlin, *"The Executioner's Face Is Always Well-Hidden": The Role of Counsel and the Courts in Determining Who Dies*, 41 N.Y. L. Sch. L. Rev. 201 (1996). See generally *infra* chapter 10.

116. David L. Bazelon, *The Defective Assistance of Counsel*, 42 U. Cin. L. Rev. 1, 2 (1973).

117. Perlin, *Death Disappears, supra* note 115, at 348.

118. 466 U.S. 668 (1984) (ineffectiveness-of-counsel standard). See *infra* chapter 10.

119. Compare Jones v. Ryan, 583 F.3d 626, 636-377 (9th Cir. 2009), *vacated* 131 S. Ct. 2091 (2011) (defense counsel ineffective at sentencing level for failing to file motion for neuropsychological testing), to Sneed v. Johnson, 2007 WL 709778, *62 (N.D. Ohio 2007) (collecting cases where ineffectiveness not found in trials where counsel failed to seek appointment of neuropsychologist); for one example, see Jones v. Schriro, 450 F. Supp. 2d 1023, 1044 (D. Ariz. 2006) (defendant presented no evidence that results of CAT scan, MRI, or EEG would support a finding of cognitive impairment; no *Strickland* violation found).

120. See Jane Moriarty, *Visions of Deception: Neuroimages and the Search for the Truth*, 42 Akron L. Rev. 739 (2009); see also, Brian Reese, *Using fMRI as a Lie Detector—Are We Lying to Ourselves?* 19 Alb. L. J. Sci. & Tech. 205 (2009).

121. See Deborah Denno, *Behavioral Genetics Evidence in Criminal Cases: 1994–2007*, in The Impact of Behavioral Sciences on Criminal Law 317 (Nita A. Farahany, ed. 2009).

122. *Id.* at 338.

123. For sample fee scales, see *supra* note 60.

124. 470 U.S. 68, 74 (1985) (indigent defendant's right to insanity defense expert).

125. I address this generally in a neuroimaging context in Perlin, *supra* note 9.

126. See *Panetti*, 551 U.S. at 952, 954 (trial court's failure to provide defendant an adequate opportunity to submit expert evidence in response to the report filed by the court-appointed experts, thus depriving him of his "constitutionally adequate opportunity to be heard," and fact-finding procedures on which the trial court relied were "not adequate for reaching reasonably correct results," or, at a minimum, resulted in a process that appeared to be "seriously inadequate for the ascertainment of the truth").

127. 573 F. Supp. 2d 804 (S.D.N.Y. 2008).

128. *Id.* at 817.

129. *Lewis* has only been cited once in a remotely relevant context. There, in United States *v.* Arenburg, 2011 WL 2421113, *1 (W.D.N.Y. 2011), the court relied on *Lewis* in ruling that retrospective competency determinations are permissible whenever a court can conduct a meaningful hearing to evaluate retrospectively the competency of the defendant, citing *Lewis*, 573 F. Supp. 2d at 822, setting out these criteria:

> (1) [t]he passage of time, (2) the availability of contemporaneous medical evidence, including medical records and prior competency determinations, (3) any statements by the defendant in the trial record, and (4) the availability of individuals and trial witnesses, both experts and non-experts, who were in a position to interact with defendant before and during trial, including the trial judge, counsel for both the government and defendant, and jail officials.

130. Holland v. Anderson, 439 F. Supp. 2d 644, 678 (S.D. Miss. 2006). The *Holland* court relied on White v. Johnson, 153 F.3d 197 (5th Cir. 1998), see *supra* note 84, in finding no "proof of substantial need."

131. See Michael L. Perlin, *"And I See Through Your Brain": Access to Experts, Competency to Consent, and the Impact of Antipsychotic Medications in Neuroimaging Cases in the Criminal Trial Process*, 2009 STAN. TECH. L. REV. 4, **33–43 (2009).

132. Reese, *supra* note 120, at 229.

133. Moriarty, *supra* note 36, at 48, citing Scott T. Grafton et al., *Brain Scans Go Legal*, SCIENTIFIC AMERICAN MIND 30, 33 (Dec. 2006/Jan. 2007).

134. Steven K. Erickson, *Blaming the Brain*, 11 MINN. J. L. SCI. & TECH. 27, 36 (2010).

135. Khoshbin & Khoshbin, *supra* note 111, at 182.

136. *Id.* at 183, 185. See also, Tancredi & Brodie, *supra* note 27, at 289; Kulynych, *supra* note 38, at 244 (all using "seduction" or "seductive" as the descriptor), and *An Overview of the Impact of Neuroscience Evidence in Criminal Law* (2004) (President's Council on Bioethics Staff Working Paper), available at http://www.bioethics.gov/background/neuroscience_evidence.html, at 10 (discussing how jurors can be "dazzled" by MRI displays).

137. Neil Feigenson, *Brain Imaging and Courtroom Evidence: On the Admissibility and Persuasiveness of fMRI*, 2 INT'L J. L. IN CONTEXT 233, 243 (2006).

138. Joelle Moreno, *The Future of Neuroimaged Lie Detection and the Law*, 42 AKRON L. REV. 717, 734 (2009) (emphasis added).

139. See Perlin, *supra* note 131, at **12–24.

140. See Michael L. Perlin, *"Baby, Look Inside Your Mirror": The Legal Profession's Willful and Sanist Blindness to Lawyers with Mental Disabilities*, 69 U. PITT. L. REV. 589, 602–3 (2008) (Perlin, *Look Inside Your Mirror*); Michael L. Perlin, *The ADA and Persons with Mental Disabilities: Can Sanist Attitudes Be Undone?*, 8 J. L. & HEALTH 15, 33 (1993); Michael L. Perlin, *Pretexts and Mental Disability Law: The Case of Competency*, 47 U. MIAMI L. REV. 625, 660 (1993).

141. Compare Henry Greely, *Neuroscience and Criminal Justice: Not Responsibility but Treatment*, 56 U. KAN. L. REV. 1103, 1104 n. 7 (2008):

> I recently organized a seminar for federal judges on legal issues in genetics and neuroscience. It was striking how uninterested judges were in violence-inducing brain conditions for issues of responsibility, sanity, and so on, and how very interested they were in those same questions

in terms of sentencing decisions. Ironically, what might be set out as a mitigating factor for a defendant in terms of responsibility is likely to increase the sentence for a convicted criminal.

142. See generally, Moriarty, *supra* note 36. On the application of *Daubert* in future dangerousness inquiries, see *supra* chapter 3.

143. Moriarty, *supra* note 120, at 747. See also, Reese, *supra* note 120, at 217 (expressing concern that jurors would "overvalue" such evidence).

144. People v. Protsman, 88 Cal. App. 4th 509 (2001); People v. Yum, 111 Cal. App. 4th 635 (2003); Clemons v. State, 2003 WL 22047260 (Ala. Crim. App. 2003), *rev'd on other grounds*, 2007 WL 1300722 (Ala. 2007); Clemons v. State, 55 So. 3d 314 (Ala. Crim. App. 2005), *rev'd on other grounds*, 55 So. 3d 348 (Ala. 2007. See generally, The President's Council on Bioethics, *Staff Working Paper: An Overview of Neuroscience Evidence in Criminal Law*, accessible at http://www.bioethics.gov/background/neuroscience_evidence/html.

145. Donnellan v. First Student Inc., 891 N.E.2d 463 (Ill. App. 2008) (personal injury case) (testimony of expert, who was board certified in nuclear medicine, about the extensive use of Single Photon Emission Computer Tomography (SPECT) scans and detailed explanation about the process of analyzing the scans was sufficient to support the introduction of SPECT evidence) (*Frye* jurisdiction); see also, Brown v. Allerton Associates, 831 N.Y.S.2d 351 (Sup. Ct. 2006).

146. E.g., Hose v. Chicago Northwestern Transp. Co., 70 F.3d 968, 973 (8th Cir. 1995). Compare United States v. Semrau, 2010 WL 6845092 (W.D. Tenn. 2010) (fMRI introduced for lie detection purposes excluded under *Daubert*).

147. 735 So.2d 1281 (1999).

148. *Id.* at 1281.

149. *Id.* at n. 1.

150. D. Michael Risinger, *Navigating Expert Reliability: Are Criminal Standards of Certainty Being Left on the Dock?* 64 Alb. L. Rev. 99, 105–8 (2000). In sixty-seven cases of challenged government expertise, the prosecution prevailed in sixty-one of these. Out of fifty-four complaints by criminal defendants that their expertise was improperly excluded, the defendant lost forty-four. Contrarily, in civil cases, 90 percent of *Daubert* appeals were by the defendants, who prevailed two-thirds of the time. For a thoughtful analysis of Professor Risinger's findings, see Deirdre Dwyer, *(Why) Are Civil and Criminal Expert Evidence Different?*, 43 Tulsa L. Rev. 381, 382–84 (2007).

Professor Susan Rozelle is blunter: "The game of scientific evidence looks fixed." Susan Rozelle, *Daubert, Schmaubert: Criminal Defendants and the Short End of the Science Stick*, 43 Tulsa L. Rev. 597, 598 (2007). See also, Erica Beecher-Monas, *Reality Bites: The Illusion of Science in Bite-mark Evidence*, 30 Cardozo L. Rev. 1369, 1371 (2008–2009). On the *Daubert* problems inherent in cases involving vaccine issues, see Joelle Moreno, *It's Just a Shot Away: MMR Vaccines and Autism and the End of the Daubertista Revolution*, 35 Wm. Mitchell L. Rev. 1511 (2009).

151. Perlin, *supra* note 9, at 906–7.

152. Beecher-Monas, *supra* note 150, at 1369.

153. *Id.* at 1371.

154. Moreno, *supra* note 138, at 1538–39, quoting, in part, Stephen Breyer, *Introduction* to Reference Manual on Scientific Evidence 3 (2d ed. 2000).

155. Perlin, *Look Inside Your Mirror*, *supra* note 140, at 599–600. See also John Q. La Fond & Mary L. Durham, Back to the Asylum: The Future of Mental Health Law and Policy in the United States 156 (1992):

Neoconservative insanity defense and civil commitment reforms value psychiatric expertise when it contributes to the social control function of law and disparage it when it does not. In the criminal justice system, psychiatrists are now viewed skeptically as accomplices of defense lawyers who get criminals "off the hook" of responsibility. In the commitment system, however, they are more confidently seen as therapeutic helpers who get patients "on the hook" of treatment and control. The result will be increased institutionalization of the mentally ill and greater use of psychiatrists and other mental health professionals as powerful agents of social control.

156. Michael L. Perlin, *"Half-Wracked Prejudice Leaped Forth": Sanism, Pretextuality, and Why and How Mental Disability Law Developed as It Did*, 10 J. CONTEMP. LEG. ISS. 3, 29 (1999).

157. See *id.* at 14–16, discussing "ordinary common sense" (OCS).

158. See generally *supra* chapter 2; see e.g., Michael L. Perlin, *"And My Best Friend, My Doctor / Won't Even Say What It Is I've Got": The Role and Significance of Counsel in Right to Refuse Treatment Cases*, 42 SAN DIEGO L. REV. 735, 750 (2005). On sanism and death penalty decision making, see Michael L. Perlin, *The Sanist Lives of Jurors in Death Penalty Cases: The Puzzling Role of Mitigating Mental Disability Evidence*, 8 NOTRE DAME J. L., ETHICS & PUB. POL. 239 (1994). On sanism and the reception of and response to neuroimaging evidence, see Perlin, *supra* note 9; Perlin, *supra* note 131.

159. See e.g., Perlin, *supra* note 9, at 900.

160. Michael Pardo, *Neuroscience Evidence, Legal Culture, and Criminal Procedure*, 33 AM. J. CRIM. L. 301, 318 (2006).

161. Joshua Greene & Jonathan Cohen, *For the Law, Neuroscience Changes Nothing and Everything*, 359 PHIL. TRANS. R. SOC. LOND. B. 1775, 1776 (2004) (emphasis added). See also generally, Dean Mobbs et al., *Law, Responsibility, and the Brain*, 5 PLOS BIOL. 0693, 0695 (April 2007) (neuroscience may play an "important role" in "updating the intuitions concerning free will and responsibility that may implicitly underlie juror deliberations").

162. See Michael L. Perlin, *"She Breaks Just Like a Little Girl": Neonaticide, the Insanity Defense, and the Irrelevance of "Ordinary Common Sense,"* 10 WM. & MARY J. WOMEN & L. 1, 17 (2003).

163. Daniel Martell, *Neuroscience and the Law: Philosophical Differences and Practical Constraints*, 27 BEHAV. SCI. & L. 123, 126 (2009), citing D.S. Weisberg et al., *The Seductive Allure of Neuroscience Explanations*, 20 J. COGNITIVE NEUROSCIENCE 470 (2008).

On the question of the extent to which the use of neuroscience testing (through an fMRI) can teach us about how brain activation is affected when jurors engage in decision making, see Jessica Salerno & Bette Bottoms, *Emotional Evidence and Jurors' Judgments: The Promise of Neuroscience for Informing Psychology and the Law*, 27 BEHAV. SCI. & L. 273 (2009) (showing how neuroscience can help illuminate certain punitive attitudes of jurors); see also, Joshua Knabb et al., *Neuroscience, Moral Reasoning, and the Law*, 27 BEHAV. SCI. & L. 219 (2009) (same).

164. Perlin, *supra* note 9, at 915 (footnotes omitted).

165. See *supra* chapter 2.

166. See e.g., Jeremy Blumenthal, *Does Mood Influence Moral Judgment? An Empirical Test with Legal and Policy Implications*, 29 LAW & PSYCHOLOGY 1 (2005); Nicole Vincent, *Neuroimaging and Responsibility Assessments*, NEUROETHICS (DOI 10.1007/s12152-008-9030-8), downloadable at http://ssrn.com/abstract=1519431.

167. Michael L. Perlin & Valerie R. McClain, *Unasked (and Unanswered) Questions about the Role of Neuroimaging in the Criminal Trial Process*, 28 AM. J. FORENSIC PSYCHOLOGY 5 (2010); H.V. Hall & D. McNinch, *Linking Crime-Specific Behavior to Neuropsychological Impairment*, 10 IN'TL J. CLIN. NEUROPSYCHOL. 113 (1988).

168. Perlin & McClain, *supra* note 167; Hall & McNinch, *supra* note 167.

169. On the question of informed consent in a neuroimaging context, see Perlin, *supra* note 131, at **25–36; Greely, *supra* note 141; Jennifer Kulynych, *The Regulation of MR Neuroimaging Research: Disentangling the Gordian Knot*, 33 AM. J. L. & MED. 295 (2007).

170. I consider it in the broader context of criminal procedure in general in Perlin & McClain, *supra* note 167.

171. J.W. Looney, *Neuroscience's New Techniques for Evaluating Future Dangerousness: Are We Returning to Lombroso's Biological Criminality?* 32 U. ARK. LITTLE ROCK L. REV. 301, 307 (2010).

172. *Id.* at 314. Cesare Lombroso, the nineteenth-century Italian criminologist, had proposed a theory of criminality suggesting that criminal behavior was biologically derived and

could be predicted by various physiognomic features. *Id.* at 301, citing Giuseppe Carra & Francesco Barale, *Cesare Lombroso, M.D., 1835–1909*, 161 Am. J. Psychiatry 624, 624 (2004).

173. On the correlation between death qualification and antipathy toward the insanity defense, see e.g., Andrea Lyon, *But He Doesn't Look Retarded: Capital Jury Selection for the Mentally Retarded Client Not Excluded after Atkins v. Virginia*, 57 DePaul L. Rev. 701, 712–13 (2008) ("Death-qualified jurors are also much less likely to accept the insanity defense, believing it to be a "loophole allowing too many guilty people to go free"), citing and quoting Phoebe C. Ellsworth et al., *The Death-Qualified Jury and the Defense of Insanity*, 8 Law & Hum. Behav. 81, 92 (1984), and Robert Fitzgerald & Phoebe C. Ellsworth, *Due Process vs. Crime Control: Death Qualification and Jury Attitudes*, 8 Law & Hum. Behav. 31, 45 (1984). For more recent confirmatory research, see Brooke Butler & Adina Wasserman, *The Role of Death Qualification in Venirepersons' Attitudes toward the Insanity Defense*, 36 J. Appl. Soc'l Psychology 1744 (2006) (study of three hundred venirepersons from a Florida judicial district).

174. *Panetti*, 551 U.S. at 956.

175. *Id.* at 951.

176. *Id.*

177. Richard Bonnie, *Panetti v. Quarterman: Mental Illness, the Death Penalty, and Human Dignity*, 5 Ohio St. J. Crim. L. 257, 282 (2007).

178. *Panetti*, 551 U.S. at 959.

179. See e.g., Therapeutic Jurisprudence: The Law as a Therapeutic Agent 121, 122 (David Wexler, ed. 1990); Essays in Therapeutic Jurisprudence (David B. Wexler & Bruce J. Winick, eds. 1991); Law in a Therapeutic Key: Recent Developments in Therapeutic Jurisprudence (David B. Wexler & Bruce J. Winick, eds. 1996); Therapeutic Jurisprudence Applied: Essays on Mental Health Law (Bruce J. Winick, ed. 1997); David B. Wexler, *Putting Mental Health into Mental Health Law: Therapeutic Jurisprudence*, 16 L. & Hum. Behav. 27 (1992).

180. See e.g., Bruce Arrigo & Jeffrey Tasca, *Right to Refuse Treatment, Competency to Be Executed, and Therapeutic Jurisprudence: Toward a Systematic Analysis*, 24 L. & Psychol. Rev. 1 (1999); Bruce J. Winick, *Competency to Be Executed: A Therapeutic Jurisprudence Perspective*, 10 Behav. Sci. & L. 317 (1992).

181. Perlin, supra note 131, at 47.

CHAPTER 9

1. Portions of this chapter are adapted from Michael L. Perlin, *The Sanist Lives of Jurors in Death Penalty Cases: The Puzzling Role of Mitigating Mental Disability Evidence*, 8 Notre Dame J. L., Ethics & Pub. Pol. 239 (1994).

2. See Kevin Doyle, *Lethal Crapshoot: The Fatal Unreliability of the Penalty Phase*, 11 U. Pa. J. L. & Soc. Change 275, 275 (2007–2008) (describing how the capital sentencing process "abounds with check, balance, and backstop, . . . and perfects the complementary of justice and mercy," then immediately noting, "Yes, all this is true—and the moon is made of green cheese").

3. 428 U.S. 153 (1976).

4. See e.g., John P. Cronan, *Is Any of This Making Sense? Reflecting on Guilty Pleas to Aid Criminal Juror Comprehension*, 39 Am. Crim. L. Rev. 1187, 1188 (2002): "A growing mountain of empirical research is concluding, with shocking accord, that jurors retain alarmingly low comprehension of the most fundamental aspects of their roles"; see generally, Joe S. Cecil et al., *Citizen Comprehension of Difficult Issues: Lessons from Civil Jury Trials*, 40 Am. U. L. Rev. 727 (1991); Geoffrey P. Kramer & Dorean M. Koenig, *Do Jurors Understand Criminal Jury Instructions? Analyzing the Results of the Michigan Juror Comprehension Project*, 23 U. Mich. J. L. Ref.

401 (1990); Michael J. Saks, *Judicial Nullification*, 68 IND. L. J. 1281 (1993); Walter W. Steele Jr. & Elizabeth G. Thornburg, *Jury Instructions: A Persistent Failure to Communicate*, 67 N.C. L. REV. 77 (1988); Robert C. Power, *Reasonable and Other Doubts: The Problem of Jury Instructions*, 67 TENN. L. REV. 45, 98 (1999); Douglas G. Smith, *Structural and Functional Aspects of the Jury: Comparative Analysis and Proposals for Reform*, 48 ALA. L. REV. 441 (1997); Paul Marcus, Stephen P. Garvey, & Sheri Lynn Johnson, *Correcting Deadly Confusion: Responding to Jury Inquiries in Capital Cases*, 85 CORNELL L. REV. 627 (2000).

5. See Shari S. Diamond, *Instructing on Death: Psychologists, Juries, and Judges*, 48 AM. PSYCHOLOGIST 423 (1993). See also, http://www.capitalpunishmentincontext.org/issues/juryin-struct (accessed May 22, 2012), on jurors' failure to understand jury instructions in capital cases.

6. See Alison P. Barnes, *Beyond Guardianship Reform: A Reevaluation of Autonomy and Beneficence for a System of Principled Decision-Making in Long Term Care*, 41 EMORY L. J. 633, 689 (1992); Robert L. Hayman Jr., *Presumptions of Justice: Law, Politics, and the Mentally Retarded Parent*, 103 HARV. L. REV. 1201, 1244–45 (1990); see generally, Lyn Entzeroth, *Putting the Mentally Retarded Criminal Defendant to Death: Charting the Development of a National Consensus to Exempt the Mentally Retarded from the Death Penalty*, 52 ALA. L. REV. 911 (2001).

7. See *supra* chapter 4. Briefly, capital sentencing juries often treat mental disorder not as a mitigating circumstance (as the law requires) but as an aggravating circumstance supporting imposition of the death penalty. See Christopher Slobogin, *Is Atkins the Antithesis or Apotheosis of Anti-Discrimination Principles?: Sorting Out the Groupwide Effects of Exempting People with Mental Retardation from the Death Penalty*, 55 ALA. L. REV. 1101, 1107 (2004); Christopher Slobogin, *Mental Illness and the Death Penalty*, 24 MENTAL & PHYSICAL DISABILITY L. REP. 667, 669–70 (2000) (collecting empirical evidence).

8. See *supra* chapter 3.

9. See *supra* chapter 4.

10. George Dix, *Psychological Abnormality and Capital Sentencing: The New "Diminished Responsibility,"* 7 INT'L J. L. & PSYCHIATRY 249, 264 (1984). See generally, Lawrence White, *The Mental Illness Defense in the Capital Penalty Hearing*, 5 BEHAV. SCI. & L. 411, 414–19 (1987); Clarence E. Tygart, *Public Acceptance/Rejection of Insanity-Mental Illness Legal Defenses for Defendants in Criminal Homicide Cases*, 20 J. PSYCHIATRY & L. 375 (1992); Christopher Slobogin, *Mental Illness and the Death Penalty*, 24 MENTAL & PHYSICAL DISABILITY L. REP. 667 (2000).

11. See White, *supra* note 10, at 414–15 (discussing findings reported in Lawrence White, *Trial Consultants, Psychologists, and Prediction Errors*, CT. CALL 1 (Spring 1986)).

12. Ellen Fels Berkman, *Mental Illness as an Aggravating Circumstance in Capital Sentencing*, 89 COLUM. L. REV. 291 (1989).

13. Lawrence T. White, *Juror Decision Making in the Capital Penalty Trial: An Analysis of Crimes and Defense Strategies*, 11 LAW & HUM. BEHAV. 113 (1987). White's research continues to be cited as authoritative to the present day. See e.g., Katherine Polzer & Kimberly Kempf-Leonard, *Social Construction of Aggravating and Mitigating Factors: How Capital Jurors Attribute Blame*, 45 CRIM. L. BULL. 982, 991 n. 68 (2009).

14. See e.g., Lockhart v. McCree, 476 U.S. 162, 171–83 (1986) (upholding process of "death qualifying" jurors by which potential jurors with "conscientious scruples" against the death penalty are excluded from jury service).

15. Phoebe C. Ellsworth et al., *The Death-Qualified Jury and the Defense of Insanity*, 8 LAW & HUM. BEHAV. 81 (1984).

16. John H. Blume et al., *Probing "Life Qualification" through Expanded Voir Dire*, 29 HOFSTRA L. REV. 1209, 1211 (2001).

17. See e.g., State Farm Fire & Casualty Co. v. Wicka, 474 N.W.2d 324, 327 (Minn. 1991) (both law and society always more skeptical about putatively mentally ill person who has a "normal appearance" or "doesn't look sick"); see generally, Michael L. Perlin, *Unpacking the Myths: The Symbolism Mythology of Insanity Defense Jurisprudence*, 40 CASE W. RES. L. REV. 599,

724–27 (1989–1990); Michael L. Perlin, *"Life Is in Mirrors, Death Disappears": Giving Life to* Atkins, 33 N. Mex. L. Rev. 315, 333 (2003) (Perlin, *Death Disappears*).

18. Andrea Lyon, *But He Doesn't Look Retarded: Capital Jury Selection for the Mentally Retarded Client Not Excluded after Atkins v. Virginia*, 57 DePaul L. Rev. 701, 713 (2008).

19. See White, *supra* note 10, at 416–18; Ellsworth et al., *supra* note 15, at 90; see also White, *supra* note 13, at 125 (besides simply feeling that "mental illness is no excuse," jurors hostile to a mental illness defense focused on the possibility that the defendant was malingering, and on his prior failure to seek help for his problems). But *cf.* State v. Perry, 610 So. 2d 746, 781 (La. 1992) (Cole, J., dissenting) ("Society has the right to protect itself from those who would commit murder and seek to avoid their legitimate punishment by a subsequently contracted, or *feigned*, insanity") (emphasis added); Gilbert Geis & Robert F. Meier, *Abolition of the Insanity Plea in Idaho: A Case Study*, 477 Annals 72, 73 (1985) (irrelevant to Idaho residents whether defendant's reliance on insanity defense was real or feigned); Henry Weihofen, *Institutional Treatment of Persons Acquitted by Reason of Insanity*, 38 Tex. L. Rev. 849, 861 (1960) (request for psychiatric assistance seen as evidence of malingering).

20. See e.g., Nita A. Farahany & James E. Coleman Jr., *Genetics and Responsibility: To Know the Criminal from the Crime*, 69 L. & Contemp. Probs. 115, 129 (Winter/Spring 2006) (discussing defense counsel's use of behavioral genetics to "distinguish between defendant's choices that arise from his bad character (presumptively within his control) and choices that are the product of his genetic predisposition (presumptively outside of his control))," as reflected in Mobley v. State, 455 S.E.2d 61, 65–66 (Ga. 1995), discussed extensively in Deborah W. Denno, The *Legal Link Between Genetics and Crime: Vile or Viable?*, 69 Law & Contemp. Probs. 209 (Winter/Spring 2006).

21. See Stephen Golding & Ronald Roesch, *The Assessment of Criminal Responsibility: A Historical Approach to a Current Controversy*, in Handbook of Forensic Psychology 395, 400 (I. Weiner & A. Hess, eds. 1987); Caton F. Roberts et al., *Implicit Theories of Criminal Responsibility: Decision Making and the Insanity Defense*, 11 Law & Hum. Behav. 207, 209–10 (1987). See e.g., Dennis v. State, 13 P.3d 434, 440–42 (Nev. 2000) (death penalty not excessive because of deliberateness of crime).

"Planfulness," of course, may bespeak the most serious mental illness. See Perlin, *Death Disappears, supra* note 17, at 332, discussing how criminal acts committed by persons with severe mental illness may be "very deliberate and planful." I often pose a hypothetical to my criminal law and procedure classes about a defendant who genuinely, if utterly irrationally, believes that the world can only be saved if he kills the seventh woman wearing a purple sweater that he sees on the second Tuesday of the month. Such a delusion clearly evidences serious mental illness, yet the killing is totally planful.

22. Mark Costanzo & Sally Costanzo, *Jury Decision Making in the Capital Penalty Phase: Legal Assumptions, Empirical Findings, and a Research Agenda*, 16 Law & Hum. Behav. 185, 199 (1992); see also, Kevin O'Neil, Marc W. Patry, & Steven D. Penrod, *Exploring the Effects of Attitudes toward the Death Penalty on Capital Sentencing Verdicts*, 10 Psychol., Pub. Pol'y & L. 443 (2004).

23. Liliana Lyra Jubilut, *Death Penalty and Mental Illness: The Challenge of Reconciling Human Rights, Criminal Law, and Psychiatric Standards*, 6 Seattle J. Soc. Just. 353, 377 (2007), citing Patrick W. Corrigan & Amy C. Watson, *Findings from the National Comorbidity Survey on the Frequency of Violent Behavior in Individuals with Psychiatric Disorders*, 136 Psychiatry Res. 153, 153 (2005).

24. Diamond, *supra* note 5, at 426–28.

25. Berkman, *supra* note 12, at 299 (footnotes omitted).

26. See William S. Geimer & Jonathan Amsterdam, *Why Jurors Vote Life or Death: Operative Factors in Ten Florida Death Penalty Cases*, 15 Am. J. Crim. L. 1, 40–41, 51–52 (1987). Compare Scott E. Sundby, *The Intersection of Trial Strategy, Remorse and the Death Penalty*, 83 Cornell L. Rev. 1557, 1570 (1998) : "The available data indicate that capital defendants whom the jury views as truly sorry are the exception rather than the rule."

27. Marybeth Zientek, Riggins v. Nevada: *Medicated Defendants and Courtroom Demeanor from the Jury's Perspective*, 30 Am. J. Crim. L. 215, 227 (1992) (reporting on research in Wayne Weiten & Shari S. Diamond, *A Critical Review of the Jury Simulation Paradigm: The Case of Defendant Characteristics*, 3 LAW & HUM. BEHAV 71, 74 (1979)).

28. Zientek, *supra* note 27, at 227 (reporting on research in Martin F. Kaplan & Gwen D. Kemmerick, *Juror Judgment as Information Integration: Combining Evidential and Nonevidential Information*, 30 J. PERSONALITY & SOC. PSYCHOL. 493 (1974)).

29. See e.g., Michael L. Perlin, *Reading the Supreme Court's Tea Leaves: Predicting Judicial Behavior in Civil and Criminal Right to Refuse Treatment Cases*, 12 AM. J. FORENS PSYCHIATRY 37 (1991) (Perlin, *Tea Leaves*); Michael L. Perlin, *Decoding Right to Refuse Treatment Law*, 16 INT'L J. L. & PSYCHIATRY 151 (1993) (Perlin, *Decoding*). Compare Riggins v. Nevada, 504 U.S. 127 (1992) (Kennedy, J., concurring) ("The side effects of antipsychotic drugs may alter demeanor in a way that will prejudice all facets of the defense.") with Heller v. Doe, 509 U.S. 312 (1993) ("The mentally ill are subjected to medical and psychiatric treatment which may involve the . . . use of psychotropic drugs"). See Scott E. Sundby, *The Jury as Critic: An Empirical Look at How Capital Juries Perceive Expert and Lay Testimony*, 83 VA. L. REV. 1109, 1168(1997) (reporting on actual death penalty cases):

> The lack of vivid imagery was likely compounded by the fact that the defendant was heavily medicated during the trial. While the defendant's drugged state was explained to the jury, his flat emotional state and demeanor meant that they had no real sense of the defendant except through the defense witnesses. As with other capital jury studies, the jurors in the Project paid great attention to the defendant's demeanor and whether he gave any indications of remorsefulness.

30. See United States v. Charters, 829 F.2d 479, 494 (4th Cir. 1987), *remanded* 863 F.2d 302 (4th Cir. 1988) (en banc), *cert. denied*, 494 U.S. 1016 (1990) (heavily medicated defendant might give jury "false impression of defendant's mental state at the time of the crime"); see also Claudine W. Ausness, Note, *The Identification of Incompetent Defendants: Separating Those Unfit for Adversary Combat from Those Who Are Fit*, 66 KY. L. J. 666, 669–70 (1978) (defendant can alienate jury "if he displays such inappropriate demeanor as grinning when gruesome details are discussed, losing his temper when witnesses maintain he is a violent man, or acting indifferent to the proceedings"); Sundby, *supra* note 29, at 1168 (jurors describing death penalty defendant as descriptions made clear that they had been observing him: They described him as "catatonic," "show[ing] no emotion . . . ambivalent," and "detached . . . totally withdrawn").

31. See Dennis E. Cichon, *The Right to "Just Say No": A History and Analysis of the Right to Refuse Antipsychotic Drugs*, 53 LA. L. REV. 283, 304 (1992) (quoting Joseph T. Smith & Robert I. Simon, *Tardive Dyskinesia Revisited*, 31 MED. TRIAL TECH. Q. 342, 343 (1985)). See generally Cichon, *supra* at 304–7.

32. That is, jurors' determinations of "what really happened" will often be strongly influenced "by the degree to which the concrete detailed stories told by the parties at trial match the instances or prototypes in the jurors' relevant schemas." Albert J. Moore, *Trial by Schema: Cognitive Filters in the Courtroom*, 37 UCLA L. REV. 273, 292 (1989). See also e.g., Nancy Pennington & Reid Hastie, *Juror Decision-Making Models: The Generalization Gap*, 89 PSYCHOLOGICAL BULL. 246, 251–54 (1981); Loretta J. Stalans & Arthur J. Lurigio, *Lay and Professionals' Beliefs about Crime and Criminal Sentencing: A Need for Theory, Perhaps Schema Theory*, 17 CRIM. JUST. & BEHAV. 333 (1990); Ronald Chen & Jon Hanson, *Categorically Biased: The Influence of Knowledge Structures on Law and Legal Theory*, 77 S. CAL. L. REV. 1104 (2003–2004); Nancy Pennington & Reid Hastie, *A Cognitive Theory of Juror Decision Making: The Story Model*, 13 CARDOZO L. REV. 519, 520 (1991); Neil Vidmar & Shari Seidman Diamond, *Juries and Expert Evidence*, 66 BROOKLYN L. REV. 1121 (2001); Jeremy A. Blumenthal, *Emotional Paternalism*, 35 FLA. ST. U. L. REV. 1 (2007).

33. J.J. Prescott & Sonja Starr, *Improving Criminal Jury Decision Making after the Blakely Revolution*, 2006 U. ILL. L. REV. 301, 335–36.

34. *Id.*

35. See *infra* text accompanying notes 52–58.

36. Lyon, *supra* note 18, at 712. See *supra* chapter 4.

37. Richard Robinson, *Irreconcilable Differences: Yet More Attitudinal Discrepancies Between Death Penalty Opponents: A California Sample*, 22 Pepp. L. Rev. 1365, 1367 (1995).

38. See *id.* n. 87, citing James Luginbuhl & Kathi Middendorf, *Death Penalty Beliefs and Jurors' Responses to Aggravating and Mitigating Circumstances in Capital Trials*, 12 Law & Hum. Behav. 263, 279 (1988); Christopher Slobogin & Amy Mashburn, *The Criminal Defense Lawyer's Fiduciary Duty to Clients with Mental Disability*, 68 Fordham L. Rev. 1581, 1634 (2000); see also Brooke M. Butler & Gary Moran, *The Role of Death Qualification in Venirepersons' Evaluations of Aggravating and Mitigating Circumstances in Capital Trials*, 26 Law & Hum. Behav. 175, 182 (2002) (finding that death-qualified jurors were more likely to endorse aggravators and excluded jurors were more likely to believe nonstatutory mitigators).

39. Craig Haney, *Exoneration and Wrongful Condemnations: Expanding the Zone of Perceived Injustice in Death Penalty Cases*, 37 Golden Gate U. L. Rev. 131, 154–55 (2006) (emphasis added).

40. Bruce J. Winick, *The Supreme Court's Evolving Death Penalty Jurisprudence: Severe Mental Illness as the Next Frontier*, 50 B.C. L. Rev. 785, 850 (2009).

41. Ellsworth et al., *supra* note 15, at 92.

42. Lyons, *supra* note 18, at 712–13, quoting Robert Fitzgerald & Phoebe C. Ellsworth, *Due Process vs. Crime Control: Death Qualification and Jury Attitudes*, 8 Law & Hum. Behav. 31, 45 (1984).

43. See *supra* chapter 3.

44. John H. Blume et al., *Future Dangerousness in Capital Cases: Always "At Issue,"* 86 Cornell L. Rev. 397, 410 (2001).

45. Brooke Butler, *The Role of Death Qualification in Jurors' Susceptibility to Pretrial Publicity*, 37 J. Applied Soc'l Psychol. 115, 116 (2007) (citations omitted).

46. See *supra* chapter 1.

47. Saul Kassin et al., *Police-Induced Confessions: Risk Factors and Recommendations*, 34 Law & Hum. Behav. 3, 22 (2010).

48. *Id.* at 24.

49. On the pitfalls of "ordinary common sense" in legal decision making in death penalty cases, see *supra* chapter 2.

50. Kassin et al., *supra* note 47, at 24–25. See *id.* at 25:

> In many documented false confessions, the statements ultimately presented in court contained not only an admission of guilt but vivid details about the crime, the scene, and the victim that became known to the innocent suspect through leading questions, photographs, visits to the crime scene, and other secondhand sources invisible to the naïve observer. To further complicate matters, many false confessors state not just what they allegedly did, and how they did it, but *why*—as they self-report on revenge, jealousy, provocation, financial desperation, peer pressure, and other prototypical motives for crime. Some of these statements even contain apologies and expressions of remorse. To the naïve spectator, such statements appear to be voluntary, textured with detail, and the product of personal experience. Uninformed, however, this spectator mistakes illusion for reality, not realizing that the taped confession is scripted by the police theory of the case, rehearsed during hours of unrecorded questioning, directed by the questioner, and ultimately enacted on paper, tape, or camera by the suspect.

51. On the willful blindness of the legal system with regard to mental disability law issues in general, see Michael L. Perlin, *"Baby, Look Inside Your Mirror": The Legal Profession's Willful and Sanist Blindness to Lawyers with Mental Disabilities*, 69 U. Pitt. L. Rev. 589 (2008).

52. See generally, Michael L. Perlin, *Pretexts and Mental Disability Law: The Case of Competency*, 47 U. Miami L. Rev. 625, 659–61 (1993); Michael L. Perlin, The Hidden Prejudice: Mental Disability on Trial 4–16 (2000).

53. See Michael L. Perlin, *Psychodynamics and the Insanity Defense: Ordinary Common Sense and Heuristic Reasoning*, 69 Neb. L. Rev. 3, 12–17 (1990); Perlin, *supra* note 52, at 4–6.

54. *See* Michael L. Perlin, *Are Courts Competent to Decide Questions of Competency? Stripping the Facade from United States v. Charters*, 38 U. Kan. L. Rev. 957, 966 n. 46 (1990) (quoting John S. Carroll & John W. Payne, *The Psychology of the Parole Decision Process: A Joint Application of Attribution Theory and Information-Processing Psychology*, in Cognition and Social Behavior 13, 21 (John S. Carroll & John W. Payne, eds. 1976)).

55. David Rosenhan, *Psychological Realities and Judicial Policy* 19 Stan. Law. 10, 13 (1984). See e.g., Perlin, *supra* note 53 at 16 n. 59, 20.

56. See e.g., Jonathan J. Koehler & Daniel N. Shaviro, *Veridical Verdicts: Increasing Verdict Accuracy through the Use of Overtly Probabilistic Evidence and Methods*, 75 Cornell L. Rev. 247, 264–65 (1990); Perlin, *supra* note 53, at 39–53; Morrison Torrey, *When Will We Be Believed? Rape Myths and the Idea of a Fair Trial in Rape Prosecutions*, 24 U.C. Davis L. Rev. 1013, 1050 (1991); see also Caton F. Roberts & Stephen L. Golding, *The Social Construction of Criminal Responsibility and Insanity*, 15 Law & Hum. Behav. 349, 372 (1991) (jurors' preexisting attitudes toward insanity defense strongest predictor of individual verdicts).

57. See generally Sharon S. Brehm & Jack W. Brehm, Psychological Reactance: A Theory of Freedom and Control (1981); Judgment Under Uncertainty: Heuristics and Biases (Daniel Kahneman et al., eds. 1982) (hereinafter Judgment); Richard E. Nisbett & Lee Ross, Human Inference: Strategies and Shortcomings of Social Judgment (1980) (all discussing heuristics in general); Hal R. Arkes, *Principles in Judgment/Decision Making Research Pertinent to Legal Proceedings*, 7 Behav. Sci. & L. 429 (1989) (hindsight and outcome biases); Perlin, *supra* note 53, at 13–18, 29–30; see also Jonathon Baron & John C. Hershey, *Outcome Bias in Decision Evaluation*, 54 J. Personality & Soc. Psychol. 569 (1988); Donald N. Bersoff, *Judicial Deference to Nonlegal Decisionmakers: Imposing Simplistic Solutions on Problems of Cognitive Complexity in Mental Disability Law*, 46 SMU L. Rev. 329, 335–51 (1992) (same); N.V. Dawson et al., *Hindsight Bias: An Impediment to Accurate Probability Estimation in Clinicopathologic Conferences*, 8 Med. Decision Making 259 (1988) (hindsight bias); Anthony N. Doob & Julian V. Roberts, *Social Psychology, Social Attitudes and Attitudes toward Sentencing*, 16 Can. J. Behav. Sci. 269 (1984) (vividness effect); Shari S. Diamond & Loretta J. Stalans, *The Myth of Judicial Leniency in Sentencing*, 7 Behav. Sci. & L. 73 (1989) (vividness effect); Baruch Fischhoff, *Hindsight, Foresight: The Effect of Outcome Knowledge on Judgment under Uncertainty*, 104 J. Experimental Psychol.: Hum. Perception & Performance 288 (1975) (both biases); Harold Kelley, *The Process of Causal Attribution*, 28 Am. Psychologist 107 (1973) (attribution); Dan Russell, *The Causal Dimension Scale: A Measure of How Individuals Perceive Causes*, 42 J. Personality & Soc. Psychol. 1137 (1982) (same); Michael J. Saks & Robert F. Kidd, *Human Information Processing and Adjudication: Trial by Heuristics*, 15 Law & Soc'y Rev. 123, 137 (1981) (availability); David E. Van Zandt, *Common Sense Reasoning, Social Change, and the Law*, 81 Nw. U. L. Rev. 894 (1987) (typification). In mental health contexts, see e.g., Harold Bursztajn et al., *"Magical Thinking," Suicide, and Malpractice Litigation*, 16 Bull. Am. Acad. Psychiatry & L. 369 (1988); David B. Wexler & Robert F. Schopp, *How and When to Correct for Juror Hindsight Bias in Mental Health Malpractice Litigation: Some Preliminary Observations*, 7 Behav. Sci. & L. 485 (1989).

58. See Perlin, *supra* note 52, at 661. In a series of papers, I have considered the power of heuristics on different aspects of the mental health disability law system. See Michael L. Perlin, *"And I See through Your Brain": Access to Experts, Competency to Consent, and the Impact of Antipsychotic Medications in Neuroimaging Cases in the Criminal Trial*, 2009 Stan. Tech. L. Rev. 4 (use of neuroimaging testimony in criminal trial process); Michael L. Perlin, *"A Change Is Gonna Come": The*

Implications of the United Nations Convention on the Rights of Persons with Disabilities for the Domestic Practice of Constitutional Mental Disability Law, 29 No. ILL. U. L. REV. 483 (2009) (international human rights law); Michael L. Perlin, *"Simplify You, Classify You": Stigma, Stereotypes and Civil Rights in Disability Classification Systems*, 25 GA. ST. U. L. REV. 607 (2009) (Perlin, *Disability Classification*) (special education law); Michael L. Perlin, *"Everybody Is Making Love/Or Else Expecting Rain": Considering the Sexual Autonomy Rights of Persons Institutionalized Because of Mental Disability in Forensic Hospitals and in Asia*, 83 U. WASH. L. REV. 481 (2008) (sexual autonomy rights); Michael L. Perlin, *"Baby, Look Inside Your Mirror": The Legal Profession's Willful and Sanist Blindness to Lawyers with Mental Disabilities*, 69 U. PITT. L. REV. 589 (2008) (issues faced by lawyers with mental disabilities); Perlin, *supra* note 53 (insanity defense); Michael L. Perlin, *Competency, Deinstitutionalization, and Homelessness: A Story of Marginalization*, 28 HOUS. L. REV. 63 (1991) (relationship between homelessness and deinstitutionalization); Perlin, *Decoding, supra* note 29 (right to refuse treatment); Perlin, *Tea Leaves, supra* note 29 (same); Michael L. Perlin, Tarasoff *and the Dilemma of the Dangerous Patient: New Directions for the 1990's*, 16 LAW & PSYCHOL. REV. 29 (1992) (application of *Tarasoff* doctrine); see also Michael L. Perlin, *Fatal Assumption: A Critical Evaluation of the Role of Counsel in Mental Disability Cases*, 16 LAW & HUM. BEHAV. 39, 57–58 (1992) (on mental disability counsel's need to familiarize herself with heuristics database); Michael L. Perlin & Deborah A. Dorfman, *Sanism, Social Science, and the Development of Mental Disability Law Jurisprudence*, 11 BEHAV. SCI. & L. 47, 63 n. 114 (1993) (on the relationship between heuristic thinking and courts' attitudes toward social science data in mental disability cases).

59. See generally, Perlin & Dorfman, *supra* note 58, at 52–54.

60. See e.g., Paul Appelbaum, *The Empirical Jurisprudence of the United States Supreme Court*, 13 AM. J. L. & MED. 335, 341–42 (1987). On *why* individuals are susceptible to these sort of prediction errors, see Jeremy A. Blumenthal, *Law and the Emotions: The Problems of Affective Forecasting*, 80 IND. L. J. 155, 176–81 (2005).

61. Michael L. Perlin, *Morality and Pretextuality, Psychiatry and Law: Of Ordinary Common Sense, Heuristic Reasoning, and Cognitive Dissonance*, 19 BULL. AM. ACAD. PSYCHIATRY & L. 131, 136–37 (1991); J. Alexander Tanford & Sarah Tanford, *Better Trials through Science: A Defense of Psychologist-Lawyer Collaboration*, 66 N.C. L. REV. 741, 742–46 (1988). See e.g., Ballew v. Georgia, 435 U.S. 223, 246 (1978) (Powell, J., concurring) (smaller than six-person jury unconstitutional in state criminal trials) (challenging the "wisdom—as well as the necessity—of . . . heavy reliance on *numerology* derived from statistical studies") (emphasis added).

62. See e.g., David Faigman, *To Have and Have Not: Assessing the Value of Social Science to the Law as Science and Policy*, 38 EMORY L. J. 1005, 1010 (1989); Sheri Gronhoud, *Social Science Statistics in the Courtroom: The Debate Resurfaces in* McCleskey v. Kemp, 62 NOTRE DAME L. REV. 688, 705–8 (1987) (on possible roots of courts' hostility toward statistical evidence). On the skepticism of capital jurors toward mental health expert witnesses testifying on behalf of defendants, see Sundby, *supra* note 29, at 1130–39.

63. Faigman, *supra* note 62, at 1016, 1026.

64. Perlin, *supra* note 61, at 136 (citing Ann Woolhandler, *Rethinking the Judicial Reception of Legislative Facts*, 41 VAND. L. REV. 111, 125 n. 84 (1988) (quoting DAVID HOROWITZ, THE COURTS AND SOCIAL POLICY 284 (1977))).

65. Constance Lindman, *Sources of Judicial Distrust of Social Science Evidence: A Comparison of Social Science Jurisprudence*, 64 IND. L. J. 755, 755 (1989); Elizabeth Loftus & John Monahan, *Trial by Data: Psychological Research as Legal Evidence*, 35 AM. PSYCHOLOGIST 270, 270–71 (1980).

66. See e.g., Perlin, *supra* note 54, at 986–93 (discussing decision in United States v. Charters, 863 F.2d 302 (4th Cir. 1988) (en banc), *cert. denied*, 496 U.S. 1016 (1990), which limited right of pretrial detainees to refuse medication). The *Charters* court rejected as incredulous the possibility that a court could make a meaningful distinction between competency to stand trial and competency to engage in medication decision making:

[Such a distinction] must certainly be of such subtlety and complexity as to tax perception by the most skilled medical or psychiatric professionals. To suppose that it is a distinction that can be fairly discerned and applied even by the most skilled judge on the basis of an adversarial fact-finding proceeding taxes credulity.

Charters, 863 F.2d at 310.

67. Gary Melton, *Bringing Psychology to the Legal System: Opportunities, Obstacles, and Efficacy*, 42 AM. PSYCHOLOGIST 488 (1987).

68. Bernard Grofman, *The Slippery Slope: Jury Size and Jury Verdict Requirements—Legal and Social Science Approaches*, 2 LAW & POL'Y Q. 285, 300 (1980); Peter Sperlich, *Trial by Jury: It May Have a Future*, in SUPREME COURT REVIEW 191, 208 (P. Kurland & G. Casper, eds. 1979); see also, David Suggs, *The Use of Psychological Research by the Judiciary*, 3 LAW & HUM. BEHAV. 135, 147 (1979) (courts have failed to develop methods to ensure validity of research used in opinions).

69. See e.g., John Monahan & Laurens Walker, *Social Authority: Obtaining, Evaluating, and Establishing Social Science in Law*, 134 U. PA. L. REV. 477, 511 n. 119 (1986) ("Anyone who can comprehend the Federal Tort Claims Act can learn what standard deviation and statistical significance mean"). For fairly optimistic assessments of *jurors'* abilities to weigh statistical evidence, see e.g., William Thompson, *Are Juries Competent to Evaluate Statistical Evidence?*, 52 LAW & CONTEMP. PROBS. 9 (1989); Neil Vidmar & Regina Schuller, *Juries and Expert Evidence: Social Science Framework Testimony*, 52 LAW & CONTEMP. PROBS. 133 (1989).

70. Appelbaum, *supra* note 60, at 341; David Faigman, *"Normative Constitutional Fact-Finding": Exploring the Empirical Component of Constitutional Interpretation*, 139 U. PA. L. REV. 541, 581 (1991); Perlin, *supra* note 61, at 136–37; Michael L. Perlin, *The Supreme Court, the Mentally Disabled Criminal Defendant, and Symbolic Values: Random Decisions, Hidden Rationales, or Doctrinal Abyss?* 29 ARIZ. L. REV. 1, 71 (1987); J. Alexander Tanford, *The Limits of a Scientific Jurisprudence: The Supreme Court and Psychology*, 66 IND. L. J. 137, 144–50 (1990).

71. On the court's heuristic misuse of social science data, see Perlin, *supra* note 52, at 664–68.

72. James Acker, *A Different Agenda: The Supreme Court, Empirical Research Evidence, and Capital Punishment Decisions, 1986–1989*, 27 LAW & SOC'Y REV. 65, 80–81 (1993) ("The prevailing opinions in the Court's recent major capital punishment decisions have increasingly displayed an unwillingness to incorporate the results of relevant social science findings"); Phoebe Ellsworth, *Unpleasant Facts: The Supreme Court's Response to Empirical Research on Capital Punishment*, in CHALLENGING CAPITAL PUNISHMENT: LEGAL AND SOCIAL SCIENCE APPROACHES 177, 208 (Kenneth C. Haas & James A. Inciardi, eds. 1988) ("The parsimonious explanation for the failure of social science data to influence the Court in death penalty cases seems to be that the outcome of these cases is frequently a foregone conclusion").

73. See Perlin, *supra* note 52, at 668–69 (discussing decisions in Barefoot v. Estelle, 463 U.S. 880 (1983) (testimony as to future dangerousness admissible at penalty phase in capital punishment case), McCleskey v. Kemp, 481 U.S. 279 (1987) (rejecting statistical evidence offered to show racial discrimination in death penalty prosecutions), and *Charters*, 863 F.2d 302 (curtailing rights of criminal defendant awaiting trial to refuse antipsychotic medication)). I discuss *Barefoot* extensively *supra* chapter 3.

74. Faigman, *supra* note 62, at 577.

75. *Id.* at 581.

76. Katheryn Katz, *Majoritarian Morality and Parental Rights*, 52 ALB. L. REV. 405, 461 (1988) (on court's reading of impact of parents' homosexuality in child custody decisions); Tanford, *supra* note 70, at 153–54. See e.g., Holbrook v. Flynn, 475 U.S. 560, 571 n. 4 (1986) (defendant's right to fair trial not denied where uniformed state troopers sat in front of spectator section in courtroom; court rejected contrary empirical study and based decision on its own "experience and common sense").

77. See e.g., Thomas Hafemeister & Gary Melton, *The Impact of Social Science Research on the Judiciary*, in Reforming the Law: Impact of Child Development Research 27 (Gary Melton, ed. 1987); Peter Sperlich, *The Evidence on Evidence: Science and Law in Conflict and Cooperation*, in The Psychology of Evidence and Trial Procedure 325 (S. Kassin & C. Wrightsman, eds. 1985); Craig Haney, *Data and Decisions: Judicial Reform and the Use of Social Science*, in The Analysis of Judicial Reform 43 (P. Du Bois, ed. 1982).

78. See e.g., Barefoot v. Estelle, 463 U.S. 880, 897–902 (1983); Faigman, *supra* note 62, at 584 (discussing Parham v. J.R., 442 U.S. 584 (1979)); see also Watkins v. Sowders, 449 U.S. 341 (1981) (refusal of courts to acknowledge social science research on ways that jurors evaluate and misevaluate eyewitness testimony).

79. The classic example is Chief Justice Burger's opinion for the court in Parham v. J.R., 442 U.S. 584, 605–10 (1979) (approving more relaxed involuntary civil commitment procedures for juveniles than for adults). See e.g., Gail Perry & Gary Melton, *Precedential Value of Judicial Notice of Social Facts: Parham as an Example*, 22 J. Fam. L. 633 (1984):

> The *Parham* case is an example of the Supreme Court's taking advantage of the free rein on social facts to promulgate a dozen or so of its own by employing one tentacle of the judicial notice doctrine. The Court's opinion is filled with social facts of questionable veracity, accompanied by the authority to propel these facts into subsequent case law and, therefore, a spiral of less than rational legal policy making.

Id. at 645; see also 1 Michael L. Perlin, Mental Disability Law: Civil and Criminal, § 2C-7.1a, at 471–76 (2d ed. 1998) (criticizing *Parham* on these grounds); Winsor Schmidt, *Considerations of Social Science in a Reconsideration of* Parham v. J.R. *and the Commitment of Children to Public Mental Institutions*, 13 J. Psychiatry & L. 339 (1985) (same). On the Supreme Court's special propensity in mental health cases to base opinions on "simply unsupportable" factual assumptions, see Stephen Morse, *Treating Crazy People Less Specially*, 90 W. Va. L. Rev. 353, 382 n. 64 (1987).

80. See generally, Michael L. Perlin, The Jurisprudence of the Insanity Defense 252–58 (1994). On visual imagery in the law in general, see e.g., Richard K. Sherwin, *A Manifesto for Visual Legal Realism*, 40 Loy. L.A. L. Rev. 719 (2007); Richard K. Sherwin et al., *Law in the Digital Age: How Visual Communication Technologies Are Transforming the Practice, Theory, and Teaching of Law*, 12 B.U. J. Sci. & Tech. L. 227, 233 (2006).

81. Valerie Hans, *Death by Jury*, in Haas & Inciardi, *supra* note 72, at 149, 169 ("We really know little about how jurors evaluate mitigating evidence"); see also, Valerie P. Hans, *How Juries Decide Death: The Contributions of the Capital Jury Project*, 70 Ind. L. J. 1233, 1238 (1995) ("particularly troubling, of course, is the misunderstanding of the concept of mitigating evidence and how it is to be used in decision-making").

82. Michael L. Perlin, *"His Brain Has Been Mismanaged with Great Skill": How Will Jurors Respond to Neuroimaging Testimony in Insanity Defense Cases?*, 42 Akron L. Rev. 885, 900 (2009). *See generally*, Sander Gilman, Seeing the Insane (1982) for a full historical overview. On the role of this demand in the development of mental disability law in general, see Michael L. Perlin, *On Sanism*, 46 SMU L. Rev. 373 (1992).

83. State Farm Fire & Casualty Co. v. Wicka, 474 N.W.2d 324, 327 (Minn. 1991), discussed *supra* note 17. See e.g., Sheldon Glueck, Mental Disorder and the Criminal Law 31 (1925) (quoting John E. Lind, *The Cross-Examination of the Alienist*, 13 J. Crim. L., Criminology & Pol. Sci. 228, 229 (1922) (setting out "typical" juror response in cases of conflicting expert testimony: "[T]he man doesn't look very crazy to us, anyhow").

To some extent, it may be necessary for a defendant to look this way in order to convince a forensic psychiatrist as well. See White, *supra* note 10, at 416–17, discussing research reported upon in Anasseril Daniel et al., *Factors Correlated with Psychiatric Recommendations of Incompe-*

tency and Insanity, 12 J. Psychiatry & L. 527 (1984), and see also *id.* (psychiatrists more likely to recommend diminished capacity when defendant exhibits "bizarre behavior").

84. See generally, Perlin, *supra* note 53; see also, Bill Ong Hing, *Raising Personal Identification Issues of Class, Race, Ethnicity, Gender, Sexual Orientation, Physical Disability, and Age in Lawyering Courses*, 45 Stan. L. Rev. 1807, 1810 (1993) ("Common sense, without training, is dangerously fashioned by our own class, race, ethnicity/culture, gender, and sexual background"). "Ordinary common sense" is comprised of "a 'prereflective attitude' exemplified by the attitude of 'What I know is "self-evident"; it is "what everybody knows."'" See Keri K. Gould & Michael L. Perlin, *"Johnny's in the Basement/Mixing Up His Medicine": Therapeutic Jurisprudence and Clinical Teaching*, 24 Seattle U. L. Rev. 339, 357 (2000).

Research reveals that the more television a prospective juror watches, the more likely he is to support punishment or incapacitation rather than rehabilitation, independent of whether or not the individual had ever been victimized. See Jared S. Rosenberger & Valerie J. Callanan, *The Influence of Media on Penal Attitudes*, 36 Crim. Just. Rev. 435 (2011).

85. Perlin, *Death Disappears, supra* note 17, at 333–34.

86. 504 U.S. 127 (1992) (discussing the right of competent criminal defendants to refuse the involuntary administration of antipsychotic medications).

87. *Id.* at 144, relying on William Geimer & Jonathan Amsterdam, *Why Jurors Vote Life or Death: Operative Factors in Ten Florida Death Penalty Cases*, 15 Am. J. Crim. L. 1, 51–53 (1987–1988); see generally, Michael L. Perlin, *"The Executioner's Face Is Always Well-Hidden": The Role of Counsel and the Courts in Determining Who Dies*, 41 N.Y. L. Sch. L. Rev. 201, 220 (1996), discussing this research. See also, Liliana Lyra Jubilut, *Death Penalty and Mental Illness: The Challenge of Reconciling Human Rights, Criminal Law, and Psychiatric Standards*, 6 Seattle J. Soc. Just. 353, 377 (2007) ("jury decisions are often impacted by jury members' perceptions as to whether and to what degree the defendants feel remorse").

88. People v. Tylkowski, 524 N.E.2d 1112, 1117 (Ill. App. Ct. 1988); State v. Brantley, 514 So. 2d 747, 751 (La. App. 1987) (defendant found to be "outgoing," "very friendly," and a "nicely dressed 'person of means'").

89. Fulgham v. Ford, 850 F.2d 1529, 1532 (11th Cir. 1988).

90. People v. McNamee, 547 N.Y.S.2d 519, 524 (Sup. Ct. 1989).

91. Richard Arens & Jackwell Susman, *Judges, Jury Charges and Insanity*, 12 How. L. J. 1, 2 (1966) (discussing results reported in Richard Arens et al., *Jurors, Jury Charges and Insanity*, 14 Cath. U. L. Rev. 1 (1965)). See also *id.* at 9 (most jurors perceive insanity defense as calling for nothing short of "highly persuasive evidence of severe psychotic disorientation"). For a more optimistic subsequent reading, see Norman Finkel & Sharon Handel, *How Jurors Construe "Insanity,"* 13 Law & Hum. Behav. 41 (1989).

92. Walter Bromberg & Hervey Cleckley, *The Medico-Legal Dilemma*, 42 J. Crim. L. & Criminology 729, 738 (1952). *Cf.* State v. Van Horn, 528 So. 2d 529, 530 (Fla. Dist. App. 1988) (state rebuttal lay witnesses provided sufficient "probative perceptions of normalcy").

93. State v. Pierce, 788 P.2d 352, 354, 356 (N.M. 1990) (finding that defendant failed to demonstrate "actual prejudice," and characterizing these remarks as merely "eccentric").

94. See Perlin, *supra* note 1, at 269.

95. State v. Clayton, 656 S.W.2d 344, 348–50 (Tenn. 1983) (reversing conviction). See also e.g., Carson v. State, 963 N.E.2d 670 (Ind. App. 2012) (affirming rejection of insanity defense in spite of unanimous expert testimony because of "demeanor" evidence).

96. Gardner v. State, 514 N.E.2d 1259, 1260 (Ind. 1987). See also State v. Alley, 776 S.W.2d 506, 513 (Tenn. 1989) (not error to allow testimony by "psychiatric technician" that "defendant was malingering and . . . did not act like persons who were really insane").

97. Louis H. Swartz, *Mental Disease: The Groundwork for Legal Analysis and Legislative Action*, 111 U. Pa. L. Rev. 389, 413 (1963), quoting Frederick Redlich, Interrelations between the Social Environment and Psychiatric Disorders 120–21 (1953):

We know what the seriously ill person in a given culture is. That we do know. In this respect we agree, incidentally, with the policeman, with the clerk in the drug store. Our crude diagnostic criteria are reasonably similar.

98. See Michael L. Perlin & Keri K. Gould, *Rashomon and the Criminal Law: Mental Disability and the Federal Sentencing Guidelines*, 22 Am. J. Crim. L. 431, 443 (1995) ("One important stereotype is that mental illness can easily be identified by lay persons; this belief matches up closely to popular media depictions and comports with our 'common sense' notion of 'crazy behavior'").

99. See Daniel A. Krauss & Bruce D. Sales, *The Effects of Clinical and Scientific Expert Testimony on Juror Decision Making in Capital Sentencing*, 7 Psychol. Pub. Pol. & L. 267, 267, 305 (2001) (concluding that "jurors are more influenced by clinical opinion expert testimony than by actuarial expert testimony" and that "the adversarial process fails to counter this bias). By way of comparison, research has shown that actuarial prediction—based on sets of indicators—is superior to clinical judgment in predicting recidivism. See e.g., Patrick Lussier & Garth Davies, *Person-Oriented Perspective on Sexual Offenders, Offending Trajectories, and Risk of Recidivism: A New Challenge for Policymakers, Risk Assessors, and Actuarial Prediction?* 17 Psychol. Pub. Pol'y & L. 530, 531 (2011); Christopher Slobogin, *Prevention as the Primary Goal of Sentencing: The Modern Case for Indeterminate Dispositions in Criminal Cases*, 48 San Diego L. Rev. 1127, 1146 (2011) ("Actuarial prediction testimony is clearly superior to unstructured clinical prediction testimony with respect to both the probative value and prejudice inquiries").

On how jurors construe types of expert witnesses and types of lay witnesses in death penalty cases, and how jurors trivialize some defense experts' testimony, see Sundby, *supra* note 29, at 1184.

100. Michael L. Perlin, *A Law of Healing*, 68 U. Cin. L. Rev. 407, 422 (2000); see, on this point, J. Alexander Tanford, *The Limits of a Scientific Jurisprudence: The Supreme Court and Psychology*, 66 Ind. L. J. 137 (1990).

101. John Q. La Fond & Mary L. Durham, Back to the Asylum: The Future of Mental Health Law and Policy in the United States 156 (1992).

102. William Bowers et al., *Death Sentencing in Black and White: An Empirical Analysis of the Role of Jurors' Race and Jury Racial Composition*, 3 U. Pa. J. Constl. L. 171, 262 (2001).

103. 476 U.S. 28 (1986).

104. *Id.* at 35.

105. http://capitalpunishmentincontext.org/issues/juryinstruct.

106. Leona D. Jochnowitz, *How Capital Jurors Respond to Mitigating Evidence of Defendant's Mental Illness, Retardation, and Situational Impairments: An Analysis of the Legal and Social Science Literature*, 47 Crim. L. Bull. 839, 841 (2011). ("Jurors who had been death-qualified, acted more punitively when the insanity defense was raised, because they viewed the defense as malingering, and a legal loophole"). On the ways that punitively minded people may be less willing to consider empirical research, see Abigayl Perelman & Carl Clements, *Beliefs about What Works in Juvenile Rehabilitation: The Influence of Attitudes on Support for "Get Tough" and Evidence-Based Interventions*, 36 Crim. Just. & Behav. 184, 193 (2009).

107. On misperceptions of "faking" in general, see Michael L. Perlin, *"The Borderline Which Separated You from Me": The Insanity Defense, the Authoritarian Spirit, the Fear of Faking, and the Culture of Punishment*, 82 Iowa L. Rev. 1375 (1997). On misperceptions of "faking" in the death penalty context in particular, see Perlin, *Death Disappears, supra* note 17.

108. White, *supra* note 13.

109. "Among the most common sanist myths are the myths that (1) persons with mental disabilities are 'faking' and (2) such persons would not be mentally disabled if they only 'tried harder.' Perlin, *Disability Classification, supra* note 58.

110. See *supra* text accompanying note 57. See also, Jennifer K. Robbennolt, *Apologies and Reasonableness: Some Implications of Psychology for Torts*, 59 DePaul L. Rev. 489, 497–503 (2010).

111. Theodore Eisenberg, Stephen P. Garvey, & Martin T. Wells, *Forecasting Life and Death: Juror Race, Religion, and Attitude toward the Death Penalty*, 30 J. Legal Stud. 277, 307 (2001).

See also, e.g., William Bowers et al., *Jurors' Failure to Understand or Comport with Constitutional Standards in Capital Sentencing: Strength of the Evidence*, 46 Crim. L. Bull. 1147, 1184–90 (2010).

112. See David B. Wexler & Robert F. Schopp, *How and When to Correct for Juror Hindsight Bias in Mental Health Malpractice Litigation: Some Preliminary Observations*, 7 Behav. Sci. & L. 485 (1989).

113. See e.g., Susan D. Rozelle, *The Principled Executioner: Capital Juries' Bias and the Benefits of True Bifurcation*, 38 Ariz. St. L. J. 769, 793 (2006), quoting, in part, William S. Geimer & Jonathan Amsterdam, *Why Jurors Vote Life or Death: Operative Factors in Ten Florida Death Penalty Cases*, 15 Am. J. Crim. L. 1, 46 (1998):

> The bias of capital jurors can be chilling in its frankness: "Of course he got death. That's what we were there for."

114. See James S. Liebman, *Opting for Real Death Penalty Reform*, 63 Ohio St. L. J. 315, 322 (2002).

115. *Id.* n. 36, quoting Tina Rosenberg, *Deadliest D.A.*, N.Y. Times, July 16, 1995 (Magazine), at 22. Elsewhere Liebman writes extensively about how the imposition of the death penalty is basically a county-by-county issue, resulting in this anomaly: over a twenty-two-year period, *sixty-six* American counties accounted for 2,569 of the 5,131 death sentences imposed. See James S. Liebman & Peter Clarke, *Minority Practice, Majority's Burden: The Death Penalty Today*, 9 Ohio St. J. Crim. L. 255, 264–65 n. 40 (2011). Perhaps even more astonishingly, just 16 percent of the nation's counties (510 out of 3,143) accounted for 90 percent of its death verdicts in the period. *Id.* at 265.

Philadelphia is discussed in this context in depth in Robert Smith, *The Geography of the Death Penalty and Its Ramifications*, 92 B.U. L. Rev. 227, 260–61 (2012).

See generally, Adam M. Gershowitz, *Statewide Capital Punishment: The Case for Eliminating Counties' Role in the Death Penalty*, 63 Vand. L. Rev. 307 (2010).

116. James Liebman, *The Overproduction of Death*, 100 Colum. L. Rev. 2030, 2032 (2000). See also, Liebman & Clarke, *supra* note 115, at 295:

> Local prosecutors stand to gain by imposing as many death verdicts as possible, regardless of the verdicts' failure rate on appeal, because they quickly realize the political gains, and the costs of review and reversal are slow to materialize and shouldered by others.

117. J. Amy Dillard, *And Death Shall Have No Dominion: How to Achieve the Categorical Exemption of Mentally Retarded Defendants from Execution*, 45 U. Rich. L. Rev. 961, 1005 (2011).

118. Brian L. Vander Pol, *Relevance and Reconciliation: A Proposal Regarding the Admissibility of Mercy Opinions in Capital Sentencing*, 88 Iowa L. Rev. 707, 709 & n. 2 (2003).

119. See Deborah C. Scott et al., *Monitoring Insanity Acquittees: Connecticut's Psychiatric Security Review Board*, 41 Hosp. & Community Psychiatry 980, 982 (1990) (persons with mental disabilities are "the most despised and feared group in society"). Compare William Berry III, *Ending Death by Dangerousness: A Path to the De Facto Abolition of the Death Penalty*, 52 Ariz. L. Rev. 889, 920 (2010) ("prosecutors, as members of the executive branch, ought to be encouraged to seek death sentences only on accepted grounds (retribution and deterrence) and not based on the perceived future dangerousness of an individual"). See Jessica Salvucci, *Femininity and the Electric Chair: An Equal Protection Challenge to Texas's Death Penalty Statute*, 31 B.C. Third World L. J. 405, 417 (2011): "A prosecutor's decision may be influenced by the public because '[t]he decision to seek the death penalty is often tied to politics and community outrage rather than to the heinousness of the homicide'" (citation omitted).

120. Gershowitz, *supra* note 115, at 347–48.

121. See Sherrilyn A. Ifill, *Using the Death Penalty to Get Re-Elected*, accessible at http://www.theroot.com/search/node/Equal%20Justice%20Initiative%20%2526%20Alabama%20

%2526%20Ifill (July 20, 2011); see generally, DAVID GARLAND, PECULIAR INSTITUTION: AMERICA'S DEATH PENALTY IN AN AGE OF ABOLITION 48 (2010).

122. Ifill, *supra* note 121. See generally, Stephen B. Bright & Patrick J. Keenan, *Judges and the Politics of Death: Deciding between the Bill of Rights and the Next Election in Capital Cases*, 75 B.U. L. REV. 759 (1995); see also, Fred B. Burnside, *Dying to Get Elected: A Challenge to the Jury Override*, 1999 WIS. L. REV. 1017 (giving examples of judges citing their decisions to override jury life sentences in their campaigns or being voted out of office for their failure to impose or uphold death verdicts).

123. State v. Brooks, 1985 WL 8589 Ohio App. (1985).

124. State v. Brooks, 2011 WL 5517300 Ohio App. 8 Dist. (2011).

125. See http://www.amnesty.org/en/library/asset/AMR51/091/2011/en/f45b68fd-043e-4990-9151-4af40f0328e1/amr510912011en.pdf.

126. *Id.*

127. See http://www.amnesty.org/en/library/asset/ACT50/001/2012/en/241a8301-05b4-41c0-bfd9-2fe72899cda4/act500012012en.pdf.

128. Natasha Minsker, *Prosecutorial Misconduct in Death Penalty Cases*, 45 CAL. W. L. REV. 373, 375–76 (2009). See also, Natasha Minsker & Daniel Ballon, *Forum Column*, SAN FRANCISCO DAILY J. (Oct. 18, 2007), accessible at http://www.ccfaj.org/documents/press/SFDailyJournal10-18-07.pdf.

129. Minsker, *supra* note 128, at 382–87, discussing People v. Babbitt, 45 Cal. 3d 660 (1988). The prosecutor's comments included these:

- "We are letting justice be decided on the basis of how well a psychiatrist can sell their bag of tricks," and, "they [psychiatrists] are so vain as to think they are capable of all these magical, mystical things they say they are capable of."
- "[W]e have a social cancer in our community now, and it is this very process of allowing psychiatrists to come in and make their moral pronouncements disguised as medical opinion in the hopes of persuading jurors to let people off the hook."
- "I'm going to find this guy crazy and let him go home."
- "[E]very time somebody gets mad, they are free to commit any crime they want, and they can be found not guilty by reason of insanity."

Id. at 697–703.

130. *Babbitt*, 45 Cal. 3d at 705.

131. ANGELA DAVIS, ARBITRARY JUSTICE: THE POWER OF THE AMERICAN PROSECUTOR 135 (2007). As Professor Davis explained elsewhere,

Defining the universe of prosecutorial misconduct is a difficult endeavor. Because it is so difficult to discover, much prosecutorial misconduct goes unchallenged, suggesting that the problem is much more widespread than the many reported cases of prosecutorial misconduct would indicate. As one editorial described the problem, "It would be like trying to count drivers who speed; the problem is larger than the number of tickets would indicate."

Angela Davis, *The Legal Profession's Failure to Discipline Unethical Prosecutors*, 36 HOFSTRA L. REV. 275, 278 (2007).

132. Marshall J. Hartman & Stephen L. Richards, *The Illinois Death Penalty: What Went Wrong?*, 34 J. MARSHALL L. REV. 409, 423 (2001).

133. Brent E. Newton, *A Case Study in Systemic Unfairness: The Texas Death Penalty, 1973–1994*, 1 TEX. F. ON C.L. & C.R. 1, 2–3 (1994); see also, Shannon Heery, *If It's Constitutional, Then What's the Problem? The Use of Judicial Override in Alabama Death Sentencing*, 34 WASH. U. J. L. & POL'Y 347, 381 (2010) (same, discussing imposition of death penalty in Alabama).

134. See e.g., Leigh B. Bienen, *Capital Punishment in Illinois in the Aftermath of the Ryan Commutations: Reforms, Economic Realities, and a New Saliency for Issues of Cost*, 100 J. CRIM. L.

& Criminology 1301, 1352 n. 207 (2010), discussing People v. Ramsey, 2010 WL 3911466 (Ill. Oct. 7, 2010).

135. Alafair S. Burke, *Revisiting Prosecutorial Disclosure*, 84 Ind. L. J. 481, 492–98 (2009); see also e.g., Susan Bandes, *Loyalty to One's Convictions: The Prosecutor and Tunnel Vision*, 49 How. L. J. 475 (2006); Daniel S. Medwed, *The Zeal Deal: Prosecutorial Resistance to Post-Conviction Claims of Innocence*, 84 B.U. L. Rev. 125, 138–48 (2004).

136. Bennett L. Gershman, *Mental Culpability and Prosecutorial Misconduct*, 26 Am. J. Crim. L. 121, 124 (1998).

137. On the special issues raised in jurisdictions in which prosecutors are elected, see Kenneth Bresler, *Seeking Justice, Seeking Election, and Seeking the Death Penalty: The Ethics of Prosecutorial Candidates' Campaigning on Capital Convictions*, 7 Geo. J. Legal Ethics 941, 947 (1994).

138. Stephen Bright, *The Death Penalty as the Answer to Crime: Costly, Counterproductive and Corrupting*, 36 Santa Clara L. Rev. 1069, 1076 (1996).

139. http://www.amnesty.org.uk/news_details.asp?NewsID=16777 (accessed May 23, 2012).

140. Jamie Fellner, *Beyond Reason: Executing Persons with Mental Retardation*, 28 Hum. Rts. 9, 12 (2002). See *supra* chapter 5.

141. Evan J. Mandery, *Executing the Insane, Retribution, and Temporal Justice*, 43 Crim. L. Bull. 981, 981–82 n. 7 (2007), quoting Andrea Weigl, *Limit to Death Penalty Sought; Bill Would Protect the Mentally Ill*, News & Observer, May 13, 2007, at B1 (noting opposition by prosecutors to a North Carolina bill excluding the mentally ill from the reach of the state death penalty statute), and Mike Smith, *Bill Would Ban Executions of Mentally Ill*, The Associated Press, Jan. 23, 2001 (noting that the Indiana Prosecuting Attorneys' Council opposes an Indiana bill to exclude the mentally ill on grounds that jurors "should be able to hear evidence and decide the issue of mental illness during the sentencing phases of capital cases" and out of concern with the "ever expanding list of what constitutes mental illness").

142. See *supra* chapter 3.

143. See Gardner v. Johnson, 247 F.3d 551, 556 n. 6 (5th Cir. 2001).

144. Russell Dean Covey, *Exorcizing Wechsler's Ghost: The Influence of the Model Penal Code on Death Penalty Sentencing Jurisprudence*, 31 Hastings Const. L. Q. 189, 257 n. 331 (2004), discussing Sterling v. Cockrell, No. Civ.A. 3:01-CV-2280, 2003 WL 21488632, at *20 (N.D. Tex., Apr. 23, 2003) (noting that state offered to make Dr. Grigson available as forensic psychiatric expert).

145. <("dr. james grigson") (james +2 grigson) & da(aft 1995)>(ALLSTATES database) (conducted May 24, 2012).

146. In Brady v. Maryland, 373 U.S. 83, 87 (1963), the Supreme Court ruled that "the suppression by the prosecution of evidence favorable to an accused upon request violates due process where the evidence is material either to guilt or to punishment, irrespective of the good faith or bad faith of the prosecution." The goal advanced by imposing meaningful sanctions for *Brady* violations is "not merely to punish the individual prosecutor but to ensure that the government does not feel empowered to violate constitutional mandates with impunity." Cynthia Jones, *A Reason to Doubt: The Suppression of Evidence and the Inference of Innocence* 100 J. Crim. L. & Criminology 415, 442 (2010).

147. Richard A. Rosen, *Disciplinary Sanctions against Prosecutors for Brady Violations: A Paper Tiger*, 65 N.C. L. Rev. 693, 701 n. 42 (1987), discussing Ashly v. Texas, 319 F.2d 80 (5th Cir. 1963) (suppression of evidence that both defendants were legally incompetent to stand trial); Powell v. Wiman, 287 F.2d 275 (5th Cir. 1961) (evidence of mental illness of key witness, including three different hospitalizations in mental institutions); Wallace v. State, 501 P.2d 1036 (Nev. 1972) (psychiatric report revealing defendant's mental illness that was relevant both to voluntariness of confession and to degree of guilt). Sanctions in *any Brady* case are virtually nonexistent. See *id.* at 730 (analyzing five-year study of *Brady* violations and finding only nine disciplinary actions taken). See also, Susan S. Kuo & C.W. Taylor, *In Prosecutors We Trust: UK Lessons for Illinois Disclosure*, 38 Loy. U. Chi. L. J. 695, 704–5 (2007), discussing research reported in Rosen, *supra*.

148. Steve Weinberg, *Turning on Their Own: A Group of Former Prosecutors Cites a Colleague's Pattern of Misconduct* (June 26, 2003), accessible at http://www.iwatchnews. org/2003/06/26/5522/turning-their-own; see also, Steve Weinberg, *Unbecoming Conduct: A Prosecutor in Nashville Is Accused of Manipulating Evidence to Send a Defendant to Death Row*, LEGAL AFF. 29 (Nov.–Dec. 2003) (same), discussing case of Abdur'Rahman v. Bell, 537 U.S. 88 (2003) (dismissing writ of *certiorari* as improvidently granted), and see Abdur'Rahman v. Bell, 999 F. Supp. 1073 (M.D. Tenn. 1998) (opinion below) (prosecutor's misconduct included suppression and misrepresentation of evidence of defendant's major mental illness).

149. Lara Bazelon, *Hard Lessons: The Role of Law Schools in Addressing Prosecutorial Misconduct*, 16 BERKELEY J. CRIM. L. 391, 399 n. 12 (2011), quoting *Preventable Error: A Report on Prosecutorial Misconduct in California 1997–2009*, NORTHERN CALIFORNIA INNOCENCE PROJECT, SANTA CLARA SCHOOL OF LAW (2010) (hereinafter *Preventable Error*).

150. Bennett L. Gershman, *The New Prosecutors*, 53 U. PITT. L. REV. 393, 445 (1992).

151. Minsker, *supra* note 128, at 400.

152. But see *id.*

153. See *supra* text accompanying note 114.

154. Ronald J. Tabak, *Finality without Fairness: Why We Are Moving towards Moratoria on Executions, and the Potential Abolition of Capital Punishment*, 33 CONN. L. REV. 733, 745 (2001). See generally, Stephen B. Bright et al., *Breaking the Most Vulnerable Branch: Do Rising Threats to Judicial Independence Preclude Due Process in Capital Cases?*, 31 COLUM. HUM. RTS. L. REV. 123 (1999).

155. Amanda Frost, *Defending the Majoritarian Court*, 2010 MICH. ST. L. REV. 757, 760 (2010), relying on Gregory A. Huber & Sanford C. Gordon, *Accountability and Coercion: Is Justice Blind When It Runs for Office?*, 48 AM. J. POLI. SCI. 247, 248, 258 (2004) (reviewing hundreds of decisions by elected Pennsylvania judges and concluding that "all judges, even the most punitive, increase their sentences as reelection nears"); Richard R.W. Brooks & Steven Raphael, *Life Terms or Death Sentences: The Uneasy Relationship between Judicial Elections and Capital Punishment*, 92 J. CRIM. L. & CRIMINOLOGY 609, 610 (2002) (finding that "criminal defendants [convicted of murder] were approximately 15 percent more likely to be sentenced to death when the sentence was issued during the judge's election year"). She notes further: "Their concerns are reasonable; judges have lost election because they were perceived as too lenient on criminal defendants." *Id.*

156. Sheri Johnson et al., *The Delaware Death Penalty: An Empirical Study*, IOWA L. REV. (2012), accessible at http://papers.ssrn.com/sol3/papers.cfm?abstract_id=2019913, manuscript at 39.

157. Harris v. Alabama, 513 U.S. 504, 521 (1995) (Stevens, J., dissenting).

158. Liebman, *supra* note 116, at 2113 n. 197 (quoting Alan Berlow, *The Wrong Man*, THE ATLANTIC MONTHLY, Nov. 1999, at 66, 80.

159. See Kansas v. March, 548 U.S. 163, 206 (2006) (Souter, J., dissenting), discussing *Roper v. Simmons*, 543 U.S. 551, 568 (2005) ("Capital punishment must be limited to those offenders who commit 'a narrow category of the most serious crimes' and whose extreme culpability makes them 'the most deserving of execution'").

160. See *supra* chapter 4.

161. See *supra* chapters 5 & 6.

162. See *supra* chapter 3.

CHAPTER 10

1. The first section and small portions of the second and third sections of this chapter are adapted from Michael L. Perlin, *"The Executioner's Face Is Always Well-Hidden": The Role of Counsel and the Courts in Determining Who Dies*, 41 N.Y. L. SCH. L. REV. 201 (1996).

2. 428 U.S. 153 (1976).

3. See *id.* at 187; James S. Liebman & Michael J. Shepard, *Guiding Capital Sentencing Discretion Beyond the "Boiler Plate": Mental Disorder as a Mitigating Factor*, 66 GEO. L. J. 757 (1978); see generally, 4 MICHAEL L. PERLIN, MENTAL DISABILITY LAW: CIVIL AND CRIMINAL §§ 12-3 to 3.8 (2002) (2d ed.) (discussing the impact of mental disorder on the penalty phase of capital punishment litigation).

4. See State v. Morton, 715 A.2d 228, 277 (N.J. 1998) (Handler, J., dissenting in part), quoting this language from Perlin, *supra* note 1, at 202.

5. Stephen Bright, *Death by Lottery—Procedural Bar of Constitutional Claims in Capital Cases Due to Inadequate Representation of Indigent Defendants*, 92 W. VA. L. REV. 679, 695 (1990) (Bright, *Death by Lottery*); KENNETH WILLIAMS, MOST DESERVING OF DEATH? AN ANALYSIS OF THE SUPREME COURT'S DEATH PENALTY JURISPRUDENCE 18 (2012) (same); see also, Stephen Bright, *Counsel for the Poor: The Death Sentence Not for the Worst Crime, but for the Worst Lawyer*, 103 YALE L. J. 1835 (1994) (Bright, *Counsel for the Poor*); David Dow, *Teague and Death: The Impact of Current Retroactivity Doctrine on Capital Defendants*, 19 HASTINGS CONST. L. Q. 23, 61 (1991) (noting that the correlation is statistically significant); Gary Goodpaster, *The Trial for Life: Effective Assistance of Counsel in Death Penalty Cases*, 58 N.Y.U. L. REV. 299, 317 (1983) (explaining why counsel's role is even more critical in death cases than in other criminal prosecutions).

6. Welsh S. White, *Effective Assistance of Counsel in Capital Cases: The Evolving Standard of Care*, 1993 U. ILL. L. REV. 323, 361 (1993).

7. See *id.* at 340–41.

8. See *id.* at 342–43. It is especially critical that the lawyer be able to so prepare *expert* witnesses in matters related to mental disabilities. See Amy Murphy, *The Constitutional Failure of the Strickland Standard in Capital Cases under the Eighth Amendment*, 63 LAW & CONTEMP. PROBS. 179, 183 (Summer 2000).

9. See Welsch, *supra* note 6, at 344–45.

10. See *id.* at 368–74.

11. See *id.* at 356–68. See generally, Laurin Wollan, *Representing the Death Row Inmate: The Ethics of Advocacy, Collateral Style*, in FACING THE DEATH PENALTY: ESSAYS IN CRUEL AND UNUSUAL PUNISHMENT 92 (Michael L. Radelet, ed. 1989) (discussing the representation of death row inmates in collateral proceedings); James M. Doyle, *The Lawyers' Art: "Representation" in Capital Cases*, 8 YALE J. L. & HUMAN. 417 (1996) (discussing the importance of shaping a client's image). On the intractable question of an attorney's responsibility when her client desires to waive postconviction proceedings in a capital case, see State v. Martini, 677 A.2d. 1106 (N.J. 1996) (holding that defendant could not waive postconviction purview).

12. On the role of counsel generally in death penalty cases, see TASK FORCE ON DEATH PENALTY HABEAS CORPUS, AMERICAN BAR ASS'N, TOWARD A MORE JUST AND EFFECTIVE SYSTEM OF REVIEW IN STATE DEATH PENALTY CASES 49–76 (1990) (ABA REPORT); AMERICAN BAR ASSOCIATION'S GUIDELINES FOR THE APPOINTMENT AND PERFORMANCE OF DEFENSE COUNSEL IN DEATH PENALTY CASES (2003) (ABA GUIDELINES); Panel Discussion, *The Death of Fairness: Counsel Competency and Due Process in Death Penalty Cases*, 31 HOUS. L. REV. 1105 (1994); Stephen B. Bright, *The Right to Counsel in Death Penalty and Other Criminal Cases: Neglect of the Most Fundamental Right and What We Should Do about It*, 11 J. L. SOC'Y 1 (2010); Eric M. Freedman, *Re-Stating the Standard of Practice for Death Penalty Counsel: The Supplementary Guidelines for the Mitigation Function of Defense Teams in Death Penalty Cases*, 36 HOFSTRA L. REV. 663 (2008); Donald Hall, *Effectiveness of Counsel in Death Penalty Cases*, 42 BRANDEIS L. J. 225 (2003–2004). On the role of counsel generally, see Symposium, *Toward a More Effective Right to Assistance of Counsel*, 58 LAW & CONTEMP. PROBS. 1–138 (Winter 1995).

13. White, *supra* note 6, at 376 (emphasis added). See McFarland v. Scott, 512 U.S. 1256, 1256–57 (1994) (Blackmun, J., dissenting from denial of *certiorari*) ("Without question, 'the principal failings of the capital punishment review process today are the inadequacy and inadequate compensation of counsel at trial and the unavailability of counsel in state post-conviction pro-

ceedings,'" quoting Ira Robbins, *Toward a More Just and Effective System of Review in State Death Penalty Cases, Report of the American Bar Association's Recommendations Concerning Death Penalty Habeas Corpus*, 40 Am. U. L. Rev. 1, 16 (1990)). See also, Carol Steiker & Jordan Steiker, *Part II: Report to the ALI Concerning Capital Punishment*, 89 Tex. L. Rev. 367, 385 (2010), discussing the "repeated accounts of extraordinarily poor lawyering in capital cases."

14. http://legis.wisconsin.gov/lrb/pubs/rb/06rb02.pdf. For one chilling first-person account, see Ernest Rideau, In the Place of Justice: A Story of Punishment and Deliverance (2011) (Rideau was the defendant in Rideau v. Louisiana—373 U.S. 723) (1963) (reversing death penalty conviction for failure to change venue).

15. Note, *The Eighth Amendment and Ineffective Assistance of Counsel in Capital Trials*, 107 Harv. L. Rev. 1923, 1923 (1994) (emphasis added) (citing ABA Report, *supra* note 12, at 7); see also Goodpaster, *supra* note 5, at 302). For a thoughtful analysis of one state's system, see Rebecca Copeland, *Getting It Right from the Beginning: A Critical Examination of Current Criminal Defense in Texas and Proposal for a Statewide Public Defender System*, 32 St. Mary's L. J. 493, 497 (2001) (quoting Texas Civil Rights Project's report, representation in Texas is part of "a grossly flawed system that appoints attorneys who are often incompetent to represent poor people," and see *id.* at 498 n. 10 (listing cases in which death penalty defendants in Texas raised postconviction ineffectiveness-of-counsel claims). Professor Sharon Dolovich goes even further, arguing that the case law reflects not just "serious incompetence but even *incapacitation* on the part of counsel." Sharon Dolovich, *Legitimate Punishment in Liberal Democracy*, 7 Buff. Crim. L. rev. 307, 436 (2004), and see *id.*, n. 291 (citing cases).

There is strong empirical evidence that a dedicated, organized public defender system does far better than an assigned counsel system. See Robert Smith, *The Geography of the Death Penalty and Its Ramifications*, 92 B.U. L. Rev. 227, 260–62 (2012):

> Philadelphia has a reputation as having one of the best public defender offices but worst private bars in the country. The public defender office is not responsible for a single death sentence from 2004 to 2009 despite handling 20% of the capital cases in the city. This is no accident. The *261 defender office assigns cases to experienced capital trial lawyers who begin mitigation investigation from the earliest possible moments, engage in aggressive pretrial litigation (filing motions that challenge the validity of the prosecution, seeking to exclude illegally obtained evidence, etc.), and are willing to spend the hours necessary to build the trust needed for a client to take a plea to a sentence less than death (often life without parole). When cases go to trial—something that is rare among the public defender office cases—the lawyers conduct comprehensive voir dire to ensure that people who could not genuinely consider a sentence less than death are excluded while those citizens who would consider both punishments are not excluded. They build a narrative for why the client should receive life, and they integrate lay and expert witnesses to help the jury understand that story. In short, they provide solid representation.
>
> Then there is the private bar. The first problem is structural. Private lawyers receive a maximum of $2000 to prepare for a capital trial and then $400 for each day of trial. The incentives are terribly wrong. Good capital trial lawyers avoid death sentences by avoiding trial as often as possible. Doing so requires resources to be concentrated at the front-end of the case rather than at trial. . . . For salaried public defenders, despite the fact that they, too, are severely overworked and under-resourced, the incentive is to spend the hours at the start of the case and avoid trial. For most private lawyers who are capped at $2000 unless they get to trial, it is not difficult to imagine how few hours they spend visiting the client pretrial.

16. Note, *supra* note 15, at 1923.

17. See Bruce A. Green, *Lethal Fiction: The Meaning of "Counsel" in the Sixth Amendment*, 78 Iowa L. Rev. 433, 433 (1993).

18. Douglas W. Vick, *Poorhouse Justice: Underfunded Indigent Defense Services and Arbitrary Death Sentences*, 43 Buff. L. Rev. 329, 397–98 (1995). For a numbing account of criminal justice

defense services provided in many states, see AMY BACH, ORDINARY INJUSTICE—HOW AMERICA HOLDS COURT (2009). For an analysis in one state, see Justine Finney Guyer, *Saving Missouri's Public Defender System: A Call for Adequate Legislative Funding*, 74 Mo. L. REV. 335, 360 (2009) ("Missouri's public defender system is being crushed by the weight of excessive caseloads").

19. Stephanie Saul, *When Death Is the Penalty: Attorneys for Poor Defendants Often Lack Experience and Skill*, N.Y. NEWSDAY, Nov. 25, 1991, at 8.

20. See Marcia Coyle et al., *Fatal Defense: Trial and Error in the Nation's Death Belt*, NAT'L L. J., June 11, 1990, at 30.

21. *Id.*

22. Saul, *supra* note 19, at 8.

23. Coleman v. Kemp, 778 F.2d 1487, 1522 (11th Cir. 1985).

24. ABA REPORT, *supra* note 12, at 52–53 (citations omitted). See Carol Steiker and Jordan Steiker, *Sober Second Thoughts: Reflections on Two Decades of Constitutional Regulation of Capital Punishment*, 109 HARV. L. REV. 355, 421 (1995): "Perhaps the most significant source of inequality in the administration of the death penalty is the unevenness of representation."

25. Robert Weisberg, *Who Defends Capital Defendants?*, 35 SANTA CLARA L. REV. 535, 537 (1995). For examples of cases litigated on appeal by Weisberg, see Mitchell v. Kemp, 762 F.2d 886 (11th Cir. 1985); Holtan v. Parratt, 683 F.2d 1163 (8th Cir. 1982); People v. Cummings, 850 P.2d 1 (Cal. 1993).

26. Vick, *supra* note 18, at 410. See also, The Constitution Project, *Smart on Crime: Recommendations for the Administration and Congress*, accessible at http://www.besmartoncrime. org/11_history.php:

> Indigent defense attorneys are overworked, underpaid, and too often lack independence and the necessary experience and skills to effectively represent their clients—especially in capital cases. With such inadequate resources, capital defendants are at a greater risk of facing death sentences that are arbitrary and unfair.

27. See *Mental Health and Human Rights: Report of the Task Panel on Legal and Ethical Issues*, 20 ARIZ. L. REV. 49, 62 (1978), discussed in Michael L. Perlin, *Unpacking the Myths: The Symbolism Mythology of Insanity Defense Jurisprudence*, 40 CASE W. RES. L. REV. 599, 654 (1989–1990). On the special competencies needed by defense counsel in *all* cases involving defendants with mental disabilities, see e.g., Danielle Laberge & Daphne Morin, *Evaluating the Case, Evaluating the Cost: Criteria for Constructing the Defense Strategy of Persons Suffering from Mental Illness*, 7 SOC'L DISTRESS & THE HOMELESS 189 (1988).

28. See e.g., Melody Martin, *Defending the Mentally Ill Client in Criminal Matters: Ethics, Advocacy, and Responsibility*, 52 U. TORONTO FAC. L. REV. 73 (1993) (discussing ethical issues facing counsel in cases involving mentally disabled criminal defendants); Kenneth B. Nunn, *The Trial as Text: Allegory, Myth, and Symbols in the Adversarial Criminal Process: A Critique of the Role of the Public Defender and a Proposal for Reform*, 32 AM. CRIM. L. REV. 743 (1995) (discussing myth in criminal cases); *Michael L. Perlin, Fatal Assumption: A Critical Evaluation of the Role of Counsel in Mental Disability Cases*, 16 LAW & HUM. BEHAV. 39 (1992) (discussing myth in mental disability cases); Vick, *supra* note 18 (discussing myth in criminal cases). On how lawyers' self-image may be negatively affected by their representation of persons with mental disabilities, see Laberge & Morin, *supra* note 27, at 203–5.

29. See *supra* chapter 4.

30. http://www.nmha.org/go/position-statements/54. On the question of whether serious mental illness should be an absolute bar on capital punishment, see *supra* chapter 6. See generally, Christopher Slobogin, *What Atkins Could Mean for People with Mental Illness*, 33 N.MEX. L. REV. 293 (2003); Bruce Winick, *The Supreme Court's Evolving Death Penalty Jurisprudence: Severe Mental Illness as the Next Frontier*, 50 B.C. L. REV. 785 (2009); Robert Batey, *Categorical Bars to Execution: Civilizing the Death Penalty*, 45 HOUS. L. REV. 1493 (2009).

31. 31 Hofstra L. Rev. 913 (2003).

32. *ABA Commentary*, 4.1, at 959.

33. Leona D. Jochnowitz, *How Capital Jurors Respond to Mitigating Evidence of Defendant's Mental Illness, Retardation, and Situational Impairments: An Analysis of the Legal and Social Science Literature*, 47 Crim. L. Bull. 839, 840 (2011).

34. On sanism in general, see *supra* chapter 2. Heuristics are simplifying cognitive devices that frequently lead to systematically erroneous decisions through ignoring or misusing rationally useful information that can contaminate the legal process. See Michael L. Perlin, *"They Keep It All Hid": The Ghettoization of Mental Disability Law and Its Implications for Legal Education*, 54 St. Louis U. L. J. 857, 875 (2010); see *supra* chapter 9 for a full discussion.

35. American Bar Association, *Guidelines for the Appointment and Performance of Defense Counsel in Death Penalty Cases*, 31 Hofstra L. Rev. 913, 1007–8 (Summer 2003), Commentary to Guideline 10.5. On the use of experts, see Alan Clarke, *Procedural Labyrinths and the Injustice of Death: A Critique of Death Penalty Habeas Corpus (Part One)*, 29 U. Rich. L. Rev. 1327, 1374 (1995):

> It is not easy for lawyers, who may lack insight into the process, to see how use of mental health experts can, without testifying to insanity, place the crime, which may otherwise appear to be inexplicable, in a mitigating context that allows the jury to see the accused as a flawed person rather than as a less than human monster.

36. See *supra* text accompanying note 19.

37. John H. Blume, Sheri L. Johnson, & Susan E. Millor, *Convicting Lennie: Mental Retardation, Wrongful Convictions, and the Right to a Fair Trial*, 56 N.Y. L. SCH. L. REV. 943, 955–56 (2011–12).

38. Michael Mello, *Facing Death Alone: The Post-Conviction Attorney Crisis on Death Row*, 37 Am. U. L. Rev. 513, 550 (1988).

39. Rebecca Dick-Hurwitz, Penry v. Lynaugh: *The Supreme Court Deals a Fatal Blow to Mentally Retarded Capital Defendants*, 51 U. Pitt. L. Rev. 699, 724 (1990).

40. *Atkins*, 536 U.S. at 321.

41. James Liebman, *The Overproduction of Death*, 100 Colum. L. Rev. 2030, 2108 n. 185 (2000).

42. See e.g., Jeffrey Wertkin, *Competency to Stand Trial*, 90 Geo. L. J. 1514, 1515–16 n. 1308 (2002), citing cases.

43. John Blume & Emily Paavola, *Life, Death, and Neuroimaging: The Advantages and Disadvantages of the Defense's Use of Neuroimages in Capital Cases—Lessons from the Front*, 62 Mercer L. Rev. 909 (2011). On how neuroimaging may play a role (or not) in determinations of whether a defendant is competent to be executed, see e.g., Michael L. Perlin, *"Good and Bad, I Defined These Terms, Quite Clear No Doubt Somehow": Neuroimaging and Competency to Be Executed after* Panetti, 28 Behav. Sci. & L. 621 (2010). This issue is discussed extensively *supra* chapter 8.

44. See Michael L. Perlin, *"And I See through Your Brain": Access to Experts, Competency to Consent, and the Impact of Antipsychotic Medications in Neuroimaging Cases in the Criminal Trial Process*, 2009 Stanford Technol. L. J. 1.

45. Michael L. Perlin, *The Sanist Lives of Jurors in Death Penalty Cases: The Puzzling Role of Mitigating Mental Disability Evidence*, 8 Notre Dame J. L., Ethics & Pub. Pol. 239, 278 (1994). See Pamela Wilkins, *Competency for Execution: The Implications of a Communicative Model of Retribution*, 76 Tenn. L. Rev. 713, 728 (2009) (the use of such medication makes it difficult for "jurors to see in the defendant's expression any indications of remorse or even humanity"), citing Scott E. Sundby, *The Jury as Critic: An Empirical Look at How Capital Juries Perceive Expert and Lay Testimony*, 83 Va. L. Rev. 1109, 1168–69 (1997).

The question of competency to be executed—with special attention being paid to involuntary medication issues—is discussed *supra* chapter 7.

46. Sanjay K. Chhablani, *Chronically Stricken: A Continuing Legacy of Ineffective Assistance of Counsel*, 28 ST. LOUIS PUB. L. J. 351, 363 (2009), citing Stephen Henderson, *Defense Often Inadequate in 4 Death-Penalty States*, McCLATCHY NEWSPAPERS, Jan. 16, 2007, available at http://www.mcclatchydc.com/201/story/15394.html.

47. Liliana Lyra Jubilut, *Death Penalty and Mental Illness: The Challenge of Reconciling Human Rights, Criminal Law, and Psychiatric Standards*, 6 SEATTLE J. FOR SOC. JUST. 353, 378–79 (2007) (emphasis added).

48. John Blume & Pamela Blume Leonard, *Capital Cases*, 24 THE CHAMPION 63, 63 (Nov. 2000).

49. 466 U.S. 668, 668 (1984).

50. See generally, 4 PERLIN, *supra* note 3, § 12-3.6, at 177–88; see also e.g., Ivan K. Fong, *Ineffective Assistance of Counsel at Capital Sentencing*, 39 STAN. L. REV. 461, 461–62 (1987); William S. Geimer, *A Decade of Strickland's Tin Horn: Doctrinal and Practical Undermining of the Right to Counsel*, 4 WM. & MARY BILL OF RTS. J. 91, 93 (1995). Although there have been multiple cases in which *Strickland* violations have been found—see *infra* text accompanying notes 87–95—there is no dispute that the "sterile and perfunctory" standard established in *Strickland*, see Perlin, *supra* note 28, at 53, has made such reversals relatively rare. See Michael L. Perlin & Valerie McClain, *"Where Souls Are Forgotten": Cultural Competencies, Forensic Evaluations and International Human Rights*, 15 PSYCHOL., PUB. POL'Y & L. 257, 260 (2009).

51. Text accompanying footnotes 52–66 is adapted from 2 PERLIN, *supra* note 3, § 2B-11.2 at 261–67 (2d ed. 1998).

52. *Strickland*, 466 U.S. at 686.

53. *Id.* at 687.

54. *Id.* at 688.

55. *Id.* at 687–88.

56. *Id.* at 689.

57. *Id.* at 691.

58. *Id.* at 693.

59. *Id.*

60. *Id.* at 694.

61. Applying these principles to the case before the Court was "not difficult." It found that respondent's trial counsel's conduct "cannot be found unreasonable," and that, even assuming unreasonableness, "respondent suffered insufficient prejudice to warrant setting aside his death sentence." The Court characterized trial counsel as having made a "strategic choice," with nothing in the record showing that his "sense of hopelessness distorted his professional judgment, and the decision not to seek more character or psychological evidence than was already in hand was likewise reasonable." In short, "[f]ailure to make the required showing of either deficient performance or sufficient prejudice defeats the ineffectiveness of the claim."

"More generally," the Court concluded, "respondent has made no showing that the justice of his sentence was rendered unreliable by a breakdown in the adversary process caused by deficiencies in counsel's assistance"; thus, "the sentencing proceeding was not fundamentally unfair." *Id.* at 698–700. See MICHAEL L. PERLIN, THE JURISPRUDENCE OF THE INSANITY DEFENSE 148–54 (1995).

62. *Strickland*, 466 U.S. at 706.

63. *Id.* at 707.

64. *Id.* at 708. Justice Marshall characterized the standard as suffering from a "debilitating ambiguity," *id.*, which will likely "stunt the development of Constitutional doctrine in this area," *id.* at 709.

Justice Brennan filed a separate opinion, concurring in part and dissenting in part. *Id.* at 701.

65. See Graham v. Collins, 829 F. Supp. 204, 209 (S.D. Tex. 1993).

66. See Paradis v. Arave, 954 F.2d 1483, 1490–92 (9th Cir. 1992).

67. See Haney v. State, 603 So. 2d 368, 377–78 (Ala. Crim. App. 1991).

68. See Young v. Zant, 677 F.2d 792, 797 (11th Cir. 1982).

69. Welsh S. White, *Capital Punishment's Future*, 91 MICH. L. REV. 1429, 1436 (1993) (reviewing RAYMOND PATERNOSTER, CAPITAL PUNISHMENT IN AMERICA (1991)). For other examples, see Stephen Bright, *The Death Penalty as the Answer to Crime: Costly, Counterproductive, and Corrupting*, 31 SANTA CLARA L. REV. 1068, 1078–84 (1996); Christine Wisermen, *Representing the Condemned: A Critique of Capital Punishment*, 79 MARQ. L. REV. 731, 742–44 (1996); see also e.g., Meredith J. Duncan, *The (So-Called) Liability of Criminal Defense Attorneys: A System in Need of Reform*, 2002 B.Y.U. L. REV. 1, 18–20 (2002) (noting that "[t]he unfortunate aftermath of *Strickland* is that a criminally accused's right to the effective assistance of counsel does not have much substance to it at all" and that "even though the Court professed to fashion a test that would lead to the just review of ineffective assistance of counsel claims, it is doubtful whether ineffective assistance of counsel claims are currently justly reviewed").

The Supreme Court has also construed *Strickland* narrowly in other contexts. See e.g., Smith v. Spisak, 130 S. Ct. 676 (2010) (defendant not prejudiced by inadequate closing argument at penalty phase).

70. William J. Genego, *The Future of Effective Assistance of Counsel: Performance Standards and Competent Representation*, 22 AM. CRIM. L. REV. 181, 182 (1984).

71. *Id.* at 196. See, for a comprehensive set of specific performance standards embodying an "efficient and functional assistance test," Note, *The Standard for Effective Assistance of Counsel in Pennsylvania—An Effective Method of Ensuring Competent Defense Representation*, 89 DICKINSON L. REV. 41, 69–71 (1985).

For excellent early reviews of all relevant issues, see Richard Klein, *The Relationship of the Court and Defense Counsel: The Impact of Competent Representation and Proposals for Reform*, 29 B.C. L. REV. 531 (1988); Melody Martin, *Defending the Mentally III Client in Criminal Matters: Ethics, Advocacy, and Responsibility*, 52 U. TORONTO FAC. L. REV. 73 (1993); Geimer, *supra* note 50; Jeffrey Kirchmeier, *Drink, Drugs, and Drowsiness: The Constitutional Right to Effective Assistance of Counsel and the* Strickland *Prejudice Requirement*, 75 NEB. L. REV. 425 (1996). For more recent considerations of *Strickland*, see e.g., Eve Brensike Primus, *Structural Reform in Criminal Defense: Relocating Ineffective Assistance of Counsel Claims*, 92 CORNELL L. REV. 679 (2007); Robert R. Rigg, *The T-Rex without Teeth: Evolving* Strickland v. Washington *and the Test for Ineffective Assistance of Counsel*, 35 PEPP. L. REV. 77 (2007).

72. PERLIN, *supra* note 61, at 16, citing Genego, *supra* note 70, at 196–98, 209–11. See also Note, *The Ineffective Assistance of Counsel Quandary: The Debate Continues*, 18 AKRON L. REV. 325, 334 (1984) (Strickland's seemingly "objective" test is "poisoned with obtrusive subjectivity"); Note, 14 U. BALT. L. REV. 335, 344, 345 (1985) (*Strickland* Court's analysis of ineffective counsel claims "self-defeating"; case's result "very well may be the expeditious disposal, if not the outright discouragement, of ineffective assistance allegations, rather than the protection of the fundamental fairness of the proceedings in such claims"). But *cf.* State v. Nash, 694 P.2d 222, 228 (Ariz. 1985) (adopting *Strickland* because its "objective standard provides better guidance to lawyers and judges" than would a "more subjective" test).

73. Genego, *supra* note 70, at 202.

74. *Id.* For a pre-*Strickland* analysis of the economic, psychological, and social factors contributing to counsel's ineffectiveness, concluding that, "unless courts are willing to police the attorney, they should candidly admit that the call for 'effective representation' is simply rhetoric," see Peter Tague, *The Attempt to Improve Criminal Defense Representation*, 15 AM. CRIM. L. REV. 109, 165 (1977).

75. Perlin & McClain, *supra* note 50, at 261. See also, Nicola Browne et al., *Capital Punishment and Mental Health Issues: Global Examples*, 25 ST. LOUIS U. PUB. L. REV. 383, 385 (2006) (case examples from other nations provide a "strong example of how important it is in

any country work to grasp fully the complex socio-cultural and socio-legal background before developing any penal policy strategies").

76. 469 U.S. 956 (1984).

77. See *id.* at 956 (discussing Michael L. Radelet & George W. Barnard, *Treating Those Found Incompetent for Execution: Ethical Chaos with Only One Solution*, 16 BULL. AM. ACAD. PSYCHIATRY & L. 297, 300 (1988)); *cf.* People v. Frierson, 705 P.2d 396 (Cal. 1985) (holding that defense counsel could not refuse to honor defendant's clearly expressed desire to present diminished capacity defense at guilt/special circumstances phase of death penalty case; question was not merely a tactical decision).

78. *Alvord*, 469 U.S. at 963.

79. But see Wood v. Allen, 130 S. Ct. 841 (2010) (argument that state-court decision involved unreasonable application of *Strickland*—because counsel failed to make reasonable investigation of petitioner's mental deficiencies before deciding not to pursue or present such evidence—was not "fairly included" in questions presented and thus would not be addressed by Court); Cullen v. Pinholster, 131 S. Ct. 1388 (2011) (state court could have reasonably concluded that petitioner failed to rebut presumption of competence mandated by *Strickland*, and could have reasonably concluded that petitioner was not prejudiced by counsel's allegedly deficient performance).

80. Williams v. Taylor, 529 U.S. 362 (2000). As pointed out by Professors Carol and Jordan Steiker, "Williams' trial lawyer failed to uncover dramatic evidence of his client's extreme mistreatment, abuse, and neglect as a child, testimony that his client was borderline mentally retarded and might have organic mental impairments, and *powerful testimony from the state's own experts that Williams might not pose a danger in the future if incarcerated rather than executed.*" Carol Steiker & Jordan Steiker, *Opening a Window or Building a Wall?: The Effect of Eighth Amendment Death Penalty Law and Advocacy on Criminal Justice More Broadly*, 11 U. PA. J. CONST. L. 155, 194 (2008); see *Williams*, 529 U.S. at 370.

81. See e.g., Rompilla v. Beard, 545 U.S. 374 (2005) (failure to adequately investigate is ineffective assistance of counsel); Wiggins v. Smith, 539 U.S. 510 (2003) (same). See, however, Kenneth Williams, *Does* Strickland *Prejudice Defendants on Death Row?* 43 U. RICH. L. REV. 1459, 1461 (2009) (survey of lower court decisions both before and after *Wiggins* indicates that capital defendants did not achieve any greater success in obtaining relief after *Wiggins* than they did before *Wiggins*).

82. 550 U.S. 465 (2007).

83. *Id.* at 482 (Stevens, J., dissenting).

84. *Id.* at 478–81.

85. See Carissa Byrne Hessick, *Ineffective Assistance at Sentencing*, 50 B.C. L. REV. 1069, 1076 (2009) (*Strickland* is "a shield for counsel's behavior against judicial scrutiny.")

86. See generally *supra* chapter 6. See Leona D. Jochnowitz, *Missed Mitigation: Counsel's Evolving Duty to Assess and Present Mitigation at Death Penalty Sentencing*, 43 CRIM. L. BULL. 3 (2007); Jochnowitz, *supra* note 33.

There are other examples of courts declining to find *Strickland* violations in cases involving other sorts of errors related to the trials of defendants with mental disabilities. See e.g., People v. Haynes, 737 N.E.2d 169 (Ill. 2000) (counsel's failure to advise defendant of his right to remain silent during examinations by state's psychiatric expert did not prejudice defendant). ABA guidelines have also considered other similar potential violations. See guideline 4.1, Commentary: "It is simply ineffective assistance for counsel to permit a mental health assessment of the client to occur before having made a reasoned decision about the purpose of the examination and having provided the examiner with the data necessary to reach a professionally competent conclusion respecting the question presented."

87. 316 F.3d 1079 (9th Cir. 2003).

88. 427 F.3d 623 (9th Cir. 2005).

89. 428 F.3d 1181 (9th Cir. 2005).

90. Compare Godinez v. Moran, 509 U.S. 389, 410–11 (1993) (Blackmun, J., dissenting) (criticizing trial judge for failure to have made sufficient inquiry to discover that defendant, at the time of his guilty plea in a death penalty case, was being administered simultaneously four different prescription drugs—phenobarbital, dilantin, inderal, and vistaril—that in combination had a "numbing effect" on the defendant, who later stated, "I guess I really didn't care about anything. . . . I wasn't very concerned about anything that was going on . . . as far as the proceedings and everything were going."

91. 458 F.3d 892 (9th Cir. 2006).

92. 463 F.3d 982 (9th Cir. 2006).

93. Issues of mental retardation are discussed separately *supra* in chapter 5.

94. 465 F.3d 1006 (9th Cir. 2006).

95. 490 F.3d 1103 (9th Cir. 2007).

96. For a nearly nihilistic view, see Murphy, *supra* note 8, at 205: "A comparison of the cases that cleared the *Strickland* hurdle and those that did not suggests that all that really matters in [ineffective assistance of counsel] claims is the appellate court's view of the case."

97. A trial attorney with the US Department of Justice has recently written that "habeas litigants make ineffective assistance of counsel arguments so frequently that those claims have largely eclipsed any other assertion of a deprivation of constitutional rights." See Tom Zimpleman, *The Ineffective Assistance of Counsel Era*, 63 S.C. L. Rev. 425, 433 (2011), citing Ellen Kreitzberg & Linda Carter, *Innocent of a Capital Crime: Parallels between Innocence of a Crime and Innocence of the Death Penalty*, 42 Tulsa L. Rev. 437, 449 n. 73 (2006).

In addition to the cases discussed *supra* text accompanying notes 87–95, see e.g., Evans v. Lewis, 855 F.2d 631 (9th Cir. 1988) (trial counsel's failure to investigate defendant's mental condition, for purpose of presenting evidence of mental condition as mitigating factor in sentencing phase of capital murder trial, was ineffective assistance); Loyd v. Smith, 899 F.2d 1416 (5th Cir. 1990), *cert. denied*, 508 U.S. 911 (1993) (same); Kenley v. Armontrout, 937 F.2d 1298 (8th Cir.), *cert. denied*, 502 U.S. 964 (1991) (counsel ineffective for failure to present lay and expert mitigating evidence of defendant's medical and psychological history); Commonwealth v. Legg, 551 Pa. 437, 711 A.2d 430 (1998) (counsel ineffective for failing to present diminished capacity defense); Brewer v. Aiken, 935 F.2d 850 (7th Cir. 1991) (counsel ineffective for failure to investigate defendant's psychiatric history); State v. Lara, 581 So. 2d 1288 (Fla.), *reh'g denied* (1991) (counsel ineffective for failing to present mitigating evidence); Dumas v. State, 903 P.2d 816 (Nev. 1995) (failure of defense counsel to obtain neurological or psychiatric testimony was ineffective assistance of counsel); Bloom v. Calderon, 132 F.3d 1267 (9th Cir. 1997), *cert. denied*, 523 U.S. 1145 (1998) (same); Taylor v. State, 1999 WL 512149 (Tenn. Crim. App. 1999) (counsel ineffective for failing to present evidence or investigate evidence of defendant's extensive history of mental problems); Wilcoxson v. State, 22 S.W.3d 289 (Tenn. Crim. App. 1999), *appeal denied* (2000) (same); People v. Morgan, 187 Ill. 2d 500, 719 N.E.2d 681 (1999), *cert. denied*, 529 U.S. 1023 (2000) (same); Smith v. Stewart, 189 F.3d 1004 (9th Cir. 1999), *cert. denied*, 531 U.S. 952 (2000); see generally, 4 Perlin, *supra* note 3, § 12-3.6, at 507 n. 181.

98. The *Strickland* standard was eroded even further in Spriggs v. Collins, 993 F.2d 85 (5th Cir. 1993) (no violation of *Strickland* in noncapital sentencing case unless defendant can demonstrate that the sentence would have been "significantly" less severe). This modification was subsequently rejected by the Supreme Court in *Glover v. United States*, 531 U.S. 198, 204 (2001) ("We hold that the Seventh Circuit erred in engrafting this additional requirement onto the prejudice branch of the *Strickland* test").

For other examples of courts rejecting *Strickland*-based claims, see e.g., Mitchell v. Epps, 641 F.3d 134 (5th Cir. 2011); Williams v. Calderon, 41 F. Supp. 2d 1043 (C.D. Cal. 1998) (counsel failed to present evidence as to defendant's diminished capacity); Brown v. State, 698 N.E.2d 1132 (Ind. 1998), *reh'g denied* (1998), *cert. denied*, 526 U.S. 1056 (1999) (counsel failed to introduce evidence that defendant suffered from battered women's syndrome); United States ex rel. Mahaffey, 978 F. Supp. 762 (N.D. Ill. 1997), *vacated in part on rehearing on other grounds*, 162 F.3d 481 (7th Cir. 1998), *cert. denied*, 526 U.S. 1127 (1999) (counsel failed to have defendant examined by clinical psychologist); Harper v. Commonwealth, 978 S.W.2d 311 (Ky. 1998), *reh'g denied* (1998), *cert. denied*, 526 U.S. 1056 (1999) (counsel failed to retain independent mental health experts); Thomas v. Gilmore, 144 F.3d 513 (7th Cir. 1998), *reh'g & suggestion for reh'g en banc denied* (1998), *cert. denied*, 520 U.S. 1123 (1999) (counsel failed to subpoena school and prison records); Parkus v. Bowersox, 157 F.3d 1136 (8th Cir. 1998), *reh'g & suggestion for reh'g en banc denied* (1998), *cert. denied*, 527 U.S. 1043 (1999) (counsel failed to obtain medical records from state hospital); Jones v. State, 504 S.E.2d 822 (S.C. 1998), *reh'g denied* (1998), *cert. denied*, 526 U.S. 1021 (1999), *reh'g denied*, 526 U.S. 1128 (1999) (counsel failed to produce mitigating evidence); Bryan v. State, 935 P.2d 338 (Okla. Crim. App. 1997), *reh'g denied* (1997), *cert. denied*, 522 U.S. 957 (1997) (counsel failed to introduce evidence of mental illness); Catlett v. State, 962 S.W.2d 313 (Ark. 1998) (counsel failed to have defendant examined by mental health expert); see generally, 4 PERLIN, *supra* note 3, § 12-3.6, at 507 n. 181.

99. 551 U.S. 930 (2007). See *supra* chapter 6.

100. See *supra* chapter 8.

101. See e.g., Crittenden v. Ayers, 624 F.3d 943 (9th Cir. 2010); Lawrence v. McNeil, 2010 WL 2890576 (N.D. Fla. 2010); Card v. McNeil, 2010 WL 4945419 (N.D. Fla. 2010); Cole v. Workman, 2011 WL 3862143 (N.D. Okla. 2011); Smithers v. Secretary, Dept. of Corrections, 2011 WL 2446576 (M.D. Fla. 2011).

102. 100 Fed. Appdx. 128 (4th Cir. 2004), *cert. denied*, 542 U.S. 955 (2004).

103. See http://www.clarkprosecutor.org/html/death/US/bailey921.htm.

104. 532 U.S. 934 (2001) (denying *cert.*).

105. See http://www.clarkprosecutor.org/html/death/US/johnson750.htm.

106. 254 P.3d 320 (Cal. 2011).

107. 188 F.3d 518 (10th Cir. 1999), *cert. denied*, 529 U.S. 1042 (2000).

108. See http://www.amnesty.org/en/library/asset/AMR51/073/2000/en/e0216822-6678-4d99-878c-d4889a31edd9/amr510732000en.pdf.

109. Messer v. Kemp, 831 F.2d 946, 951 (11th Cir. 1987) (en banc), *cert. denied*, 485 U.S. 1029 (1988).

110. See Bright, *Counsel for the Poor*, *supra* note 5, at 1859–60 (discussing *Messer* case).

111. See Russell Stetler, *The Mystery of Mitigation: What Jurors Need to Make a Reasoned Moral Response in Capital Sentencing*, 11 U. PA. J. L. & SOC. CHANGE 237 (2007–2008).

112. Perlin & McClain, *supra* note 50, at 260.

113. ABA REPORT, *supra* note 12, at 55 (citation omitted).

114. Bright, *Death by Lottery*, *supra* note 5, at 683.

115. See generally *supra* chapter 2.

116. John Parry, *The Death Penalty and Persons with Mental Disabilities: A Lethal Dose of Stigma, Sanism, Fear of Violence, and Faulty Predictions of Dangerousness*, 29 MENTAL & PHYSICAL DISABILITY L. REP. 667 (2005).

117. See *id.* ("Nowhere is [the] prejudice [of sanism] more apparent than with capital punishment").

118. Michael L. Perlin, *"You Have Discussed Lepers and Crooks": Sanism in Clinical Teaching*, 9 CLINICAL L. REV. 683, 695 (2003).

119. Michael L. Perlin, *"And My Best Friend, My Doctor / Won't Even Say What It Is I've Got: The Role and Significance of Counsel in Right to Refuse Treatment Cases*, 42 SAN DIEGO L. REV. 735, 750 (2005).

120. See *supra* chapter 4.

121. See Ellen F. Berkman, *Mental Illness as an Aggravating Circumstance in Capital Sentencing*, 89 COLUM. L. REV. 291, 299–300 (1989); CHRISTOPHER SLOBOGIN, MINDING JUSTICE:

Laws That Deprive People with Mental Disabilities of Life and Liberty 90–96 (2006).

122. Miller v. State, 373 So. 2d 882, 885 (Fla. 1979) (vacating death sentence).

123. Perlin, *supra* note 119, at 752.

124. See Perlin, *supra* note 61, at 387–92.

125. Perlin, *supra* note 1, at 227.

126. See Michael L. Perlin, *Psychodynamics and the Insanity Defense: "Ordinary Common Sense" and Heuristic Reasoning*, 69 Neb. L. Rev. 3, 61–69 (1990). "[O]rdinary common sense" refers to a "self-referential and non-reflective" way of constructing the world: "I see it that way, therefore everyone sees it that way; I see it that way, therefore that's the way it is." See e.g., Michael L. Perlin, *"She Breaks Just Like a Little Girl": Neonaticide, the Insanity Defense, and the Irrelevance of Ordinary Common Sense*, 10 Wm. & Mary J. Women & L. 1, 8 (2003). See generally *supra* chapter 9.

127. See James M. Doyle, *The Lawyers' Art: "Representation" in Capital Cases*, 8 Yale J. L & Human. 417, 445 (1996) ("[T]here will be enormous pressures to craft a representation that earns the defendant membership in a preexisting, stereotypical category of 'acute' or 'extreme' illness, and to show that he fits into that category all of the time—that he is all sickness, no function").

128. See generally *supra* chapter 2.

129. Perlin, *supra* note 1, at 233.

130. See Ford v. Wainwright, 477 U.S. 399, 411 (1986) (opinion of Marshall, J.).

131. See generally Margaret Jane Radin, *Cruel Punishment and Respect for Persons: Super Due Process for Death*, 53 S. Cal. L. Rev. 1143 (1980).

132. I use this phrase self-consciously. This was the standard employed by the Supreme Court in assessing effectiveness of counsel claims prior to the decision in *Strickland*. See Trapnell v. United States, 725 F.2d 149, 151 (2d Cir. 1983) (citing to cases from all circuits adopting this standard).

133. Murphy, *supra* note 8, at 205.

134. See Frierson v. Woodford, 458 F.3d 892 (9th Cir. 2006), discussed *supra* text accompanying note 93.

135. See generally *supra* chapter 2. This section is adapted from Perlin, *supra* note 45, at 278–79.

136. See David B. Wexler, Rehabilitating Lawyers: Principles of Therapeutic Jurisprudence for Criminal Law Practice (2008); David B. Wexler, *A Tripartite Framework for Incorporating Therapeutic Jurisprudence in Criminal Law, Research, and Practice*, 7 Fla. Coastal L. Rev. 95 (2005); David B. Wexler, *Therapeutic Jurisprudence and the Rehabilitative Role of the Criminal Defense Lawyer*, 17 St. Thomas L. Rev. 743 (2005); David B. Wexler, *Some Reflections on Therapeutic Jurisprudence and the Practice of Criminal Law*, 38 Crim. L. Bull. 205 (2002). None of these articles, nor the most important, recent critique of Professor Wexler's approach to these questions—see Mae C. Quinn, *An RSVP to Professor Wexler's Warm Therapeutic Jurisprudence Invitation to the Criminal Defense Bar: Unable to Join You, Already (Somewhat Similarly) Engaged*, 48 B.C. L. Rev. 539 (2007), responded to in David B. Wexler, *Not Such a Party Pooper: An Attempt to Accommodate (Many of) Professor Quinn's Concerns about Therapeutic Jurisprudence Criminal Defense Lawyering*, 48 B.C. L. Rev. 597 (2007)—touches on these issues. On the use of TJ in a correctional context, see Astrid Birgden, A *Compulsory Drug Treatment Program for Offenders in Australia: Therapeutic Jurisprudence Implications*, 30 T. Jefferson L. Rev. 367 (2008); Astrid Birgden & Michael L. Perlin, *"Tolling for the Luckless, the Abandoned and Forsaked": Community Safety, Therapeutic Jurisprudence and International Human Rights Law as Applied to Prisoners and Detainees*, 13 Leg. & Criminol. Psychol. 231 (2008).

137. But see, Cynthia Adcock, *The Collateral Anti-Therapeutic Effects of the Death Penalty*, 11 Fla. Coastal L. Rev. 289 (2010), discussed *infra* text accompanying notes 144–45, and Winick, *supra* note 30, on the TJ values of barring the death penalty in cases involving defendants with serious mental disabilities (discussed *supra* chapter 6).

138. See Berkman, *supra* note 121; Slobogin, *supra* note 121.

139. 509 U.S. 389 (1993).

140. Compare Indiana v. Edwards, 554 U.S. 164 (2008) (Constitution permits states to insist upon representation by counsel for those who are competent enough to stand trial but who are sufficiently ill to be incompetent to conduct trial proceedings by themselves). On the relationship between *Godinez* and *Edwards*, see 4 MICHAEL L. PERLIN & HEATHER E. CUCOLO, MENTAL DISABILITY LAW: CIVIL AND CRIMINAL § 8B-3.1c(1), at 41–49 (2010 Cum. Supp).

141. See Michael L. Perlin, *"Dignity Was the First to Leave": Godinez v. Moran, Colin Ferguson, and the Trial of Mentally Disabled Criminal Defendants*, 14 BEHAV. SCI. & L. 61 (1996).

142. See ABA report, *supra* note 12, at 56.

143. Rebecca J. Covarrubias, *Lives in Defense Counsel's Hands: The Problems and Responsibilities of Defense Counsel Representing Mentally Ill or Mentally Retarded Capital Defendants*, 11 SCHOLAR 413, 466–67 (2009) (footnotes omitted).

144. Adcock, *supra* note 137, at 291–92.

145. *Id.* at 293. See David C. Yamada, *Therapeutic Jurisprudence and the Practice of Legal Scholarship*, 41 U. MEM. L. REV. 121, 138–39 (2010), discussing Adcock's work, and *id.* at 139 (Adcock "reminds us of emotional consequences of law and legal systems that are all too easy to ignore").

146. Perlin, *supra* note 1, at 235.

147. Blume & Leonard, *supra* note 48, at 63.

148. *Id.* at 71.

149. See also, John H. Blume & Pamela A. Wilkins, *Death by Default: State Procedural Default Doctrine in Capital Cases*, 50 S.C. L. REV. 1 (1998); Pamela Blume Leonard, *A New Profession for an Old Need: Why a Mitigation Specialist Must Be Included on the Capital Defense Team*, 31 HOFSTRA L. REV. 1143 (2003); John H. Blume, Sheri Lynn Johnson, & Scott E. Sundby, *Competent Capital Representation: The Necessity of Knowing and Heeding What Jurors Tell Us about Mitigation*, 36 HOFSTRA L. REV. 1035 (2008).

150. 33 INT'L J. L. & PSYCHIATRY 475 (2010).

151. *Id.* at 481.

152. David L. Bazelon, *The Defective Assistance of Counsel*, 42 U. CIN. L. REV. 1, 2 (1973). Elsewhere, Judge Bazelon wrote memorably and disparagingly about counsel he had observed in court who were no more than "a warm body with a legal pedigree." David L. Bazelon, *The Realities of Gideon and Argersinger*, 64 GEO. L. J. 811, 818–19 (1976).

CHAPTER 11

1. For helpful overviews, see Richard Wilson, *International Law Issues in Death Penalty Defense*, 31 HOFSTRA L. REV. 1195 (2003); KENNETH WILLIAMS, MOST DESERVING OF DEATH? AN ANALYSIS OF THE SUPREME COURT'S DEATH PENALTY JURISPRUDENCE 129–54 (2012).

2. See *supra* chapter 5.

3. 536 U.S. 304 (2002).

4. *Id.* at 316 n. 21: "[W]ithin the world community, the imposition of the death penalty for crimes committed by mentally retarded offenders is overwhelmingly disapproved. Brief for European Union as *Amicus Curiae* 4"; see also, Roper v. Simmons, 543 U.S. 551 (2005) (execution of juveniles violates the Eighth Amendment). Justice Scalia dissented vigorously in both cases (see *Atkins*, 536 U.S. at 337; *Roper*, 543 U.S. at 607). I characterize his *Atkins* dissent as a "pathetic recapitulation of . . . dreary myth" in Michael L. Perlin, *"Life is in Mirrors, Death Disappears": Giving Life to* Atkins, 33 N.M. L. REV. 315, 344 (2003).

5. See Hugo Bedeau, *Death Penalty Research: Today and Tomorrow*, in THE FUTURE OF AMERICA'S DEATH PENALTY: AN AGENDA FOR THE NEXT GENERATION OF CAPITAL PUNISHMENT RESEARCH 13, 15 (Charles S. Lanier et al., eds. 2009) ("How important will international

human rights law and relevant features of international experience with capital punishment be to the future of the death penalty in this country?").

6. See *supra* chapter 2.

7. See *supra* chapter 9.

8. See *supra* chapter 2.

9. See generally, Brian Anderson, *Roper v. Simmons: How the Supreme Court of the United States Has Established the Framework for Judicial Abolition of the Death Penalty in the United States*, 37 OHIO N. U. L. REV. 221, 240–41 (2011); THE ABOLITION OF THE DEATH PENALTY IN INTERNATIONAL LAW 23 (William A. Schabas, ed., 3d ed. 1997); *Human Rights and Human Wrongs: Is the United States Death Penalty System Inconsistent with International Human Rights Law?*, 67 FORDHAM L. REV. 2793 (1999) (Panel Discussion).

10. *Capital Punishment*, GA Res. 2857, U.N. GAOR, 26th Sess., U.N. Doc. A/RES/2857 (Dec. 20, 1971).

11. Protocol No. 6 to the European Convention for the Protection of Human Rights and Fundamental Freedoms, Mar. 1, 1985, Europ. T.S. 114. This Protocol, however, only bound states during peacetime. See Greta Proctor, *Reevaluating Capital Punishment: The Fallacy of a Foolproof System, the Focus on Reform, and the International Factor*, 42 GONZ. L. REV. 211, 221 (2006–2007). Any European state that wishes to join the Council of Europe must sign on to Protocol No. 6. *Id.* at 222. See generally, William A. Schabas, *International Law, Politics, Diplomacy and the Abolition of the Death Penalty*, 13 WM. & MARY BILL RTS. J. 417, 418–19 (2004). On the limited power of UN committees to enforce treaties, see Alexandra Harrington, *Don't Mind the Gap: The Rise of Individual Complaint Mechanisms within International Human Rights Treaties*, 22 DUKE J. COMP. & INT'L L. 153, 158 (2012).

12. Anderson, *supra* note 9, at 240, citing U.N. Econ. & Soc. Council (SCOSOC), *Safeguards Guaranteeing Protection of the Rights of Those Facing the Death Penalty*, U.N. Doc. E/RES/1984/50 (May 25, 1984).

13. Liliana Lyra Jubilut, *Death Penalty and Mental Illness: The Challenge of Reconciling Human Rights, Criminal Law, and Psychiatric Standards*, 6 SEATTLE J. FOR Soc. JUST. 353, 364 (2007).

14. Simon H. Fisherow, *Follow the Leader?: Japan Should Formally Abolish the Execution of the Mentally Retarded in the Wake of Atkins v. Virginia*, 14 PAC. RIM L. & POL'Y J. 455, 461 (2005); see also, Kristi Tumminello Prinzo, *The United States—"Capital" of the World: An Analysis of Why the United States Practices Capital Punishment While the International Trend Is towards Its Abolition*, 24 BROOK. J. INT'L L. 855, 862–63 (1999); James H. Wyman, *Vengeance Is Whose?: The Death Penalty and Cultural Relativism in International Law*, 6 J. TRANSNAT'L L. & POL'Y 543, 548 (1997).

15. Bruce Winick, *The Supreme Court's Evolving Death Penalty Jurisprudence: Severe Mental Illness as the Next Frontier*, 50 B.C. L. REV. 785, 819 (2009), citing Amnesty Int'l, *Abolitionist and Retentionist Countries*, http://www.amnesty.org/en/death-penalty/abolitionist-and-retentionist-countries (accessed Mar. 17, 2009).

16. Charter of Fundamental Rights of the European Union, 2000 O.J. (L 364/01) art. II, § 2.

17. Daniel J. Brown, *The International Criminal Court and Trial in Absentia*, 24 BROOK. J. INT'L L. 763, 777 (1999).

18. *Moratorium on the Use of the Death Penalty*, GA Res. 62/149, U.N. GAOR, 62nd Sess., U.N. Doc. A/RES/62/149 (Dec. 17, 2007).

19. See State v. Makwanyane, Case No. CTT/3/94 (South Africa CC, June 6, 1995), reprinted in 16 HUM. RTS. L. J. 154 (1995); William A. Schabas, *South Africa's New Constitutional Court Abolishes the Death Penalty*, 16 HUM. RTS. L. J. 133, 133 (1995). On South Africa and the death penalty, see SANGMIN BAE, WHEN THE STATE NO LONGER KILLS: INTERNATIONAL HUMAN RIGHTS NORMS AND ABOLITION OF CAPITAL PUNISHMENT 41–62 (2007).

20. Schabas, *supra* note 19, at 135.

21. See State v. Williams, Case No. CCT/20/94 (South African CC June 9, 1995).

22. On the monitoring of Human Rights Committees by special rapporteurs, see Schabas, *supra* note 9, at 433 (discussing the views of special rapporteur Bacre Waly Ndiaye, that "international human rights law seeks the abolition of the death penalty").

23. See Panel Discussion, *supra* note 9, at 2812 (comments of William A. Schabas).

24. Anderson, *supra* note 9, at 241. See also, David Johnson, *American Capital Punishment in Comparative Perspective*, 36 Law & Soc. Inquiry 1033, 1049 (2011) (reviewing David Garland, Peculiar Institution: America's Death Penalty in An Age of Abolition (2010)), discussing scholarship arguing that "international human rights norms have contributed to the decline of capital punishment in various contexts." On the number of nations that have abolished the death penalty, see *id.* (138 abolitionist in law or practice); on the development of the trend toward abolition, see Richard C. Dieter, *The Death Penalty and Human Rights: U.S. Death Penalty and International Law* 2–3 (2003), accessible at http://www.deathpenaltyinfo.org/Oxfordpaper.pdf; on de facto abolitionist nations, see Eric Neumayer, *Death Penalty: The Political Foundations of the Global Trend towards Abolition*, 9 Hum. Rts. Rev. 241, 248 (2008) (listing twenty de facto abolitionist countries).

25. http://www.amnesty.org/en/death-penalty/abolitionist-and-retentionist-countries. For a discussion of variances in African death penalty practices, see Nicola Browne et al., *Capital Punishment and Mental Health Issues: Global Examples*, 25 St. Louis U. Pub. L. Rev. 383 (2006). On "American exceptionalism" as it relates to domestic death penalty support, see Bae, *supra* note 19, at 88–91.

26. Thomas H. Koenig & Michael L. Rustad, *Book Review: Deciding Whether the Death Penalty Should Be Abolished*, 44 Suffolk U. L. Rev. 193, 207 (2011) (reviewing Russell G. Murphy, Voices of the Death Penalty Debate: A Citizen's Guide to Capital Punishment (2010); Peter Norbert Bouchkaert, *Shutting Down the Death Factory: The Abolition of Capital Punishment in South Africa*, 32 Stan. J. Int'l L. 287, 323 (1996) ("The United States . . . , among the democratic nations, is becoming increasingly isolated in its use of the death penalty"). Interestingly, scholars have found that when authoritarian states—such as South Korea—become more democratic, recourse to capital punishment declines. See Carolyn Hoyle, *Book Review* 45 Law & Soc'y Rev. 513, 514 (2011) (reviewing David T. Johnson & Franklin E. Zimring, The Next Frontier: National Development, Political Change, and the Death Penalty in Asia (2009); see also, Bae, *supra* note 19, at 663–84 (discussing the death penalty in South Korea).

When New Jersey abolished the death penalty, in 2007, it did so to international acclaim. See James B. Johnston, *Executing Capital Punishment Via Case Study: A Socratic Chat about New Jersey's Abolition of the Death Penalty and Convincing Other States to Follow Suit*, 34 J. Legis. 1, 1 (2008), quoting John Farmer, *Rule of Law Prevailed or Did It?*, Newark Star Ledger, Jan. 13, 2008, at B2; see also, Henry Gottlieb, *An End to Death Penalty Pretense*, N.J. Law Journal, Dec. 31, 2007, at 1 ("Rome lit up the coliseum, once used for gory executions, to celebrate New Jersey's decision to abolish capital punishment").

27. Anthony Lester, *The Overseas Trade in the American Bill of Rights*, 88 Colum. L. Rev. 537, 561 (1988). Most developed countries now refuse to extradite fugitives to the United States without assurances that capital punishment will not be imposed. See Schabas, *supra* note 9, at 422; Williams, *supra* note 1, at 154.

28. See *supra* chapter 2.

29. Tony Ward & Astrid Birgden, *Human Rights and Clinical Correctional Practice*, 12 Aggression &Violent Behav. 628 (2007).

30. Astrid Birgden & Michael L. Perlin, *"Where the Home in the Valley Meets the Damp Dirty Prison": A Human Rights Perspective on Therapeutic Jurisprudence and the Role of Forensic Psychologists in Correctional Settings*, 14 Aggression & Violent Behavior 256 (2009) (Birgden & Perlin, *Home in the Valley*); Astrid Birgden & Michael L. Perlin, *"Tolling for the Luckless, the Abandoned and Forsaked": Community Safety, Therapeutic Jurisprudence and International Human Rights Law as Applied to Prisoners and Detainees*, 13 Leg. & Criminol. Psychology 231 (2008)

(Birgden & Perlin, *Tolling for the Luckless*); Michael L. Perlin & Henry A. Dlugacz, *"It's Doom Alone That Counts": Can International Human Rights Law Be an Effective Source of Rights in Correctional Conditions Litigation?* 27 BEHAV. SCI. & L. 675 (2009).

31. See, for helpful historical background, Klaus Dicke, *The Founding Function of Human Dignity in the Universal Declaration of Human Rights*, in THE CONCEPT OF HUMAN DIGNITY IN HUMAN RIGHTS DISCOURSE 111 (David Kretzmer & Eckart Klein, ed. 2002).

32. UNITED NATIONS, INTERNATIONAL COVENANT ON CIVIL AND POLITICAL RIGHTS, art. 7 (1966) (ICCPR). See generally, Dieter, *supra* note 24, at 15–17; David Sadoff, *International Law and the Mortal Precipice: A Legal Policy Critique of the Death Row Phenomenon*, 17 TUL. J. INT'L & COMP. L. 77, 111 (2008), and *id.* nn. 192–95.

33. ICCPR, *supra* note 32, art. 10.

34. UNITED NATIONS, INTERNATIONAL COVENANT ON ECONOMIC, SOCIAL AND CULTURAL RIGHTS, art. 12 (1966).

35. UNITED NATIONS, VIENNA DECLARATION ON CRIME AND JUSTICE (2001).

36. UNITED NATIONS BODY OF PRINCIPLES FOR THE PROTECTION OF ALL PERSONS UNDER ANY FORM OF DETENTION OR IMPRISONMENT, 1988; See generally, Birgden & Perlin, *Home in the Valley*, *supra* note 30; Perlin & Dlugacz, *supra* note 30; Ward & Birgden, *supra* note 29; see Christopher McCrudden, *Human Dignity and the Judicial Interpretation of Human Rights*, 19 EUR. J. INT'L L. 655, 670 (2008) (international human rights documents "adopted dignity as foundational . . . to human rights in general"). On the content of human dignity as a legal concept, see Matthias Mahlmann, *The Basic Law at 60—Human Dignity and the Culture of Republicanism*, 11 GERMAN L. J. 9, 30 (2010). On human dignity as a constitutional value, see Arthur Chaskalson, *Human Dignity as a Constitutional Value*, in THE CONCEPT OF HUMAN DIGNITY IN HUMAN RIGHTS DISCOURSE 133 David Kretzmer & Eckart Klein, eds. 2002). On the role of dignity in the trial process in general, see Michael L. Perlin, *"Dignity Was the First to Leave": Godinez v. Moran, Colin Ferguson, and the Trial of Mentally Disabled Criminal Defendants*, 14 BEHAV. SCI. & L. 61 (1996), and see *id.*, 74 n. 112, discussing US case law (see e.g., *Marquez v. Collins*, 11 F.3d 1241 (5th Cir. 1994) and scholarship (see e.g., Keith D. Nicholson, *Would You Like More Salt with That Wound? Post-Sentence Victim Allocution in Texas*, 26 ST. MARY'S L. J. 1103 (1995); Tom R. Tyler, *The Psychological Consequences of Judicial Procedures: Implications for Civil Commitment Hearings*, 46 SMU L. REV. 433 (1992)) on its significance and constitutional underpinnings.

37. See Rex D. Glensy, *The Right to Dignity*, 43 COLUM. HUM. RTS. L. REV. 65, 106 (2011), and see *id.* n. 197 (citing cases).

38. *Id.*, citing Pretty v. United Kingdom, 35 Eur. H.R. Rep. 1, 38 (2002) (noting that "[t]he very essence of the Convention is respect for human dignity and human freedom").

39. ROGER HOOD, THE DEATH PENALTY: A WORLD-WIDE PERSPECTIVE 42 (2d. ed. 1996), as quoted in Dieter, *supra* note 24, at 3.

40. Carol S. Steiker, *Capital Punishment and Contingency*, 125 HARV. L. REV. 760, 781 (2012) (book review of GARLAND, *supra* note 24).

41. *Id.*

42. Carol S. Steiker, *Capital Punishment and American Exceptionalism*, 81 OR. L. REV. 97, 129 (2002). On why the United States has "sufficient geopolitical and economic strength to resist pressure to conform to international norms," see David Johnson, *American Capital Punishment in Comparative Perspective*, 36 LAW & SOC. INQUIRY 1033, 1050 (2011) (reviewing GARLAND, *supra* note 24).

43. See Winick, *supra* note 15, at 818–19, discussing UN Commission on Human Rights Res. 2001/68, ¶ 4(e), U.N. Doc. E/CN.4/RES/2001/68 (Apr. 25, 2001) (urging retentionist countries to ban execution of persons with mental illness) (Human Rights Resolution). See generally, BAE, *supra* note 19.

44. Jubilut, *supra* note 13, at 365, citing U.N. Econ. & Soc. Council [ECOSOC], *Safeguards Guaranteeing Protection of the Rights of those Facing the Death Penalty*, U.N. Doc. RES/1984/50

(May 25, 1984), and G.A. Res. 39/118, U.N. Doc. A/RES/30/118 (Dec. 14, 1984). See also HOOD, *supra* note 39, at 85.

45. *Human Rights Resolution, supra* note 43.

46. European Union, Delegation of the European Commission to the United States, EU Policy on the Death Penalty, Letter to Governor of Georgia (Feb. 2002), available at http://www.eurunion.org/legislat/DeathPenalty/WilliamsGAGovLett.htm, cited in Laurie Izutsu, *Applying Atkins v. Virginia to Capital Defendants with Severe Mental Illness*, 70 BROOK. L. REV. 995, 1010 n. 99 (2005).

47. http://www.deathpenaltyworldwide.org/mental-illness.cfm.

This, however, should not be read to suggest that the problem has disappeared on an international basis. According to a website created by the Center for International Human Rights at Northwestern University School of Law,

> [I]t is clear that international human rights norms have not solved this problem in all nations. A vast majority of nations conflate mental retardation with mental illness, or leave out mental retardation as an exclusionary category entirely. Consequently, mentally disabled individuals continue to face the death penalty around the world. U.N. ECOSOC, Capital punishment and implementation of the safeguards guaranteeing protection of the rights of those facing the death penalty: Report of the Secretary General, paras. 86–88, U.N. Doc. E/2005/3, Mar. 9, 2005.

http://www.deathpenaltyworldwide.org/mental-retardation.cfm.

See also, Human Rights Watch, *Beyond Reason: The Death Penalty and Offenders with Mental Retardation* 28 (Mar. 5, 2011), accessible at http://www.hrw.org/reports/2001/03/05/beyond-reason-0.

48. See e.g., Jaw-Perng Wang, *The Current State of Capital Punishment in Taiwan*, 6 NAT'L TAIWAN U. L. REV. 143, 158 (2011) (Taiwan's Code of Criminal Procedure [CCP] provides that individuals diagnosed to be "mentally insane" cannot be executed until person's sanity returns), discussing CCP, art. 465; Wen San (Hannah) Chen, *On the Restorative Justice Approach to the Abolition of Death Penalty in Taiwan*, in APPLIED ETHICS: CHALLENGES FOR THE 21ST CENTURY 135 (Hokkaido University Center for Applied Ethics and Philosophy, ed. 2010) (urging the abolition of the death penalty in Taiwan); WEN-CHEN CHANG & CHUAN-FEN CHANG, MY COUNTRY KILLS: CONSTITUTIONAL CHALLENGES TO THE DEATH PENALTY IN TAIWAN (2011) (same); Ryan Florio, *The [Capital] Punishment Fits the Crime: A Comparative Analysis of the Death Penalty and Proportionality in the United States of America and the People's Republic of China*, 16 U. MIAMI INT'L & COMP. L. REV. 43, 61 (2008) (when assessing the defendant's moral responsibility, China's Criminal Code considers aggravating and mitigating factors such as mental and physical disabilities), discussing Criminal Code, arts. 14–21. On the death penalty in China in general, see HONG LU & TERANCE D. MIETHE, CHINA'S DEATH PENALTY: HISTORY, LAW AND CONTEMPORARY PRACTICES (2007).

Some of the same problems that plague the American system plague the systems in other retentionist democracies. See e.g., Wang, *supra*, at 158 (competency to be executed in the context of mental illness); Fisherow, *supra* note 14, at 460–61 (competency to be executed in the context of mental retardation).

49. 536 U.S. 304, 318–21 (2002) (holding that imposing the death penalty on a man considered "mentally retarded" is unconstitutional). See *supra* chapter 5.

50. Arlene Kanter, *The Law: What's Disability Studies Got to Do with It, Or an Introduction to Disability Legal Studies*, 42 COLUM. HUM. RTS. L. REV. 403, 464 (2011).

51. Winick, *supra* note 15, at 854–58.

52. Jubilut, *supra* note 13, at 377–78, and see Office of the UN High Comm'r for Human Rights [OHCHR], *Special Rapporteur on Extrajudicial, Summary or Arbitrary Executions Report*, http://www.unhchr.ch/html/menu2/7/b/execut/exe_mand.htm (same). See also, http://www.deathpenaltyworldwide.org/due-process.cfm:

The Human Rights Committee has accordingly held that when a state violates an individual's due process rights under the ICCPR, it may not carry out his execution. See, e.g., Johnson v. Jamaica, No. 588/1994, H.R. Comm. para. 8.9 (1996) (finding delay of 51 months between conviction and dismissal of appeal to be violation of ICCPR art. 14, para. 3(c) and 5, and reiterating that imposition of a death sentence is prohibited where the provisions of the ICCPR have not been observed); Reid v. Jamaica, No. 250/1987, H.R. Comm. para. 11.5 ("[T]he imposition of a sentence of death upon the conclusion of a trial in which the provisions of the Covenant have not been respected constitutes [. . .] a violation of article 6 of the Covenant.")

53. Margaret E. McGuinness, *Medellin, Norm Portals, and the Horizontal Integration of International Human Rights*, 82 NOTRE DAME L. REV. 755, 759–60 (2006).

54. 543 U.S. 551 (2005). See McCarver v. North Carolina, 2001 WL 648607 (2001) (*amicus* brief of diplomats Moron Abramoqitz et al.), at *16 ("International opinion has always informed this Court's understanding of the social values of the United States and, in particular, what our society considers to be 'cruel and unusual punishments.'" The Supreme Court had granted *certiorari* in *McCarver* on the same issue that it decided the next year in *Atkins*, but then dismissed that petition as moot after the North Carolina state legislature enacted a ban on the execution of offenders with mental retardation. McCarver v. North Carolina, 533 U.S. 975 (2001).

55. *Atkins*, 536 U.S. at 316, n. 21, citing Brief for European Union as *Amicus Curiae* 4.

56. *Roper*, 542 U.S. at 575–78.

57. See *supra* chapter 10.

58. 466 U.S. 668, 668 (1984).

59. See e.g., ICCPR, *supra* note 32, art. 9(4) ("Anyone who is deprived of his liberty by arrest or detention shall be entitled to take proceedings before a court, in order that the court may decide without delay on the lawfulness of his detention and order his release if the detention is not lawful"); American Declaration of the Rights and Duties of Man, art. 18 ("Every person may resort to the courts to ensure respect for his legal rights"). See also for the Protection of All Persons under Any Form of Detention or Imprisonment, G.A. res. 43/173, U.N. Doc. A/43/49 (1988), Principle 32 ("A detained person or his counsel shall be entitled at any time to take proceedings according to domestic law before a judicial or other authority to challenge the lawfulness of his detention. . . . The proceedings . . . shall be simple and expeditious"); American Convention on Human Rights, art. 7(6) ("Anyone who is deprived of his liberty shall be entitled to recourse to a competent court, in order that the court may decide without delay on the lawfulness of his arrest or detention"); European Convention on Human Rights, art. 5(4) ("Everyone who is deprived of his liberty by arrest or detention shall be entitled to take proceedings by which the lawfulness of his detention shall be decided speedily by a court and his release ordered if the detention is not lawful"). See generally, http://www.deathpenaltyworldwide.org/access-to-courts.cfm.

60. See e.g., Suarez Rosero v. Ecuador, Inter-Am. Ct. H.R., Nov. 12, 1997, at para. 63, 65 (art. 7(6) of the American Convention on Human Rights, involving right of access to a competent tribunal, is not satisfied "with the mere formal existence" of the remedy).

61. See *supra* chapter 10 at text accompanying note 152, discussing Federal District Court Judge David Bazelon's observation that many counsels he had observed in court were no more than "a warm body with a legal pedigree." David L. Bazelon, *The Realities of Gideon and Argersinger*, 64 GEO. L. J. 811, 818–19 (1976).

62. See generally, Michael L. Perlin, *"There Are No Trials Inside the Gates of Eden": Mental Health Courts, the Convention on the Rights of Persons with Disabilities, Dignity, and the Promise of Therapeutic Jurisprudence*, in COERCIVE CARE: LAW AND POLICY (Bernadette McSherry & Ian Freckelton, eds. 2012) (in press).

63. On the singular role of this Convention, see e.g., MICHAEL L. PERLIN, INTERNATIONAL HUMAN RIGHTS AND MENTAL DISABILITY LAW: WHEN THE SILENCED ARE HEARD 143–58 (2011); Frederic Megret, *The Disabilities Convention: Toward a Holistic Concept of Rights*, 12 INT'L J. HUM. RTS. 261 (2008); Frederic Megret, *The Disabilities Convention: Human Rights of*

Persons with Disabilities or Disability Rights?, 30 HUM. RIGHTS 494 (2008) (Megret, *Disability Rights*); Michael L. Perlin & Eva Szeli, *Mental Health Law and Human Rights: Evolution and Contemporary Challenges*, in MENTAL HEALTH AND HUMAN RIGHTS: VISION, PRAXIS AND COURAGE 98 (Michael Dudley, ed. 2012) (Perlin & Szeli, *Evolution and Contemporary Challenges*); Michael L. Perlin & Eva Szeli, *Mental Health Law and Human Rights: Evolution, Challenges and the Promise of the New Convention*, in UNITED NATIONS CONVENTION ON THE RIGHTS OF PERSONS WITH DISABILITIES: MULTIDISCIPLINARY PERSPECTIVES 241 (Jukka Kumpuvuori & Martin Scheninen, eds. 2010) (Perlin & Szeli, *Promise*). On the impact of UN human rights treaties on domestic law in general, see Christof Heyns & Frans Viljoen, *The Impact of the United Nations Human Rights Treaties on the Domestic Level*, 23 HUM. RTS. Q. 483 (2001).

64. G.A. Res. 56/168 (2001).

65. G.A. Res. A/61/611 (2006); G.A. Res. A/61/106 (2006).

66. See http://www.un.org/News/Press/docs/2008/hr4941.doc.htm. See generally, Tara Melish, *The UN Disability Convention: Historic Process, Strong Prospects, and Why the U.S. Should Ratify*, 14 HUM. RTS. BRIEF 37, 44 (Winter 2007); Michael Ashley Stein & Penelope J.S. Stein, *Beyond Disability Civil Rights*, 58 HASTINGS L. J. 1203 (2007).

67. See e.g., Rosemary Kayess & Phillip French, *Out of Darkness into Light? Introducing the Convention on the Rights of Persons with Disabilities*, 8 HUM. RTS. L. REV. 1, 4 n. 15 (2008):

See, for example, Statement by Hon Ruth Dyson, Minister for Disability Issues, New Zealand Mission to the UN, for Formal Ceremony at the Signing of the Convention on the Rights of Persons with Disability, 30 March 2007: "Just as the Convention itself is the product of a remarkable partnership between governments and civil society, effective implementation will require a continuation of that partnership." The negotiating slogan 'Nothing about us without us' was adopted by the International Disability Caucus, available at: http://www.un.org/esa/socdev/enable/documents/Stat_Conv/nzam.doc [accessed Aug. 23, 2011].

68. *Id.*, n. 17 (see, for example, statements made by the High Commissioner for Human Rights, Louise Arbour, and the Permanent Representative of New Zealand and Chair of the Ad-Hoc Committee on a Comprehensive and Integral International Convention on the Protection and Promotion of the Rights and Dignity of Persons with Disabilities, Ambassador Don Mackay, at a Special Event on the Convention on Rights of Persons with Disabilities, convened by the UN Human Rights Council, 26 Mar. 2007, available at http://www.unog.ch/80256EDD006B9C2E/ (httpNewsByYear_en)/7444B2E219117CE8C12572AA004C570 1?OpenDocument (Aug. 23, 2011).

69. Perlin & Szeli, *Evolution and Contemporary Challenges, supra* note 63; PERLIN, *supra* note 63, at 3–21; see generally, Michael L. Perlin, *"A Change Is Gonna Come": The Implications of the United Nations Convention on the Rights of Persons with Disabilities for the Domestic Practice of Constitutional Mental Disability Law*, 29 No. ILL. U. L. REV. 483 (2009).

70. See e.g., Aaron Dhir, *Human Rights Treaty Drafting through the Lens of Mental Disability: The Proposed International Convention on Protection and Promotion of the Rights and Dignity of Persons with Disabilities*, 41 STAN. J. INT'L L. 181 (2005).

71. See generally Michael L. Perlin, *"Abandoned Love": The Impact of Wyatt v. Stickney on the Intersection between International Human Rights and Domestic Mental Disability Law*, 35 LAW & PSYCHOL. REV. 121 (2011).

72. See e.g., Janet E. Lord, David Suozzi, & Allyn L. Taylor, *Lessons from the Experience of U.N. Convention on the Rights of Persons with Disabilities: Addressing the Democratic Deficit in Global Health Governance*, 38 J. L. MED. & ETHICS 564 (2010); H. Archibald Kaiser, *Canadian Mental Health Law: The Slow Process of Redirecting the Ship of State*, 17 HEALTH L. J. 139 (2009).

73. Janet E. Lord & Michael A. Stein, *Social Rights and the Relational Value of the Rights to Participate in Sport, Recreation, and Play*, 27 B.U. INT'L L. J. 249, 256 (2009); see also, Ronald

McCallum, *The United Nations Convention on the Rights of Persons with Disabilities: Some Reflections*. Accessible at http://ssrn.com/abstract=1563883 (2010).

74. Bernadette McSherry, *International Trends in Mental Health Laws: Introduction*, 26 LAW IN CONTEXT 1, 8 (2008).

75. See Lord, Suozzi, & Taylor, *supra* note 72, at 568; Kaiser, *supra* note 72; Michael L. Perlin, *"There's Voices in the Night Trying to be Heard": The Potential Impact of the Convention on the Rights of Persons with Disabilities on Domestic Mental Disability Law*, in EVOLVING ISSUES IN DISCRIMINATION: SOCIAL SCIENCE AND LEGAL PERSPECTIVES (R. Wiener et al., eds. 2012) (in press); Michael L. Perlin, *"There Must Be Some Way Out of Here": Why the Convention on the Rights of Persons with Disabilities Is Potentially the Best Weapon in the Fight against Sanism* (paper presented to conference at Deakin University, Melbourne, Australia, cosponsored by the Australasian Society for Intellectual Disability, June 2011) (on file with author).

76. CRPD, art. 1 and pmbl., para. e.

77. Phillip Fennel, *Human Rights, Bioethics, and Mental Disorder*, 27 MED. & L. 95 (2008).

78. Megret, *Disability Rights*, *supra* note 63; see PERLIN, *supra* note 63, at 143–58.

79. CRPD, art. 3(a).

80. *Id.*, art. 3(b).

81. *Id.*, art. 15.

82. *Id.*, art. 16.

83. *Id.*, art. 17.

84. On the changes that ratifying states need to make in their domestic involuntary civil commitment laws, see Bryan Y. Lee, *The U.N. Convention on the Rights of Persons with Disabilities and Its Impact upon Involuntary Civil Commitment of Individuals with Developmental Disabilities*, 44 COLUM. J. L. & SOC'L PROBS. 393 (2011). See also István Hoffman & György Kőnczei, *Legal Regulations Related to the Passive and Active Legal Capacity of Persons with Intellectual and Psychosocial Disabilities in Light of the Convention on the Rights of Persons with Disabilities and the Impending Reform of the Hungarian Civil Code*, 33 LOY. L. A. INT'L & COMP. L. REV. 143 (2010) (on the application of the CRPD to capacity issues); Kathryn D. DeMarco, *Disabled by Solitude: The Convention on the Rights of Persons with Disabilities and Its Impact on the Use of Supermax Solitary Confinement*, 66 U. MIAMI L. REV. 523 (2012) (on the application of the CRPD to solitary confinement in correctional institutions).

85. See Michael L. Perlin, *"I Might Need a Good Lawyer, Could Be Your Funeral, My Trial": A Global Perspective on the Right to Counsel in Civil Commitment Cases, and Its Implications for Clinical Legal Education*, 28 WASH. U. J. L. & SOC'L POL'Y 241, 252–53 (2008), quoting CRPD, art. 12.

86. CRPD, art. 13.

87. Perlin, *supra* note 85, at 253.

88. On the significance of "cause lawyers" in the development of mental disability law in the United States, see Michael A. Stein, Michael E. Waterstone, & David B. Wilkins, *Book Review: Cause Lawyering for People with Disabilities*, 123 HARV. L. REV. 1658 (2010).

89. CRPD, art. 1.

90. CRPD, art. 3(a).

91. *Id.*, para. h.

92. Dhir, *supra* note 70, at 195.

93. Gerard Quinn & Teresa Degener, HUMAN RIGHTS AND DISABILITY: THE CURRENT USE AND FUTURE POTENTIAL OF UNITED NATIONS HUMAN RIGHTS INSTRUMENTS IN THE CONTEXT OF DISABILITY 14 (2002). See also, Robert Vischer, *How Do Lawyers Serve Human Dignity?* ST. THOMAS L. REV. (2012) (in press), manuscript at 25 ("A commitment to human dignity requires lawyers to widen their gaze").

94. Michael Stein, *Disability Human Rights*, 95 CAL. L. REV. 75, 106 (2007). See also, Doron Schultziner & Itai Rabinovici, *Human Dignity, Self-Worth, and Humiliation: A Comparative Legal-Psychological Approach*, PSYCHOLOGY, PUB. POL'Y & L. (2011) (in press).

95. Cees Maris, *A Not= A: Or, Freaky Justice*, 31 Cardozo L. Rev. 1133, 1156 (2010).

96. Sally Chaffin, *Challenging the United States Position on a United Nations Convention on Disability*, 15 Temple Poli. & Civ. Rts. L. Rev. 121, 140 (2005), quoting *International Disability Rights: The Proposed UN Convention: Hearing before the Congressional Human Rights Caucus*, 108th Cong. (Mar. 30, 2004) (testimony of Eric Rosenthal, executive director of Mental Disability Rights International).

97. See *supra* chapter 2.

98. McCrudden, *supra* note 36, at 686–94.

99. *Id.* at 724.

100. *Id.*

101. CRPD, art. 15.

102. *Id.*, art. 16.

103. *Id.*, art. 17.

104. See Henry Dlugacz & Christopher Wimmer, *The Ethics of Representing Clients with Limited Competency in Guardianship Proceedings*, 4 St. Louis U. J. Health L. & Pol'y 331, 362–63 (2011). The United States has never signed a human rights treaty devoid of qualifying reservations, understandings, and declarations (RUDs). See DeMarco, *supra* note 84, at 555–56. On possible RUDs the United States might raise as a condition to signing to CRPD, see *id.* at 558–64.

At the time that this manuscript was being submitted to the publisher, President Obama—who signed the Convention three years previously—submitted the Convention to the Senate to grant final approval of the treaty, making ratification official. See Michelle Diament, *Obama Urges Senate to Ratify Disability Treaty* (May 18, 2012), accessible at http://www.disabilityscoop.com/2012/05/18/obama-urges-senate-treaty/15654.

I am optimistic that, if and when this Convention is signed, it will be taken seriously in the United States. Compare Williams *supra* note 1, at 154 (charging that the US generally signs treaties "for public relations purposes").

105. *In the Matter of Mark C.H.* 906 N.Y.S.2d 419 (Sur. 2010), citing Vienna Convention, art. 18. See Johanna Kalb, *Human Rights Treaties in State Courts: The International Prospects of State Constitutionalism after Medellin*, 115 Penn. St. L. Rev. 1051, 1160 (2011), and *id.* n. 49.

On the question of making human rights treaties actionable in US courts, see Penny Venetis, *Making Human Rights Treaty Law Actionable in the United States: The Case for Universal Implementing Legislation*, 53 Ala. L. Rev. 97 (2011).

106. Supermax prisons are ones in which "prisoners are solitarily confined in their cells for approximately twenty-three hours a day; prisoners do not have work, educational, or social opportunities; prisoners have limited access to reading materials; prisoners have nominal, or no, interaction with other humans; prisoners have no more than five hours of out-of-cell exercise a week (typically in another solitary, enclosed cell); and prisoners receive little or no natural light." See Laura Matter, *Hey, I Think We're Unconstitutionally Alone Now: The Eighth Amendment Protects Social Interaction as a Basic Human Need*, 14 J. Gender Race & Just. 265, 270–71 (2010).

107. DeMarco, *supra* note 84, at 564, quoting, in part, Nan D. Miller, *International Protection of the Rights of Prisoners: Is Solitary Confinement in the United States a Violation of International Standards?*, 26 Cal. W. Int'l L. J. 139, 167 (1995).

108. DeMarco, *supra* note 84, at 565.

109. Perlin, *supra* note 63, chapter 10.

110. See *supra* chapter 2.

111. See e.g., Ward & Birgden, *supra* note 29; Nicola Ferencz & James McGuire, *Mental Health Review Tribunals in the UK: Applying a Therapeutic Jurisprudence Perspective*, 37 Court Rev. 48, 51 (Spring 2000); Birgden & Perlin, *Home in the Valley*, *supra* note 30; Birgden & Perlin, *Tolling for the Luckless*, *supra* note 30; Bruce J. Winick, *Therapeutic Jurisprudence and the Treatment of People with Mental Illness in Eastern Europe: Construing International Human Rights Law*, 21 N.Y. L. Sch. J. Int'l & Comp. L. 537, 542 (2002).

112. On how restorative justice principles support the abolition of the death penalty, see Chen, *supra* note 48 (Taiwan). On restorative justice in Asia in general, see e.g., Marsha B. Freeman, *Comparing Philosophies and Practices of Family Law between the United States and Other Nations: The Flintstones vs. the Jetsons*, 13 CHAP. L. REV. 249, 261–62 (2010); Thomas M. Antkowiak, *An Emerging Mandate for International Courts: Victim-Centered Remedies and Restorative Justice*, 47 STAN. J. INT'L L. 279 (2011); Mark Findlay, *The Challenge for Asian Jurisdictions in the Development of International Criminal Justice*, 2010 SING. J. LEGAL STUD. 37. On the absence of restorative justice programs in Central Asia, however, see Cynthia Alkon, *The Increased Use of "Reconciliation" in Criminal Cases in Central Asia: A Sign of Restorative Justice, Reform or Cause for Concern?*, 8 PEPP. DISP. RESOL. L. J. 41 (2007).

113. Michael S. King, *Restorative Justice, Therapeutic Jurisprudence and the Rise of Emotionally Intelligent Justice*, 32 MELB. U. L. REV. 1096, 1112 (2008).

114. Alfred Allan and Marietjie M. Allan, *The South African Truth and Reconciliation Commission as a Therapeutic Tool*, 18 BEHAV. SCI. & L. 459 (2000).

115. James M. Cooper, *State of the Nation: Therapeutic Jurisprudence and the Evolution of the Right of Self-Determination in International Law*, 17 BEHAV. SCI. & L. 607 (1999).

116. Michael S. King & Rob Guthrie, *Therapeutic Jurisprudence, Human Rights and the Northern Territory Emergency Response*, 89 PRECEDENT 39 (2008).

117. Dejo Olowu, *Therapeutic Jurisprudence: Transforming Legal Education and Humanising Criminal Justice in Africa*, 1 DEJURE 95 (2010).

118. Caroline M. A. Nicholson, *The Impact of Child Labor Legislation on Child-Headed Households in South Africa*, 30 T. JEFFERSON L. REV. 407 (2008).

119. Muhammad Ahmad Munir, *Therapeutic Jurisprudence in Pakistan: Juvenile Delinquency and the Role of the Defense Lawyer*, in TRANSFORMING LEGAL PROCESSES IN COURT AND BEYOND 85 (Greg Reinhardt & Andrew Cannon, eds. 2007).

120. See *supra* chapter 7.

121. See *supra* chapter 10.

122. Juan Ramirez Jr. & Amy D. Ronner, *Voiceless Billy Budd: Melville's Tribute to the Sixth Amendment*, 41 CAL. WESTERN L. REV. 103, 119 (2004).

123. Michael L. Perlin, *"Things Have Changed": Looking at Non-Institutional Mental Disability Law through the Sanism Filter*, 46 N.Y. L. SCH. L. REV. 535, 544 (2002–2003).

124. See e.g., Dirk van Zyl Smit, *Regulation of Prison Conditions*, 39 CRIME & JUST. 503 (2010); Fred Cohen & Joel A. Dvoskin, *Therapeutic Jurisprudence and Corrections: A Glimpse*, 10 N.Y. L. SCH. J. HUM. RTS. 777 (1993).

125. Astrid Birgden, *Therapeutic Jurisprudence and Offender Rights: A Normative Stance Is Required*, 78 REV. JUR. U.P.R. 43, 59 (2009); see also, Birgden & Perlin, *Tolling for the Luckless*, *supra* note 30; Birgden & Perlin, *Home in the Valley*, *supra* note 30; Michael L. Perlin, *"With Faces Hidden While the Walls Were Tightening": Applying International Human Rights Standards to Forensic Psychology*, 7 U.S.-CHINA LAW REVIEW 1 (2010).

126. See e.g., Andrea Lyon & Mark Cunningham, *"Reason Not the Need": Does the Lack of Compelling State Interest in Maintaining a Separate Death Row Make It Unlawful?*, 33 AM. J. CRIM. L. 1 (2005); Karl S. Myers, *Practical Lackey: The Impact of Holding Execution After a Long Stay on Death Row Unconstitutional under Lackey v. Texas*, 106 DICK. L. REV. 647 (2002). Interestingly, the Judicial Committee of the Privy Council of the Caribbean has held that it would constitute inhumane or degrading punishment or treatment to prolong the period of time spent under the threat of execution for more than five years. UNITED NATIONS, HANDBOOK ON PRISONERS WITH SPECIAL NEEDS 161 (2009), discussing *Pratt et al. v. Attorney-General for Jamaica et al.*, 4 ALL ER 769 (1993).

127. Winick, *supra* note 111, at 535.

128. *CRPD*, art. 15.

129. *Id.*, art. 16.

130. PERLIN, *supra* note 63, at 159–69.

131. See *supra* chapter 2.

132. Michael L. Perlin, *"And My Best Friend, My Doctor / Won't Even Say What It Is I've Got":* *The Role and Significance of Counsel in Right to Refuse Treatment Cases,* 42 SAN DIEGO L. REV. 735, 750 (2005); see also, Michael L. Perlin & Deborah A. Dorfman, *"Is It More Than Dodging Lions and Wastin' Time"? Adequacy of Counsel, Questions of Competence, and the Judicial Process in Individual Right to Refuse Treatment Cases,* 2 PSYCHOLOGY, PUB. POL'Y & L. 114 (1996).

133. Michael L. Perlin, *"The Executioner's Face Is Always Well-Hidden": The Role of Counsel and the Courts in Determining Who Dies,* 41 N.Y. L. SCH. L. REV. 201, 235 (1996).

134. Although the phrase "therapeutic jurisprudence" is not used in her article, Elizabeth Sher's recent consideration of the impact of the mixed lay judge system in Japan on the imposition of the death penalty in that nation resonates with TJ values from this perspective. See Elizabeth Sher, *Death Penalty Sentencing in Japan under the Lay Assessor System: Avoiding the Avoidable Through Unanimity,* 20 PAC. RIM L. & POL'Y J. 635, 649–57 (2011).

CHAPTER 12

1. 536 U.S. 304 (2002).

2. Michael L. Perlin, *"Life Is in Mirrors, Death Disappears": Giving Life to* Atkins, 33 N.M. L. REV. 315, 315 (2003) (footnotes omitted).

3. See *supra* chapter 9.

4. See *supra* chapter 1.

5. As of March 13, 2012, there have been 266 exonerations. See http://www.exonerate.org/about-2/causes-of-wrongful-convictions.

6. Tracey Maclin, *A Criminal Procedure Regime Based on Instrumental Values,* 22 CONST. COMMENT. 197, 230 n. 68 (2005).

7. See *supra* chapter 9.

8. See *supra* chapter 3.

9. See *supra* chapter 9.

10. See *supra* chapter 4.

11. 463 U.S. 880 (1983); see *supra* chapter 3.

12. See *supra* chapter 4.

13. 438 U.S. 586 (1978); see *supra* chapter 4.

14. 455 U.S. 104 (1982); see *supra* chapter 4.

15. 492 U.S. 302 (1989); see *supra* chapter 4.

16. 542 U.S. 274 (2004); see *supra* chapter 4.

17. 463 U.S. 880 (1983), discussed *supra* chapter 10 *passim.*

18. 470 U.S. 68 (1985), discussed *supra* chapter 8.

19. 536 U.S. 304 (2002); see *supra* chapter 5.

20. See generally *supra* chapter 5.

21. Death Penalty Information Center, *Examples of Mentally Ill Inmates Who Were Executed,* http://www.deathpenaltyinfo.org/mental-illness-and-death-penalty#executions (accessed Dec. 20, 2011).

22. 477 U.S. 399 (1986); see *supra* chapter 6.

23. 551 U.S. 930 (2007); see *supra* chapter 6.

24. See generally *supra* chapter 6.

25. Albert Alschuler, *Bill Clinton's Parting Pardon Party,* 100 J. CRIM. L. & CRIMINOLOGY 1131, 1133 (2010); Laura Mansnerus, *Damaged Brains and the Death Penalty,* N.Y. TIMES (July 21, 2001). See Rector v. State, 659 S.W.2d 168 (Ark. 1983).

26. Panetti v. Quarterman, 2006 WL 3880284, *26 (2006) (appellant's petition for *certiorari*) (cohort of Fifth Circuit cases).

27. 466 U.S. 668, 668 (1984), discussed *supra* chapter 10.

28. See *supra* chapter 10.

29. 539 U.S. 510 (2003), discussed *supra* chapter 10.

30. But see Kenneth Williams, *Does* Strickland *Prejudice Defendants on Death Row?*, 43 U. Rich. L. Rev. 1459, 1461 (2009) (survey of lower court decisions both before and after *Wiggins* indicates that capital defendants did not achieve any greater success in obtaining relief after *Wiggins* than they did before *Wiggins*).

31. David L. Bazelon, *The Realities of Gideon and Argersinger*, 64 Geo. L. J. 811, 818–19 (1976).

32. Stephen Bright, *Death by Lottery—Procedural Bar of Constitutional Claims in Capital Cases Due to Inadequate Representation of Indigent Defendants*, 92 W. Va. L. Rev. 679, 695 (1990).

33. See *supra* chapter 9.

34. See e.g., Amanda Frost, *Defending the Majoritarian Court*, 2010 Mich. St. L. Rev. 757, 760 (2010).

35. See *supra* chapter 11.

36. G.A. Res. A/61/106 (2006). See http://www.un.org/News/Press/docs/2008/hr4941. doc.htm, and see *supra* chapter 11.

37. The United States is a signatory to the Convention but has not yet ratified it. At the time of the submission of this manuscript, President Obama has just sent the Convention to the Senate for ratification. See e.g., http://www.disabilityscoop.com/2012/05/18/obama-urges-senate-treaty/15654 (Convention submitted May 17, 2012).

38. See generally Michael L. Perlin, The Hidden Prejudice: Mental Disability on Trial (2000).

39. In *Brady v. Maryland*, 373 U.S. 83, 87 (1963), the Supreme Court ruled that "the suppression by the prosecution of evidence favorable to an accused upon request violates due process where the evidence is material either to guilt or to punishment, irrespective of the good faith or bad faith of the prosecution."

40. See *supra* chapter 1.

41. See Perlin, *supra* note 38.

42. See Michael L. Perlin, International Human Rights and Mental Disability Law: When the Silenced Are Heard (2011).

43. Connecticut has recently abolished the death penalty. See http://articles.cnn.com/2012-04-25/justice/justice_connecticut-death-penalty-law-repealed_1_capital-punishment-death-penalty-information-center-death-sentences?_s=PM:JUSTICE (April 25, 2012). For an explanation of how the abolition process has worked on a state-by-state basis, see Lyn Suzanne Entzeroth, *The End of the Beginning: The Politics of Death and the American Death Penalty Regime in the Twenty-First Century*, 90 Or. L. Rev. 797 (2012).

44. See e.g., David B. Wexler, Therapeutic Jurisprudence: The Law as a Therapeutic Agent (1990); David B. Wexler & Bruce J. Winick, Law in a Therapeutic Key: Recent Developments in Therapeutic Jurisprudence (1996); see *supra* chapter 2.

45. Michael L. Perlin, *"Things Have Changed": Looking at Non-institutional Mental Disability Law through the Sanism Filter*, 46 N.Y. L. Sch. L. Rev. 535, 544 (2003) (therapeutic jurisprudence must be used as a mechanism "to expose pretextuality and strip bare the law's sanist facade").

46. David B. Wexler, *Not Such a Party Pooper: An Attempt to Accommodate (Many of) Professor Quinn's Concerns about Therapeutic Jurisprudence Criminal Defense Lawyering*, 48 B.C. L. Rev. 597, 599 (2007).

47. Richard J. Bonnie, *Panetti v. Quarterman: Mental Illness, the Death Penalty, and Human Dignity*, 5 Ohio St. J. Crim. L. 257, 262 (2007). See *supra* chapter 6.

48. State v. Makwanyane 1995 (3) SA 391 (CC) (S. Afr.), discussed *supra* chapter 11.

49. 466 U.S. 668 (1984).

50. See David L. Bazelon, *The Defective Assistance of Counsel*, 42 U. CIN. L. REV. 1, 2 (1973).

51. 539 U.S. 510 (2003), discussed *supra* chapter 10.

52. See e.g., Valerie McClain, Elliot Atkins, & Michael L. Perlin, *"Oh, Stop That Cursed Jury": The Role of the Forensic Psychologist in the Mitigation Phase of the Death Penalty Trial*, in HANDBOOK ON FORENSIC PSYCHOLOGY (Mark Goldstein, ed. 2012) (in press).

53. See *supra* chapter 4.

54. On the implications of legislative overruling of criminal procedure rulings in general, see e.g., Anthony G. Amsterdam, *The Supreme Court and the Rights of Suspects in Criminal Cases*, 45 N.Y.U. L. REV. 785, 802–3 (1970).

55. Washington v. Strickland, 693 F.2d 1243, 1263–64 (5th Cir. 1982), *reversed*, 466 U.S. 668 (1984).

56. Professor James Ellis, appellate counsel for appellant in *Atkins v. Virginia*, 536 U.S. 304 (2002) (see *supra* chapter 5), explains how he embarked on this sort of strategy in his efforts to convince state legislatures to ban the execution of persons with mental retardation. See James Ellis, *Disability Advocacy and the Death Penalty: The Road from* Penry *to* Atkins, 33 N.M. L. REV. 173 (2003).

57. See e.g., Elizabeth Weeks Leonard, *Affordable Care Act Litigation: The Standing Paradox*, 38 AM. J. L. & MED. 410, 416 (2012): "The U.S. Constitution establishes a floor, requiring states to recognize at least that level of individual rights, but states may exceed the federal floor and accord even greater protection." See also e.g., ERWIN CHEMERINSKY ET AL., FEDERAL JURISDICTION § 10.5, at 707 (4th ed. 2003) ("State constitutions can provide more rights than exist under the United States Constitution, but the state court must make it clear that the decision is based on the state constitution").

58. For a discussion of this issue (in a non–death penalty state context), see Herbert Wilkins, *The Massachusetts Constitution—The Last Thirty Years*, 44 SUFFOLK U. L. REV. 331, 349 n. 53 (2012). I realize that, in death penalty states, this may be an almost impossible task, see e.g., Jacque St. Romain, *State V. Grier and the Erroneous Adoption of the "Punishment-Based" Standard of Review for Ineffective Assistance of Counsel Claims Based on All-Or-Nothing Strategies*, 85 WASH. L. REV. 547, 556–57 (2010) ("state courts have given . . . high deference to ineffective assistance of counsel claims"), but I believe it is a strategy worth pursuing.

59. See *supra* chapter 3.

60. See Jonathan Sorensen & James Marquart, *Prosecutorial and Jury Decision-Making in Post-Furman Texas Capital Cases*, 18 N.Y.U. REV. L. & SOC'L CHANGE 743, 749 (1990–1991), discussing the spawning of a "growing entourage of Grigson-like psychiatrists acting as hired guns for the state."

61. See *supra* chapter 9.

62. See *supra* chapters 5 and 6.

63. See Wiggins v. Smith, 539 U.S. 510 (2003), discussed *supra* chapter 10.

64. *Wiggins* incorporated the *Guidelines*, whose objective was to "set forth a national standard of practice for the defense of capital cases in order to insure high quality legal representation for all persons facing the possible imposition or execution of a death sentence by any jurisdiction." American Bar Association, *Guidelines for the Appointment and Performance of Defense Counsel in Death Penalty Cases*, 31 HOFSTRA L. REV. 913, 919 (2003), as discussed in Emily Hughes, *Arbitrary Death: An Empirical Study of Mitigation*, 89 WASH. U. L. REV. 581, 629 (2012).

65. G.A. Res. A/61/106 (2006).

66. Japan and Taiwan are the others. See e.g., Jaw-Perng Wang, *The Current State of Capital Punishment in Taiwan*, 6 NAT'L TAIWAN U. L. REV. 143, 158 (2011); Simon H. Fisherow, *Follow the Leader?: Japan Should Formally Abolish the Execution of the Mentally Retarded in the Wake of Atkins v. Virginia*, 14 PAC. RIM L. & POL'Y J. 455, 461 (2005).

67. Japan is the other. See Fisherow, *supra* note 66.

68. See *supra* note 38.

69. Vienna Convention on the Law of Treaties, art. 31(1), May 23, 1969, 1155 U.N.T.S. 331. See generally, *In the Matter of Mark C.H.*, 906 N.Y.S.2d 419 (Surr. Ct. 2010), discussed in PERLIN, *supra* note 42, at 154–55.

70. See e.g., Michael L. Perlin, *"And My Best Friend, My Doctor / Won't Even Say What It Is I've Got": The Role and Significance of Counsel in Right to Refuse Treatment Cases*, 42 SAN DIEGO L. REV. 735, 750–53 (2005); Michael L. Perlin & Deborah A. Dorfman, *"Is It More Than Dodging Lions and Wastin' Time?" Adequacy of Counsel, Questions of Competence, and the Judicial Process in Individual Right to Refuse Treatment Cases*, 2 PSYCHOLOGY, PUB. POL'Y & L. 114, 120–21 (1996).

71. Michael L. Perlin, *"The Executioner's Face Is Always Well-Hidden": The Role of Counsel and the Courts in Determining Who Dies*, 41 N.Y. L. SCH. L. REV. 201, 235 (1996).

72. Astrid Birgden & Michael L. Perlin, *"Where the Home in the Valley Meets the Damp Dirty Prison": A Human Rights Perspective on Therapeutic Jurisprudence and the Role of Forensic Psychologists in Correctional Settings*, 14 AGGRESSION & VIOLENT BEHAVIOR 256 (2009); Astrid Birgden & Michael L. Perlin, *"Tolling for the Luckless, the Abandoned and Forsaked": Community Safety, Therapeutic Jurisprudence and International Human Rights Law as Applied to Prisoners and Detainees*, 13 LEG. & CRIMINOL. PSYCHOLOGY 231 (2008); see also e.g., Tony Ward & Astrid Birgden, *Human Rights and Clinical Correctional Practice*, 12 AGGRESSION & VIOLENT BEHAV. 628 (2007).

73. See e.g., Deborah A. Dorfman, *Through a Therapeutic Jurisprudence Filter: Fear and Pretextuality in Mental Disability Law*, 10 N.Y. L. SCH. J. HUM. RTS. 805, 808 (1993) ("[W]e often presume all mentally disabled individuals are dangerous by virtue of their mentally ill status").

74. See e.g., Bruce J. Winick, *The Supreme Court's Evolving Death Penalty Jurisprudence: Severe Mental Illness as the Next Frontier*, 50 B.C. L. REV. 785, 848–49 (2009).

75. See e.g., Bruce J. Winick, *Competency to Be Executed: A Therapeutic Jurisprudence Perspective*, 10 BEHAV. SCI. & L. 317, 328–37 (1992); Bruce Arrigo & Jeffrey J. Tasca, *Right to Refuse Treatment, Competency to Be Executed, and Therapeutic Jurisprudence: Toward a Systematic Analysis*, 23 LAW & PSYCHOL. REV. 1, 43–46 (1999).

76. PERLIN, *supra* note 42, at 215.

77. See e.g., Bruce Winick, *Therapeutic Jurisprudence and the Treatment of People with Mental Illness in Eastern Europe: Construing International Human Rights Law*, 21 N.Y. L. SCH. J. INT'L & COMP. L. 537, 556–59 (2002).

78. PERLIN, *supra* note 42, at 216, and see Perlin, *supra* note 71, at 750 (on how inadequate representation violates TJ principles).

79. Compare Kathryn D. DeMarco, *Disabled by Solitude: The Convention on the Rights of Persons with Disabilities and Its Impact on the Use of Supermax Solitary Confinement*, 66 U. MIAMI L. REV. 523 (2012) (on the application of the CRPD to solitary confinement in correctional institutions).

80. See Michael L. Perlin & Valerie R. McClain, *"Where Souls Are Forgotten": Cultural Competencies, Forensic Evaluations, and International Human Rights*, 15 PSYCHOL., PUB. POL'Y & L. 257 (2009).

Bibliography

ARTICLES

Cynthia Adcock, *The Collateral Anti-Therapeutic Effects of the Death Penalty*, 11 Fla. Coastal L. Rev. 289 (2010).

Brian Anderson, *Roper v. Simmons: How the Supreme Court of the United States Has Established the Framework for Judicial Abolition of the Death Penalty in the United States*, 37 Ohio N.U. L. Rev. 221 (2011).

Paul Appelbaum, *Hypotheticals, Psychiatric Testimony, and the Death Sentence*, 12 Bull. Am. Acad. Psychiatry & L. 169 (1984).

Bruce Arrigo & Jeffrey Tasca, *Right to Refuse Treatment, Competency to be Executed, and Therapeutic Jurisprudence: Toward a Systematic Analysis*, 24 L. & Psychol. Rev. 1 (1999).

Ellen Fels Berkman, *Mental Illness as an Aggravating Circumstance in Capital Sentencing*, 89 Colum. L. Rev. 291 (1989).

Astrid Birgden & Michael L. Perlin, *"Tolling for the Luckless, the Abandoned and Forsaked": Community Safety, Therapeutic Jurisprudence and International Human Rights Law as Applied to Prisoners and Detainees*, 13 Leg. & Criminol. Psychology 231 (2008).

Astrid Birgden & Michael L. Perlin, *"Where the Home in the Valley Meets the Damp Dirty Prison": A Human Rights Perspective on Therapeutic Jurisprudence and the Role of Forensic Psychologists in Correctional Settings*, 14 Aggression & Violent Behavior 256 (2009).

John H. Blume, Stephen P. Garvey, & Sheri Lynn Johnson, *Future Dangerousness in Capital Cases: Always "At Issue,"* 86 Cornell L. Rev. 397 (2001).

John H. Blume, Sheri L. Johnson, & Susan E. Millor, *Convicting Lennie: Mental Retardation, Wrongful Convictions, and the Right to a Fair Trial*, 56 N.Y. L. Sch. L. Rev. 943 (2011–2012).

John H. Blume & Pamela Blume Leonard, *Principles of Developing and Presenting Mental Health Evidence in Criminal Cases*, 30 Champion 63 (Nov. 2000).

Richard Bonnie, *Panetti v. Quarterman: Mental Illness, the Death Penalty, and Human Dignity*, 5 Ohio St. J. Crim. L. 257 (2007).

Stephen Bright, *Death by Lottery—Procedural Bar of Constitutional Claims in Capital Cases Due to Inadequate Representation of Indigent Defendants*, 92 W. Va. L. Rev. 679 (1990).

Warren Brookbanks, *Therapeutic Jurisprudence: Conceiving an Ethical Framework*, 8 J. L. & Med. 328 (2001).

Jesse Cheng, *Frontloading Mitigation: The "Legal" and the "Human" in Death Penalty Defense*, 35 Law & Soc'l Inquiry 39 (2010).

Rebecca J. Covarrubias, *Lives in Defense Counsel's Hands: The Problems and Responsibilities of Defense Counsel Representing Mentally Ill or Mentally Retarded Capital Defendants*, 11 Scholar 413 (2009).

Mark D. Cunningham et al., *Capital Jury Decision-Making: The Limitations of Predictions of Future Violence*, 15 Psychol. Pub. Pol'y & L. 223 (2009).

Mark D. Cunningham & Thomas J. Reidy, *Don't Confuse Me with the Facts: Common Errors in Violence Risk Assessment at Capital Sentencing*, 26 Crim. Just. & Behav. 20 (1999).

J. Amy Dillard, *And Death Shall Have No Dominion: How to Achieve the Categorical Exemption of Mentally Retarded Defendants from Execution*, 45 U. Rich. L. Rev. 961 (2011).

James M. Doyle, *The Lawyers' Art: "Representation" in Capital Cases*, 8 Yale J. L. & Human 417 (1996).

Lyn Entzeroth, *Putting the Mentally Retarded Criminal Defendant to Death: Charting the Development of a National Consensus to Exempt the Mentally Retarded from the Death Penalty*, 52 Ala. L. Rev. 911 (2001).

John Fabian, *Death Penalty Mitigation and the Role of the Forensic Psychologist*, 27 Law & Psychology 73 (2003).

Alfred Freedman & Abraham Halpern, *The Erosion of Ethics and Morality in Medicine: Physician Participation in Legal Executions in the United States*, 41 N.Y. L. Sch. L. Rev. 169 (1996).

William Geimer & Jonathan Amsterdam, *Why Jurors Vote Life or Death: Operative Factors in Ten Florida Death Penalty Cases*, 15 Am. J. Crim. L. 1 (1987–1988).

Geoffrey Hazard & David Louisell, *Death, the State, and the Insane: Stay of Execution*, 9 UCLA L. Rev. 381 (1962).

Laurie Izutsu, *Applying Atkins v. Virginia to Capital Defendants with Severe Mental Illness*, 70 Brook. L. Rev. 995 (2005).

Leona D. Jochnowitz, *How Capital Jurors Respond to Mitigating Evidence of Defendant's Mental Illness, Retardation, and Situational Impairments: An Analysis of the Legal and Social Science Literature*, 47 Crim. L. Bull. 839 (2011).

Liliana Lyra Jubilut, *Death Penalty and Mental Illness: The Challenge of Reconciling Human Rights, Criminal Law, and Psychiatric Standards*, 6 Seattle J. Soc. Just. 353 (2007).

Denis Keyes et al., *Mitigating Mental Retardation in Capital Cases: Finding the "Invisible" Defendant*, 22 Mental & Physical Disability L. Rep. 529 (1998).

Jeffrey Kirchmeier, *The Undiscovered Country: Execution Competency & Comprehending Death*, 98 Ky. L. Rev. 263 (2009–2010).

Dorothy Lewis et al., *Neuropsychiatric, Psychoeducational, and Family Characteristics of 14 Juveniles Condemned to Death in the United States*, 145 Am. J. Psychiatry 584 (1988).

James S. Liebman, *Opting for Real Death Penalty Reform*, 63 Ohio St. L. J. 315 (2002).

James Liebman, *The Overproduction of Death*, 100 Colum. L. Rev. 2030 (2000).

James Liebman & Michael J. Shepard, *Guiding Capital Sentencing Discretion beyond One "Boiler Plate": Mental Disorder as a Mitigating Factor*, 66 Geo. L. J. 757 (1978).

Andrea D. Lyon, *But He Doesn't Look Retarded: Capital Jury Selection for the Mentally Retarded Client Not Excluded after Atkins v. Virginia*, 57 DePaul L. Rev. 701 (2008).

Valerie McClain, Elliot Atkins, & Michael L. Perlin, *"Oh, Stop That Cursed Jury": The Role of the Forensic Psychologist in the Mitigation Phase of the Death Penalty Trial*, in Handbook on Forensic Psychology (Mark Goldstein, ed. 2012) (in press).

Natasha Minsker, *Prosecutorial Misconduct in Death Penalty Cases*, 45 Cal. W. L. Rev. 373 (2009).

Joseph A. Nese Jr., *The Fate of Mentally Retarded Criminals: An Examination of the Propriety of Their Execution under the Eighth Amendment*, 40 Duq. L. Rev. 373 (2002).

Sean D. O'Brien, *When Life Depends on It: Supplementary Guidelines for the Mitigation Function of Defense Teams in Death Penalty Cases*, 36 HOFSTRA L. REV. 693 (2008).

John Parry, *The Death Penalty and Persons with Mental Disabilities: A Lethal Dose of Stigma, Sanism, Fear of Violence, and Faulty Predictions of Dangerousness*, 29 MENTAL & PHYSICAL DISABILITY L. REP. 667 (2005).

Michael L. Perlin, *"And I See through Your Brain": Access to Experts, Competency to Consent, and the Impact of Antipsychotic Medications in Neuroimaging Cases in the Criminal Trial Process*, 2009 STAN. TECH. L. REV. 4 (2009).

Michael L. Perlin, *"The Executioner's Face Is Always Well-Hidden": The Role of Counsel and the Courts in Determining Who Dies*, 41 N.Y. L. SCH. L. REV. 201 (1996).

Michael L. Perlin, *"Good and Bad, I Defined These Terms, Quite Clear No Doubt Somehow": Neuroimaging and Competency to Be Executed after* Panetti, 28 BEHAV. SCI. & L. 621 (2010).

Michael L. Perlin, *"Half-Wracked Prejudice Leaped Forth": Sanism, Pretextuality, and Why and How Mental Disability Law Developed as It Did*, 10 J. CONTEMP. LEGAL ISSUES 3 (1999).

Michael L. Perlin, *"His Brain Has Been Mismanaged with Great Skill": How Will Jurors Respond to Neuroimaging Testimony in Insanity Defense Cases?*, 42 AKRON L. REV. 885 (2009).

Michael L. Perlin, *"Life Is in Mirrors, Death Disappears": Giving Life to* Atkins, 33 N.M. L. REV. 315 (2003).

Michael L. Perlin, *The Sanist Lives of Jurors in Death Penalty Cases: The Puzzling Role of "Mitigating" Mental Disability Evidence*, 8 NOTRE DAME J. L. ETHICS & PUB. POL'Y 239 (1994).

Michael L. Perlin, *The Supreme Court, the Mentally Disabled Criminal Defendant, Psychiatric Testimony in Death Penalty Cases, and the Power of Symbolism: Dulling the* Ake *in* Barefoot's *Achilles Heel*, 3 N.Y. L. SCH. HUMAN RTS. ANN. 91 (1985).

Michael L. Perlin, *"Too Stubborn to Ever Be Governed by Enforced Insanity": Some Therapeutic Jurisprudence Dilemmas in the Representation of Criminal Defendants in Incompetency and Insanity Cases*, 33 INT'L J. L. & PSYCHIATRY 475 (2010).

Michael L. Perlin & Valerie R. McClain, *"Where Souls Are Forgotten": Cultural Competencies, Forensic Evaluations, and International Human Rights*, 15 PSYCHOL., PUB. POL'Y & L 257(2009).

Robert T.M. Phillips, *The Psychiatrist as Evaluator: Conflicts and Conscience*, 41 N.Y. L. SCH. L. REV. 189 (1996).

Rabindranath Ramana, *Living and Dying with a Double-Edged Sword: Mental Health Evidence in the Tenth Circuit's Capital Cases*, 88 DENV. U. L. REV. 339 (2011).

Amy D. Ronner, *Songs of Validation, Voice, and Voluntary Participation: Therapeutic Jurisprudence, Miranda and Juveniles*, 71 U. CIN. L. REV. 89 (2002).

Christopher Seeds, *The Afterlife of* Ford *and* Panetti: *Execution Competence and the Capacity to Assist Counsel*, 53 ST. LOUIS U. L. J. 309 (2009).

Christopher Seeds, *Strategery's Refuge*, 99 J. CRIM. L. & CRIMINOL. 987 (2009).

Christopher Slobogin, *Is* Atkins *the Antithesis or Apotheosis of Anti-Discrimination Principles? Sorting Out the Group-Wide Effects of Exempting People with Mental Retardation from the Death Penalty*, 55 ALA. L. REV. 1101 (2004).

Christopher Slobogin, *What* Atkins *Could Mean for Persons with Mental Illness*, 33 N.M. L. REV. 298 (2003).

O. Carter Snead, *Neuroimaging and the 'Complexity' of Capital Punishment*, 82 N.Y.U. L. REV. 1265 (2007).

Carol S. Steiker & Jordan M. Steiker, *Sober Second Thoughts: Reflections on Two Decades of Constitutional Regulation of Capital Punishment*, 109 HARV. L. REV. 355 (1995).

Ronald J. Tabak, *Executing People with Mental Disabilities: How We Can Mitigate an Aggravating Situation*, 25 ST. LOUIS U. PUB. L. REV. 283 (2006).

Douglas W. Vick, *Poorhouse Justice: Underfunded Indigent Defense Services and Arbitrary Death Sentences*, 43 BUFF. L. REV. 329 (1995).

Barbara Ward, *Competency for Execution: Problems in Law and Psychiatry*, 14 FLA. ST. U. L. REV. 35 (1986).

Lawrence White, *The Mental Illness Defense in the Capital Penalty Hearing*, 5 BEHAV. SCI. & L. 411 (1987).

Welsh S. White, *Effective Assistance of Counsel in Capital Cases: The Evolving Standard of Care*, 1993 U. ILL. L. REV. 323 (1993).

Pamela A. Wilkins, *Competency for Execution: The Implications of a Communicative Model of Retribution*, 76 TENN. L. REV. 713 (2009).

Richard Wilson, *International Law Issues in Death Penalty Defense*, 31 HOFSTRA L. REV. 1195 (2003).

Bruce Winick, *Competency to Be Executed: A Therapeutic Jurisprudence Perspective*, 10 BEHAV. SCI. & L. 317 (1992).

Bruce J. Winick, *The Supreme Court's Evolving Death Penalty Jurisprudence: Severe Mental Illness as the Next Frontier*, 50 B.C. L. REV. 785 (2009).

BOOKS

SANGMIN BAE, WHEN THE STATE NO LONGER KILLS: INTERNATIONAL HUMAN RIGHTS NORMS AND ABOLITION OF CAPITAL PUNISHMENT (2007).

DAVID GARLAND, PECULIAR INSTITUTION: AMERICA'S DEATH PENALTY IN AN AGE OF ABOLITION (2010).

THE FUTURE OF AMERICA'S DEATH PENALTY: AN AGENDA FOR THE NEXT GENERATION OF CAPITAL PUNISHMENT RESEARCH (Charles S. Lanier et al., eds. 2009).

MICHAEL L. PERLIN, THE HIDDEN PREJUDICE: MENTAL DISABILITY ON TRIAL (2000).

MICHAEL L. PERLIN, INTERNATIONAL HUMAN RIGHTS AND MENTAL DISABILITY LAW: WHEN THE SILENCED ARE HEARD (2011).

MICHAEL L. PERLIN, THE JURISPRUDENCE OF THE INSANITY DEFENSE (1994).

MICHAEL L. PERLIN, MENTAL DISABILITY LAW: CIVIL AND CRIMINAL (2d ed. 1998–2002).

MICHAEL L. PERLIN ET AL., COMPETENCE IN THE LAW: FROM LEGAL THEORY TO CLINICAL APPLICATION (2008).

THE ABOLITION OF THE DEATH PENALTY IN INTERNATIONAL LAW 23 (William A. Schabas, ed., 3d ed. 1997).

CHRISTOPHER SLOBOGIN, MINDING JUSTICE: LAWS THAT DEPRIVE PEOPLE WITH MENTAL DISABILITY OF LIFE AND LIBERTY (2006).

DAVID WEXLER, REHABILITATING LAWYERS: PRINCIPLES OF THERAPEUTIC JURISPRUDENCE FOR CRIMINAL LAW PRACTICE (2008).

DAVID B. WEXLER, THERAPEUTIC JURISPRUDENCE: THE LAW AS A THERAPEUTIC AGENT (1990).

DAVID B. WEXLER & BRUCE J. WINICK, LAW IN A THERAPEUTIC KEY: RECENT DEVELOPMENTS IN THERAPEUTIC JURISPRUDENCE (1996).

KENNETH WILLIAMS, MOST DESERVING OF DEATH? AN ANALYSIS OF THE SUPREME COURT'S DEATH PENALTY JURISPRUDENCE (2012).

CASES

Ake v. Oklahoma, 470 U.S. 68 (1985).
Atkins v. Virginia, 536 U.S. 304 (2002).
Barefoot v. Estelle, 463 U.S. 880 (1983).
Eddings v. Oklahoma, 455 U.S. 104 (1982).
Ford v. Wainwright, 477 U.S. 399 (1986).
Furman v. Georgia, 408 U.S. 238 (1972).
Gregg v. Georgia, 428 U.S. 153 (1976).
Jurek v. Texas, 428 U.S. 262 (1976).
Lockett v. Ohio, 438 U.S. 586 (1978).
Panetti v. Quarterman, 551 U.S. 930 (2007).
Penry v. Johnson, 532 U.S. 782 (2001).
Penry v. Lynaugh, 492 U.S. 302 (1989).
Rompilla v. Beard, 545 U.S. 374 (2005).
Strickland v. Washington, 466 U.S. 668 (1984).
Tennard v. Dretke, 542 U.S. 274 (2004).
Wiggins v. Smith, 539 U.S. 510 (2003).
Wood v. Allen, 130 S. Ct. 841 (2010).

Index

About the Author

Michael L. Perlin is professor of law at New York Law School (NYLS), director of NYLS's Online Mental Disability Law Program, and director of NYLS's International Mental Disability Law Reform Project in its Justice Action Center. He is the author of 23 books and over 250 book chapters and articles on mental disability and the law.